THE
SERAPH
SEAL

THE
SERAPH
SEAL

LEONARD SWEET
LORI WAGNER

THOMAS NELSON
Since 1798

NASHVILLE   DALLAS   MEXICO CITY   RIO DE JANEIRO

F
Swl

© 2011 Leonard Sweet and Lori Wagner

All rights reserved. No portion of this book may be reproduced, stored in a retrieval system, or transmitted in any form or by any means—electronic, mechanical, photocopy, recording, scanning, or other—except for brief quotations in critical reviews or articles, without the prior written permission of the publisher.

Published in Nashville, Tennessee, by Thomas Nelson. Thomas Nelson is a registered trademark of Thomas Nelson, Inc.

Published in association with the literary agency of Mark Sweeney & Associates, Bonita Springs, Florida 34135.

Thomas Nelson, Inc., titles may be purchased in bulk for educational, business, fund-raising, or sales promotional use. For information, please e-mail SpecialMarkets@ThomasNelson.com.

Scripture quotations are from the HOLY BIBLE: NEW INTERNATIONAL VERSION®. © 1973, 1978, 1984 by Biblica, Inc.™ Used by permission of Zondervan. All rights reserved; NEW REVISED STANDARD VERSION of the Bible. © 1989 by the Division of Christian Education of the National Council of the Churches of Christ in the U.S.A. All rights reserved; and the KING JAMES VERSION.

The diagram of elements reprinted on page 113 is used by permission, © Murray Robertson 1999–2008.

"Jesus, The Very Thought of You" lyrics reprinted on page 143 are by Edward Caswall, 1849 (Public Domain).

Dürer images reprinted on pages 162, 187, 261, 427, and 428 are provided courtesy of the Wetmore Print Collection, Art History Department, Connecticut College, New London, USA.

"Some Sweet Day" lyrics reprinted on page 243 are by Fanny Crosby, 1887 (Public Domain).

"City of God" lyrics reprinted on page 274 are used with permission, © 1981, OCP, 5536 NE Hassalo, Portland, OR 97213. All rights reserved.

Image of birthmark on pages 297 and 424 © Murray Robertson, 1999–2010.

Fractal on page 326 provided courtesy of J.C. Sprott, http://sprott.physics.wisc.edu/fractals/.

"Shall We Gather at the River" lyrics reprinted on page 365 are by Robert Lowry, 1864 (Public Domain).

"My Life Flows On" ("How Can I Keep from Singing") lyrics reprinted on page 414 are by Robert Lowry, 1860 (Public Domain).

Library of Congress Cataloging-in-Publication Data

Sweet, Leonard I.
    The seraph seal / Leonard Sweet and Lori Wagner.
        p. cm.
    Summary: "An epic tale of good and evil based on the four horsemen of the Apocalypse found in Revelation"— Provided by publisher.
    ISBN 978-0-8499-2077-6 (pbk.)
    1. Bible. N.T. Revelation—Fiction. I. Wagner, Lori. II. Title.
PS3619.W44265S47 2011
813'.6—dc22   2010052287

Printed in the United States of America

11 12 13 14 15 RRD 5 4 3 2 1

To Louis XVI ... and his hoards of descendents.
Please wake up.

CONTENTS

In today already walks tomorrow.

—JOHANN FRIEDRICH VON SCHILLER

Part II: Leukosis

Part III: Xanthosis

ACKNOWLEDGMENTS

Every woven tale breathes the multiplicity of stories, fragments, and memories that live within it, sometimes subtly, sometimes more evidently. As in a hand-made gift, scraps and bits of this and that are lovingly taken and threaded through the webs of our minds to make new and sometimes intricate weaves. For *The Seraph Seal*, we've gathered especially for you, the reader, many of those sticks, stones, shells, and bones that the two of us have collected along the way, and we display them here for your reading pleasure.

This project was a gift to both of us. And for many reasons, we both were thrilled to take up the challenge of this writing adventure that blurs the line between fiction and nonfiction and introduces a new literary genre—engaged fiction. We hope this project will be the first of many trailblazing quests.

As with any exciting adventure, we've had our little helps along the way. A thank-you first to our talented agent, Mark Sweeney, who patiently guides us through every weed-grown path. And second, to our risk-taking, bungee-jumping publisher at Thomas Nelson, Matt Baugher, to whom we have everlasting thanks for going out on this limb for us and trusting we wouldn't let him crash. A thank-you third to our editor, Jennifer McNeil, and our marketer, Emily Sweeney, for meticulous removal of unwanted thistles and stones and A1 pitching and peddling. And to all the rest of the devoted staff and proofers at Thomas Nelson, thank you, thank you. A special thanks to the chemistry department at Lehigh University, who provided us with the knowledge of how to effectively ignite ethanol. And to the countless sources of information, our "signs of the times," that provided us with granola for the journey.

We chose only two readers for the fledgling project—ones who we felt represented the kind of reader we were trying to reach with our story. Thank you, Michele Masterfano and Margaret (Peggy) Furmaniak, for providing those first looks and responses. We also want to thank all the members of the Sweet family (Elizabeth, Thane, Soren, Egil, and Justin), who put up with two authors for three weeks of 24/7 writing on Orcas Island. As always, Betty O'Brien located needles in the haystack that we thought were unfindable.

I (Len) never met my grandfather and namesake, Ira Sweet, but I feel I know him from his library. Ira Sweet was a tradesman by day (a glove cutter in Gloversville, New York). But by night he was a lay theologian of Wesleyan bent who read widely in apocalypticism and holiness theology. Even in death, he has had a penetrating influence on me, perhaps not unlike a westerly wind that wails and wanes when it crosses our path. His simple, wooden, homemade chair, where he sat nightly to study his precious resources on the book of Revelation and the end times, is one of my most prized possessions.

We hope you will enjoy our story and have as much fun on your journey within it as we have had in our journey writing it.

— Leonard Sweet and Lori Wagner
August 2010

ENGAGING THE APOCALYPSE

A Nonfiction Essay on Scenarios and
Semiotics for the 21st Century

The Seraph Seal is a fish story. Not the usual story told by a fanciful fisherman but from the real-life perspective of the fish.

We are now living in the ultimate fish bowl. If the fish were to tell its tale to generations to come, it wouldn't be a story of basking and boasting but of sharkish terror that defies reality. No matter how blue the water or how usual the perils of the deep, the element of surprise buckles the composure of the best of us. And red faced, we emerge, having been unprepared not for the extraordinary but for the probable and plausible ordinary that we haven't allowed ourselves to notice.

Scenario thinker Mark Vickers calls it the "Fiction Effect": "People are simply stunned by major events. One day you're plugging along, living your life, working your jobs, maybe a bit bored by mundane affairs. The next day, something happens that you can barely believe, something that is supposed to occur only in the realm of fiction or long-gone history rather than in your current all-too-real life."[1]

But life is almost always stranger than fiction. We have only to look around us at the expanse of the Gulf oil spill; the devastation of hurricane Katrina; planes flying into buildings; epidemics, such as AIDS and the avian flu; corporate and governmental Ponzi schemes;

stem-cell research; and the dark matter of quantum physics to know that we are only a hairline short of (dys)functional chaos.

So, how can we prepare for an unknown future? Are we destined to be swept down the river with the currents of change? Or can we create ways of looking at possible future realities that give us an edge when the shock waves hit? Are we reduced to always playing catch-up or put-down? Or can we get ahead of culture, *carpe mañana*, and be sowers of futures? How do we find the grey areas between utopia and dystopia, between living as an ostrich, with our faces in the sand, and sticking our heads too far into the clouds?

Global Business Network cofounder Peter Schwartz, who was hired by Steven Spielberg in 1999 to envision the future for the film *Minority Report* (2002), suggests we tell stories. But not just any stories—alternative stories about the future that reveal plausible yet challenging possibilities. These future "scenarios" are created by probing cultural patterns and connecting the dots of current events. Patterns that emerge from beliefs and choices people make now, in the present, form red flags that we can use to forecast the way the future might look, if those patterns continue on their present course.

We can also scan for probable intersections of patterns that could create other narrative possibilities. Schwartz calls the creation of such stories *scenario thinking*. I prefer to call it *scenario reckoning* or *semiotics*—paying attention to the signs of the times and following the traces and trails that lead to places of intersection, especially those junctures where our story meets God's story.

You might even call scenarios by another name: *sonograms*. Sonographers enter into relationships with reality before it presents itself—just as doctors can foresee genetic abnormalities or foreclose a wombmate's future ("selective reduction"), just as parents can "see" their offspring before they appear. Sonograms of the future are possible for those who pause to let sounds become sights, rumblings and resonances become apparitions of the future that we might call a kind of avatar.

Scenarios are not fixed strategies but recognitions that human choices, beliefs, and habits create paths toward probable and possible future outcomes. Some of these pathways are positive; some of them destructive. By identifying the patterns of meaning we see around us, we can form creative and imaginative scenarios for different faces of the future. This is the same principle behind simulation games and the various types of systems-thinking responsible for making Internet connections.

For example, let's say you want to do a research paper. Every time you type a keyword into your computer, you come up with various *scenarios* or outcomes for your topic, based on how that keyword has been valued by others. The more creatively you think about the topic you want to research, the better keywords you will come up with, and the more interesting and unusual connections you will find. Some paths you take may lead you to new and innovative ways of thinking about your subject. In the end, you will no doubt come to several possible ways to approach it and will choose the one that seems most imaginable and plausible to you.

Scenario thinking works much the same way. It is the art of seeing patterns, making connections, juxtaposing differences, tracking the drivers of change, tracing the paths of those patterns and connections, and then composing creative narratives about the potential outcomes they foretell.

"Thin slices" of information can reveal the future. For example, Matthew Hertenstein runs an emotion research center at DePauw University in Greencastle, Indiana. He has found that those who smiled the most in their old photos, whether as a child or in their high school or college yearbooks, are most likely to have successful marriages. And those who frowned were most likely to have divorces. So *smile* for the camera![2] Scenario thinking creates landscapes of meaning and bridges to the future from recognizing how the future is behind, and the past ahead.

Just as an artist might paint a tree from an impressionist, expressionistic, cubist, or Dadaistic perspective, each painting telling a different story about the artist's values and choice of meaning, so also can scenario thinking create varied stories based on the same reality. Peter Schwartz calls this a *scenario matrix*—a transformation of our creative observations into a "range of credible stories—four futures that are as different as you can possibly make them, covering the broadest range of possible outcomes."[3] Seeing the factors that lead to these scenarios, especially those identified as weaknesses, can help us avoid or confront them as they may occur in the future. Creative scenario thinking takes the shock factor and the fiction out of the "Fiction Effect" and allows instead for probable and multiple realities.

In 1958, Klaus Conrad coined the term *apophenia* to describe the experience of seeing meaningful patterns in what can appear to be meaningless or random disorder. Apophenia was first used to signify a mental illness similar to that of John Forbes Nash Jr. in the movie *A Beautiful Mind*, in which he sees messages, codes, and patterns within random numbered data. However, this term most recently describes the ability of everyday individuals to pick out purposeful patterns within the intricacies of life, leading to a state of "abnormal meaningfulness." Maybe apophenia is a condition for which we all should aim. This skill of apophenia, or art of semiotic awareness, can guide us in identifying possible scenarios based on observations we find in what Jesus called the "signs of our times."

In creating the novel *The Seraph Seal*, we have used semiotics in an apophenic way to read the signs of apocalyptic brewery all around us, and to create from it a briny scenario. Whether the novel's perspective is the worst-case scenario or the best is for you to decide, based on your own semiotic view and whether you tend to be an Eeyore or a Tigger. But within the novel, you will find a path that we have identified as probable and possible, based on the patterns of meaning we sense and the dots we connect.

In order for you to make your own connections and to evaluate the probability of our novel scenario, we have created for you a type of simulation game of our own. It is a way for us to conscript you into our ailment and for you to participate in our apophenia. You are invited to read for yourself the signs of the times to determine whether our scenario would be your scenario, or whether you might choose quite another ending to our story. We call this invitation to participate with us *engaged fiction.*

In part V of our novel, you will find a section exclusively devoted to you. In a sense, the material you find there is our rocks and gems collection—much of the raw semiotic material we have gathered and used in order to formulate our novel scenario.

We invite you to mine that material to your heart's desire and to use these tools of engaged fiction to explore for yourself whether this is the end of the old or the beginning of the new. What's ahead for the human race? The course history is now taking is arresting the attention of all the world. Nothing like it has been experienced before. Nothing of like nature has the world ever seen. Empires have fallen or teeter precariously. Economic systems have crashed or refuse to heal. The world is littered with the debris of destruction or the afterbirth of wild technological dreams. What is going on? How many more body slams can we take? What is our future?

We hope to prepare you to answer these questions and to equip you for the apocalyptic journey that our novel suggests is ahead. We admit it: the book of Revelation is as absorbing to us as it was to Sir Isaac Newton, who spent more time on his theological pursuits issuing from his reading of this text than on his scientific projects. But any apocalyptic vision is conditional semiotics: "Behold, I set before you this day a blessing and a curse; a blessing, if ye obey the commandments of the LORD your God . . . a curse, if ye will not obey the commandments of the LORD your God, but turn aside out of the way which I command you this day" (Deut. 11:26–28 KJV; cf. 30:15). Jeremiah restated the nature of human freedom: "Behold, I set before you the way of life, and the way of death" (Jer. 21:8 KJV). Or as Jesus made clear after he gave his Sermon on the Mount, what lies ahead for the human race is partly up to whether we choose the narrow gate or the broad way (Matt. 7:13–14). We need not be hurtled into some future by either the irresistible force of "scientific progress" or the horoscopic timetable of end-times pre-determinism. "Choose you this day . . ."

But remember: human freedom is trumped by something

greater—the freedom of God. The future can never slip beyond God's control. The Bible ends with a vision of a garden city, a "new heaven and a new earth," where "the tabernacle of God" dwells and where "God himself shall be with [humankind], and be their God" (Rev. 21:1, 3 KJV). The biblical answer to the question of what's ahead for planet Earth and the human race is not a crystal ball but a warning and a promise. The Bible ends not with a marionette dance but with a maranatha feast.

"The Alphabet of the Apocalypse: Reading the Signs of the Times" is a type of guide. In it, you will find those elements of our STEEP reality that contribute to our apocalyptic vision. STEEP is an acronym for *social, technological, environmental, economic,* and *political* forces. Take three elements from each category in the Alphabet and crash them together to see what the future might bring. Combine them; gather them; mix them up as you will. The combinations of many of them may lead to rather explosive deductions. For example, when you combine the *bottom billion* with *bureaucracy, consumerism,* and *high finance,* you might have a recipe for trouble brewing. If you combine *magnetic reversals, M-theory,* and *Quantum Entanglement,* you might come up with some interesting new takes on prophecies and multiple realities. We hope that you will use this apocalyptic tool not only to uncover hidden meanings within the novel but to unveil your own semiotic viewpoints of the future. The ideas in the Alphabet of the Apocalypse are a compelling tale in themselves. If you want to recognize the "signs" around you, read the Signs of the Times first. It will put the story that follows in context, and it will hand you clues that can later unlock the symbolism hidden in the story. If you want to dive into the story, go ahead. We constructed it apart from the ideas in the Alphabet of the Apocalyse, but growing from it.

In addition to the Alphabet of the Apocalypse: Reading the Signs of the Times, you will find a section called "The Journals and Notes of Paul Binder." This is the main character's notebook, filled with tidbits, scraps, notes, and materials that our character uses on his own semiotic journey. In it, you will find pieces of valuable information and bits of explanation that may help you understand some of the symbols and background in the novel. You can use this source to further investigate the discoveries that led Paul Binder on his journey to the dramatic conclusion of *The Seraph Seal.*

Thus our simulation game involves you as an engaged participant on your own semiotic journey. As you travel through the latter part of the book, we will introduce you to the warning signs of our twenty-first-century world as it is, as we imagine it. And, as you read our novel, we will take you through the twists and turns of our own Fiction Effect.

Scenario expert Peter Schwartz reminds us that "it is critical to push people's imagination out to the very edges of believability to see the full range of the possible."[4] We invite you now to stretch your imagination, to ponder the possibilities suggested by our vision, and to prepare yourself for a future that may seem stranger than fiction. For when the bird takes it into his head to swim like a fish, imagine the possibilities of a new existence! And when the fish takes it into her head to fly like a bird, proffer then the possibilities of a new reality!

Besides, there is more to fishing than catching fish. Juliana Berners (born circa 1388) was the prioress of Sopwell nunnery near St. Albans in England and was an expert writer on heraldry, hawking, and hunting. Berners (sometimes spelled *Bernes*; people were casual about spelling back then) is said to have written the first known book on fishing by a woman. She coined the phrase *Piscator non solum piscatur,* which when translated means either "fishers not only of fish" or "there is more to fishing than catching fish." It is now the motto of the Fly Fishers' Club, International.

Maybe when Jesus said we are to be "fishers of men" he was also saying that "there is more to fishing than catching fish." Maybe we are also to be catching images of the future, and feasting on the right ones.

— *Leonard Sweet*
5 July 2010

Wild, dark times are rumbling toward us, and the prophet who wishes to write a new apocalypse will have to invent entirely new beasts, and beasts so terrible that the ancient animal symbols of Saint John will seem like cooing doves and cupids in comparison.

—HEINRICH HEINE

PROLOGUE

The Key

21 DECEMBER 2012 AT 2100

TRONA, CALIFORNIA

To light a candle is to signal its demise. The law of sowing and reaping and the law of sealing and unsealing might have come from that same principle. So it was that when the clock struck the twenty-first hour of the winter solstice on that night of 21 December 2012, beginnings and endings began to merge.

The night had grown cold. The newspapers left on the stoop of Old Town Hall's decaying wooden steps flapped wildly as a gust of wind howled and swept across the porch. A crushed aluminum can rattled loudly, whisking down the frozen gutter.

The priest, dressed in hooded, black raiment, turned the corner from the abandoned hospital and disappeared into the night.

A weak glow cast shadows down the walls of the room on the fourth floor of the vacant building. The candles flickered as what appeared to be a woman dressed in a somber, loose-fitting garment cleaned yellow-white mucus from the child's face.

I stood silently with the others, eyes glancing nervously toward the dark hallway and then back to the child. *If I moved quickly, I could get to the door.* The room seemed suddenly oppressive, frightening.

The hooded figure next to me looked more nervous than I was. He licked his lips, his tongue darting out every few seconds, sweat dripping from his nose.

The wind outside had risen to an even louder pitch. Thunder rumbled, the sound growing and expanding, like high-powered jet engines hovering just a few feet from the outside of the building. The foundation seemed to tremble. The windows shook in their frames, and then all was still, except for the streaks of lightning still flashing across the walls like a muted Morse code.

The crying had stopped. The woman who would serve as Guardian turned with the child and held him up. A strange and eerie calm settled over the room as the child slowly opened his eyes. Fixed and coal black, they seemed to survey all of us with a command of knowledge and wisdom far beyond that of an infant. I shuddered.

"Look on the child who will become the savior of all nations. With his birth, the Seal has been broken." Her voice echoed in the empty room. "According to the Way of the Seal, he will be named Matthew Samael."

She held up the ancient book, its golden letters gleaming.

"May the Time of Becoming begin."

Those around me bowed slightly. I quickly did the same, not wanting to be recognized as a Messenger amid the others.

"Come and look on the child."

The Guardian nodded and held out the child, gesturing the participants to come forward.

All those in the room lined up single file, their hooded faces illuminated by the yellow glow of the candles they held out in front of them, their dark robes trailing along the floor behind them.

As I came near the head of the line, I reached under the heavy material and grasped the silver cross lying against my skin. My lips moved silently in a prayer of petition. *Lord, help me to fulfill this task.* My hands began to shake, and I released them back to my sides. *What if he knows who I am?* I tried to calm myself. *He's only a child. He's only a child.* I wiped my hands on the inside of my robe and approached the head of the line. As I leaned down to kiss his forehead, I felt his eyes follow me and hold my gaze. In a moment of panic, I broke away and hurried on past the others, out the door and into the night. My job here was done. I had witnessed the birth. There was no mistaking it. He was the one. Should Matthew Serafino grow to prevail, the world as we know it would end, as the prophecy foretold. The destiny of the earth would now be in the hands of a chosen defender. The only one to turn the prophecy and re-inaugurate the dawn of God's humanity.

*
* *

Around the world, storms, hurricanes, monsoons, earthquakes, and floods broke loose as seven more newborn cries pierced the deafening roars—all born at 2100 on 21 December 2012, all with an odd-shaped birthmark on the inside of the lower right calf. Eight births, four seraphim, seven seals. The waiting was over. The Time of Becoming had begun. Now, only the Chosen One could determine the true Way of the Seraph Seal. And the Lamb would reveal his prophet.

RANSON, WEST VIRGINIA, SEVEN MILES FROM HARPERS FERRY

Jefferson Hospital

Early in the morning hours, Deborah Binder received a package. It was wrapped in simple brown paper and addressed to Benjamin and Deborah Binder, c/o 7th Floor, Jefferson Hospital, Ranson, West Virginia. Shifting uncomfortably in the hospital bed, her distended abdomen serving as a temporary table for her perusal of the package, Deborah tore into the paper and lifted out the small cardboard box. She frowned, turning the box over in her hands. No note. No return address. Her mind began running through the events of the night. She had arrived at the hospital's emergency room at the start of her labor, just past midnight. The only four people who knew she was there were her husband, her parents, and the next-door neighbor. But her neighbor wouldn't have sent her anything, and her parents lived in Oregon.

There's no way they could have sent a package that would have arrived within the last two hours. *How would anyone know to send a package here?* Deborah continued to stare at the box, both curious and cautious about the contents. Her husband, Ben, had gone down to the hospital cafeteria to get coffee about ten minutes ago, but rather than wait for him to open the package, she let her curiosity get the better of her. Using her fingernail, she slit the tape on the box, opened the flaps, and carefully drew out a small glass case. Inside the case was a large cross-shaped key. The key looked old, yet it shimmered as though made of silver mercury infused with rainbow colors. It was ornate and appeared to be hand-cast, with some sort of design on it that Deborah couldn't quite make out. When she held it up, the early morning sun cast an array of colors onto the far walls of the room.

"Beryllium."

Deborah looked up. Ben was back in the room, looking down at the strange key.

"It's beryllium," he said. "Remember when I worked for Raycom? Every aircraft is made of the stuff. The aviation industry uses it all the time. So does national security. But I've never seen anything quite like that. Where did it come from?"

"I have no idea," Deborah replied. She was still turning the key over and over in her hands, watching the prismlike lights float about the room.

Laying the key on the bed, she picked up the box again. Neither container nor wrapping revealed any clue as to its sender. As she prepared to return the key to its casing, Deborah noticed a small white card lying in the bottom of the box. On it were seven words in script:

Paul Binder
Child of the Seraph Seal

Deborah grew quiet, and Ben looked up to find her staring off into space. Her lips were moving, and she appeared to be deep in thought or perhaps feeling the effects of her medication. Ben leaned over, placing his hand on hers.

"Deb?"

"Paul," she said out loud.

Almost whispering, she continued slowly, "Paul."

Ben moved in closer to her side. She looked up at her husband, breaking her strange reverie.

"I think we should name him Paul."

Just then, a sharp pain seared through her body, and she doubled over in labor.

Part I

MELANOSIS

In all chaos there is a cosmos, in all disorder a secret order.
—CARL JUNG

The streets were dark with something more than night.
—RAYMOND CHANDLER

Weather forecast for tonight: dark.
—GEORGE CARLIN

What raging FIRE shall flood the soul
What rich desire unlocks its door
What sweet seduction lies before us?

—"POINT OF NO RETURN"
THE PHANTOM OF THE OPERA
ANDREW LLOYD WEBBER

1

THE LETTER

21 March 2048

ROANOKE, VIRGINIA

A nimbus cloud cover lay thick and low over the Virginia hills, and Paul could tell the rain was coming. He absentmindedly waved on the light to the garage and reached for his coat from the hook by the door. He looked at his watch: 5:30 a.m. *Just enough time to stop for coffee on the way to my nine o'clock class.* He ran his fingers lightly across the touch screen on the wall, and the garage door slid upward.

Paul heard the crash just as he was closing the car door. *What now?* He slid out of his seat belt, shoved open the half-closed door, and ran out into the driveway. The moon cast a bluish hue over the vacant terrace. He crossed the lawn and stepped into the street. A block down the road, a car lay on its side in the middle of the deserted intersection, its lights flashing on and off. The back end of the coupe was torn open, and a mixture of gasoline and antifreeze poured out onto the road, causing a greenish vapor to rise over the black tarmac. Paul looked up and down the intersection. There was no one in sight.

Paul cautiously approached the vehicle, fragments of finely shattered glass crunching under his feet. It was raining now, and fog was forming around the car in wisps as the liquid from the punctured radiator continued to hiss and steam across the cold ground.

3

It was quiet. That couldn't be good. As he rounded the side of the car, Paul noticed something sticking out from under the tangled metal on the driver's side. A man's arm lay twisted in an unnatural position, crushed beneath the frame of the car. The lifeless fingers reached out, as though grasping for something just beyond reach. Paul looked around. *There's no one here.* The air was still and heavy. The only sound he could hear was the pattering of rain on metal and pavement. His mind began to race. *Someone had to have hit the car with a powerful force in order to knock it on its side and damage both the rear and front ends. But there's nothing out here.*

A cold shiver ran down Paul's spine, and he backed away from the outstretched hand. Moving slowly toward the front of the car, Paul could see that the windshield had been smashed in. What remained of the driver was slumped sideways, the side of his head covered in red, blackening blood. Then Paul noticed the letter.

The large white envelope sat on the dash, as though placed there for him to see. How it would have remained in that position during the crash, Paul could not fathom. He inched closer until he could see the scrawled writing across the front:

Mr. Paul Binder
Personal and Confidential

At first, Paul backed away, a wave of terror and revulsion building in his throat. The bulky trunk of the mutilated car blinking in the early morning darkness felt surreal, as though it were some monstrous creature lying there watching him, breathing, waiting for him to make a move. The feeling passed. Paul carefully reached into the hole in the windshield and grabbed the letter from the dash, then turned away and tuned in to his Pearl—his personally enhanced auto-relationship link—that was clipped to the base of his ear. He had just purchased the new Pearl earring last week to replace his former pendant. The new 2048 version did everything imaginable. It was a type of BMI (brain machine interface) that could not only follow commands but could interlock with Paul's every thought and body function. In a moment, the device would connect to his FirePillar, alerting emergency services.

After the police arrived and Paul answered what questions he could—*I didn't witness the accident, only the aftermath*—Paul signed his statement and walked back toward the house.

"I never saw the other car," he had told them.

Because there was nothing there to see, the voice inside his head taunted him.

Paul didn't mention the letter. If he did, he would be pressed for hours with questions he knew nothing about. He needed to think. Shivering, he drew his coat around his neck and shook off the voodoo. "To shake off the voodoo" was one of his mother's favorite expressions. Whenever he was afraid as a child, had a nightmare, or was feeling insecure about giving a speech at school, his mother would look him in the eyes, cup his face in her hands, and say, "Now, Paul, you go on and shake off the voodoo. You're gonna be fine." And she was always right. He smiled to himself, thinking how much influence she continued to have on him, even from the grave. He stopped and looked back. The police were still buzzing around the car, joined now by a fire and rescue crew working at extracting the driver from the passenger side of the vehicle. Whatever had happened that morning must have an explanation, and the authorities would find out what it was.

Paul walked back to the garage, got into his car, and set his Pearl to navigate in the direction of Charlottesville. It was already 7:30 a.m., and now he would be late for class. *No coffee today.* On the seat next to him lay the letter, his name staring up at him. Setting his jaw, he ignored it and continued to drive. He would deal with it later.

Relaxing a bit now that the rain was starting to clear, Paul interfaced with his Pearl to find station WKCI. The news ran through the usual—weather, sports, local, economics, then turned to a special address by the president. New Earth Day—he had almost forgotten. President Matt Serafino was talking now about the new technologies that would revolutionize the nation's food supply. Already in his second year in office, Serafino had mesmerized a tired and disillusioned USAmerican people with promises of superior genetically altered food supplies, increased life expectancies, innovations in avatar and touch technologies, lower crime rates, increased cyber and virtual communications, and decreased levels of aboveground contaminants. He had already mobilized forces in all the major cities to prevent looting of the hospitals and churches that were left abandoned. In the first quarter of the twenty-first century, with the introduction of the New United States and its secularized religion, the remnants of the old churches collapsed. After the faithful went underground, meeting in homes or in private settings, the old-world doctors, who refused to embrace the new manipulation technologies, followed suit and went underground, too, to form the Anti-Technology Biological Alliance (ATBA). Serafino had a plan to rebuild USAmerica once more into the most viable and economically wealthy nation in the world—harnessing the power of the oceans, winds, and the earth's core to drive the technoindustries, which would renew and replace USAmerica's failing industrial framework. The people called him the twenty-first-century Uncle Sam—the one to usher in a new and restored United States.

At thirty-six, Matt was the youngest president ever to take the oath of office. *The same age I am*, Paul thought. And he sometimes appeared to have the energy and stamina of ten men. Powerfully charismatic, the USAmerican president commanded attention everywhere he went. People gathered around him in droves, hanging on to his every word. But when Paul had seen him on the Capitol's West Front Lawn that day, 21 January 2047, something about Matt Serafino left Paul uneasy. *Could it be the president's strutting confidence? The way he cocked his head to the side before he spoke? Or the way his almost pitch-black eyes surveyed the crowd, his fiery gaze threatening to incinerate on the spot anyone who challenged him?*

The truth was, Matt's personality was both charming and deadly.

His campaign had seared into his opponents' arguments, leaving them no choice but to withdraw. And it was that same drive, accompanied by a compelling confidence, that seemed to draw people around him in support of his initiatives to make the United States a supertech world power.

That should have been enough to make him wary of the president, but Paul thought it was more than that. His mind wandered back to that day on the lawn in January, the president's inauguration ceremony. Paul remembered the way Matt (as he liked to be known to the USAmerican people—an oddity in itself for presidential stature) grasped the Bible as Chief Justice Remington Warner swore him in as the forty-eighth president of the United States. There was almost a savagery about that clutch, as though wanting to consume or conquer the Word itself. And then there was the passage he chose for his inaugural theme, Isaiah 66:

> *For the Lord will come in fire,*
> *   and his chariots like the whirlwind,*
> *to pay back his anger in fury,*
> *   and his rebuke in flames of fire.*
> *For by fire will the Lord execute judgment,*
> *   and by his sword, on all flesh;*
> *   and those slain by the Lord shall be many.*
>
> *For as the new heavens and the new earth,*
> *   which I will make,*
> *shall remain before me, says the Lord,*
> *   so shall your descendants and your name remain.*
> *From new moon to new moon.*

It was a strange passage to choose, and it cast an ominous chill over the crowd that day. Stranger still was Serafino's use of the Bible itself in the swearing-in ceremony. Even though Christianity had become an "ABC" word, something like ABC gum—rechewed and spit out by most New Selfers, Serafino had insisted on the obsolete inaugural tradition, choosing a Bible from the Library of Congress and inserting the aged manuscript into the hands of the chief justice before the inauguration ceremony, the appropriate passage marked by a golden thread.

"I, Matthew Samael Serafino, do solemnly swear that I will faithfully execute the office of President of the United States, and will, to the best of my ability preserve, protect, and defend the Constitution of the United States."

President Serafino seemed to have an answer and a solution to every problem, some of which even sounded plausible. But as professor of history and cultural semiotics at the University of Virginia, Paul knew something about politics and economics. And despite most people's fascination with the USAmerican president, what Paul knew most was that he didn't trust Matthew Serafino.

CHARLOTTESVILLE, VIRGINIA

University of Virginia

Paul reached his office at 9:35 a.m. Too late for his morning class, he stopped in the university cafeteria for coffee before settling into his office studio. He had until two o'clock that afternoon before his next lecture. He fingered the corner of the letter in his pocket, remembering the morning's events. He didn't want to open it until he was safely in his office. What could it mean? At last, armed with coffee, the virtual news report, and the latest i-issue of the *Journal of American History*, Paul reached his swivel chair and pulled the letter from his pocket. He sipped the hot, steaming liquid, gathering his thoughts. Tearing open the envelope with the edge of his finger, he took out the sheet of paper inside.

The letter was handwritten and appeared to be drafted in black ink. Rare these days. No one wrote by hand anymore. With the advent of jewelry piece BMI robotics, advanced biometrics, and Cloud computing, almost all text was now voice and touch activated. Most people didn't even use pens anymore. The only people interested in traditional paper were historians and collectors, like Paul, who loved the feel of the ancient texts. Those more interested in the dead than the living. Paul smiled. Now, the best forms of communication were in avatar space and in virtual meeting rooms. Safer too. Especially in the classroom.

Paul brushed his thumb across the black letters. The ink left a dark smudge on his pale skin, coloring the lines of his personal imprint.

Fresh. Almost as if the writer had just finished the last flourish.

Paul braced himself and began to read.

Dear Dr. Binder,

If you are receiving this letter, the year will be 2048—thirty-six years after your birth and the birth of the eight. The Time of Becoming has now reached fruition. Locate the manuscript of the Diatessaron. You have been chosen to unlock the future of your world. The cross key will guide you. Use it wisely.

Paul reread the letter three times, and finally just stared at the scripted ink intently, baffled as to what the words could mean.

For the second time that day, Paul had the uncomfortable feeling that something didn't quite fit. And his mind fought to make sense of it. The ink was fresh. He was sure of it. Yet the letter referred to the year 2048 as though written long prior. Just as the damaged car that morning seemed to appear out of nowhere with no sign of what caused the crash.

Because there was nothing there to see.

Paul swallowed hard, his eyebrows knitting together as he remembered the details of the morning hours. He read the letter again, this time holding it in his hands like a fragile piece of parchment. He turned it over, looking for some sign of identification. There was none.

What could it mean? And why is it addressed to me?

Paul knew what the Diatessaron was. That is, if the ancient Syrian manuscript he was familiar with was the one he thought the letter was referring to. More than one author had created such "harmonies of the four," but the most famous was by a second-century writer named Tatian from the region of what is still the country of Syria. With copies written in both Syrian and Greek, the text comprised a unification of the four known Christian Gospels: Matthew, Mark, Luke, and John. The message was controversial, and Tatian was later treated as a heretic. Some even feared the text had magical powers. But the harmonized Diatessaron was revered in the early Syrian church and in the Orthodox churches of the East. Paul would give his right arm to see an authentic copy of the Diatessaron manuscript. He also knew that no complete and original manuscript existed.

Paul's concentration was interrupted by his vibrating Pearl. He took the call. "This is Paul."

A male voice spoke. "Mr. Binder?"

"Yes, I'm Paul Binder."

"Is this Dr. Paul Binder, the professor of history and cultural semiotics?"

"I am."

"Dr. Binder, this is Emory Makefield. I'm calling from the Centre for Manuscript and Print Studies at the University of London. We've just received a very unusual manuscript. I think you're going to want to see this."

"What is it?"

"Dr. Binder—may I call you Paul? We believe it's a complete Syrian manuscript of what appears to be the Diatessaron."

Paul drew in his breath and paused for a moment. *It couldn't be.* He regained his composure.

"Tatian's Diatessaron?"

"I had it checked out myself by one of our experts. We believe it's authentic."

Paul's heart was beating faster. How could this be happening?

"I don't understand. Where did you get this?"

There hadn't been a discovery of a new manuscript since 1933. Paul was becoming both excited and stunned as he contemplated what finding a manuscript like this could mean, not only to historiography, but in light of what had happened today—to him. *Too many coincidences to be accidental.*

Emory Makefield continued thoughtfully, "It's unusual really, Paul. The codex of parchment leaves was apparently found by an anonymous benefactor in a remote part of the Syrian marshlands. As he told the story to me, the manuscript had been hidden in a watertight container underneath the marshes—perhaps to protect it from being burned along with the others in the early centuries. During the 1990s, under Saddam Hussein's regime, hundreds of those marshes had been drained to permit military access. So much so that the entire area experienced serious water-reduction problems for a number of years, until solutions were found. After the droughts of 2008 and 2035, the Syrians joined efforts with Turkey and Iraq to reconstitute the water supplies in the region. In the midst of excavation for a dam in the Syrian region near the Euphrates River, the container resurfaced. Our benefactor bought it from the excavation crew before the government could get wind of it. The thing is, Dr. Binder, it's a manuscript that we never thought we'd see. It's an intact original of the Syrian text, maybe the original written by Tatian himself."

Paul hesitated, his mind reeling.

"Dr. Binder? Are you there? Can you come to London?"

"Pardon me. Yes, yes." He was almost laughing now. "I'll book the first flight I can get today."

Paul hung up the phone and reached for his jacket, as his Pearl calculated the directions to the Charlottesville-Albemarle aerodock.

2

FIRE AND BRICS

Oval Office

Matt Serafino paced the office furiously. The two aides scurried from the room, returning to their offices. They knew what the president's tempers were like. The same power and presence that defined his allure could in an instant become an incinerator for venting his anger onto his victims. No one wanted to be there when that happened. And he was angry now.

Ever since businessman Murong Gui became president of the People's Republic of China, the Chinese had been gaining economic and political power not just in the East but throughout the world. Gui had invested a quarter of the country's financial resources into funding the National Center for the Study of Genetics and, with their round-the-clock staff making almost constant scientific break-throughs, China was advancing in the interrelational sciences faster than any other nation in the world. The mastermind at the center was a man named Niú Ye. Although a short and humble-looking man, Niú was an aggressively vicious businessman and a shrewd strategist. Just the kind of person Serafino wished he had in his corner in the United States. But now China had come out with a new biological

13

weapon—a genetically manufactured superkiller that would have the power to wipe out entire nations—and Matt knew Niú Ye had to be behind it. The deadly serum would elevate China far above the United States in global weaponry. How could he have let this happen? Why didn't his intel staff get wind of the project before its inception? Serafino continued to pace agitatedly. So, China wants to play with fire? Then it's time for them to feel the burn. *And Niú Ye is going to be the first to fry.*

Matt strode across the empty Oval Office to the interface panel and Pearl-activated the screen. Immediately, the image shimmered to life, all but covering the 16 x 29-foot west wall. He reduced the screen to 4 x 8 feet and stepped back.

"Niú Ye, China, Center for the Study of Genetics," he said clearly. Instantly the interface located and zeroed in to Niú's portal. In a moment, Niú would receive the signal and could accept the president's portal page. Matt Serafino steadied himself, his dark eyes glued to the screen. His face belied no emotion. Coolly, he watched as a small man's image came up onto the screen.

"Niú Ye," he said. The cold smile of greeting revealed that he would not be one to trifle with. Niú stared back, unflinching.

"President Serafino." Niú bowed slightly, then straightened.

"Your bioweapons research has caused quite a stir."

"Indeed." Niú waited, feeling like a rabbit staring into the face of a hungry jackal.

"You know what I want, Niú." Serafino's eyes fixed on Niú Ye's and held them. Niú Ye shifted uncomfortably, not willing to break contact with the president's gaze. He could feel a wave of fear well up inside him, threatening to choke his words. He opened his mouth and then closed it again, his throat constricting. Niú had never seen eyes like Serafino's before—so cold, calculating. They were pitch black, wide, and emotionless, laced with the cold anticipation of a predator relishing its prey. And Serafino was playing with him now. He could feel it. His hands went cold at his sides. Beads of sweat formed at the base of his neck. The president was still watching him.

"I'm giving you a choice, Niú," he broke out. "You can get me the research, or you can agree to head the genetics lab here in Bethesda—under my direct supervision, of course. What will it be?"

Niú remained silent, his mind working furiously like a cornered mouse trying to find its way out of a maze.

"I'll give you some time, Niú. I'll even be magnanimous. You can have until noon tomorrow. If I don't hear from you, I will find you. And Niú—don't make me find you."

Serafino's image vanished from the screen, and Niú Ye collapsed into the chair behind his portal. Hands shaking, he sipped a glass of water and tried to calm himself.

He should have known this would happen. Serafino was blackmailing him. He was sure of it. The president must know about Ye's disaster with the Capricorn Project, the human toll it had taken, and the extensive cover-up the scientist had orchestrated. He had to. Otherwise, he would never risk provoking the Chinese government. Had he even contacted Beijing? No, he hadn't gone to the president. He had come directly to him. And Niú Ye knew enough about Matthew Serafino to realize this was not an official, above-board call. This was a personal agenda. Niú shuddered.

Those eyes. They were vacant, nothing behind them.

Niú Ye tuned in to his Pearl and linked through to the lab.

*
* *

Later, in Washington, Matthew Serafino headed to his private quarters to dress. Tonight he would be hosting a state dinner in honor of the Brazilian president, Ernesto Alvarez, and the president's wife, Maria Almeida Alvarez. The República Federativa do Brasil had been on the economic rise ever since the early turn of the twenty-first century, when the BRIC nations turned their political gaze toward global capitalism. Now they were a united force in the economic and political arenas and had long displaced America at the forefront in the world economy. If Serafino could just get his diplomatic fingernails into Alvarez, maybe he could find a way to put a wedge into the BRICs.

But first things first. Matt needed to go downstairs and meet Doron at the back entrance before President Alvarez and his wife arrived at the North Portico.

He had met Doron at a stargazing party on the White House South Lawn last summer. His chief of staff, Ted Calahan, had introduced them that day, and they had spent most of the event side by side, talking about astronomy and global magnetics. Doron was a research astrophysicist at the Goddard Space Flight Center in Greenbelt, Maryland, outside D.C. A division of NASA, Goddard was responsible for the kinds of research that would define solar and space power for the coming decade. Matt liked Doron. She could be useful in making him look good in the public eye. And she was the kind of woman who would tell him anything he wanted to know. She was intelligent, a top researcher at the center, and held degrees in astronomy and astrophysics from the University of California–Santa Cruz (UCSC), but emotionally, she was still a woman. And for Serafino that meant she was an open book. Easy access. Doron was particularly easy to read— pitifully transparent. He didn't know much about her, but enough to sense she was unsure of herself, perhaps unsure of her attractiveness. She liked him. He knew that. And she liked the attention he gave her. For now, it worked. She was a suitable escort for Serafino at White House functions. He would do whatever it took to keep her happy, let her believe he was attracted to her. It was a small price to pay.

He approached the entrance and saw she was there waiting for him. She was wearing a silver brocaded gown with thinly beaded shoulder straps and a chiffon sash, and her long, dark hair was swept up into a loosely styled chignon. She smiled as he approached.

"Good evening, Dr. Anderson." He leaned down and kissed the top of her hand, scanning the hallway to see if he needed to say or do more in order to keep up his charming facade.

"Good evening, Matt," she said. Her face revealed that she was pleased with his invitation that evening.

White House state dinner invitations were a coveted commodity. With the limited number of 137 seats in the State Dining Room, only selected diplomats, friends, entertainers, and politicians would be invited. And this affair was going to be lavish. Matt wanted to make sure he took every measure he could to impress the Brazilian president. Doron's striking beauty and the way she carried herself would help with that impression.

He held out his arm. She took it, and they walked down the long corridor toward the North Portico.

Matt saw Ted, his chief of staff, striding to meet him before they rounded the corner. They were soon joined by Mullica Michaels, his executive assistant; and Brian Garvey, his contextualist and PR expert. Two bodyguards waited at the entrance for him to pass through the vestibule to the portico's main doors. The president and Mrs. Alvarez had just arrived.

"President Alvarez, Senhora Alvarez, *muito bem vindos*. Welcome to the White House. I am honored by your presence."

Matt turned and accompanied Doron and his guests into the hallway, where they would be announced to enter the State Dining Room.

The room was stunning. Doron had outdone herself. He had asked her as a favor to assist Mullica with the planning of the occasion, and she had agreed. Although the dinner was indoors, the tables were set with green and yellow linens and offset with dark blue glass place settings to accent Brazil's national colors. The long tables were likewise strewn with the country's national flowers—vases containing long stalks of yellow ipê-amarelo adorned the entryway and side tables. Upon the guests' entrance, musicians began playing the *Hino Nacional Brasileiro*.

President Alvarez and his wife looked pleased. Matt smiled charmingly as he ushered them to their seats.

*
* *

Inside the White House gate, a man in a dark woolen coat handed something to the guard and began striding across the lawn. The guard couldn't see who it was, but he engaged his Pearl and directed his frequency to the ground floor. Manuel Vamos answered.

"This is Javier on the third floor. I just saw a man enter on the north side, near the White House kitchen entrance. Thought you might check it out."

"Checking."

Javier waited. He turned to the window again and peered out. The garden and grounds were empty. Whoever it was, he was no longer in his line of sight.

"Manuel here. Checked around. Don't see anyone on the grounds. Will keep alert."

"Right. Let me know if you see anything. Over and out." Javier looked again out over the White House lawn. Nothing. But just in case, he would alert the guards at the gate to be sure to identify the man when he exited the grounds.

*
* *

The president was raising his glass for the official toast of the evening. The guests turned in their seats to listen to Serafino's official welcome to the Brazilian president: "My dear President Alvarez and your lovely wife, Senhora Alvarez, on behalf of the United States of America, I welcome you to the White House.

"In recent years, the United States has celebrated the emergence of Brazil as an economic and political world power, and we are pleased to engage with you as a partner in world commerce. Tonight, I hope we can continue to celebrate the vitality of both our countries and to support each other as partners—two great nations moving forward toward a common world future." Matt raised his glass.

One of the staff had come up behind Ted Calahan, who had turned and was listening intently, nodding. He turned now to Matt and motioned. The president excused himself from the table and followed Calahan out of the room.

"Not a good time to be interrupted, Ted."

"Yes, Mr. President, I understand. But we have a situation." He motioned the president into a room off the hall. Inside, a man dressed in a black silk suit rose to his feet and bowed quickly, never taking his eyes off Serafino. In his hand was a small digidrive.

"I can handle this from here, Ted." Serafino nodded to his chief of staff, and Ted Calahan walked out the door, shutting it behind him. The man spoke, his English carefully enunciated.

"I have come representing Niú Ye. I believe I have something you wanted from him."

Serafino nodded and reached out his hand to retrieve the tiny digidrive. He activated the drive and waited for his Pearl to connect with the coordinates. Engaging his Pearl again, he projected the image onto the far wall, and a long string of codes streamed out from the file, displaying what looked like a complex series of numbers, letters, and holograms. He looked over at Niú's messenger and nodded.

"I'll check this out with the government lab."

The little man nodded.

"And tell Niú I'll see him soon."

The man nodded again silently.

The president shoved the drive into his coat pocket, turned, and quickly exited the room. In the dining room, the guests had just applauded the Brazilian president's second toast.

BEIJING, CHINA

National Center for the Study of Genetics

Niú Ye watched on his screen as his operative exited the White House and got safely into the limousine that would carry him back to the aerodock. He set down a glass of scotch on the office desk and chewed his lip thoughtfully. It would take Serafino's lab a few days to find out that the file was a fake. By then, he would find a way to destroy the records he had for the Capricorn Project. He wasn't sure how Murong Gui would react if he knew about the operation. On one hand, he had wiped out hundreds of lives—their own people. But on the other, through his research, he had made China one of the leading, if not the leading economic power in the world. It was a risk he had to take. But whatever the cost, he would never bow to Serafino.

3

THE DIATESSARON

BUCKINGHAMSHIRE, ENGLAND
English Countryside

The sheep pushed against the front bumper, halting its progression down the winding path that served as a road outside the village of Hambleden. Paul slowed, then stopped. *There must be hundreds of them.* The car was surrounded now, and there was no way to pass. Paul shut down the engine. He was still tired. He put his hands over his eyes and sat back, thinking about the night before. He had gotten into London on the latest flight and had checked into the Montague on the Gardens near Russell Square. The hotel had been comfortable and well-appointed, a beautiful display of organic and artistic beauty. Paul wasn't an expert in architecture, but he could tell the hotel was a work of exceptional artistry and considerable historical significance. Exquisite marble foyers reflected large carved-mahogany staircases that curved up into an internal balcony strewn with foliage. To the right of the lobby was a large glass sunroom with an attached green-house, and to the left, a four-star restaurant with antique furniture and potted palm trees.

His room was equally inviting, but Paul hadn't slept well. He was still reeling from the experiences of the past two days, and he was becoming increasingly excited about viewing the Diatessaron manuscript. He had risen early, intending to pass the morning reading and enjoying the sunrise over the hotel gardens. But instead he had sipped his coffee only briefly, and then requested a map of the surrounding countryside from the hotel concierge. His appointment with Emory Makefield was not until three o'clock that afternoon, when he was invited for tea and then a discussion of the Diatessaron manuscript. He had decided, therefore, to spend the morning exploring. What could be more relaxing than to rent a car and drive forty miles outside the city, where the picturesque landscape looked like something out of a Jane Austen novel? But he hadn't been prepared for the rugged dirt roads and multitude of livestock that made traveling by car less than desirable in rural England. Now he was stranded. He sat restlessly, waiting for the sheep to pass.

The three-hour flight from Charlottesville to Heathrow had been uneventful. Paul had used the time searching the Cloud with his Pearl for information on any recent findings of Tatian's Diatessaron manuscript. There were no new discoveries recorded. The original had been written around 172 CE, both in Syriac and in Greek, making Tatian's the oldest compilation of the four New Testament Gospels, composed from the original precanonical texts and possibly with influence from several other noncanonical texts that were circulating at the time.

The Syriac churches used Tatian's Gospel harmony exclusively until the fifth century before finally giving in to using the four separate Gospels, along with the Peshitta Old Testament—an early independent translation from the Hebrew Bible.

A commentary on the original by Ephraem the Syrian was still available in the Syriac language, containing approximately 80 percent of the original papyrus leaves and remaining the closest witness to the existence of the original gospel text by Tatian. The manuscript was available in Dublin at the Chester Beatty Library. But otherwise, the most complete and oldest versions of the actual text still remaining were those translated into Arabic.

To date, no complete version of the Diatessaron in either Syriac or Greek had been recovered. Only the medieval translations had survived in Arabic and Latin, relying on texts that had been "corrected" to conform to the separate Gospel versions. The most recent fragment to date had been the one in Greek found in 1933. And even that one now was thought to be a fake. To have found an original—whether in Syriac or in Greek—would be beyond comprehension. But that seemed to be exactly what Emory Makefield was telling him had occurred.

It wouldn't have been unusual, though, for the manuscript to have been hidden. Syrian bishop Theodoretus of Kyros destroyed more than two hundred copies of the Diatessaron to make way for the canonical gospels in the early fifth century. And although revered early on in the Eastern churches, the Diatessaron was later declared heretical by the Western institutional church. Some had even feared the text, feeling it was imbued with some kind of mysterious and unusual power.

The ink was fresh.

Paul startled in his seat to discover that the sheep had now cleared the road and were gathering in the grassy meadows to the west of the vehicle. He glanced out his left window, adjusted his Pearl earring with his right hand, and reignited the car. But as he turned forward again to put the vehicle in gear, his eyes widened in surprise. In front of him, standing on the edge of the road, was a single goat. Unlike the sheep, the goat was pure black from head to toe, with a bearded tuft and coals for eyes. Even its stubbed horns were black. It stood there, staring at him, and Paul got the strange feeling that it was deliberately watching him, could see right through him. He looked away, then back, but the goat continued to stare at him without moving. Paul pressed the accelerator, and the car started forward. The car lurched to the right, rounding the animal, and then Paul awkwardly pulled the car back onto the dirt roadway. Satisfied, he glanced once more in the rearview mirror, but now the goat was nowhere to be seen. He turned, surprised, his eyes scanning the field, but he couldn't see it anywhere. Paul shook his head and smiled. He really needed to get more sleep.

UNIVERSITY OF LONDON, ENGLAND

Centre for Manuscript and Print Studies

At precisely three o'clock, Emory Makefield motioned for Alyce, his assistant, to bring them tea. Afternoon teatime in England was still a treasured tradition, and Paul looked forward to the treat.

"I took the liberty of ordering us a cream tea with scones, jam, Pekoe black tea, and lemon cream." Emory Makefield was pouring the hot, steaming liquid into delicate china cups. He reached over and handed one of the cups to Paul. Paul nodded politely and sipped. He smiled as the warmth slid down his throat and into his stomach.

As the two of them munched on their scones, Emory talked about the history of the center. Founded in 2001 at the turn of the century, the center's partners were proud of their forty-seven-year commitment to paleography and other print and manuscript studies. Attracting prominent researchers and scholars and renowned for their expertise in early languages, they had come to be known as the leading manuscript specialists in the world. Paul didn't doubt their dating of the Diatessaron, but he was eager now to see the manuscript for himself.

At last, Emory Makefield rose and asked Alyce to clear the tea trays.

"Come," he said. "I have someone I want you to meet."

The two men walked through the rear door of the library that served as the center's main sitting room and entered a narrow hallway that led to a studio in the back of the building. As they entered, a woman stood up from one of the long tables in the back of the room. She had long, golden-blonde hair that cascaded down her back and shoulders, porcelain skin, and bright hazel eyes. She smiled as she greeted them, and Paul stood transfixed for a moment, staring.

"Paul, this is Angela Matthews Krall—our ancient manuscripts specialist. Angela is also an art historian and something of an artist herself." Emory moved aside so that Paul could shake Angela's hand.

"Pleased to meet you." Her voice was still and confident and hinted subtly of what Paul knew had to be a considerable intelligence.

"Pleased to meet you," Paul replied. He was still staring.

Emory Makefield was now moving toward the door. "I'll leave the two of you to examine the Diatessaron, then, shall I? Let me know if I can be of service." He nodded, smiling, and left the room, shutting the door behind him.

"I hear you had tea with Emory," Angela said, flashing her brilliant smile again. "He loves to have guests for tea. And I'm sure the scones were delectable. Emory has excellent taste. But now I think you're in for the real treat."

With gloved hands, she lifted a cover off one of the worktables to reveal a set of parchment leaves spread out under transparent mylar sheets. Paul could tell they were old, but they seemed to be in almost perfect condition, as though they had been sealed away in an airtight vacuum while waiting to be discovered.

"I've tested the manuscript several times," she continued. "It's authentic. And it's in Syriac. This may well be close to the original, if not *the* original, manuscript written by Tatian."

Paul was stunned. This was an unimaginable find.

"I'm working on translating the text now." She showed him the beginnings of what appeared to be at least ten pages of notes written on her electronic tablet.

Paul peered closely at the pages. The script may well have been penned by Tatian himself. Could it really be the original Diatessaron?

Angela continued to speak, explaining the procedures she had used to date the text and the way she was translating the document. Paul noticed the slight lilt in her voice—she was Irish. Paul found himself distracted both by the manuscript and by Angela's voice, which seemed to almost sing as she spoke.

"I should be able to have the document officially dated and translated for you by the end of this month," she was saying. "Possibly in a few weeks."

Paul nodded his approval.

"In the meantime, you're welcome to use the British Library and any of our university libraries if you'd like to study some of the other fragments. I've also obtained permission for you to view the commentary from the Beatty Library in Dublin. When you're through, perhaps in about a week, come back here and you can study the manuscript as long as you like."

Paul thanked Angela and shook her hand again as he prepared to leave. It was late March, and Paul still had another month of his semester to go at the University of Virginia. But he didn't want to miss out on the opportunity to prime himself on the Diatessaron research. He wanted to be ready to study the original when Angela was done with it. He would need to request permission from the university to finish his classes via the avatar classroom. But Paul didn't think that would be a problem. After all, most of the classes were taught that way today, except for some of the special lectures and workshops for disciplines requiring live sensory-visuals. The History Department was one of those, but the dean had always been supportive of Paul's research, especially in his studies of the relationships between history and semiotics, and Paul felt sure he would have his support now.

Paul's research had not always been specific to early Christian documents. His first studies had been in ancient historical texts. Interest in manuscripts from now barely extant Christian scholars had dwindled among the New Selfers. But Paul had always been fascinated by the early renderings of the now crumbling numbers of the Christian faithful. Why had they felt so strongly about maintaining the texts of a man whose ministry lasted only a few years and who lived to be barely thirty years old? How had the infrastructure lasted so long? What drove these people to protect their faith no matter what the cost? Where did this faith come from? Paul sometimes envied their surety. The faithful. These disciples of Jesus the messiah. Paul connected to the University with his Pearl and asked to speak with the chair.

An original manuscript was a rare find. How could he not want to examine it?

And then there was the letter.

Although Paul was thrilled to be able to work with the Diatessaron, Emory Makefield had still not really told him why he had singled him out to come to see the lost manuscript. True, he had achieved some notoriety in the field, but was it enough to warrant this? Now Paul's mind began to plague him. How had Makefield found him, and why? Paul reminded himself to ask the director that question the next time he visited the center.

Don't forget about the letter.

Paul forcibly pushed the letter out of his mind. He was tired. His morning excursion and now his visit to the center had depleted his remaining energy reserve, and he was still suffering from jet lag. It was almost eight o'clock now—only three o'clock in Virginia, and he had slept fitfully the night before because of the time change. Now he found himself needing to sleep. He headed on foot through Russell Square toward the Montague. He would rest well tonight and then make an appointment with the manuscripts and rare books clerk at the British Library in the morning.

LONDON, ENGLAND

Hotel Montague

Paul heard a rumbling somewhere from the distance. It sounded like thunder. Bright jags of light streaked across the sky. The night was dark. He was straining his eyes but couldn't see anything in front of him. The wind seemed to whip up from nowhere, and he began to feel himself being pulled backward into the darkness. The rumbling sounds became louder and louder, until they sounded like jet engines roaring next to his ears. He was still moving backward and now his body was being sucked into what felt like a vortex. Was he dying? Was he still on the plane? Paul couldn't remember. Suddenly, a bright light flashed around him, blinding him, and he was falling . . . down . . . down . . .

Paul jerked up to a sitting position in the bed, sweat streaming down his face and neck. His clothes were soaking wet, and his body began shaking in the cool room. He got up, stumbled into the bathroom, and turned on the hot shower. He deposited the wet clothes in a heap on the floor and stepped into the steaming water. Paul rubbed his eyes and leaned against the shower wall. He hadn't had a nightmare like that since he was a young child. It had left him shaken, the feeling of falling still planted surreally in his waking brain. Gradually, he stood straight, recovering and shaking off the memory of the dream. What had it been about? He couldn't remember . . . something about jets. All he remembered was the feeling of falling, and the sound, like a roaring in his ears.

It was 7:00 a.m. Paul dressed in a tailored shirt and brown tweed sport jacket and went downstairs to the dining room for breakfast. On the way, he tapped into his Pearl and connected to the British Library.

Before he could finish the call, his device began to vibrate, indicating an incoming call. Quickly, he paused his connection and picked up the other caller.

"Paul Binder."

"Paul, this is Angela at the Centre for Manuscript and Print Studies. I apologize for calling you so early in the morning, but something very odd has come up. The Diatessaron manuscript—it seems to be a type of palimpsest. There seems to be another text superimposed in between the Syriac lines of the Diatessaron. This one is in Greek, and it looks like the same hand script. I think Tatian superimposed the Diatessaron over another manuscript—or perhaps not over it, but deliberately in between it. It looks as though the Greek had not been entirely wiped clean, but had been covered over, so as not to call immediate attention to it within the new text. In other words, to notice it, you would have had to to be looking for it. Or be a manuscript specialist." She smiled. "Can you come to the center today?"

"I'll be there within the hour."

Paul finished his breakfast and prepared for the walk across the square. As he picked up his coat, he felt the letter from a week ago, still in his pocket. He pulled it out again and reread the text.

Dear Dr. Binder,

If you are receiving this letter, the year will be 2048—thirty-six years after your birth and the birth of the eight. The Time of Becoming has now reached fruition. Locate the manuscript of the Diatessaron. You have been chosen to unlock the future of your world. The cross key will guide you. Use it wisely.

Why would anyone send him something like this? The Diatessaron. He hadn't located it; it had somehow located him. But who were the eight? What kind of seal was the letter referring to? What was the Time of Becoming? And what was the cross key? More important to Paul, who had given him this letter? The man in the car? Or was he just a messenger? And how had the dead man so neatly laid the letter there on the dash for him to find?

Paul decided to talk personally to the Roanoke Police Department to find out if the man had been identified. Perhaps then he could make sense of who had sent the letter and why. In the meantime, an opportunity to study the Diatessaron was too good to pass up. He pulled on his coat and headed for Russell Square and Malet Street to see Angela.

When he arrived, Emory Makefield greeted him at the door. Paul walked with him through the main hall to the back of the building.

"Dr. Makefield, I wonder . . ."

"Please, call me Emory." Makefield held open the door for Paul to enter the back studio.

"Thank you. Emory—I never asked you. But I've had this on my mind. What made you think to call me that day about the Diatessaron manuscript? I am, of course, a historian and have been interested in early Christian texts, but so have many other scholars. Why me?"

Makefield laughed. "Well, it was the letter, of course."

"The letter?"

"Yes. Our benefactor specifically requested you. He said it was the only way he would gift the manuscript to the center. Only if you would be the one to study it."

Paul didn't know how to respond. But for now at least, he didn't want to think about it. He was glad that he would be the one to examine the Diatessaron. It was an unheard-of opportunity, and he could figure out the whys later. He pushed open the doors of the studio and headed for the back table to view the palimpsest.

4

CERASTES, CERASTES

CAIRO, EGYPT

National Research Institute of Astronomy
and Astrophysics (NRIAA)

The sun shone red over Cairo, baking the streets in the eighty-six-degree air, hot for the end of March, even in Egypt's desert climate. The humidity hung over the Nile delta like a wet blanket, and Youhanna Nasim Lachier panted for oxygen as he headed up the steps to the national lab. Lachier was president and head research partner at the lab in Helwan outside Cairo. Born in France, he barely remembered the place of his birth. His mother, a native Egyptian, had brought him to Cairo after his father's death when he was only four years old, and young Youhanna Lachier quickly rose in the educational system, finally completing his doctoral studies at the University of Cairo after acquiring multiple degrees in astronomy, engineering, and astrophysics at the Arab Academy for Science and Technology. Having an amazing capacity for scientific invention, along with an acute sense of vision and a fiercely competitive spirit, Lachier became the country's most promising scientist for government aerospace and weapons development and the youngest research partner at the institute. He was well liked. He had connections. And he wasn't afraid to use them.

"What's the word?" Lachier turned, distracted, as Hassan Masih hurried up the steps to join him.

Lachier smiled. Hassan was young, and sometimes too excited. But he was a good research assistant, and Lachier knew he could be trusted. And that was most important. He didn't want anyone rooting around in his lab. Hassan was like a watchdog. As long as he was around, Lachier's work was safe.

"Good morning, Hassan. You're here early." He took the latest report drives from Hassan and continued up the steps.

"You're not going to tell me?" Hassan's mouth was hanging open like a golden retriever, eager to catch the slightest morsel thrown his way.

"Nothing to tell. The prime minister hasn't yet called me back."

Hassan's smile collapsed, his excitement fading.

"I wouldn't worry, Hassan. When the government gets wind of our project, there'll be plenty of celebration. Come, now; let's get to work."

The two men entered the building, placing their palms on the side code panel, and disappeared inside the institute's huge, reddish-brown walls.

As soon as he saw that Hassan had settled into the lab, Lachier grabbed a parcel from his desk, slipped from the workroom at the rear of the building, and drove to the warehouse that sheltered his private jet. Maslow would be waiting for him. In a few minutes, the aerojet was soaring over the city and heading in the direction of the Libyan border.

SAHARA DESERT

Egypt, near the border of Libya

The cloud of dust rose high over the red dunes of the Sahara as the Egyptian Zephyr swooped its shadow like a giant eagle flying over the barren wasteland. Called the "sea of sand," the Sahara stretched across northern Africa, its dry and dusty climate unfriendly to cultivation or extended habitation. It was here that Lachier agreed to meet Jonathan Maslow.

Maslow was there waiting for him in a dark-grey Sand Trekker, a small 4x4 nanoblast-drive desert jeep that could wrangle across even the most formidable sand dunes. The jet set down on its large sand skimmers and skied to a halt a short distance away, kicking up more sand and dust in its wake. Maslow held his khaki jacket over his face and eyes as the wind blew reddish sand into the front of the jeep and across the windshield of the Trekker. Within a few minutes, Youhanna Lachier emerged from the side door of the aerojet, his long, white tunic and head cloths flapping about his body. In his arms, he carried what looked like a large canvas bag.

"Mr. Maslow, greetings."

Maslow nodded and stepped down from the vehicle. He stretched out his hand, and Lachier took it firmly.

"Do you have the coordinates for me?" Lachier began to unwrap the canvas bag, revealing a medium-sized tent, which he erected, keeping Maslow in his sight.

"Do you have the funds?" Maslow stood his ground, waiting.

Lachier rose. "Have a seat, Mr. Maslow." He motioned to the ground at the side of the tent, where he had laid two large foamlike flat seats, covered with a red and black decoratively striped material. Maslow sat. Lachier sat down beside him, pulling out two large canteens and two small stacking cups.

"Egyptian coffee." Lachier handed one of the small cups to Maslow and filled it with a brown, thick substance that smelled like pungent coffee grounds. It was still hot. He sipped cautiously.

Then Lachier reached into his tunic and pulled out a large envelope.

"Ten thousand EGP. The equivalent of approximately twenty-five thousand US dollars, as you requested." He held the package out to Maslow.

Maslow took the envelope, glanced inside it briefly, then tucked it away in his inside coat pocket, zipping the enclosure. He handed Lachier a digidrive.

"The coordinates and all the information you requested about the site are on here."

"I thank you, Mr. Maslow. Your help has been greatly appreciated. And I hope you will have a safe trip home."

At that moment, Maslow heard the sound of an engine. He stood up to see the Sand Trekker fleeing across the sand, away from the tent. Alarmed, he turned toward Lachier.

Lachier smiled. "I can't have anyone trace you here, Mr. Maslow. Don't worry about the Trekker. You can recover it when you return to Cairo. You will remain here for the night. I am leaving with you provisions for an evening meal and enough water to sustain you for another day. In the morning, you may leave. I'll have a camel sent to you, and you can ride out."

Shaken, Maslow looked with mistrust at Lachier, noticing how his elongated nose almost curved over his lip as he smiled.

"You'll be fine, Mr. Maslow." Lachier held out his hand once more. Maslow hesitated, but finding he had no other options, took Lachier's hand. Then he stepped back as Lachier strode off in the direction of the aerojet.

Within moments, the small white plane with red and black Egyptian colors covering its flank roared to life and circled the air above the dunes. Then it was gone.

The sun was hot, and Maslow looked about, his lips already becoming parched by the heat and wind. He grabbed the canteen and pouch that Lachier had left for him, along with the foam pad, and crawled into the makeshift tent to wait out the afternoon glare.

After a few hours, as the sky began to darken with the red and purple glow of the setting sun over the desert, Maslow opened the pouch and unwrapped a type of rolled sandwich and what appeared to be some marinated vegetables. He ate hungrily, washing the food down with water from the canteen. Then he lay down and tried to rest. He hoped the camel would arrive early. He didn't like being in the desert at night. As the wind continued to whip sand around the tent, he could hear the sounds of the desert evening, and he was fairly sure he didn't want to meet any of the animals that spent their nights in the Sahara wasteland. After what seemed like hours, his mind exhausted from the ordeal, he closed his eyes at last and fell into a restless sleep.

Sometime in the night, Maslow woke, his head pounding. His body felt heavy and hot. His eyelids were stuck together, and he struggled to open them. He tried to sit up. Immediately, dizziness flooded his brain, and he fell back down hard into the sand, his head lolling to one side. As his vision cleared slightly, he saw that something was with him in the tent. It looked like a miniature dragon. The thing was pale buff in color, pallid as a rotted corpse, with darkish-yellow spots that swam and seemed to move in and out of his line of vision. Its small, glassy eyes were black, and over its flat head were two horns, pointed, like the horns of the devil. It was making a rasping sound, like someone struggling to breathe, and it reminded Maslow of the death rattle in the dying patients he had seen on his trip through Nigeria. It was then that he noticed his hand, bleeding and swollen, lying motionless below the thing that was now staring at him, gasping viciously. If he tried to move, it would bite him again. He wasn't sure how many times it had bitten him already.

Suddenly, a searing pain jabbed through his chest, causing him to jerk upward. The thing reared back and struck at his face, catching him in the neck just below the jaw. Maslow screamed, the sound dying in his throat, as the venom began to constrict his windpipe. He felt what seemed like hands squeezing his heart in his chest, squeezing harder and harder until he thought it would explode from his ribs. His body began convulsing, spraying red sand into the sides of the tent. And then he lay still.

GREENBELT, MARYLAND
Goddard Space Flight Center (NASA)

The report came in on the large screen in the center hub of NASA communications as Doron Anderson was finishing her evening stats. A terrorist alert. Someone had infiltrated the Novitia Plant's mainframe. A red alert was sent out to all government agencies to shut down entrances and activate all security measures.

Novitia was the newest and most powerful air and flight arms manufacturer in the United States. Its founder was a longtime friend and companion of the president's, and since the turn of the century Novitia had been the sole provider for the newly discovered TechnoJet technology. Matthew Serafino had hoped that the new Night Streamer jet would place the United States in the lead for aeronautics intelligence and infiltrative flight weaponry. The company had been unstoppable and had been pouring needed financial resources into the States with the sale of some of its lesser arms to Middle Eastern countries. The company was the hope of the future. Doron knew Matt was going to be furious. No doubt, he had already gotten the news.

Using her touch pad, Doron entered the high-security area and stepped down into the main conference studio. She sat down in one of the black padded chairs and motioned the sensor to direct-link the president's official reportage. Nothing. She wondered if he had heard. She connected to her Pearl and activated her private number for Matthew Serafino.

CAIRO, EGYPT

The Lachier Residence

The smell of sweetmeats and lentils filled the room as Lilith set the table for the evening meal. Youhanna Lachier had met her at a government event in 2038 when he was twenty-six and she was nineteen. She was the daughter of a Syrian air division officer. She smiled at him now, setting his dinner in front of him and waiting for him to pick up his utensils to signal the start of the celebration. It was his son's first initiation into school, and the family had invited relatives and friends to congratulate young Nezih on his acceptance into the elite training center for the children of government officials. Youhanna smiled at his son, nodding in approval. Nezih smiled back and followed his father in taking the second bite of the evening. Just as Youhanna prepared to give his speech as head of household in honor of his son and to toast his success, his Pearl began to vibrate, signaling an incoming call. Youhanna excused himself and walked outside to the balcony.

"Lachier here."

"The infiltration was successful." The voice on the other end of the line sounded jovial, and Lachier knew his young disciple would be seeking his approval. *Well-deserved approval.*

Youhanna smiled. "As I knew it would be, Ammon, as I knew it would be." He paused, then added, "Congratulations, Ammon." He could practically hear the pride in the man's voice.

"Thank you, Monsieur Lachier."

Youhanna Lachier hung up the phone and breathed deeply. Soon, he thought. Soon he would reap his rewards. He breathed in deeply and returned to the dining room and to his guests.

WASHINGTON, D.C.

The White House

The strains of piano music wafted down the halls from the staff offices. It was a recording of Arnaud Chevalier, playing Beethoven's Ninth Symphony, the 1831 piano arrangement by Richard Wagner, no doubt, and Mullica Michaels paused in her preparation of the president's schedule to listen for a moment. It was a beautiful piece, carefully constructed, and extremely difficult to perform. About ten years ago, Chevalier had been one of the best-known pianists in France and could have been one of the best of the twenty-first century. But he was an unusual case. A gifted pianist from childhood, he began performing in France at an early age and would have traveled the world, if he hadn't felt suddenly compelled at the age of twenty-five to enter the ministry as an Orthodox priest. In France, Christian orthodoxy still clung to its roots, though much like the ABC phenomenon in the New Selfer United States, it had lost its foothold years ago and hung on now to only a small faction of followers. But Chevalier had proved gifted in many ways. He was now gaining renown as a scholar of ancient and early cosmology.

Something Mullica knew nothing about. But she still loved listening to his music. She wondered if he still played.

Her thoughtful mood was broken suddenly by the sound of Matt Serafino's voice coming down the corridor. And he didn't sound happy. Quickly, she resumed her work.

"Turn that music off," he snarled, gritting his teeth.

Mullica grazed her fingers across the touch screen on her studio panel, and the music ceased, leaving an uncomfortable silence as the door of the Oval Office slammed shut.

Inside, Matthew Serafino was smoldering. He adjusted his Pearl and put a call through to Novitia's corporate headquarters. The call would not connect. His eyes blazing, he tried Derrick Martin's private number. The line rang, but again with no connection.

Barely controlled, he touched the panel for his executive assistant, and her face appeared on the screen.

"Mullica, I want Derrick Martin on the line within fifteen minutes. Find him."

"Yes, sir," Mullica replied as she hurried to make the connection.

Meanwhile, the rest of the White House staff was gathering at the windows. Ted Calahan strode into the central office and, seeing the strange assembly, pushed by them to stare out at the White House lawn. His brows wrinkled, his mouth opening slightly in perplexed surprise. The sky appeared to be covered with migrating birds. They looked like crows. *Do crows migrate?* Wondering where they were headed, he twisted his head for a better view out the window and recoiled. The birds were not migrating anywhere but were gathering in clumps on the roof of the White House. *Odd. There must be hundreds of them.* It had to be some fluke of nature. Well, they had better things to do in the White House than look at birds. Ted shrugged off the strange phenomenon and motioned his staff to get back to work. But all afternoon he noticed the birds continued to gather. One after another, they appeared from the sky and settled onto the roof, pushing one another, squawking and pecking, until now the roof was black with them. And throughout the day, one by one, the staff members rose and went to the windows to look out in fascination and mild alarm at the blackening gardens and pathways.

Oblivious to the surrounding cacophony, Matthew Serafino prepared his coordinates and began activating his avatar module. Avatar conversion technology had been around for the last few decades, and communications had used avatar classrooms since the early twenty-first century. But only a few people had the means or the connections both to acquire the module and to undertake the preparatory procedures for creating their own avatar likenesses, in both traveling physical form as well as virtual hologram form. Matt had done both, compliments of Novitia's technology resources and the scientific finesse of his most recent tech acquisition, Roland Tarkland. As far as Serafino knew, he was the only one who had a working version of both physical and holomorph avatars, and he liked it that way. The president stepped into the module. He smiled. *Let's see what you can do.*

5

THE PALIMPSEST

ISLAND OF PATMOS, GREECE

Monastery Museum of St. John the Divine

"Casimir, come! It's time to go."

The boy was stooped flat against the cool rock wall in the back of the cave, holding up his electronic detection device and poking gingerly at a small, shadowlike crevice underneath one of the over-hanging rock formations. A golden mane of curls hung from his head down his back.

"Mama! Mamusia! I've found something."

"Casimir, come, now; we don't have time for you to play games."

"No, Mama, I've really found something. There's something in here. There must be some opening somewhere behind the cave wall."

Ester Marceli turned and, holding up the edges of her skirts, descended the steep stairway back down into the Cave of St. Anne.

"Casimir, we can't be poking around down here. You're going to get in trouble." Her voice echoed in the small, silent chamber.

"But Mama, look at the light. Look how it's flashing. Right here."

Casimir held up a flat, elongated panel that looked like a type of flashing remote Pearl and pointed it toward the corner of the ceiling. The panel light was blinking rapidly, its laserpoint pin light centered on a small hairlike fissure that ran across the side of one of the rocks.

"Look, Mama!"

Ester hesitated, glancing nervously at the stairs. The tour guide had already moved to the upper level, and she could hear him speaking from one of the chapels above them. Casimir continued to stare at the wall.

"You know my nanodetector works, Mama. Remember, it found your gold necklace last week. It's blinking now right here. There's got to be something in here."

Ester felt torn, knowing they shouldn't be poking around the walls of one of the monastery's most treasured tourist attractions, yet she also knew to trust Casimir's intuition. Was it intuition? Or was it his almost bizarre understanding of the intricacies of twenty-first-century technology? Ester didn't know. But she did know her son had a gift. Even at four years old, young Casimir was able to take apart the family's robotic and computing systems and put them back together, creating new features out of the old ones. One time, about five years ago, he had taken her old portable Pearl and made a toy robot capable of integrating the neighbor's household sound systems, and he had frightened the young girl next door with what must have sounded like the voices of disembodied people talking in her room. Now he was older, and his mind moved at a phenomenal pace. The Institute for Technology, Science, and the Arts near their home in India had allowed Casimir to attend courses there. And although he was still in most ways a child, he had stunned them with his ability not only to create new Cloud apps, but to understand complex quantum systems and to hack into almost any of those created by other students. Easily bored, at home he had taken to building unique and sometimes useful household apparatuses, and so when he invented his nanodetector a few weeks ago, she had thought it was just another of his toy pastimes. But now his detector was pointing him in the direction of the cave wall, telling him he had found metal, and Ester knew he was probably right. She took a deep breath and ran upstairs to find someone in charge.

The Monastery of St. John the Divine, now run by Greek Orthodox monks, had been built on the very site where John, the writer of the Christian book of Revelation, had spent his last days in exile, having received the strange images for the book in some sort of vision. The cave where he had the vision was now named the Cave of St. Anne, and this was where Casimir now doggedly searched for signs of metal. Ester had heard about the man, but she had never read the Revelation or any of his other writings herself. Although her family was of Jewish descent—her family lineage was traced once by one of her relatives all the way back to the old city of Jerusalem in the first century—no one practiced the ancient faith anymore, and she wasn't even familiar with the old writings of her own heritage, let alone those of the old Christian Scriptures. Her husband, Josek, was Polish, and they had lived all their lives in Poland, until recently when Josek had taken a job as a manager of the E-World Bank in India, where they lived now. A huge conglomerate, the bank had branches in most countries of the world and had transferred Josek from their home near Gdańsk, Poland, to the suburbs of Chennai. In return for taking the promotion and uprooting his family, they had given him a two-week paid vacation anywhere in the world. And he had chosen Greece.

Ester had just reached the front desk and had asked one of the tour guides to locate the manager when she heard her son shout all the way from the floor below. Turning, she ran through the monastery museum back toward the chapel area.

As she reached the entrance to the narrow staircase, Ester saw Casimir approaching her from the bottom of the cave. The rock where he had been poking had been pushed upward to reveal a small stone cavity. In his hands he held a small but elaborately carved gold box. And below the ornately styled keyhole was a shining silver-colored cross. In the light from the stairway, the strange metal shone with ribbons of rainbow colors.

LONDON, ENGLAND
Centre for Manuscript and Print Studies

Paul stood hunched over the Diatessaron's parchment sheets, studying the scrawled text. He moved the sliding scope slowly over the mylar, magnifying the letters. As he did, he could see the faint outlines of a second set of script appearing between the Syriac lines. Greek. The ink also appeared to be of different constitution.

"It's iron based."

Paul was so intent on studying the yellowed manuscript that he hadn't noticed Angela behind him. She was telling him something about the ink.

"In the first and second centuries, most of the ink was carbon based, made from soot, something like our lead-based pencils. Sometimes they also used resin or even wine dregs. Worked great on papyrus. But in the beginning of the second century, when parchment codex sheets started to replace the bulky papyrus leaves, another type of ink was used, made from iron and tanning compounds. The new brownish ink was now easier to use and more versatile. The writers discovered they could rub the writing surface partially clean and use the sheet again, creating a palimpsest—two texts on one manuscript. That's the ink you see here, in the Greek. It's iron based. And it's been deliberately rubbed and essentially hidden beneath the new text—your Diatessaron."

"What is it?" Paul continued to examine the letters.

"That's a good question. I'm still working on the translation, but from first glance, it appears to be some kind of prophecy—maybe some kind of apocalyptic text. But it has other text in it too. Symbols, numbers, descriptions, even some diagram-like images. I'll start working on the Greek today, and hopefully, I'll be able to tell you more soon."

Paul leaned closer, moving the scanning scope randomly through the manuscript. As he moved over one of the pages of parchment, something caught his eye. Quickly, he pulled the scope back over the prior page and searched for the symbol.

There, staring up at him, was a picture of a key. Not just any key. The top of the image was a large, somewhat ornate cross with the bottom formed into an elaborate sort of key. Paul paled visibly, still staring at the image on the page, his head shaking slowly and deliberately in disbelief.

Angela came around the side of the table and looked into the glass. "Paul?"

"I know that key." His voice was low and sounded dazed, as though he had just stepped out of a virtual space simulator.

"You've seen it before?" Angela looked curious, still trying to assess his strange reaction.

"I've not only seen it. It exists, and I know where it is—or at least one like it."

"Where is it?"

"In my attic."

MARSEILLE, PROVENCE-ALPES-CÔTE D'AZUR, FRANCE

St. Seraphim Orthodox Cathedral

Father Arnaud Jerome Chevalier had just finished his morning coffee before walking back to the cathedral. Café Marseille had the best croissants in the city, and he had made it a cherished habit to have his breakfast there each morning before starting into his duties for the day. Today was no exception.

Tucking his hands into his pockets, he lifted his face into the morning sun and breathed in, savoring the smells of the city—fresh coffee, baking bread, the perfumes and colognes of men and women hurrying to their workplaces, and the rising mist of the city streets, still damp from the evening rain. He loved Marseille. And he loved the way art and history blended together into almost every part of the city's life. Known as the cultural capital of France, Marseille was still a thriving place, even in the current world economic and financial crises. It seemed to have found a niche of its own, like a sacred relic, refusing to be devastated as so many of the cities were today.

Coming into his office, Arnaud closed the door and reached for the touch screen on his studio pad. The morning news flashed onto the screen:

"This morning, the body of NASA scientist Dr. Jonathan Maslow was found lying in his jeep in the Sahara Desert just outside Cairo in Egypt."

Arnaud absentmindedly waved up the volume, his eyes glancing toward the screen as he began to sort through his desk for his morning prayer book.

"Maslow's death has been determined to have been caused by a lethal dose of venom from what appears to have been a desert horned viper. The snake apparently had attacked him several times, biting him on the neck and arms, causing almost immediate death. No cause for the attack could be found nor other clues as to why Maslow was in Cairo or what he was doing there. He is survived by his wife, Ann, and daughter, Rachel Maslow.

"A funeral is planned on Friday for the family and friends of the deceased. NASA has issued a statement denying any knowledge of a planned trip to Egypt by the deceased or any reason why Jonathan Maslow should have been in the Sahara that day.

"This is Sarah Connelley, reporting for World News France. Now back to the weather report for the day."

Arnaud Chevalier took out the cross he wore under his dark-red robes, kissed it, and said a prayer for the dead man. Although he didn't know him personally, Arnaud always filled his morning prayers with petitions for everyone and anyone he could think of who might need them. Arnaud sighed. Hardly anyone even believed in prayer anymore. But for Arnaud, it had been the turning point of his life— the place where the music met the magic.

He stood in the doorway and glanced in at the cathedral's sanctuary. The ebony grand piano had been the source of a huge dispute at one time within the cathedral community. Although the historic Syrian Orthodox cathedral in France had adopted wooden chairs somewhere around the turn of the century, it was only in the past few years that some cathedrals began using pianos within the elaborate sanctuaries. But when Arnaud was installed at the cathedral in Marseille, his reputation as a renowned concert pianist followed him, and several members of the small-but-wealthy faith community had donated the expensive instrument to the parish sanctuary. He had never played it.

He turned his back to the piano and the intruding memory and crossed his office to the winding stairs that led to the tower.

He smiled to himself as he headed into his observation room. Arnaud's private observation study was a gift by the archdiocese in honor of his cosmological research. Located in the upper levels of the cathedral, the room was round, with a domed ceiling and glass windows that rose from floor to ceiling on three sides of the room. Each window was lined with dark mahogany panels in beautiful, intricate patterns that looked like gothic diamonds. Red Oriental rugs covered the dark wooden floors. Lining the back circle of the room were mahogany bookshelves, also floor-to-ceiling, filled with volumes on cosmology, ancient languages, and various models of the universe down through history. And in the center of the room stood a round worktable, littered with papers, books, and diagrams, along with a small framed visual screen.

In front of the table, a telescope jutted out from the floor, reaching into the tops of the skylight windows. The rosewood and gold scope appeared to be a model from the turn of the century but clearly had every twenty-first-century device for viewing the constellations. The observatory was not only aesthetically pleasing but delightfully anachronistic—a meeting of ancient and future. It was Arnaud's favorite place to be. It was here that he had found the sign.

He hesitated for a moment, running his hands over the oiled leather of one of his sacred volumes, and then turning, Arnaud went back downstairs and entered the sanctuary to prepare for the morning Eucharist.

RUSSELL SQUARE

London, England

Paul sat on one of the benches lining Russell Square, eating a corned beef sandwich and watching the blackbirds splash in the center fountain. It was a beautiful March day, and the temperature was somewhere around sixty-two degrees, warm, with just enough breeze to feel slightly balmy. The bright square, filled with people dipping their hands into fountains and children running across the lawns and gardens with their dogs, seemed for the moment to pull Paul out of his experience of the morning and back into the world of city sights and sounds. It had been a week of strange circumstances. And Paul was not one to embrace strange.

But he couldn't help wondering about the key in the manuscript. The coincidences were beginning to seem a bit creepy. He hadn't seen his own cross key since he was a young child and had nearly forgotten that he had it. His mother had told him the story many times of how she received the gift meant for him on the day he was born, and she cautioned him always to keep the key in a safe place. But Paul had never thought much about it. For years it had remained in a box in the attic trunk, along with some of his other baby things—pictures, bits of hair from a first haircut, his first lost tooth, and a scrap of blanket that he had dragged around for the first two or three years of his life, growing up in West Virginia. He assumed the keepsake would still be exactly where he had left it, perhaps a bit tarnished with age.

His mother had told him she never knew who sent the gift. It had arrived at the hospital with a note addressed to him. He thought of his mother, always kind and smiling. She had succumbed to an infection a couple of years ago, caused by an experimental operation to repair her spine after a fall. Even with the advent of the new technomedical sciences, they couldn't save her. He still missed her. He leaned forward, dipping one hand into the fountain thoughtfully.

Paul's thoughts were broken by the vibrating of his Pearl. He leaned back and answered. The call from Virginia came through with just a hint of static.

"Mr. Binder, this is Sergeant Morris from the Roanoke Police Department. You had called us, asking about the driver of the car that crashed about a block from your home a few weeks ago? I just wanted to let you know—and this is a strange thing—we haven't been able to identify the driver. We've checked out all his prints, dentals, DNA, everything we could think of, but we can't find a record anywhere. It's the strangest thing. It's as though he never existed. He'll be held in the morgue as a John Doe for a couple of months, but then the remains will be cremated. I'm sorry. I know you were hoping to contact the family. If we come across any further information as to the identity of the victim, we'll be glad to let you know. But for now, I'm sorry we couldn't be of more help. You have a good day now."

Paul thanked the sergeant and ended the call. The dark cloud of confusion had once again settled over his countenance.

6

SMOKE AND MIRRORS

International Conference for Genetics and Technology (ICGT)

It was almost Niú Ye's turn to speak. The International Conference for Genetics and Technology (ICGT) drew scientists and scholars from all over the world. Last year's conference had been held in India, but this year, Beijing was hosting the prestigious group. Held at the Beijing International Convention Center, in 2048 it was the largest annual world conference, except for the International World Conference on Economics. The IWCE was fast becoming the new powerhouse of the political-economic arena, especially with the leadership of what everyone now called the "magic bricks" (MK BRICs)—Mexico, Korea, Brazil, Russia, India, and China—the building blocks of the world economy. For the most part, the same countries that were excelling economically were also excelling in the new sciences. *And that's the way we want to keep it,* Niú thought to himself. The audience was applauding now. Niú smiled, walked out onto the platform, and took the podium.

In another part of the conference, Malik Haider Asvaka shifted his black taqiyah and kurta and headed to his next conference session. Malik was head technoscientist at one of the largest companies in Afghanistan. The company was gaining ground as a leader in the interrelational sciences, combining the best of genetics, robotics, information technology, and nanotechnology. Their advances had stunned the world more than once—and had frightened some of its leaders. The ability to manipulate biology to the level they had discovered was unprecedented, trumped only by the Center for the Study of Genetics here in Beijing.

Malik Asvaka knew of the center's director, Niú Ye, but he had never met him. He would need to seek out the Chinese scientist here at the conference. Malik believed in keeping his competition right where he could see them. And at this point, China was Afghanistan's top competitor. Of course, that was in visual and legal trade. Malik had some other trade avenues he was pursuing that would fry bigger fish. And he knew of enough buyers to keep the world hopping and gasping for air for a good, long time. Malik smiled, showing his large, unnaturally white teeth as he entered the conference room for the next session.

GREENBELT, MARYLAND

Goddard Space Flight Center (NASA)

"What was Maslow doing in Egypt!?"

The director brought his fist down hard on the table next to him. The sound reverberated through the large conference room. No one spoke.

"Maslow was not sent by NASA. We have no idea what he was doing there or whom he saw. But we have to assume we've been compromised. And Novitia may well be only a part of that disaster. If any of you have even a scrap of information that might lead us in the right direction regarding this mess, see me. Otherwise, we are now activating high-security measures. Only those in the innermost circle will have access to classified information. There will be no entrance for anyone into any of the information access areas, unless you are personally touch-coded by my office. Understood?"

Doron filed out of the conference room with the others from

Goddard. She hadn't heard from Matt since she had called him regarding the breach. She was confident he'd taken some sort of action by now. No one could better take care of the situation than Matt Serafino.

Doron glanced over her shoulder as she moved through the exit door, and that was when she noticed Katherine. The dark-haired, slender woman looked as though she hadn't slept in days. She had dark circles under her eyes, and her cheeks looked sunken and sallow. *Why hadn't I thought of Katherine?* Doron knew, as did almost everyone at Goddard, that Katherine and Jonathan Maslow were seeing each other. Although they were discreet, these things always made it through the grapevine. Doron didn't think the director knew, but everyone on their floor did.

Doron inched to the side of the hallway and waited for Katherine to exit. Then she stepped up alongside her, gently guiding the distraught woman to a copy room at the end of the hall. She ushered her inside, shutting the door behind them.

Katherine was absentmindedly dabbing at her eyes and brushing a strand of hair out of her face as she lifted her head to look at Doron. Her eyes pleaded with Doron not to ask her what she didn't want to tell.

"How are you, Katherine?" Doron sat down at the opposite end of the table and waited.

After a long silence, the dam broke. "Doron, I told him not to go. He wouldn't listen to me. I knew something like this was going to happen." Katherine looked as if she were about to burst into tears at any moment.

"Who did he see, Katherine?"

Katherine brought her lips together, shaking her head slowly. She looked away, her eyes staring at the side wall.

"You know how important this is, Katherine. I won't let anyone know it came from you. I promise. But Matt needs to know."

Katherine looked down at her hands in her lap, silently contemplating what she wanted to say. Then, slowly, she raised her head and looked at Doron. "Please don't tell anyone I told you," she whispered.

Doron nodded, listening.

"Maybe this way, Jonathan's death will at least have meant something." She paused again, looking down. Finally, she nodded slightly and raised her head, her eyes clear and focused.

"His name was Lachier."

Doron waited. "Do you know his first name, who he is, where he's from?"

The woman shook her head. "I never asked."

Her eyes welled up again, and she lowered her face into her hands. When she raised her head again, she found herself alone in the room. The door was open, and she could hear the sound of footsteps hurrying down the hall. The emergency door opened and then shut. Then silence.

In less than two minutes, Doron had exited the building to the parking lot and Pearl-set her car in the direction of the White House.

OUTSIDE WASHINGTON, D.C.

Novitia Tech

Matt Serafino strode down the halls of Novitia's main computing framework and into the company's executive center. The CEO's assistant, Susan, stood up as he passed by, quickly opening the door to Derrick Martin's office. She knew better than to ask the president to wait to be announced. When Matt Serafino arrived, he didn't wait for anyone. Nor should he, she thought. He was, after all, the president. She looked around, expecting to see the president's bodyguards lurking in the hallway or trailing not far behind him, but the hallway was empty. She stood, puzzled. President Serafino had closed the door behind him. She returned to her desk and began to sort through the mail, occasionally glancing out at the empty hallway.

Derrick Martin stood up from his chair as Serafino walked in.

"Mr. President. Matt. Thanks for coming." He reached out to take Serafino's hand. Serafino didn't respond. Derrick smiled. He was only mildly surprised to realize Matt had sent his avatar. The president liked the freedom to move around at will. Although avatar hologram technology gave him that freedom, holography was still imperfect. Matt could function through his robotic likeness, but the avatar couldn't yet sense all the intricacies of human social functions. Not yet. But the time would come. Avatar holography was one of the biggest growth technologies on the market. Now personal avatar holographs belonged to only a select few with the money to support them. But soon they would become as commonplace as Cloud technology or the personal Pearl.

"I tried to reach you on your private line." Serafino was looking at him now.

"Yes, I wasn't wearing my Pearl when I went down to the mainframe. I apologize for that, Matt. But I'm glad you got here. Let me show you what happened."

The two men headed for the private hallway through the door in the rear of Martin's office. They soon came to the mainframe central core.

Derrick Martin spoke the pass code into the voice detector, and the panel board came to life.

"Code Breach," he then said.

The main computing system began digiting out information from the core. As Serafino watched, Martin showed him where the system had been infiltrated. Whoever had hacked into the central core had not only been able to retrieve all of Novitia's engineering diagrams, including that of the Night Streamer, but was also able to gain access to its key intelligence information. Included was a list of overseas potential targets and government access codes.

Matt Serafino swore under his breath.

"You'll have to build it up from the ground again."

"Already done." Derrick Martin was busy showing him the protective measures they were taking to prevent any further damage.

"We're currently reprogramming all of our data into new formats. But our locations are compromised, and so is our model for the Night Streamer. It's a real blow to our aeronautics division and to national security, not to mention our intelligence network."

"Any idea who did this?"

Serafino's avatar wore a blank expression, and Derrick was secretly glad to have the vacant-looking substitute next to him in the place of Serafino's fiery temper.

"No idea. We're working on it."

The light on Matt Serafino's avatar wrist was blinking now, and Matt excused himself.

"My Pearl indicator is blinking, Derrick. It's Doron. I need to take this." The avatar seemed to shut down for a moment, then reanimate, as though waking from a brief memory lapse.

"I have something I have to take care of, Derrick. I need to use your avatar holomorph portal. I don't have time to go back."

"Of course, Matt. Right this way."

Derrick led the president to the avatar deck, where Novitia's dream of viable avatar technology had been realized with the inception of Matt Serafino's request for the first module. At least they still had that. The designs for the avatar had been kept in separate files belonging to its lead scientist and were never placed in the company's mainframe. Derrick had argued against allowing the inventor to keep the designs as his own intellectual property. Now he was relieved. He would hate to see Matthew Serafino's temper flare if the president thought he no longer had the monopoly on avatar tech, especially the holomorph. The holomorph had the ability to read the coordinates from Serafino's physical avatar and to re-create it in a virtual version of the same. The holotar looked like the real thing, but the virtual hologram could appear and disappear at will, allowing its operator to be almost anywhere in the world at any time. The invention was Serafino's ultimate prize.

Matt's avatar stepped into the portal and closed the glass dome of the holomorph simulator. In a moment, the virtual avatar appeared in the holoconnector dome. Matt's physical avatar stepped out, went over to the touch panel, and set his coordinates for Cairo.

"See you in a few minutes."

Serafino's avatar returned to the module and shut down. His virtual holotar had vanished.

CAIRO, EGYPT

National Research Institute of Astronomy and Astrophysics (NRIAA)

Hassan Masih finished the notations on his technotablet and sat back, waiting for Youhanna Lachier to return from his meeting with the prime minister. At last they would know if their project would be approved with the funds they needed to launch the Moonbeamer space jet. Hassan had helped Lachier engineer the project. It had the power and the technology to reach not only the moon but any of the neighboring planets. Now their dream of establishing vacuumed living on these other planets would finally be within their reach. And Egypt would own the first land in space.

He knew Youhanna should be thrilled. And yet, his boss had seemed distracted lately. Hassan knew his director had other projects, ones he was not aware of, but he thought Youhanna Lachier would have been more concerned about the grant. Something was on his mind. Hassan knew enough not to ask what he wasn't told.

Hassan's thoughts were interrupted by the sound of footsteps coming down the hall to the lab. He turned, ready to greet Lachier as he entered the door. But it wasn't the director.

Hassan rose as President Matthew Serafino entered the lab. He recognized the president of the New United States from the news visuals, but he had never met him in person. *Why is he here in the lab?* Hassan nodded in respect to the world leader.

President Serafino got right to the point. "Where's the director? Where's Youhanna Lachier?"

"Uh, he's in a meeting right now with the prime minister, sir. Is there anything I can do for you?"

Hassan still could not imagine why the president of the United States would come to the lab. Why wouldn't he go to the government headquarters? Or to Lachier's private office? Or had he already gone there? Young and inexperienced in government protocol, Hassan paused, uncertain of what to do next.

"Just give Lachier a message from me, would you?"

The president's dark eyes now seemed to bore right into Hassan, and a cold line of irrational fear ran from the base of the young man's spine up through the top of his skull.

"Tell him we need to talk. Privately."

"Yes, sir, Mr. President."

Hassan moved forward to shake the president's hand but recoiled in shock as his hand passed right through the president's arm. Backing away, Hassan glanced nervously to the rear door. When he turned again to face the front of the lab, the president was nowhere to be seen.

WASHINGTON, D.C.

Oval Office

Back in the Oval Office, Matthew Serafino stepped out from the avatar module and stretched his legs. He would still need to deal with Niú. But not today. When the Maryland genetics lab had called to let him know that the formula in the Chinese scientist's digidrive contained a compound for advanced respiratory influenza, Matt knew he would have to come down hard on Niú Ye. But first he would need ammunition, so for the moment he would let Niú sweat.

Matt's studio panel flashed just as he was contemplating what he would do to the Chinese conspirator, and Mullica Michaels appeared on the screen.

"Mr. President, sir, you have an emergency call."

Matt tuned in to his Pearl and accessed the call from his chief-of-staff, who sounded out of breath.

"What is it, Ted?"

Ted Calahan exhaled hard. "Mr. President, we've just had a terrorist attack."

Matt Serafino knew what was coming before Ted could finish his first sentence. He smirked. What else would someone want with Novitia's mainframe coordinates?

"What's the hit?"

"The missile plant in Texas. Novitia."
Serafino's eyes narrowed. *Lachier.*

HOUSTON, TEXAS
Novitia Missiles Manufacturing Plant

In the Houston, Texas, branch of Novitia, its missiles manufacturing plant, a deafening explosion ripped through the manufacturing company's central engineering platform before the alarms could even signal the presence of an intruder. From miles away, Houstoners could see the cloud of smoke rising over the city, thick and black like a giant twister. One of the members of the local union ran inside to connect to his Pearl and activate its FirePillar. Emergency services would need every man it could get for this one. The burning remains of what had been Novitia's primary missiles manufacturing plant for the New United States lay in a heap of ash, rubble, and twisted metal.

7

THE ARIES SEAL

Centre for Manuscript and Print Studies

The key arrived in a brown paper carton from Virginia. Paul had asked his housekeeper, Amanda, to go upstairs to the attic, find the key, and then wrap it carefully before sending it. She had done that, and now the package lay in the foyer of the center, waiting for him to open it. Paul hesitated briefly, not quite knowing if he wanted to see the strange piece again in light of all that had been happening during the course of the week. But at last, after staring at the unassuming parcel for another few minutes, he cut the strings, tore away the paper, and snapped open the box containing the beryllium cross key.

The key looked new—probably just the way it had looked the day his mother received it in Jefferson Hospital in West Virginia on the morning of his birth, thirty-six years ago. As he pulled the multishaped keepsake out of its packaging, Paul noticed that although the key itself was ancient in its ornate design, the odd silverlike metal shone like new, casting rainbow colors across the walls and rounded ceilings of the center's entryway. He held it in his palm, turning it this way and that. The key gleamed effervescently in the morning sun as Paul rotated it between his fingers.

Paul's fascination with the strange lights was broken by the abrupt opening and closing of the front door of the foyer as Emory Makefield walked in, talking animatedly to someone through his Pearl. Paul moved to the side of the foyer to allow the director to walk by. He lifted a hand to Paul, nodding and smiling briefly as he continued to speak to the unseen caller, and entered the study area, closing the door behind him.

The moment broken, Paul returned the key to its case and exited the building in the direction of the British Museum. Not only had he allowed time today to visit the museum, but he planned to catch the 10:30 a.m. train from Euston to the Dublin Ferry. Ephraem's Diatessaron commentary fragment was housed in the Chester Beatty Library in Dublin. There he hoped to get a base of information on the already translated texts and notes of the more recent Diatessaron fragments in order to see if the new original contained any differences or aberrations from the known manuscripts.

Angela was still engaged in translating the two texts set together within the strange codex, but Paul made plans to meet her for dinner the evening following his return. They had agreed to Calaghan's Irish Restaurant on Coram Street at seven o'clock in order to talk about whatever Angela may have found out so far about the nature of the palimpsest's hidden document. Paul hoped that between them, they could begin to decipher the messages between the lines of the strange new codex.

Paul shoved the box with the key into his left pocket and shut the door of the center behind him. The sun was shining brightly on Russell Square, and as Paul moved across the park, the spray from the center fountains reflected the rays, making it seem as though the fountains were made of pure light. It was deserted this morning. The mothers and children who usually visited the gardens were apparently off to other sites today, and Paul could hear the songs of the blackbirds as they echoed through the early morning air, surprisingly brisk and clean for twenty-first-century London.

LONDON, ENGLAND

Euston Station

The train arrived on time, and Paul looked forward to the six-hour ride through the green, velvety countryside from London's Euston Station to Holyhead Station in Wales, then on to the Dublin Ferryport. As he gazed out the windows, taking in the sun-drenched gardens laced with ribbons of colored flowers and the multitudes of black and white sheep scattered across the landscape, Paul thought about Tatian and why the second-century writer would have thought it necessary to hide his unusual manuscript in the marshes of northern Syria.

The second-century regions of the Middle East had been experiencing a time of unsettled "truths" and apocalyptic visions—and even more uncertain fates for those scholars who often found themselves and their beliefs at odds with the political rulers of the day, or with those of the newly forming church hierarchies and orthodoxies. Yet Paul found it hard to imagine that anyone would risk death just to promote a set of stories, gathered and written down from the life experiences of a single man who called himself the Son of God (*could anyone actually have believed that?*). And why would someone go to the trouble to preserve a manuscript containing these stories, even to the point of hiding an additional subtext under an already disputed one, and then burying it under a bog just to protect it from burning and destruction? But that was exactly what Tatian had done. *Why was this manuscript so valuable to him? Who did he hope would find it?*

Paul shook his head in disbelief. Although as a historian, the ideas and myths behind the early religious documents fascinated Paul, especially the Christian ones, he himself didn't subscribe to any of the old belief systems. Who did anymore? Twenty-first-century New Selfer sciences had all but proved religion to be nonsensical. No one even had to mention the inherent and obvious failure of the old order churches to positively impact anything that might have convinced anyone of their stake in some sort of God, or humanity. Their buildings now lay as barren as their "faith," decaying and moldering relics in the midst of the New Selfer cities, especially in the New United States.

But these days, Paul also found it hard to believe in anything the New Selfers had to offer. Did New Selfers actually believe in anything? Paul wasn't sure. Secular or not, New Selferism had morphed into just another belief system with a myth of its own. Much like the numb-brained New Agery of the early twenty-first-century, the religio-philosophical system called New Selferism was a smorgasbord of spiritualities. Like a tray of divine canapés, you could pick the one most pleasing to your tastes. Whenever anyone said, "I am spiritual but not religious," it did not mean that person had no religion, but that religion was self-organized, self-indulgent, and self-governing, free of authority and constraints. New Selferism was solipsism gone spiritual. *If we don't learn from the past, we are destined to repeat it.* Wasn't that how the old saying went?

It wasn't that New Selfers believed in the supernatural. They believed in the technologically *supra*natural. If anything, they were too sure of their own ability to conceive of and acquire anything they wanted. The most universal component of New Selferism was this one creed: *No God but God, and you are God.* For New Selfers, the gods were visible to mortals. Just look in the mirror. The sacrament that made the godhead possible was science and technology, and New Selfers worshipped at the golden calf of the next upgrade and beta distribution that would make them better and safer. Bioinformatics was the alchemy of deity.

New Selfers even had their own demonology. Some despised the underground religions as murderous and violent, centrifugal forces pulling society apart. They were convinced that they knew what turned faith sour: antiscientific superstition. Others saw the traditional religions as humorous and sometimes heartwarming attempts to justify life's meaning, when life had no meaning other than "to thine own self be true."

New Selfer USAmericans believed in politics and a return to what they named the Old American Way, a hope based in acquisition, power, and the advances of science that they had felt sure Matthew Serafino, their beloved Uncle Sam, would usher in. The last fifty years had been hard for USAmerica. The country had lost its footing to the "magic brick" (MK BRIC) nations, and little by little, the country that used to be known as the world's leader in politics, economics, and business had taken a dive headfirst into the muck of devolution. The country had been gradually unraveling, and most had blamed its inconvenient demise on a lack of spine. For USAmericans, *security* was the new catchword, and only power could create peace. Only wealth could create stability. Only control could create order. Only those with the best technology could ensure survival in a world that was now fast losing its natural resources, food supplies, and resistance to the ever-advancing superbug viruses of the new generations. Only the Underground doctors resisted this combination of past "embrasion" and encompassing scientific power, but their impact had been inconsequential at best.

For Paul, the New American way left him with an ever-growing discomfort. He didn't think the replacement of postmodern ideals with New Selfer values had gotten anyone anywhere, and he instinctively distrusted Matthew Serafino. But he had nothing better to offer. As most now relatively isolated Americans had done for the last century or more, Paul remained numbly grounded in his own existence, happy for his reasonably uncomplicated lifestyle, a moderately successful career, and a relatively safe place to live.

That is, until the day of the accident, when everything changed . . .

But what had changed? Being spooked by a few circumstantial coincidences was certainly not enough to indicate that anything in his life had changed. Yet Paul had to admit he was intrigued by the Diatessaron manuscript, which seemed to be from a time when *meaning in life* meant more than the successful procurement of the next genetically produced food supply.

Paul's seat jerked forward as the train came to a halt midway through a vacant pasture. The train was still several hours away from Holyhead Station. Through the windows, Paul could see that the sky was blackening. A thick cloud cover moved in rapidly from the eastern horizon, bringing torrents of rain that beat down on the roof of the train cars. The storm had come up quickly. Paul hadn't even noticed the change in the weather until the deluge was already upon them. But why had the train stopped?

Paul leaned toward the doors of his train compartment and peered out into the aisle. He didn't hear anything but the pounding of rain on metal and the now approaching rumbling of thunder as the storm roared across the countryside. Outside, the fields were blowing with wind and rain, the grasses thrashing wildly.

Paul stepped outside the compartment doors and walked cautiously up the main aisle. He could see no one else in the carriage. Streaks of lightning lit up the abandoned train car, illuminating the windows of the empty cabin compartments. The lights had gone out, and Paul could only vaguely make out the back end of the next car through the rain-beaten window of the exit door.

Feeling a slight wave of fear in the base of his stomach, Paul reached to his ear for his Pearl and tested the sensor. No response. The Pearl was inactive. *How could that be?*

The storm was getting louder now, and the rain rushed like a waterfall onto the roof, so loudly that Paul was sure it would burst right through the ceiling and into the cabin.

Paul stepped back into his compartment, not knowing what to do.

And then he saw them. Paul rubbed the window with his palm, as though to clear away the rising wisps of fog that covered the landscape, and looked again, plastering his face against the cold, dark glass.

Around the front of the train appeared four horses. They were larger than any horses he had ever seen. They were running, charging forward, their nostrils spewing out steam or rain as they pushed across the field in front of him. As they ran, their hooves reverberated on the ground like gathering thunder, pounding the earth with a terrible fury. Their eyes glistened and shone, as if reflecting the lightning around them. Stopping not ten feet from the train, they rose on their haunches, their legs kicking and beating the oncoming wind and rain, and then continued down the rippling pasture toward the far woods, finally disappearing into the darkening fog.

In what seemed only a few moments after that, the rain cleared. The sky appeared to open up as the clouds dissipated and moved toward the west, while hazy rays of sunlight shone through the remaining wisps of fog that hovered over the warm ground and glistened in droplets on the water-drenched fields.

The cabin lights flickered on just as Paul's Pearl sprang to life, vibrating the base of his ear, and the train began slowly to inch its way forward. Paul cracked his window but now could hear only the sound of birds as they flapped through the afternoon air. The dark had lifted.

LONDON, ENGLAND

Centre for Manuscript and Print Studies

Angela leaned over the parchment, carefully and expertly applying the cellulose-acetate mixture to the almost flawless pages. She needed to make sure to fix the ink, so that neither of the two texts of the palimpsest document, the almost faded Greek nor the more dominant Syriac text, would deteriorate as she continued to examine the manuscript. Although kept out of the air and tightly sealed, parchment of this age was prone to a variety of paper- or ink-related calamities, and Angela wanted to make sure nothing within the manuscript suffered damage of any kind. The cellulose acetate would not only protect the document but would ensure no further loss of visibility as she cleaned any additional debris from the ancient pages.

As she worked, she thought about the commentary that Paul would examine when he arrived in Dublin that evening. She had seen the manuscript fragment a few years back but hadn't taken the time to read it. In 1993, an English translation of the commentary was published, and although she hadn't checked, she was fairly sure that the center kept a copy of it in the main library. She would tell Paul about it when he returned to London.

Angela had been at the Centre for Manuscript and Print Studies for several years now, leaving her native Ireland for London as a student and never returning. And she had been happy in London. The center was at the heart of the cultural section of the city, and Angela liked being a part of the hustle and bustle of metropolitan life. But in her heart, she was Irish. She loved the beautiful rolling hills, the rocky coastlines, and the quaint country villages in County Clare where she had grown up, near Galway Bay. At times, even now, when the night grew quiet, she could almost hear the soft sound of the incoming tides as they crashed into the rocks on the shore, the sound of the gulls, and in her mind's eye she could see the smooth green of the hills that seemed to roll out like an endless carpet across the land with its woods, paths, and footstones.

It wasn't just that her family had lived on that land for generations, but the place had a feel about it that breathed history. Every place had a tale to share, secrets to be discovered, and a landscape that told a story of its own, as though offering a glimpse of a different reality, a different eternity. It was a place still nearly untouched by twenty-first-century culture, with all its gadgetry and pollutants. And there was a serenity about it, a quiet, as though the earth were remembering its past, a time in which people and soil lived a different kind of unity. Angela smiled to herself.

It was then that she smelled the burning liquid. Acetone. Angela ran to the far corner of the lab where she had prepared the restoration treatment. Inside the boiler pot, the acetone had caught fire and was burning, sending fumes and smoke into the lab. Quickly, she grabbed the oxygen mask from the corner of the wall, fastened it around her head, and began to extinguish the flames.

The fumes would take hours to clear now. She wouldn't be able to work any further on the manuscript until morning. How had the acetone caught on fire?

Angela was sure she had turned off the burner. It wasn't like her to make mistakes in the lab. She tried to remember exactly what she had done after preparing the cellulose acetate. She had turned it off. She was sure of it. But no one else had entered the lab while she was there . . .

Angela sighed and latched the door of the lab, leaving its vents and blowers on to clear the air for the next morning's work.

I must be getting tired.

She paused for a moment, holding her hands over her eyes. They were still watering slightly from the fumes. She would need to wash them out. Angela did what she could to rinse her eyes in the kitchen of the building, then gathered her belongings and headed for the front exit. As she passed through the archway, she noticed a small white parcel on the table in the front foyer. On it were scripted letters:

Angela Matthews Krall

Angela opened the library doors and called out for Emory, but he seemed to have left. The library and offices were deserted. The package did not appear to have been mailed. There was no return address, nor was it addressed to the center. It simply bore her name. She hadn't heard anyone arrive to make the delivery, but then again, she had been busy in the lab since the early morning.

Setting down her coat and keys, she picked up the small, neatly wrapped box and gingerly turned it over. By the weight of it, she could tell it was something substantial.

Angela carefully removed the wrapping, preserving the scripted lettering, set the covering aside, and proceeded to open the white cardboard container.

Inside was a flattened, rounded stone. It appeared to be some kind of quartz—pale, with an almost pinkish-white hue. The front of the rock was plated with what Angela knew to be pure gold, poured onto the stone and thickly sunken into the base. Over the top of the plate was the figure of a ram, in the center were the Greek letters A and Ω, and toward the bottom of the plate were engraved the following words:

The Word was made flesh and it dwelt among us.

Angela turned the stone over. The bottom appeared to be just the rough underside of the quartz stone. Only the front section that was pressed into the stone had been engraved. It was a seal of some kind. Angela had seen samples of that type of seal in some of the old artifact books in the British Museum. They were used often to identify family crests or to use in sealing contracts or treaties. The one before her appeared to be quite old, yet the letters were perfectly legible, as though cast a few moments ago.

As Angela held the seal in her hand, the gold seemed to grow warm, absorbing the heat from her body. Its shining yellow plate cast a warm glow onto her skin, making her face appear almost luminous in the dimly lit foyer.

She would ask Paul about it at dinner the following evening. In the meantime, she needed to get home. She still had a lot of work to do the next day if she wanted to work on the palimpsest.

Angela placed the golden seal back into the box and placed it gently in the drawer of the table. If the gift was a contribution to the center, she would find out about it in the morning. It had been a long day, and she was tired. With that thought, she reached for the doorknob, pulled open the latch, and stepped out into the warming April air.

8

THE DEVOLUTION REVOLUTION

WASHINGTON, D.C.

The White House

The crowd lined the streets surrounding the White House, pushing in toward the South Lawn. The sun was just rising, but already the heat was baking the black streets. At eighty degrees, it was warm for mid-April. But in the last thirty years summer had begun to arrive earlier and earlier, making spring almost obsolete.

"Who are they?" Serafino stood sipping his morning coffee and staring out across the White House grounds.

"It appears to be several groups this time." Ted Calahan rose from the conference table and joined the president at the window. "Some are from ATBA, the Anti-Technology Biological Alliance. Others are apparently aligning themselves with them. Mostly old orders and under-grounders, but they are numbering in the tens of thousands, and they're demanding answers about our role in the attacks on the Shrubs."

Matt Serafino smiled, shaking his head slowly.

The Shrubs were outliers, dilettantes who didn't appreciate Serafino's increase in government regulation in order to rein in power for the struggling economy through the new and interrelational

71

sciences. They opposed the funding Serafino was driving into the techno fields and accused him of creating a new elite. Only those in government-sanctioned tech companies were thriving. The rest of the country's population continued to grow weaker economically and educationally, they said. Serafino was widely supported by the conservative, consumer elite in the east, but he was fast gaining critics from the western masses for what they deemed unethical uses of the country's technological advances, financial resources, and political power. Not only was Serafino tapping the country's water and core resources without creating renewal and restoration systems, but the Shrubs had blamed Matt for the destruction of the country's already weakened economy through big spending in the technosciences and poorly managed resources for the country's growing middle- and lower-class populations.

With the rise of the powerhouse MK BRIC countries, the new economic world giants, the United States had tumbled to a standard of living well below that of its world counterparts. For the Shrubs, increased technology was not the answer. And they began to align more and more with the underground doctors and bioscientists from the alliances—those who wanted to impose heavy restrictions on robotics and nanogenetics and now protested regularly for a decentralization of Serafino's Interrelational Sciences Health-care Program (ISHP), a system from which all biological and natural medical professions were now banned.

The Shrubs had gotten too powerful in the western parts of the country, and Serafino had needed to control them. He wasn't directly responsible for the attacks. He had to make sure only that several of the Shrubs' key leaders were effectively removed, thus making a firm statement. *Just enough to cripple the resistance.* And he knew if he released their names to certain factions within companies such as Novitia, the problem would take care of itself. And it had. The door had opened for Matthew Serafino to begin to increase the country's tech resources. And he was doing that. He also had begun to work on chipping his way into the BRICs. *Until the infiltration of Novitia.*

Matt clenched his teeth. He would still have to deal with Niú, and now Lachier. If he had to, he would buy their loyalty. He still had the support of those in the Senate and the House, more than any president had ever had. But he needed China's scientific prowess. China was already the largest of the world economic leaders. And now the Middle East was fast rising in the sciences, faster than he had predicted they would. He would need to put a wedge between them and the other MK BRIC countries, before nations like Egypt and Afghanistan could add themselves to the new world economic structure.

Matt turned from the window.

"What do you want to do about them?" Calahan was still staring out onto the lawn.

"Nothing. The matter will take care of itself."

Ted Calahan turned at the president's nonchalant statement, but he had left the Cabinet Room.

Matt Serafino knew he would need all his energy in the next few weeks to deal with the International World Conference on Economics and his visits to the BRIC countries. It was time to start calling the shots. Soon the United States would be back in the forefront of the global powerhouses. Then the resistance movements would have no one to back them up.

Matt sensored to Mullica, asking her to prepare a trip itinerary to China, Russia, India, and the Middle East. He felt confident about Brazil. His state dinner had been a success, and he was sure he could get Ernesto Alvarez in his corner. Now he needed to work that same magic on the other MK BRICs. He would begin by talking. And if that didn't work, he had other ideas, other ways of gaining power.

And there was also the ritual. He knew where his power came from.

Serafino knew his heritage. Since the day he was born, he'd been destined to find the Way of the Seal. And the rituals had served him well up until now. True to the prophecy, he had excelled in everything he did, had risen quickly in all the government channels, and had become the youngest president of the New United States. But he also knew this was only the beginning. And he would need every bit of force—natural and supernatural—that he could muster to unify the four and to fulfill his final destiny. Then no one would be able to get in his way. The world would be his for the making.

Matthew Serafino peered out the door of the Oval Office. Mullica had taken her break, and his staff was down the hall, arguing over some mundane matter concerning corned beef. He slipped out of the office and shut the door so they would think he was still inside. In a rolling suitcase, he had secreted the large book. The thing was heavy, and he needed all of his strength to pull it after him. The codex in the case was made of aged leather with brittle parchment pages, and he needed to take care not to damage it. He would need it for the ritual. He hurried down the corridor into the lower level of the building, watching to make sure no one was following him. Matt stopped at last near the basement corridor, where the furnace rooms and White House mainframe were housed. Looking around to make sure no one was coming down either hallway, he slipped quietly into a small storage room. After lifting away several boxes and an old carpet, he pulled up a wooden trapdoor from the rear center of the little room to reveal an old wooden stairway that led downward in a slow spiral and then wove around to the right as far as the eye could see. Grabbing a flashlight that he had left in a corner of the room, Serafino lowered himself and the suitcase into the dark stairwell, repositioning the door over his head before he inched precariously down the stairway.

The stairs wound around several times and then emptied into a long passageway. The passage had the dank smell of rotted wood and untouched earth, but Serafino pressed onward, his feet echoing on the wooden planks strewn along the floor of the earthy corridor. At last, he came into a rounded room.

The room appeared to have been built as some sort of emergency shelter. There were boxes of candles lying on shelves in the corners and shelves with gas lamps lining the upper walls. In the center of the room was a wooden table, and around the table a geometric figure had been hand-sketched onto the floor. The circle, which spanned most of the room, was drawn in pale paint and contained in its center a triangle, within which was a square, and inside that a smaller circle in the center completed the figure.

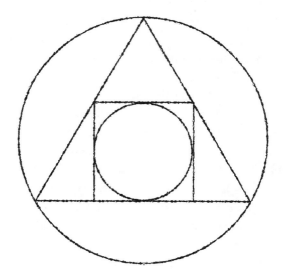

Quickly, as though time were of the essence, Matt Serafino lit a candle and with some difficulty laid the book on the table, opening it to a colorfully illuminated manuscript page. And then standing upright with his hands lifted, he began to recite the Latin words.

Just as he started the last part of the ritual, his Pearl began to vibrate, and Mullica's voice rang out in his ear. Matt threw down his hands in disgust. Then, gathering his composure, he tuned in to the call.

"Yes, Mullica?"

"Sir, I have your travel schedule ready. I can get you on a plane later today. You should arrive just in time for the International World Conference on Economics in New Delhi. In fact, you may just get there a bit early. Can you be ready in a few hours, sir?"

Serafino smiled. "Yes, Mullica, I can."

MOSCOW, RUSSIA

International Environmental Organization (IEO)
Fund-Raising Event

The fund-raising event in Moscow's Bolshoi Theatre was attended by donors and organizations from all over the world. In recent years, funding for the nongovernmental organization had dwindled as Russia had managed to catapult itself into a major economic world power. But now, with new concerns for greening its industries, as well as building a massive fifty-mile-wide and five-mile-high domed greenhouse for growing native food supplies, Russia had drawn the attention of the world's bio- and enviroscientists. Whereas other countries depended upon molecular genetics to develop new types of foodstuffs for their growing populations, Russia had depended on the IEO's funding to preserve the arts of natural and sustainable food production. As the country progressed politically and economically in the last thirty to forty years, working with the government had become more and more palatable. And now the IEO had garnered the respect of most political leaders, as well as serving as an interesting anomaly in the scientific community.

The director of the IEO was Oksanna Anya Galina, a Russian-born doctor and an environmentalist almost from birth. Her family had led one of the largest sustainable farming projects in Russia, developing a new model for growing crops in the Siberian wastelands through bubble-dome farming. Oksanna had been leading the International Environmental Organization for the last twelve years, providing not only the funding to systematize farming to feed an entire country of people in her native Russia, but also donating vast amounts of crops to countries in need of food. In the farming industry, Galina's efforts had made Russia the good neighbor of the eastern half of the world.

Oksanna was a large-boned but classically beautiful woman with sleek, dark hair; olive skin; and a broad face that hinted at a prior Mongolian ancestry. Dressed in a musk-ox fur coat and her signature golden hoop earrings, she stepped into the spotlight on the large auditorium stage to the sound of loud applause. The screens surrounding the back of the stage burst to life with visions of Russia's bioinitiatives.

"Ladies and gentlemen"—Oksanna smiled, turning her face to scan the large audience—"today is a proud day for the Russian people and for the international community. With the success of the Siberian Biofarming Project, the 'World Greenhouse,' the International Environmental Organization has been approved to begin a similar project in cooperation with a companion country. In a humanitarian spirit, our plan is to build, grow, and help sustain the new biofarming initiative within the chosen country and then train citizens to continue with its maintenance and growth, providing sustainable agriculture for yet another nation on our globe. All we ask is that when the project reaches fruition and a surplus is achieved, that the host might pass on a similar model to another country. In this way Russia, as supported by the IEO, can assist in extending a hand of friendship and in building a better world. In order to make this initial project happen, we need support from you, the citizens of the world, first with your generous donations, without which this initiative could not be realized; and second in nominating a country to receive the world's second biofarm. With that, I hope you will enjoy your evening here tonight. And I look forward to greeting all of you—and of course to receiving your donations." Oksanna smiled as the crowd stood and applauded.

The shot rang out through the crowd before Oksanna left the stage, and people began screaming and pushing their way to the exits. A shadow moved across the screens from the sound and visual booth in the back upper level of the theater and disappeared into the darkness toward the back recesses of the storage areas. The storage door opened onto a side alley that led into the busy streets of Moscow.

Oksanna pointed a finger in the direction of the door, clasped her left hand to her side, and buckled to the ground, her fur coat swaddled around her. Two men from the front of the stage rushed up the stairs and knelt beside Oksanna, cradling the woman's head and checking for vital signs as two hundred–plus Pearls simultaneously activated emergency services.

LONDON, ENGLAND
Centre for Manuscript and Print Studies

The night was dark with the new moon. A light wind rustled through the trees in the courtyard of the Centre for Manuscript and Print Studies. At the midnight hour, a soft yellow glow began to illuminate the glass foyer of the center's front entrance. The dim gleam seemed to fluctuate, brightening then softening. Then suddenly, the light flared bright white. It flashed only briefly, and then after a moment the room returned to shadowy black. No one saw the strange occurrence. But in the morning, Angela would find that the strange seal had been broken, the golden front piece separated from the rock into which it had been infused. There was no indication of how the two pieces had been molded together in the first place. No clasp or wedge was evident on either part, nor was there evidence of any kind of bonding substance. It was as though the pieces were held together by some type of magnetic force that had just simply broken apart.

NEW DELHI, INDIA
2048 International Economic Summit

President Aishwarya Kapoor welcomed her guests to the 2048 International Economic Summit, where the MK BRIC countries would meet privately during several of the sessions. Since the turn of the century, the BRICs had organized in order to consolidate their economic strength within the world economy. With the addition of Mexico and South Korea several years ago, they had begun meeting at the yearly summit. Their presence within the world economic community was a given, and their ability to meet among the other sessions of the conference made their union especially convenient for all the countries' leaders. Most of them had in fact gotten to look forward to the yearly meetings, and the gathering had become a mixture of business and pleasure. Each year to date the summit had been meeting in one of the original BRIC countries. This year, for the first time,

Aishwarya Kapoor would suggest Mexico City as the meeting place for 2049. They had earned it. She smiled, then, resuming her role as hostess, walked forward to the entrance as she saw the French official limousine arrive at the front gate. She held out her hand, welcoming France's first female president.

The presidents of Brazil, China, and Mexico had already arrived. They now awaited the arrival of the South Korean president, Kim Sun Lee, and Russian president Igor Petrov. Chinese president Murong Gui and Brazilian president Ernesto Alvarez stood talking earnestly in the far corner along with their interpreters and economic officers, and Mexican president Bernino Bruno had moved toward the coffee table and was laughing and nodding to Aishwarya Kapoor, who had left the entryway to greet him.

Meanwhile, in another part of the summit, Matthew Serafino waited for Afghan president Abdul Gulzar to arrive. Afghanistan had been rising fast in the technosciences, especially in genetics and informatics, and Serafino knew it wouldn't be long before the fledgling country joined the MK BRICs. He needed Afghanistan in his corner. He was sure that their advances in the sciences were minimal compared to their advances in weapons. The right partnership could more than make up for the momentum that America had lost with Novitia's collapse. If he played his cards right, the United States would join Afghanistan in the MK BRIC community—and would reconstitute its place in the global power frame. Serafino smirked. At first, he had asked Mullica to arrange for the tour of Afghanistan's largest technoscience and weapons manufacturing company. But he had quickly reconsidered, preferring to take the top-down route instead. He wanted to take care of this one himself. He looked at his watch. Abdul Gulzar would be arriving any moment. In less than a half hour, he would have an invitation to tour the Scitheon Corporation; he was sure of it.

Serafino watched Gulzar get out of the black limousine outside the conference center and enter through the side doors. As the Afghan president entered the room, Matthew Serafino stood to greet him. As Gulzar's eyes met the American president's and locked for a moment, a startled look came upon the face of the Afghan leader. Serafino's dark eyes shone with an intensity that indicated either extreme intelligence or mere madness. Serafino smiled. He knew the Afghan president would do anything he asked.

MOSCOW, RUSSIA
Central Clinical Hospital

Oksanna Galina stirred in her hospital bed, wincing in pain as her shoulder shifted against the sheets. As her eyes opened and adjusted to the darkness, she could see the far side of the room where the door opened into the hallway. One of the doctors stood holding a chart and talking quietly to a team of nurses at the station. She felt for the button under her right hand and pressed it hard. Immediately, a sharp pain seared into her shoulder, causing her to gasp for breath.

One of the nurses rushed in, motioning to the doctor. "She's awake."

The doctor held up a light and looked into her eyes while the nurse took her pulse.

"You've had quite an evening." He smiled at her, showing clean white teeth that seemed to match his coat. "But I assure you, you are quite safe here."

"I don't know what happened." The words came out muffled and thick, and Oksanna felt as though her tongue were stuck to the roof of her mouth.

One of the nurses lifted a cup with a straw to her mouth. "Water." She smiled.

The doctor, whoever he was, sat down on the side of the bed. Oksanna couldn't read the name tag on his coat. Her eyes seemed to swim every time she tried to focus. She squinted, trying to get her bearings.

"You've been shot. Do you remember that?"

Oksanna looked confused. Her head began to move back and forth slowly.

"No. I remember giving my speech, and then . . ." She paused, her eyes growing large. "Yes, the shot. I do remember." She looked more animated now. "But I didn't feel anything. I just remember everything going black, and then falling . . ."

The doctor glanced briefly at one of the nurses, nodded, and then looked back at Oksanna.

"You're going to be fine. Your shoulder will take a while to heal, and the muscles will be sore for some time, but there's no permanent damage. You're lucky. The thick hide of your coat seems to have taken most of the impact. The bones weren't even shattered."

"Do you know who . . . ?"

"The police will want to talk to you in the morning."

He was rising now and, Oksanna saw, preparing to leave.

"For now, rest. Your room is guarded. You have nothing to worry about."

Oksanna felt her eyes growing heavy again. Before the doctor could exit the room, she had drifted off to sleep.

LOS ANGELES, CALIFORNIA

"Revolution? Do you know what you're saying, man?"

The man in the black overcoat appeared nervous as he looked around the room at the others.

The man known to the group only as the Alpha stared pointedly at his compatriot.

"We need to know if you're in. This will only work if everyone does their part."

The man in black looked around. The others stood unmoving in the abandoned warehouse, avoiding his gaze.

What the group was suggesting was treason. If they were caught, they would be imprisoned for life, or worse. Then again, if they did manage to disable national systems, knocking out communications, maybe the ensuing panic could help them finally get that idiot Serafino out of office.

He stood for a moment, his teeth grinding together.

"You know we can't do this without you, Dan." One of the others had spoken up, and now he noticed they were all looking at him, waiting for him to respond. They were moving together now, forming the bond of agreement.

He lowered his head, lips pursed, then, looking around, he stepped forward, reached out his hand, and placed it into the center with the others.

The Alpha nodded. Avoiding each other's eyes, the group left quietly, each disappearing cautiously into the night.

9

THE PROPHECY

Hotel Montague

Paul sat in the Skylight Room of the hotel, watching the news. It would be another half hour before he would meet Angela at Calaghan's Restaurant. The trip back from Dublin had been uneventful. Paul saw no further sign of the four horses he had witnessed in the English countryside, nor did the train stop for any reason on the return trip. It seemed almost like a vision, a bad dream, in hindsight.

Paul rubbed his hands across his face, massaging his tired temples. Examining the Diatessaron fragments had led to nothing unusual. But he had taken copious notes and waited anxiously to see if the original lying on the lab tables at the Centre for Manuscript and Print Studies differed from the later versions. It wouldn't be unusual. The longer the unified Gospel had circulated, the more others had tried to conform it to the prevailing orthodoxies. Reading the untouched original not only would be fascinating but would shed light on just how different early Eastern Christianity had been, especially in Syria.

Paul's thoughts were interrupted by the news screen, which now buzzed loudly, indicating an emergency news report. He lifted his head to see anchor Monika Edwards appear on the large screen.

"This just in. The United States was shaken this morning by a complex cyberattack on its centralized computer framework. The attack disabled the financial data of the country's nearly four hundred million people, including America's top companies, banks, the IRS, Wall Street, government salaries and records, and the financial data of the MSHP health program. With its systems disabled, the United States is facing a catastrophic loss of trust as its leaders struggle to find temporary solutions. Meanwhile, riots and demonstrations have broken out all over the country, as citizens rise up against a leadership it now holds to be leading the country into a disenfranchised and dysfunctional state. State and local governments are stepping in to try to keep order in the country, as all over the world, nations step back from the crippled country's economic interests. No information is yet available as to who launched the attack or why. Monika Edwards, reporting for News Abroad Network, Great Britain."

Paul pulled his portable screen from his coat pocket and requested his Pearl to tap into his banking and financial data. Nothing. The message on the screen indicated the system was down. Paul rolled his eyes, exasperated. He could feel the back of his neck stiffening, and he leaned back into his chair and closed his eyes for a moment. At least for now, he would not be able to access his funds. Paul wondered if the hotel would keep his expenses on tab until the situation could be straightened out. At least he had his credit card. Without that, he would have nothing to get by on. He hoped it would still be honored. *Serafino.* The president was losing his grip. Now he'd have a very hard time convincing even his closest supporters to keep him in office.

Paul glanced at his watch: 6:45. Time to meet Angela. Quickly, he gathered up his sport coat and technotablet with the notes from his trip and exited the Skylight Room, heading toward Coram Street.

MARSEILLE, PROVENCE-ALPES-CÔTE D'AZUR, FRANCE

St. Seraphim Orthodox Cathedral

Father Arnaud Chevalier sat across from the young French woman, watching her eyes squeeze shut, as though hoping to force back her grief, as she told him about the death of her son. Arnaud leaned forward and reached out his hand. As she took it, the dam burst forth, and her shoulders heaved as she sobbed and wailed—the deep, wrenching grief only a mother could know. After a period of what seemed a half hour, she raised her head and looked him straight in the eye.

"Why?" she asked. Her eyes looked vacant but pleading. "Why?"

Arnaud felt his heart freeze for a moment. His eyes issued pain, and he pressed his lips together solemnly. Then his reason kicked in.

"The boy was baptized?"

"Yes, Father," she whispered.

Arnaud continued. "It is difficult to answer why. But I can tell you that God did not intend for your child to die. God does not love death. God triumphs over death. What happens sometimes in this world is a tragedy. But we know, we are assured, that in Christ's resurrection, we have a life that goes beyond all experience of death. Your son is with God now. He is in a beautiful place. You miss him because you were close to him. He was your son. But if he could speak to you now, he would tell you not to worry—that he is surrounded by love and is living a life without pain or fear. No one knows why something like this happens to one person or why something else happens to another. But we do know this: death has no power and no final word for us."

The woman looked down at her hands as though contemplating the truth of his words. Then she nodded her head slowly.

"Let me know if there's anything else I can do." Arnaud rose, escorting the woman to the entrance, holding her coat for her as she stepped through.

"I will. Thank you, Father."

Arnaud nodded, closing the door behind her. He glanced out the front window and watched her as she exited the cathedral and made her way down the Rue de la Trinité. Then he turned back to his office and breathed a sigh of relief. It was still hard for him, dealing with the grief. *How long has it been?* Too long. He shoved the memory aside and reached into the large bag beside the birdcage that hung from a large hook in the far side of his office.

"Some seeds, Seraphim?"

The bird cocked its head and looked at Arnaud eagerly. He lifted one claw from his perch and let out an exuberant squawk as Arnaud opened the cage and filled the tiny cup with honey seeds and yogurt drops for the young cockatiel. He had found Seraphim in a pet shop one fall while visiting a parishioner in the Frioul Archipelago off the Bay of Marseille. Arnaud had been walking past the little shop when he heard singing. Curious, he entered to find a beautiful white bird, with rosy cheeks and a large yellow plume on the top of its head, singing "O Sacred Head, Now Wounded" in the most haunting voice he had ever heard. Captivated by the little fellow, he leaned toward the cage, and as he did, the bird bowed and said, "Beautiful." Arnaud smiled.

"You are beautiful," he said.

"Beautiful," the bird repeated.

At this, the bird began singing again, this time an old French folk melody.

Arnaud turned to the shopkeeper. "The bird is for sale?"

"Seraphim? Yes. He was the pet of the local Lutheran pastor there on the island. When the man passed away just recently, the bird was given to us to care for until a new home could be found for him. He's a beautiful bird, and quite tame. Are you interested?"

Arnaud smiled. After making his visits, he returned to the shop, collected the bird and its belongings, and returned to the rectory, placing the bird and its cage across from his desk in his office. Every morning, the bird would sing a new hymn or folk song. Arnaud still wasn't quite sure how many the bird had memorized.

Finishing the seeds, the bird bowed and said, "Thank you. God bless you."

Arnaud made sure the cage door was latched, gathered his notes, and prepared to make his way to his observatory study. He had been making notations from a chapter of Newton's *Principia Apocalyptica* and wanted to get back to his research.

Mathematics fascinated Arnaud. In ways he was only beginning to understand, nature seemed to be filled with mathematical abstractions, infinite, yet comfortingly decipherable if only one had the right formulae. Recently, his cosmological studies had taken a turn when he discovered that most of Sir Isaac Newton's apocalyptic astronomical predictions based on his studies of Revelation were strikingly familiar to his most recent observations. Curious, he began spending most of his evenings in the observatory, comparing and making notes in a notebook. Soon, he hoped, he would have something to show for it.

LONDON, ENGLAND
Calaghan's Restaurant

Paul met Angela as she was coming through the doorway of the restaurant. After a brief exchange, Paul could see Angela was excited to talk about what she had found at the lab. They found a table, ordered quickly, and Angela wasted no time in pulling out the manuscript notes she had brought with her in her brown leather bag.

"It's a section of John's Apocalypse." Angela's face seemed to light up as she spoke, blond hair strands framing her face like a halo.

"What is? Where?" Paul looked confused.

"In the Diatessaron." Angela passed one of the translated sheets across the table to Paul. "The Greek in the palimpsest? It's part of the Apocalypse of John—you know, the book of Revelation. Somehow, the apocalyptic text was deliberately inserted between the lines of the Gospel and then hidden. But there's more, Paul. In addition to the known section of the Apocalypse, there are instructions, diagrams, and a sort of prophecy, and it indicates the year 2012."

"The year I was born." Paul glanced up, smiling.

"And the year I was born, too." Angela laughed. "Guess it was a pretty interesting year."

Paul read quickly through Angela's translation. The Greek text began with what appeared to be chapter 4 of the Revelation text, ending after chapter 6. Paul scanned quickly through the text translation:

Coming from the throne are flashes of lightning, and rumblings and peals of thunder, . . . a sea of glass, like crystal. Around the throne, . . . four living creatures, . . . the first living creature like a lion, the second living creature like an ox, the third living creature with a face like a human face, and the fourth living creature like a flying eagle . . . Then I saw in the right hand of the one seated on the throne a scroll written on the inside and on the back, sealed with seven seals . . . Then I saw between the throne and the four living creatures and among the elders a Lamb standing as if it had been slaughtered . . . He went and took the scroll . . .

Then I saw the Lamb open one of the seven seals, and I heard one of the four living creatures call out, as with a voice of thunder, "Come!" I looked, and there was a white horse! Its rider had a bow; a crown was given to him, and he came out conquering and to conquer.

When he opened the second seal, I heard the second living creature call out, "Come!" And out came another horse, bright red; its rider was permitted to take peace from the earth, so that people would slaughter one another; and he was given a great sword.

When he opened the third seal, I heard the third living creature call out, "Come!" I looked, and there was a black horse! Its rider held a pair of scales in his hand, and I heard what seemed to be a voice in the midst of the four living creatures saying, "A quart of wheat for a day's pay, and three quarts of barley for a day's pay, but do not damage the olive oil and the wine!"

When he opened the fourth seal, I heard the voice of the fourth living creature call out, "Come!" I looked and there was a pale green horse! Its rider's name was Death, and Hades followed with him; they were given authority over a fourth of the earth, to kill with sword, famine, and pestilence . . . When he opened the fifth seal, I saw under the altar the souls of those who had been slaughtered for the Word of God and for the testimony they had given . . .

When he opened the sixth seal, I looked, and there came a great earthquake; the sun became black . . .

Paul stopped and glanced to the next section. Angela had made notes in the margins as well.

"What's this?"

"It's a text addition, presumably made by Tatian to the original, but written into the margins. It's from the first chapter of Ezekiel. Tatian seems to indicate he made these notes on a trip to Patmos just before his death. "

Paul continued on.

As I looked, a stormy wind came out of the north: a great cloud with brightness around it and fire flashing forth continually, and in the middle of the fire, something like gleaming amber. In the middle of it was something like four living creatures. This was their appearance: they were of human form. Each had four faces . . . the face of a human being, the face of a lion, . . . the face of an ox, . . . the face of an eagle . . . Each creature had two wings . . . In the middle of the living creatures there was something that looked like burning coals of fire, . . . the fire was bright, and lightning issued from the fire. The living creatures darted to and fro, like a flash of lightning . . .

I saw a wheel on the earth beside the living creatures, one for each of the four of them . . . Their appearance was like the gleaming of beryl; and the four had the same form . . . Their rims were tall and awesome . . . When the living creatures rose from the earth, the wheels rose . . . I heard the sound of their wings like the sound of mighty waters, like the thunder of the Almighty, a sound of tumult like the sound of an army . . .

Paul looked up briefly.

"Go on, Paul. Read the next part. This next section is one I guarantee you've never seen." Angela seemed anxious now. Paul smiled faintly and looked to the next section.

God's decision to make a Seal has been set. This Seal will determine the final path of humankind. If humankind chooses at last to seal their covenant with God, all of creation will be spared. But if not, humankind will choose its own death. The Seal is the Final Hour. It is a Choice. The Seraphim have placed the Seal into seven parts. But the unity of the four will prevail. When the first seals are broken, the Time of Becoming will begin. One who will be chosen will serve to help others choose. And the Lamb will choose him. The future of mankind will be sealed, but with the possibility of redemption. In the year 2012, the horsemen will appear upon the earth. They will appear in the birth of the eight. And they will be scattered. If four who choose death prevail in uniting together, the earth and all that is in it will be destroyed forever. If four can be found and brought together who choose life, then they will lead a remnant of humanity into a new age, a new dawn, the new Eden. The Chosen One holds the key to their unity. His task will be to find them. But first, he must find himself.

To the one chosen by the Seraph's Seal: At the appointed time, you will find this prophecy. When you do, you must find the others. You will know them by their attributes. Use the key. Find the box of John of Patmos. From there, you will know what to do. The Society of Messengers will help you and guide you on your way. They are entrusted to carry the Way of the Seal into the Time of Becoming. You are not alone. Start now. Choose well, Paul.

—Patmos, 723

Paul continued to stare at the page, not wanting to lift his head. He knew Angela was staring at him. Finally, he got up, pushed back his chair, excused himself, and headed for the front entrance. He pushed open the door and leaned against the brick wall of the building. He needed air.

Was this some kind of joke? Did Angela put his name into the text to give him a good laugh?

He glanced inside the restaurant. He could see Angela standing by the table. She wasn't laughing. She looked as though she wasn't sure whether to stay at the table or follow him. He just needed a few more minutes.

Everything that Paul knew contradicted what he had just encountered, what he had been encountering in the last few weeks—the strange car crash, the letter addressed to him with almost the same language as he had just found in the Diatessaron's apocalyptic prophecy, finding the Diatessaron itself, the cross key, the odd dreams he had been having, the experience just yesterday on the train, and now his name inserted into a prophecy from the year 723.

He couldn't deal with this right now.

Paul looked at Angela inside the restaurant, still standing by the table. He went inside, murmured a quick good-bye, then fled from the restaurant. He strode briskly down the walk, turned the corner into an alley, and then disappeared into London's central district.

10

THE GRIFFIN'S EGG

BEIJING, CHINA

Center for Sleep and Hypnosis

"He's recording something."

The interns stood behind the glass enclosure, watching as the MF-Unit typed the visual descriptions coming from Niú's brain. New hypnosis was the latest version of post-traumatic stress therapy. It allowed the subject not only to tap into prior memories, but to transcribe them into a type of narrative, told from a current adult perspective. In other words, the patient could objectify himself, could see himself and his memories as though standing as a dispassionate observer within his own dream. And then narrate them to the observer.

"Couldn't a patient do that without hypnosis?"

"Maybe, but very young memories aren't verbal. They're sensory. Descriptive. It's hard to access those early sensory memories and to translate them into adult verbal speech. The device helps to do that. When the sensory experiences are transcribed as descriptions, doctor and patient can go back and analyze them, identify them, and put them into contexts that the adult brain can reconfigure. Essentially, an old truth can be transformed into a new truth, eliminating the mind's hyperprotective fight-or-flight response. In a sense, post-traumatic stress reactions tell us that we are in survival mode. New hypnosis hopes to disable it."

"How long has he been suffering from the disorder?"

"I think the doctor said he's been having headaches since he was a child. But this one also wanted to try the hypnosis for personal reasons of some sort. And he's government. He can do what he wants, I guess."

"What's it say?"

"I can't read it from here. Doc will keep it confidential, though. We won't get to see it. Wait, he's turning on the speaker. Tell the others to be quiet."

"Looks like he's moving around down there. He must be under. What age did the doc take him back to?"

"Shhh . . . One or two, I think."

They could see the doctor talking to Niú Ye through the device. Ye's memories were solidifying now, forming themselves into a narrative. The device began to register sentences.

"Go ahead now, Ye, tell me. Tell me what you are experiencing."

The machine hummed as Niú Ye's hypnotic narrative spoke from the device

"Where are you, Ye?"

"I'm in a room."

"Are you at the orphanage?"

"No, it's before the orphanage. Somewhere else."

"Tell me, Niú. Enter the dream. Tell me what you see."

Niú's eyes fluttered briefly and then began to swim back and forth as he entered his past.

I can smell cedar. Can smell it hanging over the room. Thick, oppressive. I can see walls. They're brown, and they look gritty. It's a wooden box, I think. There's no real light. Only a thin streak of sun. It's jutting out—kind of like a beam, straight across the room. I like it. The room is filthy. I'm looking at the light again. It looks strange, filled with particles of dust. I can see a fruit fly. It's darting in and out of the ray. In and out. In and out. It's making swirls. I laugh. The air around it looks filmy, gold from the sun, and I'm fascinated by it. I want to watch it longer, but then

I get bored. I turn my head again to wait. But no one comes. No one ever comes. I don't cry. I never cry. My thumb is my solace. It's never taken away. It's my constant, my relief. I suck it raw.

Niú seemed to pause. The doctor looked up, about to speak, when Niú began again.

I hear wailing now. The air is suffocating, and the space is dark where I am lying. Everything is in shadows. I'm still staring upward, but now I can see moving lights. I continue sucking ravenously at the thumb, until it feels a little like a shriveled prune. I want to remain unnoticed. I know not to cry. I've learned to live inside myself. To expect nothing. To pay attention to everything.

Now it's quiet again. I listen, but I can't hear any sound—just the hum of a fan and something rumbling from the street below the window somewhere on the far side of the box.

Niú began to stir in the chair. The narrative began to transcribe faster as Niú's heart rate seemed to rise suddenly. The doctor stayed by the monitor, ready to stop the session if Niú's vitals continued to soar. And then, the computer's voice grew low and steady, dropped to a cold calm.

A low, growling feeling started creeping into the pit of my stomach one day. I could feel it growing more and more. Like someone had bored a hole in the center and left it open to fester. Fear settled into my core and hunkered down deep like a dark seed. In time, it grew distant and dormant, but like a slumbering ox, it could awaken in an instant in the night, jarring me from dreaming. In the terrifying night where no one ever came, I feared it. At any time, the sleeping beast could turn, rear its head, and howl.

The narrative abruptly ended, and Niú's body seemed to slump and return to a sleeplike state. The doctor turned off the machine and waited. He glanced up at the window where the interns were watching. They were also silent, looking at each other and then back into the room at the sleeping man. The doctor tore the narrative pages from the device, placed them in a file, and left the room. Soon the interns filed out from the glass observation deck, returning to their posts. No one spoke, nor would they ever speak about the session again.

Niú woke feeling troubled. The back of his head felt stiff and sore, and his eyes hurt and felt as though the sockets were stuffed with cotton. Slowly, he raised himself onto one arm, allowing his vision to clear. The headaches were becoming more frequent now. And the sessions seemed to exacerbate them rather than relieve them.

"Niú, I'd like to terminate the treatment." The doctor stood beside the cot, waiting for Niú Ye to steady himself.

"Anything?"

"Nothing." The doctor frowned thoughtfully. "You know, Niú, we may never find out what you want to know this way. I thought I explained that to you. Hypnosis is a wonderful tool to relieve post-traumatic stress symptoms. But it isn't meant to be a memory recovery tool. Your origins, your parents, your birthplace—you were only two years old when you entered the orphanage. The memory of a child that age is mostly visual, sensory memory, based on very primal experiences. You may be just stirring up uncomfortable memories. And your symptoms are not abating—the headaches, the difficulty sleeping are getting worse instead of better. Perhaps it's time to stop."

"I can't stop. Not yet."

The doctor stood in front of Niú, looking directly into his eyes, as though searching for some fragment of what he had just heard. But Niú's eyes stared back, showing determination with perhaps a trace of sheer stubbornness. If there was a beast inside, it was sleeping now.

"I won't hypnotize you again, Niú. I'm sorry. You can see someone else. But I won't do this again."

The doctor nodded respectfully, then quietly walked to the end of the lab, opened the door, and left, closing it gently behind him.

STOCKHOLM, SWEDEN

National Library of Sweden

The director stared at the empty case in the library's Main Hall, which housed the museum's medieval collections. The section had been shut down for the last few weeks for repairs, and no one had noticed the missing artifact until this morning. The Codex Gigas, otherwise known as the Devil's Bible, had been housed in the Swedish library since 1649, when the illuminated manuscript was stolen as plunder by the Swedish army in the Thirty Years' War. The largest medieval manuscript in the world, the codex weighed 165 pounds. And yet someone had carried it off, leaving no trace of its presence or theirs. A strange manuscript, the codex was filled not only with pictures and diagrams to complement the biblical passages but with information on every known discipline of the thirteenth century, from medieval sciences and philosophy to spells and exorcisms. It was essentially an almanac of sorts for the spiritually inclined. The director shook his head. He couldn't imagine who would want to take the calfskin-bound volume. He sighed and contacted the police to make a report of the theft.

CAIRO, EGYPT

National Ballroom

"Good evening, Monsieur Lachier."

Youhanna Lachier nodded to the doorman, his elongated nose accented by his widening smile.

"Would you care for a mask, sir?"

Lachier nodded, accepted a red eagle's-head mask from the man, and entered the ballroom. The Masquerade Ball was an annual event, put on by the National Research Institute of Astronomy and Astrophysics, the NRIAA of Cairo, to raise funds for the center's most promising scientists' research projects. His own research had been funded by one of the institute's prime grants, and he fully intended to see it continued into the following year. He knew his presence at the event would draw attention. He was the institute's most well-renowned—and highest paid—scientist, and that meant he would always have his share of finessing to do for the institute's wealthy donors. He would rather be back at the lab, working on his private projects. It was hard to get time now that Masih seemed to follow him everywhere he went, loitering in the lab until all hours, working on the technology for the Moonbeamer.

But Lachier knew the secrecy of his plans depended on his ability to put on a popular face to the public. And so Lachier gritted his teeth, plastered on his best smile, and positioned his mask as he prepared to greet the roomful of guests.

KABUL, AFGHANISTAN

Scitheon Corporation

The gates leading to the headquarters of the largest weapons manufacturer in Afghanistan opened to allow the U.S. president's entourage to enter the site. The car was escorted on either side by guards on motorbikes until it reached the entry point to the corporation's main doors. From there the president was assisted from the car by several Afghani guards and escorted along with his bodyguards to Scitheon's main lobby, where they would remain, as Matthew Serafino and Dr. Asvaka had requested to be left alone to tour the building in privacy.

"Greetings, Mr. President."

Matt Serafino nodded in return.

"My name is Malik Asvaka. I am the head bioinformatics scientist here at Scitheon. I will be happy to escort you today. While we are touring the building, I will give you a brief overview of what we do here and will try to answer any questions you may have."

"Thank you. I look forward to the tour." Matt watched Asvaka out the corner of his eye. He was an unusual-looking man with a broad face, large dark eyes, and sallow skin. His nose was somewhat flattened to his face, and his mouth boasted the largest, whitest teeth Serafino had ever seen. His black taqiyah had shifted slightly to reveal hair that was a dark brownish-gold color, not the usual for an Afghan male. Serafino wondered about his heritage.

"And what is your interest in Scitheon, Mr. President?"

Serafino glanced up quickly, his thoughts interrupted. The two men were walking now through the main part of the building toward the central manufacturing warehouses.

"It seems your company is one of the largest weapons manufacturers in the world, Dr. Asvaka. I'd be very interested in knowing the types of weapons you manufacture here and the types of technology you are using. I understand Afghanistan is becoming one of the world's leaders now in advanced bioinformatics. What do you intend to do with this technology?"

"Well now, Mr. President, you know I can only answer that question in part." Asvaka's teeth seemed to gleam in the light, his deep bass voice resonating through the warehouse of the manufacturing plant. "We make your standard weapons, but we also work to create infiltrative weaponry, as I know you are aware. Components derived from a combination of nanotechnologies and genetics—combinations of biomimetics and molecular biology—are used to build new types of creative weaponry, some of which are open to public view, some of which are still in development. All on the up-and-up, I assure you." Asvaka again smiled his big, toothy grin.

"Will you be looking to sell those weapons, sir?" Serafino stopped walking and stared at Asvaka.

Malik Asvaka stared back, his jaw now set. His dark eyes seemed to glint with interest. "Mr. President, I'm sure we could have much to discuss if you are really interested in buying."

"I'm interested." Serafino continued to hold Asvaka's gaze.

"Come, then." Asvaka motioned to Serafino to follow as he moved down an adjacent hallway toward a rear office. Looking around to make sure no one was following them, he ushered Serafino into the room and shut the door.

"Well then, Mr. President, what do you have in mind?"

WASHINGTON, D.C.

The White House

Ted Calahan, the president's chief of staff, gestured vehemently and sat back in his chair. The president's advisory team sat in the meeting room along with his contextualist, Brian Garvey, and his executive assistant, Mullica Michaels. One of the president's advisers spoke up next.

"With all due respect, sir, how can Matt Serafino leave the country and expect us to deal with this mess! The country has no working systems! Our financials have crashed, our mainframe is still not back up and running, and it looks like the president has flown the coop! People are angry! What are we supposed to tell them?"

Brian Garvey agreed. "Ted, I don't know how to cover him on this one."

Ted looked tired as he sought to keep order among the staff. The circles under his eyes had grown so heavy in the last few days that they formed flaps over his cheekbones. The US technology team had still not restabilized the computer mainframe, and the country was panicking. He knew Matt Serafino had a plan, but he had told Ted to keep quiet until he returned. Easier said than done. If Matt didn't do something soon, the local governments would start taking matters into their own hands. Many of them already had. The potential for a revolution was red-hot. Without serious intervention, in a matter of months or less, the whole country could dissolve into a civil war. And yet, the day before, Serafino had looked at him calmly and told him he had it in hand. Whatever he was up to, he was doing it on his own, and that made Ted nervous. But Ted had been Matt's right hand for years. And he wouldn't desert him now. He sat up in his chair and prepared to give his "loyalty" speech to the president's inner circle.

GREENBELT, MARYLAND

Doron Anderson's Condominium

Doron Anderson entered her condo in the historic district of Greenbelt and dropped down onto one of the green and burgundy upholstered chairs in her sitting room. She was exhausted. She was due at the White House in the morning to go over particulars with Mullica for the president's planned meeting with the press upon his return. She had gotten into the habit of doing him these favors, and now he pretty much expected it of her. Despite his criticism by the press, just before he had left, Matt had asked her to invite all press and interested others to a White House lawn afternoon tea in order to address the state of affairs and his proposed solutions. She never questioned Matt. But she hoped he knew what he was in for. Then again, he never failed to surprise her.

Doron removed her shoes and massaged her tired legs. She startled. The package Matt had asked her to pick up for him at the post office still lay on her dining room table. He said it was important that she deliver it to his private apartment right away. *Where had he wanted me to put it?* Doron struggled to remember. *Ah, on the hall table.* She got up, grabbed the package from the dining room table, hastily put on her shoes, and headed for the car.

Matt had kept the apartment in Falls Church as a private escape residence. Doron was the only other person as far as she knew who had a key. After what seemed like a long time in Washington, D.C., traffic, she finally entered the apartment and headed for the hall table to deposit the package, kicking off her shoes as she went.

As she padded down the hardwood floor, her left toe caught on a nail. She flinched. Where had that come from? She bent down to examine the errant piece of metal that had skewered her foot. It seemed to have been recently placed into the floorboards. She wondered if Matt knew about it. One of them could be seriously injured if the nail entered the foot. Doron went into the kitchen and retrieved a hammer. Prying the nail from the board, it lifted slightly. She wiggled the plank to reposition and secure it, and in less than a moment, the board dislodged from the floor, revealing the corner of a small, white envelope that had been stuffed into the flooring. How had that gotten there? Doron looked around her, as though expecting an intruder to step out of one of the rooms. She lifted the board and retrieved the envelope. Walking back to the living room, Doron stared at the sealed envelope. *Should I open it? Who could have placed it there?* Could it be something Matt should know about? She hesitated only a moment, her curiosity finally getting the best of her, and gingerly, she opened the sealed envelope.

Photographs. She gasped as she flipped through the set of pictures. They were shocking to say the least, and Doron had to look away several times, as she realized what she was viewing. It was some kind of sacrificial rite. A large slab lay in the midst of an octagonal room, lit with multiple candles. The floor appeared to be earthen. And a large, ornate book lay on a nearby table stand. A woman, who appeared to be in her early twenties, lay upward and naked on the sacrificial stone, her wrists and ankles bound to the four edges with metal rings. Below the table, two large, elaborately decorated urns were set up underneath the wrist bands. Doron peered closer. It appeared that blood from the woman's wrists, which appeared to be slashed, dripped from the table into the twin urns. Doron looked away again before proceeding to the next photograph. Then she recoiled in horror. A man was engaged in some kind of rite with the paling woman, who appeared to be drugged. She looked closer. *It couldn't be!* But there was no mistake. It was Matt. And he was engaging in what appeared to be a sacrificial ritual. Had he killed her? What else could she think? Where was he? Doron had never seen this room. She couldn't imagine where he had done this horrid thing.

The urns.

Doron got up and walked cautiously through the apartment. Being careful not to leave anything out of place, she searched for the urns in the picture. Finally deducing that he would never leave them out in the open, especially if they were filled with blood, she sat back down, her head in her hands. What should she do? At that moment, her Pearl began to vibrate. It was Matt.

"Doron, good afternoon! I wanted to make sure you were able to pick up the package for me that I had asked you to deliver to my apartment?"

Doron collected herself.

"I did. I just dropped it off."

"Great. Great. OK. Well, I'll see you tomorrow at the press conference, then."

"Yes." Doron hesitated. "Matt?"

"What is it, Doron?"

She glanced down at the pictures. "Nothing. I'll see you tomorrow."

Doron took one more look at the pictures on her lap. Why would Matt have these printed? She looked closely into the crevice under the floorboard. She saw no sign of a digidrive. She wondered where he had the original file. Hastily, she had put the envelope back into the hideaway and replaced the board, trying to reposition the nail the way he had left it. Then she left the apartment, locking the door behind her, and headed back to the city.

11

THE KEY AND THE DOVE

MOSCOW, RUSSIA

Central Clinical Hospital

The night was dark, and the moon glowed faintly between shadowy tree branches and creeping vines. She emerged from the woods and continued running through a dark field, brambles and small branches slicing into her ankles. Faster and faster she ran, looking back only briefly to see if he was following her. She couldn't see him, but she knew he was there, following her, gaining ground, almost at her heels. She stumbled over a tree stump and kept running, sweat pouring down the sides of her face. She could see the outer edge of the woods. Only a few feet, and she would make it. She heard the shot echo behind her. Something hit her hard in the back, the impact pitching her forward and knocking the breath out of her. Her body exploded in pain, and her head reeled. Just as she reached the edge of the woods, she felt herself falling . . .

Oksanna woke with a start. The wind blew softly through the half-open window of her room. She put her hands over her face and tried to shake off the nightmare. The hospital was quiet. Oksanna could see a small sliver of light from the hallway streaming through the gap at the bottom of the door, creating shadows on the far walls. She was aware now that her shoulder was throbbing again. Sweat had beaded on her forehead, and her entire arm felt as though it were immersed in a vise. Had she missed taking her medication? Oksanna glanced to the nightstand and saw that the nurse had left two white pills for her in a small plastic cup, along with a glass of fresh water. Perhaps she hadn't wanted to wake her. *Odd.* Then again, Oksanna was too tired to think about what was odd. She shook the pills from the cup and thrust them into her mouth. Taking a sip of water from the glass on her nightstand, she wiped the sweat off her face with the corner of the sheet and fell back into an exhausted sleep.

The monitor's high-pitched sound was joined by the rushing of feet, sounds of voices, and moving of equipment. The doctor applied the defibrillator paddles and yelled, "Clear!"

In a moment, the monitor began to slow to a steady, rhythmic beeping, and the technicians began pumping liquids through the intravenous line and through Oksanna's stomach tube to clear out any residue.

"What happened here?" The doctor was looking at the chart now.

"Doctor, the lab results just came back. They indicate poisoning from secobarbital."

"Secobarbital! How much?" The doctor flipped through the charts, looking for a record of prescriptions.

"Enough to put down an ox!" He looked up again from the chart.

"I didn't prescribe secobarbital. No one did. Who gave her the pills?" He looked angrily at the nurses and lab staff. No one spoke, just looked at one another and shook their heads.

"Was the room guarded?"

"The police were here the first evening. But they left after speaking with her two days ago."

The doctor looked alarmed.

"We can't have this kind of thing happening in our hospital. Keep this quiet. Call the police. I want this room guarded every second of every day. We almost lost this patient."

"Yes, sir." The nursing staff hurried from the room.

Oksanna lay breathing steadily, her face pasty white. The movement of her eyes underneath closed lids seemed to indicate she was dreaming.

CHENNAI, INDIA
The Marceli Household

"Mama, do I have to go on this school trip?"

Casimir Marceli slumped down defiantly on the couch, his golden curls pressed into the black leather. His huge brown eyes implored his mother.

"You know I hate history, Mama! Think about what I could be doing instead. I want to be working on my science projects. That's what I'm going to do all my life. What do I need history class for?!"

Ester Marceli poked her head into the room from the kitchen, wiping her hands on a towel. She smiled, shaking her head.

"Casimir, you are going to have a wonderful time. France is a beautiful country. It's only a few days. You're going to see some of the best museums in the world, some of the most famous artworks of all time. Not everything in life is about science and technology, *moja droga.*"

"Mama, you just say that because you love history."

Ester came into the room and sat by Casimir. "Look at me, *moja kochana.*"

Casimir obediently turned his head and looked at his mother's face. She held the boy's face in her hands and kissed the top of his head. Then she looked him in the eyes and smiled. "Some day, Casimir, you will see that not all knowledge comes from the Cloud. Sometimes the best knowledge is what you find in places you least expect it. Just remember the beautiful box you found in Greece! A work of art and a valuable historic piece! Go on, now. Your bus is here."

"But I found it—with my technology!" Casimir laughed as he charged out the door to meet the tour bus. "Bye-bye, Mama. I'll see you soon."

Marseille, Provence-Alpes-Côte d'Azur, France

St. Seraphim Orthodox Cathedral

The cathedral reverberated with the sound of the priest's powerful voice. "As man ultimately strives for perfection, for unity with God, he seeks and ultimately desires that which transcends time and space—those qualities that characterize perfect unity with God: truth, beauty, goodness, and love. And these are all in relationship within the unity of God. Where there is truth, there is also beauty, love, and goodness. Where there is goodness, there is also truth, beauty, and love. Just as the Holy Trinity of God, Christ, and the Holy Spirit is bound together in a unity of love, so also are the attributes of truth, beauty, and goodness bound together by the unity of love."

Arnaud Chevalier stepped down from the pulpit and strode to the center of the cathedral to prepare for the eucharistic ritual. The pews were almost empty today. Most people would show up for service only on a holiday, for a birth, or for a death. The few who came more regularly looked at him sometimes with such blank stares that he couldn't imagine they were listening to him at all. No doubt daydreaming about what they would cook for Sunday brunch or how the weather would turn out that afternoon. Did anyone really care anymore? Did anyone trust in a God they couldn't perceive to act within the realm of their daily lives? Did anyone believe in the divinity of a man who lived now almost three thousand years ago and hadn't been seen since? Did anyone pray? Really pray? Believe in anything? Did they? More important, did he?

Prayer was what had originally brought Arnaud to the priesthood. Or was it? Actually, it was Giselle. Giselle, who was now dead. Giselle, who had been the joy of his life. Giselle, whose death nearly devastated his own life, until the priesthood had saved him—given him something to believe in again. She had been so beautiful. Young. Both musicians, they had played together, composed together, created together. And together they had reached a level of ecstasy most people could never imagine. She had been the most beautiful creature he had ever seen, had ever known. That was before the accident.

Arnaud looked up, realizing the organ had stopped and was waiting for him to begin the Eucharist. He reached down and picked up the chalice.

LONDON, ENGLAND
Hotel Montague

Back in the Skylight Room, Paul watched as the full moon appeared from behind a wisp of clouds. Even through the branches of the trees outside the hotel, Paul could see that the moon was large and bright tonight, lighting up the sky so well that the darkest of night looked like a luminous dawn. Paul sat holding the box containing the cross key on his lap. No one was in the Skylight Room at this hour of the night. The hotel had quieted down for the evening. Paul could see the marble floors of the lobby shining in the moonlight through the far windows of the glass room. The only sound was a muffled voice from the screen across the room. Monika Edwards was still reporting the nightly news.

Paul knew he needed to deal with what had come to light that day with the Diatessaron manuscript. But his entire mind resisted the implications of what had been happening to him. What was happening to him? Too many coincidences to make sense. That's all he knew. He was a historian. A semiotician. He dealt in facts. Signs. Symbols. But all of this—this was beyond his understanding. And he just couldn't wrap his mind around it. How could he believe that he was somehow—what was the word?—*chosen*, years ago, no less, to somehow unite some sort of horsemen in an ancient Christian prophecy that he didn't even believe in. *Nonsense.* There had to be some reasonable explanation for all this. Perhaps that is what he should be focusing on—who might be responsible for setting up this elaborate ruse in order to entice him into pursuing some kind of trail to find a lost box. *"Find the box of John of Patmos."* That was the question he should be asking. What was so special about this box? Where was it now? Patmos.

". . . *on the island of Patmos.*" Paul looked up, his eyes widening in surprise. The reporter was talking with the director of the Museum of the Monastery of St. John the Divine in Patmos, Greece. The director was holding up a gold box with a cross on the front of it. Cut into the front of the box was a large, rather elaborate keyhole.

"So, Dr. Kontos, you say the box was found by a young boy?"

"Yes. We had no idea the relic was there. It had apparently been hidden away in a carved-out cavity within the cave wall since the time of John of Patmos. The boy and his family were visiting the Cave of St. Anne, and he had been using some sort of metal-locating device. Before you know it, he had discovered the location of the box and had found a way to move back the cache in the rock where it had been secreted. Quite an industrious and intelligent young man."

The news anchor was now speaking to the television camera again: "We tried to contact the boy, whose name is Casimir Marceli of Chennai, India, to interview him on the show today, but his family declined the appearance. They said they didn't want the boy thrust into the public eye. We do know, however, that apparently young Casimir is quite a prodigy in the biomechanical information sciences and at the age of twelve already attends the Institute for Technology, Science, and the Arts near his home in India."

"We are grateful," Dr. Kontos spoke up, "for the expertise of young Casimir Marceli in finding this very valuable artifact for us."

"Where is the box being kept now, Dr. Kontos?" Monika had turned back to the director now to conclude the interview.

"For now, the box will remain housed within the museum at the Cave of St. Anne. It is there for anyone to see; however, for security reasons, the artifact is being kept in a locked glass case. I'm sure you can understand why."

"And have you investigated the contents of the box, Director?"

"We have not. At this time, no key that opens the box has been located in or around the area where the box was found, and we are not yet ready to have a team come in who can further investigate the box and perhaps open it by other means. For now, it will remain locked, and its contents, if any, will remain a secret."

"We thank you, Dr. Kontos, for appearing on News Abroad Network. This is Monika Edwards reporting. Good night."

Paul was still staring at the news screen. Slowly, he lifted the lid on the box resting on his lap and took out the cross key. Immediately, it seemed to catch the rays of moonlight, sending muted colored patterns of light into the area. The colors reflected softly off the glass in the Skylight Room and began whirling about the space, as though in a rotating prism. Paul accessed his Pearl and called Angela. She answered on the first ring. Paul didn't even give her a chance to speak.

"Angela, we need to go to Patmos. Can you be ready tonight?"

Angela paused on the other end of the line. The last time she had seen Paul, he had left her sitting in Calaghan's Restaurant. Now he was asking her to go to Greece? She knew Paul was going through a difficult time. The Diatessaron prophecy had spooked him, and Angela was sure he hadn't meant his hasty exit personally. But still, he hadn't apologized. She hesitated again.

"Angela?" Paul sounded hopeful.

Angela sighed and relented. "I can be ready in an hour."

KABUL, AFGHANISTAN
Hotel Kabul

Matt Serafino sat watching the European nightly news from his hotel room in Afghanistan. His dark pupils narrowed as he watched the director of the monastery hold up the box of John of Patmos. The prophecy. What if the secret was in that box? John of Patmos was the author of the Revelation. A find like this could be just what he was looking for. Perhaps it held some clue as to how to locate the four horsemen. He knew the horsemen in John's text, like himself, had to be somewhere within his reach. But he also suspected there could be others. Others who might have a different idea about how the new earth should be. He needed to make sure he would be the one to locate the others. And to figure out the way—the location of the gateway—into the new earth. He would use the rituals and his intuition. Surely, he was destined to figure it all out. It was just a matter of looking around him. He had thought the Codex Gigas, the Devil's Bible, might have held a clue to the location of the gateway or the identity of the four. But the Devil's Bible hadn't answered his questions. Not at all. It had given him only the most rudimentary information. He needed to know more. He needed to gain all the power he knew belonged to him before the country disintegrated beneath his fingertips. With everything in place as it should be, he would be the most powerful man in the world, would control the entire world's resources. And every country would have to serve the New Order. It was his destiny. He needed to have that box.

Matt picked up the phone and dialed. Time to put Doron to use. She was turning out to be very useful. Matt smiled. He had no interest in her personally, although he would let her think so. But he did have her under his charm—under his control—and that's exactly where he wanted her.

ISLAND OF PATMOS, GREECE

Monastery Museum of the Cave of St. Anne

Paul and Angela arrived in the early hours of the morning at the airport in Leros and took the first ferry to the island of Patmos. Paul had made a research appointment with Dr. Anthony Kontos, the director of the Monastery Museum, and now he and Angela were sitting side by side, waiting to examine the box that had been found in the Cave of St. Anne.

As the director brought the box to them, Paul reached into his coat pocket and extracted the container holding the cross key. He held the key up next to the box. The cross symbol was a duplicate of the one on the box, both made of the same silver-like beryllium. Paul held up the key to the director.

"May I?"

Anthony Kontos looked at Paul and then at the box. "Where did you get this?"

"It's a long story. But I assure you, it's legally in my possession."

The director nodded and waved his hand toward the box, welcoming Paul to try the lock.

"Be gentle," he cautioned.

Paul turned to the box, lifted the cross key, and inserted the ancient artifact into the gold box. It slid in with no difficulty. Paul slowly turned the key to the right. They heard a small click as the key triggered the lock. Paul looked at the others and then proceeded to lift the lid of the box.

Inside was a set of diagrams, notes, and a book of Psalms.

Some of the ancient diagrams appeared to be scientific, some philosophical, others geographical, and some related to pictures and descriptions of the four horsemen of the Apocalypse, each bearing various symbols related to their identities. Paul lifted out one of the diagrams. It appeared to be an ancient depiction of the four earthly elements: fire, water, earth, and air. It was surrounded by what looked to be some kind of cosmological signs, along with other text and symbols.

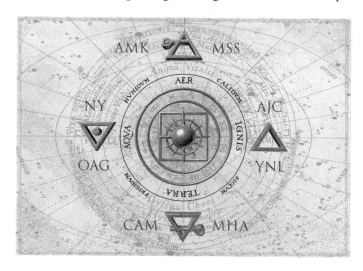

He would need more time to examine the documents.

"Sir, would you allow me to copy these?"

Kontos nodded, still amazed that Paul was able to unlock the box. Slowly, pursing his lips together in thought, he said, "Perhaps we could arrange for a brief study grant for the box and its contents, being that you obviously have a vested interest in the box and the key to its entry. Perhaps a month's loan for study to the Centre for Manuscript and Print Studies would be sufficient? I would be happy to take care of the paperwork and have the box and its contents legally and officially transported to you within a few days."

Paul smiled and nodded his approval. As he was replacing the documents inside the box, he noticed a pair of numbers etched into the wood on the inside of the box: 21, 21. He mentally stored them away, closed the lid of the box, and returned the key to his pocket.

After Paul and Angela left the Orthodox monastery, they sat down on one of the benches outside the grounds. The monastery was built on a hill and looked down over the island and the sea. The day was clear, and the sky bright white.

"You know, Angela, I need to apologize for leaving you at the restaurant."

"Don't worry about it, Paul." Angela laughed. "I'm just glad you're up to investigating the manuscript's prophetic notes. Your training in semiotics makes you invaluable. The worst that can happen is that you will have made a discovery of ancient Christian literature, right?" Angela smiled.

Paul smiled back. "Yeah, right."

"But, since you owe me, how about joining me for dinner? I know a wonderful little restaurant here on Patmos. What do you say?"

"Sounds good to me."

Angela got up and extended a hand to Paul, who took it and followed her down the path to the island.

12

SULFUR AND ICE

Agrimar Bioenergia

"*E aí*, Eduardo! How's it going?"

"Gabriel! I'm great. How's your wife?"

"Ah, she's great. And how's your family?"

"Fine, fine. Listen, I thought I smelled sulfur awhile ago down the back hallway. The smell usually doesn't get in there from the refinery, does it?"

"I don't know. I don't remember smelling anything before. Think we ought to check?"

"This your only break of the day?"

"Whadya think?" Gabriel laughed sarcastically, rolling his eyes.

Eduardo smiled, sat back, and drank his second cup of coffee.

In the refinery, unnoticed, sulfur trioxide was pouring through a punctured pipeline, forming a white mist that began to fill the room and to seep out through the cracks in the windows and doorways. And in the cellulose manufacturing plant, just outside the fermenting bins, a section of tubing had been cut away, allowing ethanol gas to begin to evaporate into the enclosed boiler room.

After his extended coffee break, Eduardo walked down the hallway to the back entrance of the refinery. As he approached the doorway, he saw a white mist seeping through the bottom of the doorway and into the hall area, forming a cloud of fumes in the air that had already filled half the corridor.

"What the—"

Before he could finish his sentence, Eduardo's hands flew to his eyes, and he began to back away in the direction of the office area. His eyelids were burning. As he went to rub them, he began to have the same burning sensation in his throat. His stomach cramped in alarm as he ran for the exit. Breathing in the fumes, his breath shortened, and he doubled over, clutching his chest as the sulfuric acid began to eat away at his organs from the inside out.

In the sealed boiler room, the air grew thick and heavy as ethanol continued to evaporate into the enclosed space.

The spark was minimal, but the ethanol in the boiler chamber had evaporated steadily. In only seconds, the explosion blew through the agrofuel manufacturing plant, sending smoke and flames into the darkness of the Brazilian night, taking every life for miles around with it.

MEXICO CITY, MEXICO

Bio-Conference

"Agrofuels are the 'new oil.' Soon, Mexico will join our Brazilian neighbors in supporting the largest agrofuels production in the southern hemisphere."

The audience applauded. The advent of agrofuels production—already going strong at the turn of the twenty-first century—had spurred a great divide between those in favor, primarily those making megabucks off the industry; and those against, who supported environmental issues and who lived in countries stripped of natural resources and food supplies. Similar to America's reactions to Serafino's New America initiatives, the world's countries as a whole seemed to be separating into greater and greater divisions between the haves and the have-nots, with the powerful preying on the weak, an elaborately advanced example of survival of the fittest.

The yearly Bio-Conference was a forum for both sides to debate issues of industry and environmentalism. Little had been done in pursuing wind and ocean power. The real power was in money, and everyone knew it. The agrofuels industry had been masquerading as an environmental solution for years. But now the dissenting voices were beginning to grow louder, and once again the Middle East was in a place to reassert its power and position in world energy production. Malik Asvaka had oil. And he was willing to share it—for a price.

Malik stood and walked regally to the podium, his stride sleek and sure.

"Ladies and gentlemen. Greetings from the Republic of Afghanistan, one of the world's greatest suppliers of natural oil resources, and from the Scitheon Corporation, the largest nanotechnical and biogenetics manufacturer in the world. I am here with you today on behalf of my country not only as a supplier of top-quality, energy-efficient petroleum, but as an environmentalist and a member of the World Environmentalists Group, opposing the use of agriculture as commodity. As most of you must know, the energy efficiency of processing cellulosic ethanol is only approximately 27 percent. The current production of agrofuels, especially second-generation agrofuels, combined with genetic engineering and plant modifications, has had an enormous negative impact on the planet's ecosystems, accelerating biodiversity loss, reducing carbons, stripping and burning forests, increasing global warming, and causing extensive droughts and nutrient deficiency within the world's food supplies.

"Furthermore, our planet does not have the resources to provide enough food for its people. Yet companies such as Agrimar Bioenergia, Brazil's largest predatory agrofuels manufacturing plant, are using up supplies of sugarcane and maize grown by some of the poorest countries of the world, exploiting not only nature but human nature, in the interest of capitalism. There is a good reason why the Republic of

Brazil calls herself the 'green Saudi Arabia of the South.' While the people of our world are being deprived of adequate and healthy food and water supplies, Brazil continues to exploit uses of government and foreign funding to perpetuate this rapacious use of our world's resources, taking valuable time and funds away from exploring more-equitable means of power. In the meantime, I would like to point out that Afghanistan continues to provide safe, clean, and energy-efficient means for the production of energy through its country's rich and ample oil resources. I want to remind you that in comparison to agrofuels production, petroleum refineries are 88 percent energy efficient and do not have a comparable negative impact on our world's ecosystems. I beg you, therefore, to consider your relationships.

"Will you continue to pour funding and resources into the Republic of Brazil and other countries, such as Mexico and India, who threaten to strengthen the economic power and monopoly of the MK BRIC countries? Or will you turn to those countries now in the Middle East who are successfully creating alternative, clean energy by means of more efficient and creative production of petroleum resources? I invite you to take another look at Afghanistan's energy-efficient refineries and to ask yourself if it isn't time to reevaluate the effects of your so-called alternative energy sources, which have replaced natural oil to the desecration of our planet. What has been propositioned to you by your countries are not more efficient ways of preserving our planet through alternative energies. What has been propositioned to you has been a propaganda of capitalism. The only resource you are providing more efficiently to countries using these systems is 'economic power'—not to your countries' peoples, but to your capitalist governments and big businesses, such as Agrimar Bioenergia. Thank you."

A section of the auditorium stood and applauded as Malik Asvaka exited the stage, though others murmured in disapproval. The next speeches would be by the Bio-Defense Alliance of USAmerica (BDA) and the Russian-based International Environmental Organization (IEO).

MOSCOW, RUSSIA

Central Clinical Hospital

"Due to possible global warming conditions, a large ice shelf in the East Siberian Sea broke loose suddenly and unexpectedly earlier today at approximately 4:00 p.m., sending tidal wave–like waters and chunks of ice rushing toward the shores of northeastern Siberia. So far, reports of deaths and injuries are inconclusive. We do know, however, and regret to report, that the World Greenhouse Bio-Farming Project, led by global environmentalist Oksanna Galina, has been washed away in the floodwaters that are devastating Siberia at this time. The World Greenhouse has been the pride of Russia's humanitarian efforts to support the obliteration of world poverty through the cultivation of old bio methods of natural and sustainable agriculture. This is Juliette Martinez, reporting for World News Europe."

In her hospital bed, Oksanna sat stunned, her hand flying to her mouth in numb surprise. To her mind, already paralyzed by the events of the past month, this was the final blow. She slid slowly onto her back, staring at the network of cracks in the ceiling of her room. Then, she turned her head to the side and disengaged her mind to enter the euphoric world of painkillers.

BEIJING, CHINA

Pasture (Scientific Test Site) outside of Beijing

The testing site for the serum that would genetically alter any food supply that it came in contact with was set. The cattle were brought in, and Niú Ye lifted the covers off the troughs holding the food mixture. The prior testing had been done with serum. But this test would determine whether the genetically altered foodstuffs would cause the same reaction as the direct injections. The results should be visible within twelve hours. In the meantime, Niú had other problems. He knew it was only a matter of time before Serafino would confront him about the false formula. But he couldn't let Serafino get hold of this power. This serum was a covert weapon that could put China in control of the entire world's politics. Whoever controlled the food supplies controlled the people and their governments. China had already risen far above the rest of the world in technology and genetics. Only the Middle East had been slowly and stealthily advancing, much ignored by the rest of the world. But Niú paid attention. Nothing got past him. And he knew the demand for food imports in the Middle East was increasing steadily. Soon healthy, untainted food would be a rare commodity, and China would be ready to provide whatever was needed—for a price.

Niú walked from the pasture site back to his waiting car. The driver waved from the window as Niú slid into the backseat.

"Back to the lab." Niú settled into the leather and began to scan his Pearl for messages.

After a period of time, Niú looked up. The car was speeding down an unfamiliar road in the midst of hilly and barren terrain. Confused and somewhat alarmed, Niú sat up and called to the driver. The driver didn't answer. Niú began to bang on the glass, but the driver ignored him. He tried the doors, but they had been secured and wouldn't open. Niú wasn't in favor of throwing himself from a speeding car; so he nervously sat back and waited, chewing on the end of his fingernail and trying to work out alternate escape scenarios in his head. In a few more minutes, the car finally came to a stop. Niú looked out of the window and could see dust flying everywhere as a black helicopter, with no markings that Niú could ascertain, sat waiting.

The driver approached his door and opened it. Immediately, Niú was surrounded by ten or twelve armed men, all in black clothing. Without a word, they handcuffed Niú's hands behind him and pushed him to the entrance of the helicopter. He was led inside and seated. And within minutes the helicopter took off, hovering only moments over the ground before skimming off over the hills to the US Air Force base in Mongolia.

As Niú entered the US Osprey Copter, Serafino stood, smiling at him from the cabin.

"Come, Niú. Time for us to have a talk."

Niú Ye grimaced and clenched his teeth, his jaw set.

"Not feeling conversational at the moment, eh, Niú?" Serafino chuckled, his low and powerful voice resonating from his chest. "Ah, but you'll be staying with us for quite some time. Don't worry. No one knows you're gone yet. And when they do, they'll find no trace of you. How long you have to get used to your new lodgings will depend upon your willingness to cooperate. It seems you are at a loss for words at the moment, Niú. I'll give you some time to adapt to your new situation. And I'll see you at dinner. Perhaps you'll feel more amenable to talking then. The food on the plane is quite good. I think you'll like it."

With that, Serafino motioned to three of the men, and they escorted Niú Ye to a room near the back of the plane. The room was bare except for a low cot, where Niú sat, quaking with rage, staring at the blank white walls of the plane.

Meanwhile, in a pasture in China, cows dropped like flies into troughs and mud.

MARSEILLE, PROVENCE-ALPES-CÔTE D'AZUR, FRANCE

Someone screamed as the bus hit the growing crevice in the road and tipped to one side, sliding backward off the lurching asphalt and down the incline, coming to rest at the bottom of the ravine. The frame of the tour bus was still shaking as students and teachers grasped hold of seats and one another, plastering themselves against the floor and sides of the toppled vehicle. Above them, they could see rocks and debris sliding down the hill around them. Someone was praying loudly. Others squeezed their eyes shut. Still others desperately fumbled with their Pearls and earpieces. No signal was available. Casimir Marceli was aware that someone was grasping his arm so hard that it was beginning to grow numb. He turned to see the young girl who had sat behind him, her eyes wide and wild, her fingers white as they clutched his skin. He pulled her toward him, removing her hand from his arm, and gripped it in his left hand, allowing the circulation to return to his upper forearm.

Within a few minutes, the quake had stopped. Initially, no one wanted to move, afraid that the rumbling and shaking would start again. When it seemed that wouldn't happen, frightened heads began to peer up over the seats, and the teachers began to dislodge themselves, stepping gingerly through the bus to check on each student. Eventually, they would all reach the doors of the bus, half stepping, half tumbling onto the grassy ground of the ravine. For what seemed like hours, those who were uninjured attempted to help others who had broken limbs or received lacerations. When all were accounted for, two of the students were chosen to accompany one of the teachers in scaling the ravine to check out the situation above and to retrieve help. Having no injuries, save a few bruises here and there, Casimir volunteered to accompany the other two. The teacher was an Indian man just a bit taller than Casimir, with strong arms and legs and a shock of dark, wavy hair. The other student, Banaj, was much taller than both Casimir and the teacher, with lanky arms and legs. He was adept at climbing and had won several rock-climbing competitions back in India. Now would be his time to test his skills in real life. Though not tall himself, Casimir was, despite his thin frame, unduly strong, with muscular arms and legs and a firm chest. His dark golden locks splayed across his shoulders as he began climbing the jagged edges of the ridged ravine wall.

As the three approached the top, they could see that what had been the road was now a jumble of rock and broken pavement, jutting up in uneven ledges. For as far as they could see, the entire landscape looked like a pile of dirt and debris where only an hour before, the French countryside had stretched out green and lush for miles. The three sat down on the edge of the upper meadow and tried again to connect to their Pearls. Still no response. *How wide had the quake been?* They looked at one another silently and then began to climb over rocks and dirt, following the road into town.

CAIRO, EGYPT

National Research Institute of Astronomy and Astrophysics (NRIAA)

It was almost midnight, and Hassan Masih had been working on computations for the Moonbeamer Project all day. He set down his technotablet and leaned back in the lab chair. Hassan hadn't seen Lachier in the lab since the prior morning, and he wondered what his boss could be doing. Youhanna Lachier never told him much about his activities. In fact, Hassan had felt frequently embarrassed when approached or called on by those wanting to speak with Lachier. Hassan always sounded vague and confused, never able to relay to anyone his boss's whereabouts. But that was the way Lachier wanted it, and Hassan never asked him any unwanted questions. Today, however, Hassan wished Lachier would return. He had come across some computer files in the system that looked as though they corresponded to some kind of code. They seemed to have been separated from another document and had randomly appeared in Hassan's inbox that morning. Hassan wanted to ask Lachier about the files. He wasn't sure if they belonged to the lab or if someone had infiltrated their information systems. Hassan was concerned, but Lachier hadn't answered his Pearl all day. As Hassan was packing up to leave for the night, one of the night guards poked his head into the lab. He looked distressed.

"Hassan. Hey—there's been an explosion in the desert outside of Egypt. Have you heard?"

"An explosion?"

"The military has been called out there to find out what's happened."

Hassan continued to gather up his things, wondering at the news. "I'm going home now, Rasui. I'll check it out on the news." He looked up at the guard. "Have a good night." He waved to Rasui as he packed the last of his equipment into his lab bag.

Just as Hassan prepared to leave, a bright light seemed to come out of nowhere, blinding him and throwing him to the floor of the lab.

LONDON, ENGLAND
Centre for Manuscript and Print Studies

Somewhere in the adjoining apartment for the Centre for Manuscript and Print Studies, a teapot began to shrill and boil over, as Emory Makefield lay slumped in his chair, a bullet shot cleanly through the back of his head.

Part II

LEUKOSIS

*Truth, like gold, is to be attained not by its growth, but by
washing away from it all that is not gold.*

—LEO TOLSTOY

The purpose of art is washing the dust of daily life off our souls.

—PABLO PICASSO

All will come out in the washing.

—MIGUEL DE CERVANTES SAAVEDRA

If there is magic on this planet, it is contained in water.

—LORAN EISELEY

Water, not unlike religion and ideology, has the power to move millions of people.

—Mikhail Gorbachev, 2000

Only those people that have directly experienced the wetlands that line the shore . . . can appreciate their mystic qualities. The beauty of rising mists at dusk, the ebb and flow of the tides, the merging of fresh and salt waters.

—Governor's Task Force on Marine and Coastal Affairs, "Delaware Wetlands," 1972

Water, water, see the water flow
Glancing, dancing, see the water flow
O wizard of changes, water, water, water

—The Incredible String Band

13

STIRRING THE SOUP

The White House

"I can't believe it wasn't there."

Doron gazed at Matt, trying to hide her thoughts. She wasn't ready to confront him about the photographs, nor was she sure she should. He had surely killed the young woman. *Where did he hide her body? Where is the blood from the urns? Or the urns themselves?* Doron jolted. She had to focus, or he would know something was bothering her. She looked over at Matt. He wasn't paying attention.

She continued. "I'm sorry I couldn't get the box for you."

Matt Serafino smiled absentmindedly at Doron, glancing up from his panel screen.

"It's not your fault, Doron. Don't worry about it. I should have had you call first before sending you all the way to Patmos to retrieve the box."

Matt smiled to himself again. He could have gotten the box himself it he wanted it. And would. What he really had wanted was to get Doron out of the way for a while. He needed space to take care of some private matters, and Doron was too close.

"Are you sure you don't want me to call the Centre for Manuscript and Print Studies?" Doron looked as though she desperately wished she could find the box and place it in Matt's hands at that very moment.

"No, I've decided not to pursue it," he lied.

Doron raised her head in surprise. "You don't want it anymore?"

"It's not worth what I thought it was." Matt kept his eyes focused on the screen, glancing only intermittently toward Doron, noting when her eyes seemed to relax and she let the matter of the box go from her mind.

Doron gazed out the window, her mind working. But she wasn't thinking about Matt's box.

Should I tell him? Maybe now would be a good time. What should I say? Should I keep his secret? Will he think I would?

"Matt . . ."

Matt looked up from the panel again. He had already gone on to another topic.

"Doron, is everything ready for the press conference?"

"Yes," Doron burst out perhaps a bit too quickly.

"Well, let's go, then. We'll talk about strategy during lunch."

Doron gathered up her coat, somewhat relieved, positioned her Pearl, and followed Matt dutifully out the door of the Oval Office. Mullica Michaels smiled at her as they left. Doron wasn't sure if it was out of admiration or sympathy.

The crowd of press on the White House lawn was growing angry. The roads surrounding the Capitol Building were filled with people carrying signs and banners. As the president appeared in the doorway, the shouts increased, filling the air with complaints, threats, and obscenities. Matt Serafino's bodyguards moved closer, eyeing the crowd. Poised and positioned, they appeared ready to leap at the slightest movement. The press was spread out on the lawn. To Doron, their equipment looked like some strange sort of mechanical lawn art. They filled the first several hundred feet of space. Elaborate sound system mics stood out from the White House porch, so that the president's voice could be heard by the entire group in front of him. Matt walked up to the edge of the portico to begin the press conference and waited until the sounds of the crowd died down.

"If you know one thing about Matt Serafino, you know this: I'm a promise keeper. And I am here today to make you some promises. I want you to look me in the eye today, so that you will know these promises will be kept. Our great nation is under attack. A terrorist group has sabotaged our mainframe systems. So here's my first promise: We will hunt down who did this, and we will punish them severely. They will wish they'd never attacked the United States of America. Now, for my next promises. Look into my eyes. I promise you that all your financial assets will be honored and protected. Backup systems are already in place, and banks will be up and running by Monday morning. And I promise you that full restitution will be made to anyone who has suffered any kind of financial hardship or loss. Terrorists of the world, now I'm looking at you. We are the United States of America."

The crowd applauded, and Ted Calahan noticed that several had laid down their picket signs and were now listening intently. The president was, if anything, a dynamic speaker, and he seemed to command and calm the entire group of people now. They appeared mesmerized, as though under a fairy-tale spell that would enchant them for the next hundred years. Ted shook his head in disbelief. The president continued.

"Some of you know that the real song I wish could be our National Anthem is not 'The Star-Spangled Banner,' but 'America the Beautiful.' It's a song I can sing. I can make America once again the most beautiful nation in the world. America is beautiful not only because it has spacious skies, but limitless advances in the sciences and technologies and limitless standards of living. America does not have just amber waves of grain but waves of financial success, waves of prosperity, waves of progress, waves of power. America is beautiful, and it will become more and more beautiful. I assure you today that the New United States of America will again lead the nations as the most formidable center of economic and political power and prestige in the world."

The sun had risen high in the afternoon and shone brightly, reflecting off the white bricks of the Capitol Building. The walkways shone as the ingrained bits of quartz gleamed and glittered in the sunlight, which seemed brighter than usual for this time in April. An almost translucent haze seemed to surround the portico. Yet, despite the sun's glare, no one seemed to want to disengage from the president's message. Ted Calahan looked out at the gathering. People all across the White House lawn were standing and applauding now, completely taken up in Matt Serafino's vision.

Smiling, Matt stepped down to take questions from the press.

LONDON, ENGLAND

Centre for Manuscript and Print Studies

The police and forensics team were finishing up in the small apartment at the rear of the Centre for Manuscript and Print Studies. As the stretcher emerged with Emory Makefield's body, the police chatted with two of the lab technicians. It seemed no one had seen anything. The center had been locked up for the night. Nothing appeared to have been taken.

As the police were getting ready to leave the scene, an armored truck drove up to the entrance of the building.

"We have a secured delivery for the Centre for Manuscript and Print Studies, in care of Mr. Paul Binder. It's a delivery from the Museum of the Monastery of St. John the Divine on Patmos in Greece."

One of the center's manuscript technicians stepped forward.

"Mr. Binder has not yet returned from Greece. But I'll sign for the package and make sure it's put into the center's vault to await his arrival."

The grief-weary technician signed for the box and took it through the main foyer and into the back room, where the vault was housed.

The police looked at one another, then back at the technicians. "Who is this Paul Binder?"

"He's an American historian from the University of Virginia

who is here to study a special codex that was donated to the center. He's working with our manuscript specialist, Angela Matthews Krall. They both went to Greece a few days ago to follow up on a lead concerning their research. They should be back anytime, I should think."

One of the policeman nodded. "Do you have contact information for the two of them?"

"Yes, sir. And I'll let them know what happened."

WASHINGTON, D.C.

National Holding Center

Niú gasped for air as he was lowered back into the water for the sixth time. He came up sputtering and coughing, scarcely able to catch his breath again before the table dipped back into the water a last time. When he was finally released from the board, he lay huddled on the floor, wheezing, coughing, and throwing up warm, salty water. His eyes were burning, and he could barely see from the salt. His skin itched all over. One of the guards threw him a coarse towel, and he scrubbed furiously, trying to rid himself of the residue. Shivering on the cold cement, he quickly tried to remove as much water from his body and hair as he could. His lungs were still heaving from the ordeal, and his legs, arms, and neck ached from the strain of the rope and metal bonds. The metal board had left rough contact burns on much of his back and buttocks, and Niú winced as he rubbed the coarse terrycloth material across his back and shoulders. One of the men present threw him a loose garment. When he had pulled it on, they yanked him from the floor and led him back into his cell.

The cell was dark, small, and windowless, the only light coming from a bare bulb down the whitewashed cinder-block corridor. Niú sat on the wooden bench that served as a cot and leaned his head against the rock-hard wall of the cell. *How did this happen? How did Serafino manage to fly me out of the country without anyone knowing?*

Niú realized he wasn't dealing with just any other world leader. There was something different about Serafino. He had known it from the beginning. *Those eyes. I could see it in his eyes.* And now Niú had come to an impasse. He would have to at least try to work with Serafino. Otherwise, he would be killed. He was sure of it. He wasn't entirely sure what Serafino wanted. But Niú was fast becoming compliant.

ISLAND OF PATMOS, GREECE

Thermia Hot Springs

"This island has got to be one of the most beautiful places in the world, and I'm an islophiliac."

Angela lay back into the water, her blond hair lying across her shoulders in golden-white strands. Her skin seemed pearl-like, with just a flush of pale color in the steam of the warm water. If Paul hadn't noticed before how beautiful she was, he did now.

"I'm glad we decided to stay in Hora. The beaches, the restaurants, the landscapes here are all fabulous."

Angela smiled. "Yes, and I'm sure we'll have enough work to last us the rest of the month when we get back to England. Do you think the box has arrived yet?"

"Well, there's only one way to find out."

Paul pushed himself out of the spring and reached for a towel. Then he connected to his Pearl and requested the Centre for Manuscript and Print Studies. The line rang about eight times and then went into voice mail.

"Hmm, no one answers." Paul put the Pearl down and slid back into the water.

"Well, perhaps they're all out to lunch or engrossed in the lab. We can try later."

Angela looked at Paul. He appeared to be more relaxed than she had ever seen him. "Paul, can I ask you something?"

Paul smiled. "Of course."

"Do you believe there are forces in the world or in the universe that are beyond our sensibilities, beyond our control, our understanding?"

Paul laughed. "That's quite a question, Angela."

"I'm thinking of the manuscript, Paul. The Diatessaron. The key. The box. Everything. Do you think there could be something 'out there,' more vast than we can imagine, trying to tell us something, trying to tell you something?"

"Here's what I think: I think someone very clever has been guiding me toward finding out some information that I'm certain must be very valuable to someone. And whoever it is, he or she is going to a great deal of trouble to get me to take a look at this box."

"And that doesn't make you nervous? Thinking someone could be out there who wants to manipulate you into finding something? What if that person is dangerous? Does that really feel more comfortable than believing that something unusual, something perhaps supernatural, could be going on here?"

Paul laughed. "Yes. As a matter of fact, it does feel more comfortable. I'm sorry, Angela, I just can't accept the kinds of superstitions that other people in the past have accepted as truth."

"It's not in the past for everyone, Paul. You know, back in Ireland, we feel we have a knowledge of our land, our people, our stories, a type of intuitive knowledge, and it goes way beyond superstition. When I'm back home in Ireland, I am attuned to it. Can feel it. Just as you can feel the water in this spring, I can feel somehow that there is life in all things, an energy in the air, a feeling that everything is created, connected, and has a purpose."

"I'm glad you feel that, Angela. It sounds like a wonderful experience. But I don't feel that. I've never felt anything like that. My life is built on facts, signs, symbols. Life is life, and history is history. For me, history is only the sediment of leftover life. And the only life is the one I am living right now. If there were some mysterious powers in the world, don't you think the religions of the world would have lasted longer than they did? Not died out to the extent that they have? If there were some wonderful being like the God and the Christ that everyone believed in back in the time of the Diatessaron, don't you think the world would be a better place than it is right now? But I envy your naïveté." Paul smiled.

Angela was staring hard at him now. "Do you believe in love, Paul?"

Paul lifted his hands from the water and brushed back the brown strands of hair from his face. "Of course."

"But you can't see it. You can't touch it. You can only feel it."

"Are you trying to convert me, Angela?" Paul laughed.

"I just think we need to be open to every possibility. If you can believe in love, I don't see why it would be such a stretch to believe that other types of experiences in life could also be felt and not experienced with the senses. Maybe we have a left brain and a right brain for a reason. Perhaps some things must be left wrapped in mystery."

"Perhaps." Paul reached out his hand and helped Angela out of the spring. "But for now, I'll settle for the mystery of what we're going to have for dinner."

As the two gathered up their clothes and belongings, Angela's Pearl pendant began vibrating around her neck. As she answered, her eyebrows seemed to knit together in pain, and her face fell.

"What is it?" Paul was still drying the remaining water from his hair.

Angela looked at Paul. "Paul, Emory is dead."

SIBERIA, RUSSIA

Oksanna sat in the cockpit of the small plane that was now circling the remains of the World Greenhouse in Siberia. The floodwaters covered the entire area, as though the ocean had expanded and swallowed up the land in a single gulp.

She had left the hospital the previous week, still sore but fully recovered from her injuries. The police insisted on assigning her a personal bodyguard to accompany her until more could be learned about the two attacks on her life. But otherwise, she spent most days trying to reassess and make some sense of her future. The Greenhouse Project was gone. To start over now would take years. Oksanna didn't know if she was up to it. And the crops that would have served as seed for the expansion of the project in a companion country were also now all washed away in the flood. Oksanna peered down into the waters. The sun seemed abnormally bright as the light reflected off the bluish-white waters, still filled with chunks of unmelted ice, making it hard to see. Her land had become a sea. The land that had been in her family for generations. The labor of her parents and everything they had created was gone. Her last twelve years of work—all gone.

"Let's go back home." Oksanna motioned to the pilot, and the plane swung back around and headed for Moscow.

14

OIL AND WATER

BEIJING, CHINA

National Center for the Study of Genetics

"Where's Niú Ye?" President Murong Gui looked agitated.

"No one has seen him, sir."

The president stood in the doorway of the ransacked lab of the National Center for the Study of Genetics' Department of Interrelational Sciences. Broken equipment and shattered glass covered the floors. Files and lab notes were strewn everywhere. The main computer had been bypassed and its systems scrambled. Even the safe, where high-security serums and digidrives were kept, had been opened and its contents cleaned out, so that very little remained of the country's leading scientific power base. The defrocking of the lab, all its secrets exposed now, was equivalent to stripping China of its greatest political leverage. Murong Gui looked as white as the paint on the walls as he told the lab technicians to make notes of all the losses and to submit a report to the government's investigative division.

"Keep trying to reach Niú."

"Yes, sir." The head technician bowed and retreated to the back of the lab to survey the remaining contents of the storage room.

KABUL, AFGHANISTAN

Scitheon Corporation

"Did you get the serum?"

"I've got it, Dr. Asvaka."

"Excellent, Asa. Good work. Your payment is in the envelope on the table. Keep this to yourself, eh?"

"Absolutely, Dr. Asvaka. Don't worry, sir."

"I won't, Asa. I won't."

Asa picked up the envelope and hurried from the building's back entrance, retreating to the Scitheon parking lot. He got into a white van and pulled out the exit and onto the main road leading away from Kabul. After a short while, he exited the van down a side road toward one of the small outlying villages. As he approached a barren area, he stopped the van and took out the thick yellow envelope. The envelope was bulging with the weight of the money: five hundred thousand Afghani. Asa smiled and began to open the seal. As he reached his hand into the envelope, pain shot up his right arm.

"Huh . . . what?"

Asa pulled his hand from the envelope to reveal two puncture wounds on the side of his index finger. He peered inside the envelope just in time to see a large, elongated spider the size of his hand with long, thin, black, bulging legs; a white head; and a yellow, saclike body. The spider was rearing up on its hind legs and hissing. Startled, Asa dropped the bag onto the floor of the van. In a moment, the thing had jumped onto his leg. Asa screamed and tried to brush the spider from his body. As he did, it bit him again on the back of the hand. Frantically opening the door, the man lunged from the van and tumbled into the dusty road. The spider seemed to leap from the vehicle, scuttling quickly underneath it and disappearing into the desert brush.

Where was the nearest hospital? Back in Kabul, Asa realized as he clambered back into the van. Throwing the envelope into the backseat, Asa floored the van's gas pedal and turned the wheel sharply to the left. The vehicle made an abrupt about-face, sending clouds of dust into the air. He sped back toward Kabul. *How long do I have?* Asa wasn't sure. He didn't even know what type of spider it was. He had never seen anything like it before in Afghanistan. *Asvaka.* *He had to have done this.* Asa felt his stomach begin to cramp. He began to perspire. With the edge of his shirt, he wiped his face and forehead, which were now beaded with sweat. The cramps began rising into his chest as Asa sped the van forward toward the highway to Kabul. *How long did it take me to get here? An hour? More?* His skin felt feverish, and his mouth began to salivate. Suddenly, his stomach began to wrench. Asa stopped the van, threw open the door, and wretched onto the side of the road. Just as he thought he had recovered, his stomach heaved again, and again, until he was heaving only water and stomach bile. Sweat was pouring from his neck and body now, dripping from his face and nose. His clothes were drenched, and he could tell his fever was rising. The back of his hand was only slightly red and swollen, but Asa knew this was no ordinary spider bite. He forced himself back into the van and stepped on the gas.

He was only a few miles from the hospital. He could make it. He had to. He floored the accelerator, and the engine shot forward with a scream. Just as he rounded the exit ramp to the hospital's main entrance road, his breathing started to become erratic. His heart was palpitating. He thought he would be sick again and leaned to the right, wretching into the passenger seat. Then, as Asa floored the gas pedal one more time, the van darted forward across the intersection and directly into the path of an oncoming truck. The last thing Asa heard as his heart failed was the truck's horn blaring loudly through the afternoon air.

The black car rounded the corner and stopped a short distance away from the crashed vehicle. A lone man got out and walked up to the smoking van. He looked briefly at the man in the driver's seat, assuring that he was dead. Asa's face was rapidly turning a bluish-black, his head smashed against the front wheel. With no expression, the man reached into the backseat and retrieved the yellow envelope. Then he exited the scene, just as the hospital emergency team came running toward the van. The man rounded the rear of the vehicle and walked nonchalantly back toward the black car. He got in, gave one last glance toward the now teeming intersection, and then drove away in the direction of the Scitheon campus.

CAIRO, EGYPT

Capitol Building

"The way to control the Middle East is through water." Youhanna Lachier was presenting his research in a private meeting with the Egyptian president, Menes Mubarak.

"Our imagers have identified all the underground water sources in the entire area throughout Turkey, Syria, Iran, and Iraq—all areas experiencing severe water shortages due to drying marshlands. If we were to severely drain these sources, we would essentially control all these countries, make them totally dependent upon our water resources. They would have to beg us for help. Without us and our resources, they wouldn't survive. And we would then have complete access to the best oil fields in the region. Whoever controls the water has the oil, and whoever controls the oil has the power."

"And how would we go about draining these water sources? And without being traced?" The president looked solemnly at Lachier, waiting for his reply. He knew his top research scientist had been working on strategies for dominating the Middle East. He had given him special privileges and funding to find a way to harness the power and oil of the Middle East for Egypt. He hadn't expected this. But then again, he would never underestimate Lachier. The man was brilliant, and if he had figured out how to use and adapt astrophysics technology to identify the entire quantity of water sources, he had no doubt that the man could come up with a plan to execute the massive drought.

"Strategic underground drainage siphons. A network of them. I've already created the blueprints. And the technology." Lachier waited silently. The Egyptian president nodded his head slowly.

MARSEILLE, PROVENCE-ALPES-CÔTE D'AZUR, FRANCE

Father Arnaud Chevalier stepped from the cathedral and ventured out into the devastated remains of Marseille. Due to its location and the strength of its stone foundation, the cathedral had sustained only mild damage from the quake. But almost everywhere in Marseille, buildings had collapsed in heaps, cars lay on their sides, and chunks of roadways and sidewalks stood up like stalagmites. Clouds of dust hovered over the entire town, and everything blended together under a coat of thick brown haze. Arnaud could hear people screaming everywhere and see others trying to pull friends and family from debris. Rescue teams were at work tirelessly to assist the injured and bring order to the chaotic mass of rubble. He had counseled and consoled family after family who came seeking solace at the cathedral. In times of trouble, suddenly those without faith were willing to rethink anything that might give them a release from their pain, a hope for answers, and a future free from their agonizing grief. And those with faith came more often to the sanctuary, kneeling in prayer and lighting candles for the dead.

Gingerly climbing over heaps of rock, Arnaud looked toward the edge of town. He could see people coming his way, waving their hands. He stepped forward and saw a man with what appeared to be two young boys making their way across the jumble of dirt and stone toward the town's main road.

"Over here." Arnaud waved back, the arms of his red robes flowing outward like the wings of a large, soaring bird. His silver cross gleamed in the sun—which felt unusually hot for this time of year, now that he thought about it.

The boys were laughing and shouting now as they climbed over the last of the rubble and ran to meet Chevalier. The man behind them caught up as quickly as he could.

"We made it, we made it!" Casimir smiled, his blond curls framing his brown face.

"Where have you come from? Are there others?" Arnaud said to the man now coming up behind the boys.

The man extended his hand, and Arnaud took it, nodding gently.

"We're from the Institute of Technology, Science, and the Arts in Chennai, India. We had just arrived here yesterday on a school trip to visit Marseille when the quake threw our tour bus from the road into a ravine."

Arnaud looked alarmed.

"There are no deaths. All the students are safe. Some are injured, though, and we have no food or water. The three of us weren't sure how far we were from town, and the driver is injured as well. Can you help us?"

"How many are you?" Arnaud waved the three into the cathedral doors as he spoke. "Come, come inside. Get some water. Rest a few minutes."

"About forty, I'm afraid."

"It will be all right. We'll get help. I'll call the authorities to help get all of your group out. Not to worry. But right now, rest. Here, come into my office."

Arnaud led the three into his office and motioned to three of the chairs.

Immediately, Seraphim began to sing: *"A mighty fortress is our God, a bulwark never failing . . ."*

The boys looked up in surprise.

Arnaud grinned. "The bird of a former Lutheran pastor."

While the boys began trying to initiate conversation with the energetic cockatiel, Arnaud set about gathering water, tea, and biscuits for the hungry travelers. He then contacted his Pearl and began calling for assistance.

"We'll get your group out as soon as possible. Just relax now. Have some tea."

The man smiled and turned toward the boys, who were still

engrossed in Seraphim, the talking bird. He was now singing another song, this time in French:

> *No voice can sing, no heart can frame,*
> *Nor can the memory find,*
> *A sweeter sound than Jesus' Name,*
> *The Savior of mankind.*

LONDON, ENGLAND

Centre for Manuscript and Print Studies

"I thought you'd want copies of these."

Angela held out two copies of the set of documents that were in the box sent from Patmos. "It's saved on a digidrive, but I know you need to work with the printed versions." She nodded. The two of them understood the need for the paper copies when it came to examining the historical documents. For historians and manuscript specialists, nothing would replace the human eye's ability to analyze the originals, no matter how advanced technology would get.

"And I also got you this." Angela smiled and handed Paul a large brown leather satchel. Inside were pockets and a large leather-bound notebook, similar to the ones used in the early twentieth century.

"Where did you get this?" Paul's eyes lit up as he stroked the oiled leather.

"I found it in one of the shops when we were in Patmos. I wanted to surprise you. I thought, in light of everything that's been happening, you might want to start keeping notes. I couldn't think of a better place to keep all your documents and notes than this."

Paul laughed. "This is incredible. I haven't seen anything like this in years. And you're right. I want to examine these documents firsthand—not as scanned pictures in my Pearl. And I have some other documents as well—the letter I received in Virginia and copies of the Diatessaron prophecies. I've been thinking, anyway, that I may just want to take some handwritten notes. Haven't done that in a long time! I'll have to see if I remember how to write real script." Paul laughed again, delighted with the historical find in the box, and even more delighted that Angela had given him the gift. He lifted out the leather binder. Inside were crisp white sheets of real paper and an antique twentieth-century ballpoint pen with black ink. Paul's eyes flashed appreciation.

"You're wonderful, Angela. Thanks!"

Angela nodded, her face beaming. She was pleased she had at last brought a smile to Paul's face. He had been troubled from the time he had arrived in London. This was the first time she had seen his eyes light up. And something told her he would need this gift. That his journey was just beginning.

Angela replaced the original documents in sealed plastic holders and put them in a container in the vault. She placed the box inside one of the locked glass cases in the library, on display, returning Paul's key once again to his coat pocket, where he kept it with him. Although Paul said he didn't believe in anything beyond factual evidence, Angela noticed that, almost like a talisman, he kept the key securely in his inside coat pocket, close to his heart.

The two were interrupted by the news as Angela activated the screen in the library study.

"Seems we've missed a lot." The frown was back on Paul's face as the two of them surveyed the list of disasters on the nightly news report.

"Earthquakes, floods, explosions—all in the last week?" Paul looked at Angela. She was biting her lower lip, and her eyes looked troubled.

"I know what you're going to say, Angela. It's not possible."

Angela looked at Paul silently, letting him talk.

"Maybe I'd better record current events in my notes as well?" Paul glanced at the leather notebook in his hands, almost expecting it to begin recording at will. He glanced up at Angela.

Angela remained silent, waiting.

"I'm going to go back to the hotel for a bit," Paul said slowly. "I want to catch up on recording some events that have happened so far. See you tomorrow?"

Angela nodded. She watched Paul round the courtyard of the center and head toward the square. Then, turning, she returned to the lab to examine the copies of the Patmos documents and finish her translations.

15

THE CROSSROADS

MOSCOW, RUSSIA

Oksanna stood in her signature fur coat as the two men approached. She had agreed to meet them in the park outside the city, as long as her bodyguard could attend with her. Shivering slightly in the spring wind, she motioned them to sit down on one of the benches surrounding the fountains.

The two looked around and then, satisfied that no one was listening and no surveillance cameras lay hidden nearby, leaned closer.

"We represent a group of scientists, all of us Greens. We've learned that the Russian government is not planning on pursuing the World Greenhouse Project."

Oksanna stared at the scientists, not understanding their concern. "The World Greenhouse has been destroyed. It would take years to rebuild, nourish, and replenish the crops and seeds, if ever, that we used to cultivate our natural crop growth. I'm not sure we could ever recover what's been lost. It's no surprise that the Russian government is not allocating funding now."

"It's more than that." The one on the right was leaning closer now, his voice almost a whisper. "We have word that the government is planning on developing agrofuels. All of the MK BRIC countries

147

are getting on board, and Russia has no reason now not to pursue the big bucks."

"They can't. We don't have the resources," Oksanna said, incredulous.

"They'll take it from the land, the people, same as all the other countries are doing, same as Stalin did years ago. Russia will suffer. All the work you've done to raise the standard of living through natural food production will not only stall but reverse dramatically and quickly. The nation will be thrown into a food crisis. Not only that, but they're planning on establishing a lab to develop genetically altered foods, just like the rest of the capitalist high-tech countries."

Oksanna sat back, stunned. *Would they really do that?* she wondered. *After all they had invested to make Russia the most humanitarian agricultural country in the world?*

"I don't understand. Why are you telling me this? What do you want from me?"

The two men exchanged glances. The one on the right sighed, then spoke. "We want you to lead the Underground Greens."

Oksanna pursed her lips. Behind her dark eyes, her mind seemed to be working intensely.

"Ms. Galina, there are many of us. Not just from Russia. We represent a worldwide environmental movement in opposition to what's happening all over the globe. We know we can't accomplish anything through regular channels. That's why we're going underground. We need you."

Oksanna stood up. "Gentlemen, I understand your concern. But two attempts have recently been made on my life. I don't think this is the time for me to be sticking my neck out any further. I just want to be left alone."

"Ms. Galina, with all due respect, I can't believe you, of all people, would choose to be passive about something like this."

"Look,"—Oksanna remained standing—"the only reason I led the World Greenhouse Project was to carry on the work of my family.

I'm not as invested in this as you think. I have no ethical or personal investment in any of it. All I want is to preserve my life and find some kind of meaningful work to do for the rest of it."

"I don't believe that." The two men stood now as well, meeting Oksanna's eyes.

"Believe what you want. But leave me alone." Oksanna motioned to her bodyguard, and without another word left the two men standing amid the trees surrounding the fountain.

KABUL, AFGHANISTAN
Department of Pathology, Jamuriat Hospital

The police detective led the family out of the identification room, then returned to speak with the pathologist. "What were the results of the autopsy?"

The doctor held out a copy of the report for the detective. "Death was caused by intensive neurological failure. Spider bite. Specifically, venom of a South American banana spider. Found primarily in Brazil and some other South American countries. They're not indigenous to Afghanistan. Either it was deliberately brought here or it arrived by accident in fruit or some other produce. It's a rare occurrence."

The detective wrinkled his forehead and tilted his head incredulously. "South America. But where would he have encountered it? When we found him, he had been driving his van. There was no sign of anything in or around the van."

"There's really no way to know. Unless we have the spider, we have no way to determine how or in what way he was bitten. We only know the bites were the cause of his death. It takes only one to three hours for the poison to completely devastate the human system. In his case, he was somewhat dehydrated. It was probably within one."

The detective swore under his breath. "Poor guy."

The doctor nodded. "It wouldn't have been pleasant."

The detective moved toward the door. "Thank you, Doctor."

The doctor nodded and returned to his lab, the report under his arm.

WASHINGTON, D.C.

The White House

"The press conference was brilliant, Matt. Simply brilliant."

Ted Calahan followed Matt Serafino from room to room like an eager puppy.

"Is Doron here?" Serafino threw a glance in the direction of Mullica Michaels as he entered the office suite.

"Yes, sir. She's waiting in the sitting room down the hall."

"Ted." Serafino nodded at Ted Calahan, dismissing him with his eyes as he hurried down the hallway to the sitting room. Doron was seated by the window, pretending to admire the roses on the White House lawn. When she saw Matt, she got up and went to greet him, trying to look engaged.

He smiled and put out his arms to embrace her. "How are you, Doron?"

"Matt. You're charming as always." She smiled back. "I'm fine. That was quite a press conference."

"Yes, I think we've stalled that little uprising for now."

"Indeed." Doron sat back down, and Matt joined her in the opposite chair.

"You wanted to talk to me?" Matt feigned concern, sneaking a look at his watch.

"Yes." Doron paused, looking somewhat uncomfortable. "Matt, you know, we've shared a lot about ourselves. And I'm sure each of us has done things in the past that are . . ." She hesitated. ". . . perhaps somewhat out of character."

"I'm not concerned about the past, Doron. Only the present and the future." Matt smiled, wondering what Doron could want to confess.

"Yes," Doron continued hesitantly. "But I felt I should bring something up that might be . . . important." Doron licked her lips nervously, glancing at her hands, which were now fumbling with the edge of her suit jacket. "You know, when—"

Doron's voice was interrupted by the president's panel loudspeaker. It was Mullica.

"Mr. President, a call for you from Afghanistan, sir."

Matt stood up. "I'll take it in my office, Mullica." He turned and looked at Doron. "I'll be right back. Hold that thought." He smiled at her again and hurried off to the Oval Office, leaving Doron still nervously clutching the edge of her suit, her hand now gripped around it. She sighed and turned back to the rose garden.

GREENBELT, MARYLAND
Goddard Space Flight Center (NASA)

"Was the mission successful?"

The director, Hal Goodman, nodded, smiling. He reached out and tapped the panel monitor to connect Matt Serafino to the live speaker function. Matt's image appeared on the screen in the NASA headquarters director's portal.

"Mr. President, per our military liason, the targets were hit. We leveled the main lab in Cairo and struck a hit on Lachier's personal aircraft in its dock in the Sahara."

"Excellent. Can anything be traced?"

"Not a chance. We took them by surprise. No one saw our sonics. We're positive. They were launched under protective radar-blockers. They never saw us coming, sir."

"Good work, Hal. Keep me posted."

"Yes, sir."

Matt Serafino's eyes darkened and sparkled, his mouth widening into a satisfied smile. *That was for Novitia. Now for the stolen coordinates.* He motioned off the sensor for the White House screen and went back to find Doron.

LONDON, ENGLAND

Hotel Montague

Paul stirred in his sleep, tossing and turning in the hotel bed. The dreams were coming more and more frequently now, and each time he woke, sheets drenched, wondering what the dream had been about. But this time, it stayed with him.

He had been wandering in some sort of cave. It was dark, except for a dimly glowing candle. It looked similar to the cave they had seen in Patmos. Then, all of a sudden, he was in his mother's attic back in West Virginia, holding a candle and looking at the box containing the cross key. As he picked up the key, he found himself standing in marsh water. Someone was holding a large, rolled-up manuscript in front of him. The figure was dark, and Paul could barely see through the fog over the marshes. As the shadow held out the manuscript in front of him, he could see it was bound in some sort of casing. The casing had seven pressed-wax seals running down the edges, all of them holding the manuscript together. The figure held out the scroll to him and motioned. And in the dream, Paul reached out and broke open the seven seals, one at a time, separating them from the brittle paper and releasing the manuscript pages, which seemed to transform into a huge book. Then a wind rose up, and the pages seemed to flutter about, opening to a passage that he couldn't quite make out. The figure pointed to the passage. Paul leaned forward to look, and the shadowy form disappeared. Startled, Paul became suddenly aware of the wetness around his ankles as he stood in the marshes. The figure was nowhere to be seen. He looked down, and that was when he awoke, wrapped in his wet sheets and trembling in the cool room.

After standing in a hot shower and putting on fresh clothes, Paul went to the leather satchel and retrieved the notebook. From now on, he would record everything.

LONDON, ENGLAND

Centre for Manuscript and Print Studies

The alarm sounded for the second time that week, and the police rushed to the source of the break-in. The center's back door had been forced open and the emergency lights smashed. In the library, the case holding the Patmos box had been pried open, and the shelf where the box had been was now bare. The police had called Angela, and she stood now in the center of the library, shaking her head in disbelief.

"The box had only just arrived. I didn't think anyone was even aware it was here," she told the police, her voice betraying her surprise. Then, with an alarmed look on her face, she rushed into the back room to the vault. The doors were still intact. Putting in the combination, Angela turned the latch and entered the vault. The originals and the copies of the papers from the box were still there in the plastic sheets. Angela breathed a long sigh of relief, returned the papers to the shelf, and resealed the vault. As she returned to the library, the detective looked at her quizzically.

"Anything wrong?"

"Nothing," she replied. "Let's do the report."

Whoever had broken into the center must have known that the box contained something. She was sure whoever it was could not have known what was inside. Only she and Paul had examined the documents. And only Paul had the key. If someone broke into it now, that person would find only an empty box, except for the numbers carved into the side of the box: 21, 21. And even she and Paul had no idea what the numbers meant. They would need to be more careful. Something strange was going on, and Paul was right. It wasn't just about strange occurrences and personal prophecies. This had to do with a very real person—an intruder or intruders, and Angela didn't want to take any more chances with their lives. Emory Makefield was already dead, and she didn't want herself or Paul to be next. They would need to work somewhere other than the center. She would talk to Paul about it tomorrow. Rubbing her eyes, she finished with the detective's report before making her way, along with an armed escort, back to her apartment for the remainder of the night.

Beijing, China

Capitol Building

President Murong Gui took the sixteenth call of the day reporting deaths throughout China. He stood in front of his portal screen, talking to his second-in-command scientific officer.

"What's going on? Is it an epidemic? What are the symptoms?"

"Sir, we don't know. People are dying. The closest we can tell, it appears to be some sort of encephalitis. Almost like a version of the turn of the century's mad cow disease. We have no idea where it's coming from."

"Have you checked the meat?"

"Yes, sir. The meat's clean."

"Well, find out, will you? I'm getting calls by the hour. Something needs to be done. I'll expect to hear back from you within two hours. Get your staff out there, and find out exactly what's causing these casualties."

"Yes, sir." The man bowed and disappeared from the portal screen.

President Murong Gui buried his face in his hands. "What else?"

16

THE WETLANDS

SOUTHERN IRAQ

"What's happened to the water?"

The people of the marshes in the once fertile land of Mesopotamia gathered in the muddy trenches of what had been the village's primary water supply. In the last two weeks, the bodies of water permeating the area around the Fertile Crescent had begun gradually dissipating, leaving only muddy ditches and the remains of reeds and rushes. The area's only source for agricultural sustenance, the depleting water supply now threatened the village's scant crops. And with no source of water or food, people began to panic. Some began evacuating the region in hope of locating better supplies of water. Those with less nomadic tendencies waited out the drought in hope that the water would return to the marshes.

Gradually, all areas of Iran, Iraq, Syria, and Turkey began to suffer the effects of water loss. It was as though the water had simply evaporated. Each day, the marshes grew thinner and smaller and the water levels drained lower and lower until, eventually, the entire region had to declare a state of national emergency.

In a state of confusion, each country sent scientists to investigate the marshes, but to date, no conceivable explanation for the water losses had been found. The leaders of the four countries met in Baghdad along the now draining Tigris River to discuss options.

The Syrian prime minister looked around the table at his confederates.

"Our countries suffered similarly before the turn of the century under the regime of Saddam Hussein. But we had restored our marshes and irrigation systems after the destruction of the extensive dams and walls, and the areas had almost fully recovered. We can find no scientific reason currently why the water is evaporating. We do know, however, that it has greatly affected the state of our agriculture already, and no harvestable crops will survive if the drought continues for months on end. We must find a way to return water to the region and to provide food to our citizens, even if it means we need to import both water and food."

The others nodded in agreement as the prime minister finished speaking.

"We have a proposal from the Egyptian government." The Iraqi leader touched the panel, and a document appeared on the screens surrounding the conference area. "It's from President Menes Mubarak himself."

The members of the group looked at one another silently.

"Why would he do this?" The Turkish prime minister spoke up, his eyes betraying his suspicion of their Arab neighbor.

"Perhaps we ought to first read the document." The prime minister from Syria began to read aloud:

To our Arab brothers and sisters in Iraq, Syria, Iran, and Turkey,

Our country has become aware of the dire circumstances of your marshes and riverbeds, and we sympathize with the plight of our Middle Eastern neighbors. While Egypt continues to be challenged with our own issues regarding adequate water supplies and irrigation, particularly in our desert regions, we still have ample resources and our people are living comfortably. We would therefore like to extend the hand of peace and offer a temporary resource of water and food to your countries as you seek solutions for your current situation. We know you must be in a position of need, and in order to provide food and water to your vast populations, emergency procedures must be put into place.

Therefore, Egypt offers you the use of supplies, both agricultural staples and adequate water for your populations, in return for specified quantities of oil and access control to established oil fields in your respective countries. We feel this is a fair exchange in light of your current need and hope you will consider Egypt's offer of support.

President Menes Mubarak

"We can't do this." The Syrian prime minister looked angry.

"This isn't an offer of support. It's extortion," the Turkish prime minister said in agreement.

"On the other hand, what other choices and options do we have?" The prime minister from Iran looked up grimly from the table. "Despite the drawbacks, if the drought continues as it is, all our populations will be jeopardized. I think we need to seriously consider this option, unless and until we can think of anything better."

The leaders exchanged nervous glances.

"We have no choice but to meet with our respective governments and return in one week for a decisive vote." The four nodded in agreement and filed out of the meeting room.

It would be another month before they would meet again.

MOSCOW, RUSSIA

Oksanna's Residence

Oksanna sat absentmindedly stirring her tea and staring at the model of the World Greenhouse that occupied the entire left corner of her sitting room. The dream her family had of creating sustainable agriculture was apparently as fragile as the glass case surrounding the replica of her life's work. Her mind wandered to the meeting in the park.

The Underground Greens. Oksanna had spent years working through government systems and red tape, all on the up-and-up, in order to establish her reputation as the director of the IEO. The Underground's movements were always something shadowy and disreputable in Oksanna's eyes, restless dissenters with nothing better to do than roll out cyber leaflets and lead marches that were always squelched before they began. And what was the good of it, anyway? Nothing would come of it, except the deaths of the objectors. If the Russian government wanted to do something, no movement was going to stop it. Oksanna had better things to do with her life.

"*Don't I?*"

Her voice echoed in the large, empty room. She hadn't realized she had spoken aloud.

Oksanna sat back in her chair, surveying what served as her study. Her entire life seemed to stare out at her from the various corners and spaces housing her most prized possessions. Surrounding the walls of this room, her favorite room in the entire house, were her collections, floor-to-ceiling glass cases filled with figurines from around the world. Each one was made from lead crystal. She had collected them throughout her lifetime, arranging them neatly inside the cases, in groupings, like little communities of glass. They seemed to mock her now, goading her to declare them meaningful. Oksanna looked away.

I won't do it.

MARSEILLE, PROVENCE-ALPES-CÔTE D'AZUR, FRANCE

St. Seraphim Orthodox Cathedral

The music from the loudspeakers filled the rear rooms of the Orthodox cathedral, spilling out through the walls and into the devastated streets of a despondent Marseille. Concerto no. 2 by Rachmaninoff.

"Is it really you?" asked Casimir Marceli, the young boy from the ravaged bus that had crashed the day before. He was feeding Seraphim yogurt drops as he examined every artifact in the rector's formal office.

The boy was becoming immensely curious, with an inexhaustible mind and an insatiable thirst for knowledge. He hadn't stopped asking questions since he had arrived the day before and had nearly exhausted Arnaud with his inquiries on art, music, religion, and the history and culture of Marseille. Now he was asking questions about Arnaud, and Arnaud began to feel slightly uncomfortable.

"It's my recording. From many years ago." Arnaud was searching through his collections for his most recent version of French folk songs. He wanted to introduce the boy to the folk music of his country. If Casimir would miss his school trip, surely he could learn at least something here. He was, after all, in France.

The others were still sleeping. The rescue squad had delivered them all safely to the cathedral, bringing the last of them in toward the wee hours of the morning. Exhausted, the crew, teachers, and students had all bunked down in the sanctuary and in the monastery rooms for the night, some even having curled up on chairs and in the padded corners of the aisles, covered with blankets from the rectory. They would be here for a few days until the roads were sufficiently repaired to send for a bus that would take them to the nearest functional aerodock and then back home to India.

It was still early, but Casimir Marceli was up almost at the crack of dawn, wandering about the halls. Arnaud saw him and ushered the boy into his office while he prepared for the day's meditations. He doubted anyone would show up for services. The quake had leveled most of the city, and rescue teams were still working to free people from the rubble, the remains of businesses, houses, museums, and shops. But Arnaud wanted to be prepared nevertheless. In times of devastation and trouble, people seemed to suddenly want to believe in something greater than themselves. They needed something or someone to trust in who could assure them that a reprieve from their grief was in sight. It was at these times that people were most open to hearing about the saving power of Christ. But often, as quickly as their dilemma passed, so, too, did their faith. As he worked on his sermon, Arnaud watched the boy out of the corner of his eye, every so often breaking into an amused smile.

Father Arnaud instinctively liked Casimir. The boy was clearly intelligent and had the mental hunger and physical agility of a cheetah. Tiring of feeding Seraphim, he was now perusing the books on Arnaud's shelves, taking each one out and scanning the pages for interesting tidbits of information, every so often blurting out some phrase that must have taken him by surprise. He wondered what the boy would become as an adult.

"Do you like history, Casimir?" Arnaud sat back, watching the boy intently as he scanned through a book on French architecture, *The Cube and the Cathedral.*

"Not really." The boy smirked shyly, tilting his head so that a dark gold curl fell over one of his almond-shaped eyes.

"Why not?" Arnaud watched as the boy contemplated his answer, as though it were an inquiry into his very soul.

"I guess . . ." He paused, his eyes searching the air. "I guess I just think more of the future than the past."

"The past can be a portal into the future sometimes, you know."

The boy sat silently, waiting for Arnaud to continue.

"It is in the richness of the past that we find our way into our own individual and collective future, the same way that we find within our souls the strength and faith to carry on with the complexity of our lives." Arnaud paused.

"Do you understand that, Casimir?"

"I'm not sure."

"The leaves of the present fall and form the mulch of the past from which the tree of life grows and produces green leaves, fresh fruit, and new futures."

"I don't know much about my past. I am Hebrew from my mother's side. My father's side is Polish. Of course, my mother is Polish, too. But she often talks about her Hebrew heritage—although I don't think she understands much of it either. She just likes to talk about it." Casimir grinned, his boyish face sporting a mischievous expression.

"Let me show you something." Arnaud got up and moved the ladder in his study to one of the far shelves. Climbing to the top of it, he retrieved a large, ornate book. On the cover were the words *Sefer Yetzirah.*

"What is it?" Arnaud could see that Casimir's eyes had the intrigued look of a curious cat.

"Kabbalah."

"What?"

"Kabbalah." Arnaud repeated the word. "It's the ancient secrets of the universe recorded from the Hebrew traditions."

Casimir was definitely fascinated, and he reached out and took the book. Laying it carefully on the table next to him, he began opening each illuminated page as if it were made of crumbling parchment.

"Take a look at it. I'm going to check on the others."

With that, Arnaud left the office, leaving the study door cracked ever so slightly so he could observe the boy as he made his way through the sacristy into the back of the sanctuary.

LONDON, ENGLAND

British Museum

"It's *The Four Horsemen of the Apocalypse*."

Angela was guiding Paul through the museum's prints and collections, stopping at the Dürer woodcut and studying its intricate precision.

The Centre for Manuscript and Print Studies was closed for the day as the police finished their investigation of both the homicide and the theft of the box from Patmos. The police had graciously agreed to keep the theft out of the press, and Angela had procrastinated in contacting Dr. Anthony Kontos, hoping the box would be returned and no harm done. She couldn't bear to let him know of the loss so soon after he was kind enough to authorize the loan to the center. If the box wasn't returned within the week, she would call him. But for now, she and Paul were spending the day working in the British Museum's main conference area with permission from the staff.

Angela had almost forgotten about the Dürer. But there they were, the four horsemen, displayed with the symbols of their characters. The first rider would be the white horse, mounted by a horseman carrying a bow; the second, the red horseman, carrying a large sword. The third was black, and the rider bore a set of scales. The final horse, which seemed to trample all the others in the drawing, was the horseman of death and the plague. The seraphim hovered above the four, most likely declaring the release of the first four seals. The woodcut had been completed in 1498 in Nuremberg, during the time of the Black Plague in Europe.

Angela looked over at Paul. She wondered what he was thinking. He had been quiet today, studying the documents from the box and making notes in his leather binder. From time to time, he would raise his head and appear to be contemplating something. Then he would return to his notes again. Angela left him alone. She sensed he was struggling with something, and that in time he would talk to her. For now, he stared intently at the Dürer print, his mind almost visibly working. Angela left him to his thoughts and returned to the front conference room to wait.

17

COOKING GOOSE

National Holding Center

Serafino sat watching Niú Ye as the Chinese scientist hungrily shoved meat and rice into his mouth from the large bowl. Ye hadn't eaten in days, and he could feel his stomach cramping. But he didn't care. He downed the contents of the bowl. Who knew when he would get another? He could feel Serafino's eyes on him, observing him as though Ye were a helpless rabbit. When he was finished, he sat back against the cell wall, waiting for Serafino to pounce. Although Niú was a strong man with a stocky build and strong arms and legs, he knew in his current condition he would be no match for Serafino. And the guards remained just outside the cell, as though they thought Niú could somehow wrench his way through the iron bars.

As a young man just out of the orphanage, Niú had worked in the fields, pulling heavy carts and lugging pails of rice. He might still be there if it hadn't been for the English missionaries. They were going through the fields and villages that day, recruiting people to work in their hospitals. They didn't care where he came from. All he had to do was listen to their stories and agree with their propaganda, and he could work in town in a clean environment, with regular meals—and books. It didn't take long for several of the leaders of the group to recognize that Niú Ye had potential. He quickly taught himself to read in both Chinese and English, and he immediately took to assisting the medical staff with preparing medications and assisting in operations. It wasn't long until he was reading medical and scientific texts and soaking up whatever knowledge he could glean from the staff. During all this, Niú continued to attend their morning and evening prayer sessions and to pretend to read the Bible. After a period of time, they arranged for him to go to the university in Beijing, with his tuition paid by the Christian Mission. He spent six years there studying science and the new genetics, making the highest grades in the class. Before graduation, he had been approached by the government to work in the National Center for the Study of Genetics, where he had been ever since, rising to the position of head biogenetics scientist at the young age of twenty-eight. He never saw any of the missionaries again.

Niú Ye recovered from his thoughts to find Serafino still staring at him as though he could see right through his mind. Ye shivered.

"So, someone already is in possession of the serum for the genetic manipulation of foodstuffs. What's the official name of the project, then, Niú?"

"Project Angel Cake."

"Angel Cake. Nice." Serafino smiled, his eyes squinting into dark slits. "So, who has it, hmm?"

"I don't know what you're talking about. China has it."

"But oh yes, I forgot, you haven't been listening to the news, have you, Niú? It seems your home country is going through a bit of a crisis. The country is dying of something akin to encephalitis, and no one seems to have a clue as to what's going on. Now, we both know what's going on, though, don't we, Niú? Someone got their hands on the serum and is using it to bring down your own country."

Niú Ye paled.

"Well, we both have something in common now, don't we? We both want that serum."

Serafino smiled coldly.

"So, are you ready to work with me, Niú?"

LONDON, ENGLAND

Angela's Apartment

The smell of cooking wafted from the apartment in London as Angela prepared her family's recipe of roast goose for the spring holiday. Not many people really celebrated it as a Christian holiday much anymore, but still, the businesses had closed, and everyone generally still cooked the traditional Easter-style feast for friends and family. In England, that feast included roasted lamb, spring vegetables, and roasted potatoes, accompanied by hot cross buns and biscuits. But Angela had always made duck or goose, roasted in butter sauce and topped with herbs. As she opened the oven door to marinate the bird, the warm, succulent smell of the seasoned meat steamed through the kitchen and permeated the small apartment. Pussy willows decorated the table, and Angela included some additional white roses from the gardens outside the apartment complex. When her parents were still alive, Angela always went home to Ireland for holidays. But now, with only distant relatives remaining, she remained in London, instead inviting friends and acquaintances to her small but festive celebrations. This year, Paul had accepted her invitation, along with several others from the Centre for Manuscript and Print Studies, who for one reason or another would be alone for the spring holiday.

Angela hummed softly as she prepared a seasoned gravy and then lifted the warm rolls from the small oven. It was just about time for her guests to arrive. She hung her apron from a hook on the kitchen wall, smoothed her skirt, and went into the dining room to inspect the table.

The bell to the apartment rang, and Angela let Paul enter the building. She looked out through the glass and could see he had brought the leather binder. She smiled. They had agreed to look at the materials from the Patmos box later that evening. Paul had indicated something very cryptic on the phone, and Angela had no idea what he wanted to show her. But she had agreed to take a look. Besides, she was beginning to like spending time with Paul.

As Paul reached the doorway to the apartment, Angela let him in and steered him toward her favorite chair, just as the others arrived at the lower floor. Angela buzzed again, and soon the apartment was overflowing with people, the scents of meat and spices, and blended conversation.

After dinner, they settled into a satisfied comfort.

"The dinner was fantastic, Angela."

"Indeed, Angela, the goose was cooked superbly." The guests were sitting back now, satisfied and ready to relax into comfortable conversation.

"Thank you all." Angela hurried to clear the dishes from the table and to serve the afternoon coffee and teas.

While they were waiting, Paul had taken a copy of the Dürer out of his satchel and was staring again at the strange horsemen.

"What's that, then?" One of the guests was staring at the illustration, intrigued.

"It's *The Four Horsemen of the Apocalypse.*" Paul smiled. "Here, take a look at this." He reached into his binder and pulled out a sheath of notes, along with diagrams from the Patmos box and a magnifier.

"In most of the artistic depictions of the horsemen, they appear like odd-shaped, winged creatures, but the Dürer illustration depicts them as men, just like in the prophecy of Ezekiel, all bearing the qualities of the four. So, I was thinking. What if these horsemen were really to exist? What would they be like?"

"Okay, I think you've had enough tea now." One of Angela's guests, Ian, a preservationist at the Centre for Manuscript and Print Studies, was laughing, stopping only to send a humorous jab Paul's way in a loud Irish brogue.

Paul smiled wanly. "But seriously, what if we were to experience the equivalent of an apocalypse? Look at what's happening around us—earthquakes, floods, devastation, more each day. What if the predictions from all those years ago from the Revelation of John were right, and we just hadn't reached the right time before now? It's possible."

"Anything is possible." Ian was laughing even harder now. "We could see a herd of purple gazelles and imagine it a sign of the earth's descent into madness."

Paul's smile faded. He nodded his head and slipped the documents back into the satchel. He would wait to talk to Angela alone. Paul was never one to believe in the truth of the materials he had devoted his life to. But something strange was happening to him, and he had found something. Something personally captivating and luring about the intertwining links between his letter and the manuscript. Something that challenged even his meager faith, and he wasn't so sure about anything anymore.

BEIJING, CHINA
Capitol Building

"We have a message coming in on the portal, sir."

Murong Gui bowed his head slightly and walked toward the portal screen. "Who is it?"

"Someone named Malik Asvaka, chief scientific officer with Scitheon in Afghanistan, sir. He says he represents President Gulzar."

Gui clenched his teeth. He knew what was coming. The genetics lab had traced the source of the illness killing his people by the tens of thousands to a rice manufacturing plant. The Angel Cake serum had been stolen and used on his own people. And Niú Ye was still nowhere to be found. No one had seen him since the cattle test of the serum more than a week ago. The lab had created the serum but had not yet created an antidote. People were dying everywhere in the country, and there was nothing Murong Gui could do about it. It was worse than the Capricorn Project. Niú didn't think Murong Gui knew about Capricorn. But Gui knew. Hundreds of villagers had been guinea pigs to an early form of the serum. Gui would have objected, but he knew

Niú Ye was onto something big, and he cleared the path for him to succeed. But now he was missing, and the lab was a disaster. Whoever had the formula now had the power. Gui waited.

Malik Asvaka's image floated onto the screen.

"Good morning, Mr. President. I'm sure you know why we are talking."

Gui bowed solemnly but remained silent, waiting for Asvaka to continue.

"I am a fair and just man, Mr. President. And so is our Afghan president, Abdul Gulzar. China has resources we can use. Your innovations in technology and science are impressive. Your Center for the Study of Genetics has made stunning advances, and you have achieved international economic leadership. We want to partner with you. Obviously, we would take over the leadership of your country, but if you are willing and don't resist, we will continue to use you and your people in leadership for the new Afghani-China. We are a wealthy country. Our oil and proceeds from weapons technologies sustain us and allow us to help your people with food and energy in exchange for your loyalty. It is a partnership that will help both our countries."

Murong Gui smirked, shook his head slowly, and looked directly at Asvaka. "Surely, you can't imagine that I would just simply hand over my country because of your terrorist tactics."

Asvaka's dark eyes glinted and flashed with anger. His broad face seemed to take on a wild look but then calmed again, his big teeth breaking through in a cold smile. "I really don't see that you have much choice, Murong."

Asvaka stood. "The president will be sending an entourage in the morning to your office to make the arrangements. I hope you will be cooperative. If so, we will hold off on the second round of serum infiltration." Asvaka continued to smile.

Murong Gui started but remained calm until Malik Asvaka's image had left the screen.

A second round. That means they've already infiltrated another food source.

Gui looked silently around the room at his staff. They all sat waiting for him to speak. He bowed his head, staring at his hands. Then suddenly, he waved them from the room. He needed to be alone.

MARSEILLE, PROVENCE-ALPES-CÔTE D'AZUR, FRANCE

St. Seraphim Orthodox Cathedral

When Arnaud looked into the office, he saw that Casimir was still deeply engrossed in the Sefer Yetzirah. He smiled. The boy had a freshness about him, a blatant honesty and blunt truthfulness that Arnaud found charming. In fact, it caught Arnaud off guard, challenged his own sense of being. For Arnaud, his faith had become more of an insurance policy, a set of beliefs that he could count on when everything else in life had let him down. His parishioners counted on his rugged sense of reason, his ability to offer sound theological arguments for almost any question. But spiritually, Arnaud was becoming as dry as Ezekiel's bones. And he knew it all too well. The accident had left him at first devastated, then cynical, then seemed to drain the life out of him. Desperate for control and order in a life he no longer understood, he had reached out to the priesthood in the hope that he could uncover some meaning for Giselle's death. But instead, he had retreated inside himself, clinging to tradition and doctrine in order to assuage his grief, or perhaps to negate it.

He was a good priest. He was functionally and intellectually more than admirable. But as time went on, it was as though his wings had been clipped, and he could no longer see the heavens, only read the signs in the earth. By the time he had realized the consequences of his sacrifice, it was too late. Christ was in danger of becoming for him a remnant, his truth cast like a rune among the forgotten icons in the Orthodox cathedrals. Arnaud believed in the comfort of rules, of science, of books, of knowledge, and of wisdom passed down through centuries of history. But did all this really connect to a God who existed beyond the dogmas of tradition? Arnaud wasn't sure. He had rarely encountered God as a priest. He learned about religion, inquired about the philosophical basis of faith, argued about the ontological questions of God's existence, but he hadn't experienced the assurance of God's presence since he had played as a concert pianist. He had sensed God then. In the music. Felt God's presence, as though the music were the very breath of the divine.

Then came the accident, and the music in him had died.

Arnaud left the office to ring the heavy cathedral bells for the celebration of Easter morning. Casimir stood in front of the deserted cathedral gates, watching as the sun rose above the eastern horizon. It looked somehow larger than he had ever seen it. And from the office came the strains of Mor Ephrem, as Seraphim burst into his morning song in Syriac:

> *By a flood of tears you made the desert fertile,*
> *and your longing for God brought forth fruits in*
> *abundance.*
> *By the radiance of miracles you illumined the whole universe.*

Sahara Desert

The crews were gathering up the last supplies from the cleanup. The explosion had devastated Youhanna Lachier's private aerodock located in the Sahara, and had destroyed two of his three planes. The third had been in the air at the time, transporting Lachier himself from a conference with President Menes Mubarak in Cairo.

Lachier stood and surveyed the damage. The explosives had also hit his lab at the National Research Institute for Astronomy and Astrophysics (NRIAA) in Cairo. Hassan had been in the lab at the time and had sustained extensive burns. He now rested somewhat uncomfortably at the Alzadra Hospital in the city of Cairo.

Much of Lachier's research was destroyed, but not his most important, private projects. He hadn't kept that research in the main lab, due to Hassan's presence. Now he was very glad indeed. However, he had surely lost time and notes for the Moonbeamer Project. And the way things were going, Egypt would need those notes. Of any who might desire to successfully establish a domed and sealed community in space, Egypt had the technology to do it. Lachier needed to find out how much of a setback the explosives had caused. The fact was, President Mubarak was worried. Floods, hurricanes, earthquakes, and fires all had been increasing. It was as though the earth had reached a climax, and it couldn't take any more. It seemed to erupt from within and without at random, sweeping whole countries into havoc. It remained perhaps only a matter of time before the earth would no longer be viable for human existence. And Egypt would be the country to establish a safe zone on another planet, a habitable community that would be the start of a new time and place.

Lachier turned from the remains of the desert aerodock and climbed back into his red plane. He would need to survey the damage to the lab and find out what had been preserved. Then he would set up his new headquarters, this time in a secret location.

18

REVELATIONS

The White House

The underground room felt cool and damp. But Matthew Serafino had broken out in a light sweat as he carefully removed the last pieces of the lock from the box of Saint John of Patmos. At last, reaching a small tool inside to move the trigger, he lifted the lid of the box to reveal an empty casement. Serafino snarled. Whatever had been inside had already been removed. He lifted the box, examining its underside. Running his finger alongside each edge, he could find no hidden compartments, no unusual seams. Not on the inside of the box either. Just then, Matt's fingers came upon several rough indentations in the bottom corner of the box. He felt inside again. There was something carved into the wood of the box. Lifting his small flashlight, he peered at the place where he had felt the anomaly in the wood. There, carved into the grain, were two numbers: 21, 21.

Matt stared at the numbers, as though their meaning would rise up out of the box and embed itself in his brain. *What can they mean?*

"Stay calm, Matt; think. What reference would John of Patmos have?" Matt's voice echoed in the empty underground space. His eyes rested on the Codex Gigas, still sitting on the wooden table in the center of the room. He walked toward it and began flipping through the brittle pages until he found Revelation 21:21: "The twelve gates were twelve pearls, each gate made of a single pearl. The great street of the city was of pure gold, like transparent glass."

Matt snarled again and flipped to the Gospels. In the early times, the four Gospel writers had been associated with the attributes of the four horsemen of the apocalypse. The only problem was, the gospel of Mark ended with chapter 16. There was no chapter 21. But he continued to look up the others. There had to be a clue somewhere in one of them or in the combination of the three.

He found Matthew 21:21: "Jesus replied, 'I tell you the truth, if you have faith and do not doubt, not only can you do what was done to the fig tree, but also you can say to this mountain, "Go, throw yourself into the sea," and it will be done.'"

Matt smiled. Power. Yes, perhaps he was getting somewhere.

Next he found Luke 21:21: "Then let those who are in Judea flee to the mountains, let those in the city get out, and let those in the country not enter the city."

The mountains. Matt continued to page forward.

John 21:21 read, "When Peter saw him, he asked, 'Lord, what about him?'"

Matt stared at the three passages again. Beginning to grow frustrated, he randomly shoved the pages of the book forward; when they settled, they revealed an ancient map. As Matt's gaze centered on the map, taking in the peripheral lines and spaces, his eyes began to narrow, and his lips curled into a satisfied grin. *Latitude and longitude.*

SAHARA DESERT

The plane landed in the dust of the desert just as the sun was going down. Matt Serafino knew it would soon grow cold, and he pulled his jacket around him. The others were filing out of the plane now with picks, shovels, and other machinery that would dig, drill, and sift through mounds and miles of sand, if necessary. Matt wasn't sure what he was looking for, but he knew the numbers had to correspond to this area of the desert, on the border of Libya and Chad.

Using his Pearl, he located what should be the exact location—21, 21—and then he motioned to the group to begin excavation of the site. There had to be a clue somewhere in this desert. Matt sat down on one of the nearby dunes and prepared to wait out the night.

At nearly 9:00 a.m., Matt began to feel restless. His team had drilled miles around into the sand of the Sahara but found nothing. He checked the latitude and longitude again. The location was indisputably correct. Something was wrong. *Had someone gotten here before him? Or had he made a mistake?*

Matt called out, "One more sweep."

"*Rien, rien.*"

One of the workers scowled as he rejoined the team and once again swept their indicators over the several-mile radius that would indicate the presence of anything beneath the disturbed sand.

At last, Matt Serafino motioned to the men to leave the site and carry the equipment back to the plane. He stood looking out over the desert, now heating up as the morning sun beat down on the dunes.

"Nothing."

LONDON, ENGLAND

Hotel Montague

The call came in during the middle of the night, and Paul had to strain over the side of the bed to grab his Pearl, which was still in the pocket of his coat from the night before. It was Angela.

"Paul, do you remember the papers from the Patmos box we were looking at? The map of the four elements?"

Paul rubbed the sleep from his eyes.

"Yes." He couldn't imagine what Angela could find so important at this hour of the night.

"And do you remember the small manuscript, the book of Psalms, along with the other papers?"

"Yes, of course. A book of Psalms."

"Well, there's something different about this group of psalms."

Paul could tell Angela was excited. He let her continue.

"Paul, how many psalms are in the Bible text?"

Paul stopped for a moment, his mind now waking a bit. "One hundred fifty."

He rubbed his eyes again. What time was it? He looked at the clock: 2:30 a.m.

"Well . . ." Angela paused. "In this book, there are 151."

Paul startled, completely awake now. "Yes, of course. There *are* 151 psalms in the Septuagint, the Greek version of the Hebrew Bible. Not many people know about it, though. Most versions of the Hebrew Scriptures never mention it, although the psalm appeared in Syriac. Our friend Tatian could easily have known about it, as could John of Patmos. The Eastern Orthodox Church has accepted it for years. They have 151 in their Bible."

"Oh." Angela sounded surprised, then confused. "Well . . ."

Paul continued, "In fact, the Dead Sea Scrolls contained a number of psalms that were never numbered or accepted into the official version of the Scriptures." He paused for a moment. "Now that you mention it, I'm not sure why only one of them was chosen to be numbered."

Paul adjusted his Pearl and connected to his databases. "I'm familiar with most of them. And I think I may have a listing in my data file—"

Angela interrupted. "I don't think you've seen this one."

"No?" Paul stopped to listen.

"Well, it sounds . . ." She seemed to struggle for the right word. "It sounds . . . prophetic."

"Prophetic?" Paul was curious now.

"Look, Paul." Her excitement was returning. "It really doesn't read like any psalm I've ever heard. Listen."

Paul could hear Angela rustling a sheet of paper. In a moment, she began to read from her translation:

"Praise to God on high who
Sends the Holy Seal upon us.
All of the people shall praise him.
Let the hills rejoice and
May the chosen see the dawn of the new day.
Find the
Hidden hills."

"What do you think it means?" Angela paused, waiting for Paul's reaction.

"Can you bring it over here? In fact, bring all the documents. Can you come within the hour?" Paul sounded excited now.

"Better. I can come within ten minutes." Angela grabbed the documents and headed for the Hotel Montague.

Angela arrived at the hotel just as Paul was slipping on his jacket. He rubbed his hand over his cheek. He hadn't had time to shave, but it would have to do. Running a comb quickly through his hair, he answered the door to find Angela grinning at him from the hallway. He invited her in, and they spread the documents out across the hotel table.

Paul opened the book of Psalms and looked at the translated text. It appeared to be a psalm like any other. But the language was strange and smacked of the same prophetic tone he had encountered in the Diatessaron prophecy. He read through the psalm several more times.

Praise to God on high who
Sends the Holy Seal upon us.
All of the people shall praise him.
Let the hills rejoice and
May the chosen see the dawn of the new day.
Find the
Hidden hills.

Paul stopped. "Praise to God on high who sends the Holy Seal upon us." There was that language about the seal again. The rest began to sound like a typical psalm until the last line of the paragraph: "May the chosen see the dawn of the new day." No other psalm seemed to have that kind of reference. It came across to Paul as apocalyptic, just as the text from Revelation embedded in the Diatessaron. *Who are the chosen? What is the dawn of the new day?* But the oddest part of the psalm was the ending—two lines set apart from the rest of the text, given as a command. "Find the Hidden hills." Paul remembered other psalms, including 121, that talked about the hills: "I will lift up mine eyes unto the hills." But nowhere else in the psalms was there a command like that. And to whom would it be addressed? There was no indication in the rest of the psalm as to whom the psalmist was speaking.

Paul read through it again. Several of the sentences were interrupted and continued onto the next line but with a capital letter beginning it. *Odd.* Paul sat back and looked at the psalm again, his eyes focusing on the strange style. While breaks and capitalization are typical in poetry, the last seemed awkward. Suddenly, he sat straight up.

"It's an acrostic."

Angela turned the sheet to see what Paul was looking at.

"An acrostic," she repeated.

"Look at this." Paul was excited now, and taking Angela's finger, he traced the letters to the left margin of the psalm downward: PSALM FH.

"Psalm FH?" Angela looked confused.

Paul shook his head. "The letters of the alphabet correspond to numbers. F is the sixth letter and H the eighth. Psalm 68."

Paul paged backward in Angela's translation of the book to Psalm 68. But as he did, he noticed that several of the other psalms had been underlined. Carefully, Paul scanned through the entire book of Psalms, writing down the underlined passages in his notebook:

> *Lord, who may dwell in your sanctuary?*
> *Who may live on your holy hill?*

He whose walk is blameless,
  and who does what is righteous,
who speaks the truth from his heart. (Psalm 15:1–2)

Who may ascend the hill of the Lord?
  Who may stand in his holy place? (Psalm 24:3)

How good and pleasant it is
  when brothers live together in unity! (Psalm 133:1)

In the first entry, the number 15 was underlined twice. Paul paged back to Psalm 68 and read verse 15:

The hill of God is as the hill of Bashan; an high hill as the hill of Bashan.

He then read through the next two lines:

Why leap ye, ye high hills? this is the hill which God desireth to dwell in; yea, the Lord will dwell in it for ever.
The chariots of God are twenty thousand, even thousands of angels: the Lord is among them, as in Sinai, in the holy place.

Paul looked at Angela. "It's a message."

NEW HAVEN, CONNECTICUT
Yale University

Rich Lavater grabbed his coffee from the lab table and headed out the back door of the Environmental Building at Yale. It was a beautiful April day, and the sun shone on the early morning dew, making the lawns look like sleek, sparkling green ponds. Rich loved the peace and quiet of Yale's campus grounds, often filled with birds, small animals, and especially pigeons. Yale's pigeons were a cherished part of the Yale community, and many of the students fed them, named them, and spent time loitering with them on the greens and pathways, where the birds nested within the corners and archways of the century-old neo-Gothic stone buildings. Usually, their coos and trills could be heard throughout the campus in the morning as they strutted out for food to greet the new day. But today the air was oddly quiet, and Rich found himself listening intently in the silence. It was too quiet.

Rich stepped forward onto the lawn, and his foot bumped against something lying motionless and half buried in the grass. He looked down. It was a pigeon. He could see it was lying on its side, its wings pressed close to its sides and its head tucked unnaturally into the grass. It was already stiffening. Rich moved it slightly with his foot, turning it over to reveal a body half eaten away, its feathers bare, innards spilling out like the broken springs of a cuckoo clock. Quickly, Rich stepped away, allowing the bird to fall back down into the earth. He stepped forward again and came across yet more grey and white bodies, all lying still in the dewy earth. Instinctively, Rich grabbed his pocket binoculars and peered out over the lawn. It was littered with feathery bodies. *What is going on? Is it poisoning?* Quickly, Rich entered the lab and returned holding several plastic containers and a set of vinyl gloves. He scooped three of the birds into the containers and returned to the lab. Accessing his Pearl, he contacted the biosciences lab. They would need to do extensive autopsies and tests on the birds, and he would need to have someone clean up the small bodies before the students began to appear on the grounds.

At the same time, Miranda Culler left her dorm for the cafeteria early, since she was on the first shift as student cashier. She screamed as she approached the walkway. There in front of her lay the bodies of at least forty or fifty pigeons. She ran back into the building and called security.

Back at the lab, the two scientists continued to try to locate the virus.

"Rich, I think you better take a look at this."

Alan Richter looked up from the microscope and motioned for Rich to look into the eyepiece at the pressed plate teeming with microbes.

"Is this what I think it is?" Rich stood back, stunned.

"Sure is. *Streptococcus pyogenes.* But I've never seen a strain quite like this. This is a potent one. Looks like death occurs almost within days, maybe hours."

"What are the symptoms?" Rich recorded the information in his lab digidrive as Alan read off the list of symptoms.

"My guess is that the incubation period is minimal. Might feel some initial pain, blistering. But the fever and vomiting probably start immediately, and the flesh and internal organs probably begin disintegration within hours of onset. We're going to need a lockdown."

Miranda Culler stepped into her dorm room after her morning class and ran for the trash can. Heaving, she wretched into the can again and again, sweat breaking out on her forehead and running down her chest and back. Her body felt clammy and warm. Reaching into a small box in the corner of her room, she felt for a thermometer. Hands shaking, she shoved it into her mouth and scarcely removed it in time before she was wretching again into the can, her stomach now cramping with dry heaves. *Could I have gotten food poisoning? What did I have to eat?* Miranda couldn't remember. Her mind seemed to be focusing only on steadying her shaking body enough to see the thermometer readout: 105 degrees. *How can that be?*

Fumbling once again in her plastic box, Miranda found a bottle of Tylenol and, grabbing a bottle of water from her bedside, downed three of them. Then she lay down on the bed, her body a wet mass of sweat and tears.

In three hours, she would be dead.

US health officials swarmed the periphery of the campus. Bright red tape labeled "Quarantined Area" covered every edge of the university grounds. No one was allowed within a mile of the campus borders without appropriate sanitary gear. Those who monitored the edges of the campus wore gas masks that made them look something like giant metal anteaters.

"My daughter is a student." A distraught father was attempting to push past the guards to enter the campus gateway.

"I'm sorry, sir. The entire campus is on lockdown due to an outbreak of what appears to be a rare and lethal form of staph."

"I have to get my daughter out of there. She's been calling me from her dorm. I need to take her home. She doesn't have the disease. She told me."

"I'm sorry, sir. But no one is allowed to either enter or leave the campus. Orders of the United States Centers for Disease Control and the US Army. The disease has been extremely infectious and quick to strike. We've already had nearly four hundred deaths reported today so far. We have no idea yet how to contain the infection." The guard hesitated. "I'm sorry about your daughter, sir."

Pacing back and forth along the taped area, the agitated father fingered the Pearl on his wrist and tried once more to contact his daughter. There was no answer.

19

IN THE VINEYARD

FERTILE CRESCENT

The earthquake began at 5:00 a.m. Far beneath the Mediterranean Sea, the earth's crust shifted violently, sending eighty-foot tidal waves crashing into the coasts of Egypt, Syria, and Turkey. The banks of the Nile quickly overflowed, and the Fertile Crescent began to flood.

The meeting of the prime ministers of Syria, Iraq, Iran, and Turkey, which had been set for that morning to discuss how to address Egypt's offer of irrigational and agricultural support, was hastily canceled as all four countries prepared to evacuate to the south and the east.

MARSEILLE, PROVENCE-ALPES-CÔTE D'AZUR, FRANCE

St. Seraphim Orthodox Cathedral Observatory

The observatory was filled with light. A dark figure sat huddled over a large volume, occasionally looking up to peer into the end of the telescope that rose up in the glass enclosure and pointed out into the night sky. The heavens were riddled with stars. The man's left hand held the end of the telescope, while the right scribbled frantic notes into a dog-eared notebook. Slowly and intently, he traced the numbers from his notebook across the sky. The constellations would be nearly perfectly aligned on 12/21/2048 at 9:00 p.m., the twenty-first hour.

My birthday. Arnaud sat back, his eyes pensive. An odd coincidence. *Or is it?* He was beginning to wonder.

Littering the large observatory table were volumes of cosmology, notes from Pythagorean theory, notes on the number four, Leibniz's *Monadologie*, volumes on alchemy and the Kabbalah, maps of almost every kind, Newton's *Observations upon the Prophecies of Daniel and the Apocalypse of St. John*, and a copy of an ancient Mayan prophecy.

Newton's book lay open to the page where Arnaud had underlined a group of passages:

> This prophecy is called the Revelation, with respect to the Scripture of Truth, which Daniel was commanded to shut up and seal, till the time of the end. Daniel sealed it until the time of the end, and until that time comes, the Lamb is opening the seals.

Newton believed that Christianity went astray in the fourth century, when the first Council of Nicaea propounded what Newton thought to be erroneous doctrines of the nature of Christ. But although the controversial mathematician and theologian did not believe in the divinity of Christ, he did believe that the patterns of the universe displayed themselves as the mind of God. In fact, he spent more time pursuing apocalyptic trails than he did his scientific endeavors. Newton believed that a mathematical code ran as a subtext beneath the surface complexity of the natural world—a rudimentary theory in an Enlightenment generation, but how dissimilar was it really to the current twenty-first-century M-theory?

Horace Milkins had recently theorized a twelfth extension to the current M-theory, what he called the "liminal zone," and which some in the scientific fields were now calling the mind of God, cosmic music of the universe, the matrix of all parallel worlds. Could Newton have presupposed any of this? And what could he have really known, using the limited cosmological equipment available in the early 1700s?

Like some of his contemporaries, Bacon, Descartes, Turner, and Dee, Newton believed that a lost "pure knowledge" could be discovered in mathematical truths and symbolic language. Robert Turner in particular fascinated Newton in that he believed the language of the Hebrews contained a supernatural power that could unlock the secrets of nature. Newton regarded the universe as a kind of cryptogram, designed by God and open only to the intuitive and introspective imagination. His orthodoxy may have been askew, but his cosmological deductions were uncannily similar to other prophecies, including the ancient calendar of the Mayans and the time predictions of the Kabbalah. *Could they all be wrong?* Had Newton somehow found something that made him believe something godlike would happen in December 2048? *This year?* The idea was disturbing at best. Yet, it was Newton's descriptions of the biblical seraphim that particularly fascinated Arnaud:

> The four beasts are therefore four Seraphim, . . . the first in the eastern side with the head of a lion, the second in the western side with the head of an ox, the third in the southern side with the head of a man, the fourth in the northern side with the head of an eagle . . . These animals are therefore the Seraphims.

It was getting late. Arnaud leaned back in the chair for a moment, his arms folded across his chest, his head swimming. Within minutes his head drooped, resting sideways on his collarbone, as his eyes fluttered and closed.

Sometime during the night, Arnaud found himself in the cathedral sanctuary, seated at the large, ebony grand piano. He wasn't sure how he got there, nor was he certain what was propelling him now, as he began to play a melody he hadn't heard for many years. The strains of Franz Liszt's *Mazeppa* echoed through the building, bouncing off the stone walls and domed ceilings, flowing out of the cracks in the stained glass like water through rock. As the strains of the tune progressed, Arnaud's countenance grew more severe, and his left hand pounded out the sounds of galloping horses, his right hand whisking across the keyboard in a spread he wouldn't have thought possible for his modest hand width. He was like a man possessed, needing to play, needing to play this piece. *This piece.*

Arnaud was so engrossed that he didn't see the small, dark figure standing at the edge of the sanctuary wall, not moving but transfixed, eyes wide, listening to the music that seemed to seep into his small soul like a slow honey. Casimir Marceli had been studying the Kabbalah documents, the Zohar and the Sephir Yetzirah, for several days now, his sturdy frame pressed against the library's mahogany walls, his eyes boring into the yellowed and frayed pages of the books. The words seemed like magic itself to Casimir. It was the first time anything had caught his attention other than technology. And he didn't know why. But now, in similar fashion, he found himself captivated by this music. Casimir was not a musician. He had not studied an instrument nor had any prior interest in learning one. His mother had once suggested that he join the school chorus, but because he was always ahead several grades, he felt awkward. Yet he had a powerful, resonant voice for such a small boy, and he used it now, beginning to hum to the melody, this melody that he had never heard before.

LONDON, ENGLAND

Hotel Montague

After Angela left, Paul continued to pore over the contents of the Patmos box. *Air, fire, earth, and water; Mark, Matthew, Luke, John; ox, lion, eagle, angel.* The number four seemed to be turning up everywhere. Even the Diatessaron was built on the number four. The word *diatessaron* meant "fourth" in Greek. In Pythagoras's music of the spheres, the diatessaron was the ratio 3:4, the most harmonious musical interval, according to the Greek Pythagoreans. Harmony resulted from two unequal intervals drawn from dissimilar proportions. For the Pythagoreans, all the universe revolved according to these musical ratios, creating a beautiful harmony, a music of the spheres. A unity of all things.

Paul scanned the psalms again. *Find the Hidden hills.* If line 15 of Psalm 68 was a clue, then the hidden hills were the hills of Bashan. Paul didn't understand what it meant or how it related to the rest of the box's materials, but the language about the chariots seemed to resonate also with the symbolism in the hidden Diatessaron prophecy. *Horsemen, chariots, wheels.* Paul sat back, perplexed. His eyes settled again on the Dürer print. *The Four Horsemen.* Paul glanced then at a second Dürer sketch, one he had made a copy of when he and Angela were in the British Museum. *The Adoration of the Lamb.* In this woodcut as well, the Lamb, the symbol of Christ, was surrounded by the four Gospel writers, each in the form of an animal—the four horsemen. Was this an apocalyptic message as well?

Drawing out his leather notebook, Paul began to form a chart of what seemed to be a pattern in the descriptions of the four horsemen that he had discovered as he researched.

Air/Wind	John	Eagle	Sword	Red	War
Water	Luke	Ox	Bow & Crown	White	Strife
Earth	Mark	Lion	Balances	Black	Famine
Fire	Matthew	Angel	Scythe	Pale	Disease

The tetrasomia, or doctrine of the four elements, dated back to Empedocles in the fifth century and could be found in the Kabbalah, on Native American medicine wheels, in the Pythagorean tetractys, and in the early texts of almost every medieval chemical and medical manuscript. *Aer, ignis, terra, aqua.* Current science knew that the four elements of carbon, oxygen, hydrogen, and nitrogen (C, O, H, N)—earth, air, water, and fire—made up 96 percent of all living matter. They also represented the elements in all known fuels: charcoal and agrofuels, solar energy, petroleum, and fertilizers and explosives. Dürer drew on the idea of four again in another drawing, the *Melancholia* (the four temperaments), creating the first magic square using 4x4 after Agrippa claimed a square using the four elements couldn't be done. The only other 4x4, although imperfect, was created by sculptor Joseph Subirachs and engraved into the Sagra Familia Church in Barcelona. Later, drawing on the idea of the temperaments, Carl Jung would establish eight personality types based on the idea of four elemental traits. *The birth of the eight.*

Paul's thoughts were interrupted by a knock on the door. When he opened it, Angela stood there smiling, an elaborate invitation in her hand.

"Would you like to take a trip?"

"Okay, I'm game. Where?"

"To Italy. Siena. We have an invitation to dine with a Dr. Pietro Engiolo, the curator of the Cathedral of St. Catherine. He says he has something he wants to discuss with us regarding our work with the

Diatessaron manuscript. And he promises in addition to our meeting to give us a tour of the cathedral and tickets to the Palio Horse Races at the Piazza del Campo."

"Sounds great. But how did he know we were working with a Diatessaron manuscript?" Paul looked suddenly suspicious.

"Well, listen to this. He claims he is the benefactor who donated it to the museum."

Paul looked startled.

"And in the letter, he asked me to give you this." Angela pulled out a small slip of yellowed paper and handed it to Paul.

> *Everything comes from love,*
> *all is ordained for the salvation of man,*
> *God does nothing without this goal in mind.*
> *2, 1, 19, 8, 1, 14*
> *— Saint Catherine of Siena*

Paul stuffed the paper, along with his copies of the other documents from the Patmos box, into his leather binder and stood up.

"Let's go."

TUSCANY, ITALY

Vineyard outside the Village of Siena

The drive from the Peretola Aerodock in Florence to Siena in Tuscany took about a half hour on the superstrada, but Paul and Angela drove off the Italian highway and into the beautiful hill country of Tuscany, with its winding roads and vineyards. It was early, and they had ample time before their appointment with Pietro Engiolo.

"Look, Paul, let's take a peek!"

Angela was pointing to a small sign that pointed the way up a winding hill toward a winery: WINE TASTING TODAY. The building looked old but quaint, and a stone path led up to a large wooden door, which led farther into a chamber with huge barrels and stocks containing bottles of wine of all kinds. Excitedly, Angela pulled Paul toward the long wooden counter and stools, where a man in a long white apron stood, nodding and smiling. He motioned to them to sit down on the rounded stools and then proceeded to bring out small glasses that he now set in front of them. Continuing to smile and speak in a polite Italian, he motioned to the bottles behind him, bringing them out one by one to Angela and Paul, gesturing for them to choose four of their favorites.

After tasting a selection of the wines, Angela chose a deep, red Tiare Mate merlot, and armed with the wine and a selection of cheeses and fruits, she and Paul left the vineyard and settled onto a blanket on the edge of the property, which looked out over the Tuscan countryside. They could see the Village of Siena not far off in the distance. They still had several hours until they needed to be in Siena, and in the warm summer breeze, thick with scents of grapes and lavender, leaning back against the vines and hand in hand, Paul and Angela soon fell asleep.

20

EXPOSÉ

TUSCANY, ITALY

Vineyard outside the Village of Siena

"The distilling and fermenting process of the wine is the most important for bringing character to the fruit."

Paul could feel Angela tugging him now, pulling him along the edge of some kind of flowing waterfall or spring, surrounded by brilliantly colored wildflowers in a meadow of silvery goat willows, their reddish branches striking against the cottony white. The water seemed to glisten in the morning sun, shimmering bright in Paul's eyes as he tried to focus on where they were. He turned to Angela but found she had left his side, no doubt wandering among the white rocks at the edge of the embankment. He tried calling out to her but struggled as his voice died in his throat, most likely from too much wine. Dizzy from the sun, the glare, and the blood pounding in his chest, he sat down on the tall grass.

Steam seemed to rise now above the water, creating an almost prismlike haze across the meadow. Through the glinting of water and sun, he saw a figure coming toward him. *Angela?* But it didn't look like Angela. She was dressed in flowing white, holding bloodred flowers in one hand and some kind of chalice in the other. As she approached,

Paul could see that her face almost glowed. *"Sollemnitas Sanctissimi Sanguinis Christi . . . Exsultent Divina Mysteria! Veritatem facientes in caritate."* She reached out to hand Paul one of the red roses. He wanted to reach out to her and grasp it, but he felt himself suddenly being pulled up from the edge of the bank and turned to look into the face of Angela, who was looking down at him, concern in her eyes.

"Paul, it's time to go."

Paul sat up, leaning on one arm, his eyes adjusting to the midday light. The blanket still lay under him, the bottle of red wine sat propped against the silver branches of the vines. Angela was smiling at him.

"We both fell asleep. Come on, it's time to meet Pietro Engiolo."

Paul rubbed his eyes. The dream had seemed so real. He looked up. Angela was already folding up the edges of the blanket. He stood then and helped her gather up the remnants of their feast, and the two trudged to their car. In a little while, they would be rounding the curved road to Engiolo's villa, just outside Siena.

WASHINGTON, D.C.

The Cavendish Inn

The restaurant bustled with people. Doron fingered the napkin on her lap nervously as she waited for Matt to arrive. It was now or never. She would need to tell him what she had seen. She needed to know what he would say, why he had done this. Or perhaps she needed him to convince her it was all just a sad mistake. Above all, Doron knew the possibility existed that he would leave her then, would not be able to face her again. But if she kept it from him, she wouldn't be able to live with herself. Wouldn't be able to feel good about him.

And there was also the press. If they got hold of something like this, it could harm Matt's presidency. Although the uprisings against Matt Serafino had died down significantly since the restoration of the banking systems, enough hate groups persisted who would like nothing more than to bring Matt down. The possibility of a US civil revolution was not so far-fetched any longer. Some of the states, especially in the West, were taking matters into their own hands; others were talking secession, and Doron knew the state of the union was no trifling matter. The withdrawal from the Union of eleven of the Southern states in 1860 and 1861 had resulted in the first Civil War. Now, with the US systems in disarray and the country politically and economically fragmented, it would take something virtually miraculous on the part of Matt Serafino to restore the country to its former glory as a world forerunner in science, culture, and economics. America seemed to be splintering from within, ready to implode into shrapnel of subterritories and micronations. If the country knew Matt was engaged in something so horrendous as this sacrificial ritual, who knows what could happen to Matt Serafino and the new United States. She would need to keep it quiet. To let Matt know she would.

*
* *

From the moment Matt's black limousine pulled to the curb at the front of the restaurant to the moments in the aftermath at Washington Hospital seemed like a strange dream to Doron—like a moment of timelessness in which everything seemed to disappear into some kind of slow-moving other reality. Doron saw the gunman from inside the restaurant and rose, toppling the contents of the table to the floor. She thought the shooter had aimed for Matt, but the president's security team of bodyguards had thrust the US president quickly into the lower reaches of the limousine. In a split second, she thought she had seen Matt turn for a moment to look at her in the doorway. The gunman took aim from the corner of the building. One of the bodyguards tackled the gunman to the ground, cuffing him and shouting to a bystander to call emergency services. Everything went grey then as Doron tumbled to the ground, blood surging from her side.

Waking later to the sound of the beeping and whirring of the hospital machinery, she opened her eyes to look into the faces of the doctors at Washington University Hospital.

Matt cut all ties to her and became as unreachable as the pictures that still lay hidden in the apartment floorboards. To Matt Serafino, she had never existed.

MARSEILLE, PROVENCE-ALPES-CÔTE D'AZUR, FRANCE

Arnaud was enjoying the five-hour drive from Marseille to Siena. He had received an invitation from Dr. Pietro Engiolo to officiate in a baptismal ceremony at the Cathedral of St. Catherine and then to accompany him on a visit to the Basilica of San Domenico. He had accepted the invitation, even though it seemed strange for an Eastern Orthodox priest to be invited to do a baptism in the very Catholic town of Siena, especially that of Tuscany's patron saint. But Arnaud didn't ask questions. He was glad for the opportunity to get away from Marseille for a while. The aftermath of the devastation had exhausted him, and he needed the break. The drive through Tuscany was one of the most beautiful in the world, much of the land still untouched by the ravages and devastations of the world's most recent natural and human disasters.

The students and teachers had all boarded a flight back to India the day before, and the cathedral seemed quiet without them, especially without young Casimir. Arnaud had taken quite a liking to the young boy and hoped he would have the pleasure of seeing him someday as a young man, surely making a great impact on the world in some way. He hoped the flight would not encounter difficulty passing over the flooded regions of the Middle East. He had asked Casimir to call if he ran into any trouble and looked forward to inviting the boy back to Marseille perhaps for a visit during the summer months, for an internship of sorts. In the meantime, they had vowed to keep in touch on LifeStream, the latter twenty-first-century version of Facebook, which allowed for an almost moment-by-moment portrait, a 'life-logging,' if you will, of a participant's life in virtual, including hologram messaging, integrated blogging forums, and a holistic life history of every user. Although Arnaud didn't like to admit it, the boy had somehow had an effect on him, and he found himself wanting to play for the first time since the accident, found himself opening up to a spirituality he had long presumed dead within him. And now, in the midst of the vineyards and rolling hills, Arnaud breathed in the fragrant air and welcomed a new sense of peace.

MOSCOW, RUSSIA

Ethics over Power. The cyber leaflets covered the lighted kiosks and digital screens all over Moscow, and Oksanna knew the Underground Greens had to have disbursed them in the night, overriding the city's marketing systems in what once would have been called hacking but today was merely operative free speech. Cyber was cipher, and anyone with a competitive edge knew how to infiltrate the most simplistic advertising systems.

Oksanna paused and leaned down to rub her leg. The odd-shaped birthmark on the inside of her lower right calf had been swollen for days, taking on an almost bluish tone, and Oksanna hoped it wasn't somehow infected. She absentmindedly made a mental note to see a dermatologist. She had had the spiral-like mark all her life, and it hadn't given her any trouble, but lately it had begun to emerge and puff out like a brand, as though the result of some isolated allergic reaction. She straightened and stared at the billboard screen flashing in front of her in the city square. It seemed to be getting brighter. She stared harder. No, it was the sky that was getting darker, an almost unnatural darkness for midmorning. Was it supposed to rain? Oksanna didn't think so. People were stopping now in the middle of the square and looking up toward the sky, which was fast turning from grey to pitch black. Some began running toward their cars and speeding out of the city; others just stared as though transfixed to the spot. Still others took shelter in nearby buildings and storefronts, reaching for umbrellas, not quite knowing what to expect from the still-darkening and clouding sky.

Oksanna herself moved to a nearby building, standing just inside the brick-and-glass enclosure and wondering how long the storm would last before it would pass. In what seemed like a split second, a large flash of light streaked across the sky, followed by thunder louder than anything Oksanna had ever heard. From her shelter she could see huge bands of lightning emerging from the now thick black mass of clouds, emitting almost deafening explosions as the lightning touched down across the city and landscape, starting fires. Sirens began screaming through the air as the rumbling increased to an ear-splitting pounding and nature seemed to take on the explosive energy of TNT.

The bizarre electrical storm must have lasted fifteen or twenty minutes, although it seemed much longer, and Oksanna's ears were still ringing from the explosions. If she hadn't seen it with her own eyes, she would have been certain it was a nuclear attack. She wasn't sure what kind of radiation would affect any of them from the solar energy still heavy and alive in the air.

In the sky now were what appeared to be celestial lights, a kind of aurora borealis that glowed like a neon fractal, shimmering in colored waves across the Russian atmosphere. Oksanna wondered how widespread the storm and the lights really were. Was it an isolated phenomenon? Or had it affected the entirety of northern Europe? She touched her Pearl but found it was dead. The ever luminous signal would not turn on. She reached for the touch screen in the foyer where she stood. Nothing. In the square, no lights were on and no traffic signals were operable. The city's entire power structure seemed to have been wiped out.

Within twenty minutes, Moscow had regressed from the twenty-first century to the Stone Age.

CAIRO, EGYPT

The skies were blackening all over Cairo, and Youhanna Lachier could feel the trembling as the second earthquake within weeks began shaking the foundations of the Middle East. Since the mass flooding of every country surrounding the Mediterranean, Cairo appeared to be a ghost town, an echo of its former life as a buzzing and vital metropolis. Lachier had fled to the south, setting up a makeshift lab on the outskirts of the desert as he awaited word from the president to continue work in the nation's underground headquarters, where his new fully equipped lab was being hastily constructed. *Now* more than ever, Egypt would need to complete the Moonbeamer. The project would have to be his first and foremost concern.

After assessing the situation in the south, he had to return north to retrieve whatever equipment was still salvageable and to collect the test results of the country's surviving marine scientists, who were now reporting a kind of Black Death in the dark floodwaters of the Mediterranean Sea. Somehow within the earth's tectonic shift, the sea had changed—and all life within it seemed to be swallowed up or rendered stagnant, sucked lifeless in a single sweep. And now, despite every concentrated test and inquiry, no marine life could be found. It was as though the sea had reconstituted itself into a fetid but still-rolling death swamp. Egypt's primary food source had vanished as though a vacuum or vortex had simply whisked it away, replacing it with a soup of metallic mud and silt.

New Haven, Connecticut

The city of New Haven lay quiet and desolate, strips of yellow caution tape flapping in the wind. Suited figures wearing army-grade gas masks pounded heavy poles with warning lights into the ground around the farthest peripheries of the city, preventing access and hoping to keep in whatever bacteria had swept through the city. Not since the Black Plague had anyone seen a bacterium this virulent. There was no time to develop a cure, no antibiotic that would take effect before the bodily disintegration had already begun, literally dissolving and eating away the victim's flesh from the inside out. Within the day, the disease had spread across the Yale campus and throughout the region, causing widespread panic. Those living within fifty miles of the outskirts were asked to evacuate in an attempt to contain the plague.

BEIJING, CHINA

Capitol Building

President Abdul Gulzar stood with Malik Asvaka close by his side in the central hall of the Capitol Building in Beijing as the new president of Afghani-China prepared to give his opening speech to the crowd below. Malik's yellow-brown eyes gleamed, his teeth a sharp contrast to his dark golden beard and smooth brown skin. Former Chinese president Murong Gui stood solemnly by Malik's side, looking discouraged and disconsolate. The decision was hard, but not as hard as watching his entire country die a slow and agonizing death from a poison his own lead scientist had created. No one had heard from Niú Ye in weeks, and Gui assumed he had been killed by the Afghani government. Neither Gulzar nor Asvaka would offer any clue to Niú's whereabouts however and for the moment almost seemed to share in his concern about the missing scientist. But it was clear also that the disappearance of Niú Ye was a convenient issue as the Afghani government prepared to take over operation of the National Center for the Study of Genetics, placing Asvaka in Niü's former role of executive director and head scientist. Those who would work with Afghani-China could remain in their research labs. Those who chose not to had already left or were eliminated. As long as Gui cooperated, he would be given a place in the new system. For now, he felt he had no choice but to concede.

WASHINGTON, D.C.

National Lab

Niú Ye sat in front of the news screen along with Matthew Serafino in the government lab just outside Washington. He had long before decided he would work with Serafino, even if it meant swearing temporary loyalty to the US National Lab. And it no doubt wouldn't be the last time. He hated and feared Serafino to his utmost core, but he also knew Serafino was smart, cunning, and not one to be trifled with. If Serafino wanted the Angel Cake serum, he would get it, and if Niú played his cards right, he would be along for the ride, could perhaps, with Serafino's help, rid China of Afghani rule. Even if it meant an American China, Niú wanted Afghanistan out. And besides, Niú trusted his own ability to think creatively under pressure. He was certain that, by the time Serafino got his hands on the serum, Niú would be able to figure out a way to gain Serafino's trust and recover control of his lab. And then, who knows what could be worked out? Niú nodded to himself imperceptibly, pressing his lips together, and prepared to get to work.

21

LATITUDE AND LONGITUDE: 21, 21

WASHINGTON, D.C.

"It couldn't have been latitude and longitude."

Matt Serafino ran his hands across the carved indentations in the Patmos box and scowled. He stared again at the Gospel that bore his name.

> *Jesus replied, "I tell you the truth, if you have faith and do not doubt, not only can you do what was done to the fig tree, but also you can say to this mountain, 'Go, throw yourself into the sea,' and it will be done."*

Bringing his fists down on the wooden table in frustration, he slammed the ancient box shut, and with his right hand swept it off the table. It flew through the air, smashing into the rocklike wall of the underground room and landing hard on the dirt floor. He glared at it angrily. The impact had broken one of the box's hinges, and now it lay on its side, its lid hanging precariously.

His temper abating, Serafino knelt down to pick up the mangled box. As he did, his fingers felt a set of ridges under the inner hinge.

How appropriate, he thought. *Where better to place a message than in the very place where lid and box come together. The point of unity.*

He reached for a flashlight and illuminated the scratchings on the inner ledge:

God's Sanctuary
5500

"God's Sanctuary" was obviously Jerusalem. Every prophecy pointed to Jerusalem as the site of the Apocalypse. Excited now, Serafino leafed through the pages of the Codex Gigas until he came to the passage he knew would verify his find, Ezekiel 42:15–20.

The passage clearly stated that the temple's land would stretch 5,500 feet in each direction in order to separate the holy temple from the rest of the world. But how did the numbers 21, 21 correspond to the Jerusalem temple?

Serafino began to play with the numbers. He accessed his Pearl and issued a command for combinations. In a few minutes a surprising variation emerged as the numbers arranged themselves in mirror images, four sets of numbers, back to back.

"Ah, yes." Serafino smiled. The birth of the eight: 21, 12, 12, 21. 21 December 2012, at 9:00 p.m., or 2100 hours—the date of the opening of the seals, and the inauguration of the Time of Becoming. It only makes sense, then, that the next date should be the date times four. And that would be 21 December at 2100 hours in the year 2048.

Six more months. Matt Serafino closed his book and set his jaw. He had work to do.

TUSCANY, ITALY

Village of Siena

As Paul and Angela approached the gates of the villa, they saw Pietro Engiolo waiting for them.

"Dr. Engiolo."

Paul reached out to shake the gentleman's hand, but the elderly professor quickly smiled and embraced both Paul and Angela in his wide arms, laughing and guiding them past the courtyards and through the large rounded doorway of the household. They walked across a large foyer beset with bas-relief tiles and elaborate frescoes that spiraled up into a domed cathedral ceiling, painted with Baroque-style cherubs and seraphim. Glancing at each other in amazement, they followed their host to the rear of the villa through a greenhouse and out onto a large balconied patio, which was lined with large pots of flora and ceramic fountains. The balcony looked out onto a wide estate with vineyards as far as the eye could see. To the right of the estate, they could make out the historic outlines of Siena, the cathedral rising out of its midst, much like the medieval paintings of the site that Angela had seen in the British Museum.

Paul and Angela were so fascinated by their surroundings, they barely noticed that Engiolo had begun speaking.

"You probably wonder why I've brought you both here."

Engiolo walked over to an enclosed case sitting on a nearby patio table. He reached in and extracted what seemed to be an old piece of parchment. It was enclosed in a kind of plastic preservative and appeared to be an original of some kind of manuscript document. Angela was immediately both impressed and intrigued as her interest in the composition of the manuscript superseded her curiosity over whatever meaning lay within it. But Engiolo continued.

"This is an original poem by our patron saint, Catherine of Siena, one of the sisters in a long line of messengers who vowed to make sure the clues to the last times would be passed on and brought to you, Paul, at the appropriate time. I realize both of you are only beginning to recognize your role in what will become a major turning point in the future of the world as you know it."

Angela and Paul exchanged glances.

Dr. Engiolo turned to Paul. "Dr. Binder, the Society of Messengers has been avidly waiting for you. You have been selected from before the time of your birth by the Lamb of God to determine the Way of the Seal—to locate and lead those together who might choose to bring hope and a new dawn for the earth—for all creation, and for those who will choose to embrace Truth and to welcome the resurrection hope of Jesus the Christ. The earth as you know it is fast fading away, as I'm sure you've been noticing by now. But God always opens new possibilities for life, even in the midst of the darkest hours of humanity. The Way is being revealed to you, but your path is one you must discover for yourself. We help where and when we can. You'd have no doubt found your way to this place if I hadn't invited you. But time is of the essence. And you are going to need this."

Engiolo reached out and handed Paul the manuscript. It appeared to be a rather simple text, but below the poem's title was a set of what looked to be unrelated Hebrew letters. The poem was titled "The Sanctuary." Paul read it out loud.

The Sanctuary

וְשָׁב

It could be said that God's foot is so vast
that this entire earth is but a field on His toe,
and all the forests in this world
came from the same root of just
a single hair of His.
What then is not a sanctuary?
Where can I not kneel
and pray at a shrine
made holy by His
presence?

"Have you brought with you the poem I sent to you in your invitation?"

Engiolo was looking at Paul intently now as the latter speechlessly reached into his leather binder and drew out the poem.

Everything comes from love,
all is ordained for the salvation of man,
God does nothing without this goal in mind.
2, 1, 19, 8, 1, 14
                              —Saint Catherine of Siena

"Do you know Hebrew, Mr. Binder, Ms. Krall?"

"I studied it long ago as a historian of the Hebrew and Christian traditions," Paul answered. "It certainly doesn't make me an expert, but I would say the letters are *N, S,* and *B.*"

Angela was getting excited now. "They would be *N, S,* and *B* if you read it as you read English, but—"

"Ah yes, of course," Paul chimed in. "Hebrew is read from right to left. So the letters are actually *B, S, N.* And the geresh above the *s* would make it a *sh* sound instead of an *s.*"

"Yes," Angela added. "And in Hebrew, only the consonants are written. The vowels would be inserted into the pronunciation of the word. *B sh n* . . . Bashan."

"Bashan," Paul echoed. "Bashan."

Paul leafed through his folder, pulling out the notes from Psalm 68. "The hills of Bashan."

Paul grabbed the second poem. "Here they are—2, 1, 19, 8, 1, 14—just as in the acrostic we found in Psalm 151, the numbers adapt to letters of the alphabet. Bashan."

Angela and Paul both looked at their host. Paul spoke first.

"The psalm in the Patmos box told us to 'Find the Hidden hills.' Find the hills of Bashan."

"Indeed," said Engiolo. "And now, if you'll excuse me. I will leave the two of you for a while. Dinner will be served in the dining room at seven o'clock. In the morning, my driver will meet you in front of the villa to transport you to St. Catherine's Cathedral, where you will be my guests for the day."

With that Engiolo bowed slightly and retreated into the hallway, walking back in the direction they had come from.

Angela looked at Paul.

"I don't know, Angela." Paul laughed uncomfortably. "I just don't know."

Evening dinner at the villa had been lovely if not unusual. Their host had invited an unexpected guest, a Syrian Orthodox priest named Arnaud Jerome Chevalier, and the conversation was filled with discussions on almost every imaginable topic—music, history, French and Italian culture, and art. Pietro's chef had made a unique version of antipasto, along with minestrone and a local dish of wild boar in a sauce of tomatoes, olives, and rosemary. He brought out an endless array of Morellino Tuscan wines, and for dessert, the four dined on crostata di ricotta, a traditional Tuscan cheesecake, served with rich Italian coffee. By the end of the meal, both Angela and Paul had become comfortable with Arnaud, as well as relaxed from the food and wine, and the conversation turned to a discussion of Arnaud's theology of the divine transcendentals.

"What is beautiful is true, what is true is based in goodness, and all of these are unified in love. All of these attributes can be found together in the divine."

"Wait a minute." Paul left the room for a moment and returned with his leather satchel. He pulled out the notes he had made from the passages in the book of Psalms.

> *Lord, who may dwell in your sanctuary?*
> *Who may live on your holy hill?*
> *He whose walk is blameless,*
> *and who does what is righteous,*
> *who speaks the truth from his heart. (Psalm 15:1–2)*

> *Who may ascend the hill of the Lord?*
> *Who may stand in his holy place? (Psalm 24:3)*

> *How good and pleasant it is*
> *when brothers live together in unity! (Psalm 133:1)*

"'Who shall dwell in thy holy hill? Who may ascend the hill of the Lord? The righteous or good, the true, and the beautiful—all in unity!'" Paul quoted from the notes.

"You study the Psalms?" Arnaud nodded at Paul, pleased he had found another believer.

Paul smiled wanly. "Not exactly."

CHENNAI, INDIA

Bay of Bengal

The Marine Biology Center on the outskirts of Chennai was buzzing with energy as scientists pondered the daily spread of dead sea life lining the shores of the Bay of Bengal.

Citizens were warned to avoid eating any fish recently caught in the bay—formerly one of the richest, largest, and most diverse marine ecosystems in the world. And the area's many reservoirs were being tested daily to determine the safety of the rain deposits, as the waters of the bay began to visibly darken. It was nearing the time of the Bay of Bengal monsoon, when the East Indian current progressed in its yearly circular motion. Now fishermen were reporting no catches at all or only nets full of the dead and rotting corpses of sea mammals, fish, and crustaceans. Entire coral reefs seemed to blacken and die almost from the inside out as the Indian Ocean was overtaken with what appeared to be a spreading blackness.

When the tsunami hit, that night of the new moon in June, no one had anticipated the waves of darkness that would cover the city and wash it into the Indian Sea. The Ganges had been rising steadily for weeks, and scientists had been watching the pressurized area between the Indian and Burma tectonic plates, worried about volcanic eruptions in the area of Myanmar and the Sunda Arc. But on the night of 21 June, a massive submarine earthquake would jam the two plates together in a head-on collision, sending killer waves toward the shores of India, Burma, and Southeast Asia, and causing miles and miles of land to crumble and sink into an angry sea.

MARSEILLE, PROVENCE-ALPES-CÔTE D'AZUR, FRANCE

St. Seraphim Orthodox Cathedral

Casimir Marceli huddled in Arnaud's chair in the office in the dark Marseille cathedral. As the others had left to board the plane back to India, he had hid in the sacristy, not yet ready to return to the rigors of the Institute for Technology, Science, and the Arts. Surprisingly, no one had seemed to notice that he wasn't among the other boys, shouting and singing in the back of the bus. Now he shivered uncontrollably as he stared at the news screen from Arnaud's office. He had tried with his Pearl several times to reach his parents, but the calls wouldn't go through. There was no connection, only a deafening silence. Casimir watched the screen in horror as the entire city of Chennai appeared to dissolve and disappear into the Indian Ocean.

Seraphim seemed to sense the boy's terror and hopped nervously back and forth across his cage, occasionally shouting out in squawks and sputters. At last, toward midnight, as Casimir fell into an exhausted sleep, still huddled in the chair, the bird began to sing:

> *You shall cross the barren desert,*
> *but you shall not die of thirst.*
> *You shall wander far in safety,*
> *though you do not know the way.*
> *You shall speak your words in foreign lands,*
> *all will understand,*
> *you shall see the face of God and live.*
> *Be not afraid,*
> *I go before you always.*

22

SILVER MOON

TUSCANY, ITALY

Village of Siena

The moon rose high over the vineyards, and Paul turned restlessly in the crisp white linens of the feather-lined duvet amid mounds of pillows in the large antique bed. Their host had put them up for the nights they would be in Italy at the villa, showing each of them to upper-level rooms filled with Italian art and painted frescoes. Paintings of winged seraphim and cherubim guarding the ark of the covenant and the Holy Grail led upward into the domed circular hallway that surrounded the entryway to the guest rooms. Each room had large double doors that led to narrow ornate patios, with elaborately styled iron grating and spectacular views of the surrounding Italian countryside.

In his dream that night, Paul followed a path that led through the vineyards and down into a small grotto. A freshwater spring flowed over the white stones that lined the edges of the water. White water lilies gleamed translucent in the silvery light as the moon cast a shimmering glow across the stones. The path led into a small cave, lined with wildflowers and adorned with a wooden plaque that read, "God is my Sanctuary." Somewhere in his dream, Paul could hear footsteps across the stones. He turned, and the woman in white, the same woman he had seen in his dream after visiting the winery, stood smiling in front of him. Paul watched, transfixed, as she reached out and handed him the chalice that she held in her right hand. The golden metal was studded with sapphires that seemed to cast a faint blue sheen around it like a halo of divine light. The cup was filled with a deep, red wine, and as she spoke, Paul could hear the words that came from her mouth, even though her lips barely moved. Her words sounded far away, as though echoing from somewhere underneath the waters of the spring: "The Blood of Life, the divine Mystery."

He lifted the chalice to his mouth and could taste the metallic traces of the cup on his lips. The liquid surged into his mouth and down his throat like fire. Startled, he looked up, but the woman was gone. He could hear now the sound of horses, galloping from somewhere nearby. The sound grew louder and louder as they approached, whinnying and snorting, until one of them, a large, pale horse, rounded the corner and stopped in front of him. The horse bowed its head slightly, as if beckoning Paul to mount its gleaming back. Paul laid down the chalice and pulled himself up onto the horse. Without hesitation, the horse began to run. Paul could feel the wind and dew on his face as the countryside swept by in the glow of the moonlight. He looked back and could see the outlines of the villa far behind him as the horse continued to gallop through the vineyards to some unknown destination. Paul turned, laced his fingers deeply into the silvery mane of the horse's neck, and cast his eyes forward into the moonlit night.

Breakfast was served on the villa's main balcony. Paul came down still looking tired, his eyes slightly puffy in the morning light. Angela smiled.

"Wake up, Mr. Sandman. We've got only ten minutes before we leave for the tour of the cathedral."

Paul smiled, absentmindedly brushing his hand along the back of

Angela's chair as he took a seat and reached for one of the still warm and steaming biscuits in the center of the table. One of Engiolo's staff came out and poured hot, dark Italian coffee into Paul's cup, and he sipped eagerly, savoring the warm liquid. In a few moments, he looked like a different person as he began animatedly talking with Arnaud and Pietro about the history of St. Catherine's Cathedral and the eccentric nun herself.

"She was an unusual woman for her day, no doubt about that." Pietro smiled broadly, leaning back into his chair.

"Catherine, as you know, was a Dominican, and she loved her Tuscan wine dearly." Pietro paused to laugh to himself.

"She believed, as did the other Dominicans, that the imbibing of wine was a way of deeply partaking in the mystery of Christ. For all of them, truth lay in the mystery, the astonishment, the ecstasy and joy of God's Word, found experientially in the wine of the Eucharist—and they found all kinds of ways to enjoy that eucharistic experience."

Pietro laughed again good-naturedly. "The knowledge of God through the experiential in wine, in nature, and in other forms of medieval mysticism was a confirmation of the amazement of Christ, the awesome nature of God. Interestingly, the cathedral, completed around 1215, was built on the original site of a ninth-century church dedicated to the Roman goddess Minerva, the equivalent of Athena for the Greeks. Sometimes I think those ancient values of wisdom and music somehow rubbed off on the early Catholic mystics. But at any rate, our Catherine was, for a woman of her time, a strong figure, politically, religiously, and spiritually."

Pietro stood up then and motioned for his guests to follow him back through the villa to the front of the courtyard. "But come then, see for yourselves. I believe our driver is ready for us to embark on our tour."

The trip into Siena took fewer than ten minutes, and soon Angela, Paul, and Arnaud found themselves at the forefront of the huge Gothic facade. Angela gasped and pointed to Paul. Surrounding the front of the huge structure were elaborate statues of the four horse-men, each in the form of its representative animal, with the wings of seraphim, depicted almost exactly as the ones in the paintings from the British Museum.

Piegro Engiolo was nodding. "These were carved in the early 1200s by Giovanni Pisano, who did most all of the sculptures on the cathedral facade. The original cathedral was begun much earlier by Manuello di Ranieri and his son Parri, but Pisano is the artist for the facade. Oddly, he left Siena around 1296 and seemed to disappear. At that time, most all of the country's artists and sculptors belonged to an organization called the Cathedral Masons Guild, the Opera di Santa Maria. Often, several architects and sculptors would work together on a single structure. Same with Leon Battista Alberti, another of the great Dominican architectural geniuses. I think you'll find him espe-cially interesting."

Angela and Paul exchanged looks as they followed their host into the narthex of the cathedral.

"This narthex was excavated only in the early twenty-first cen-tury. It had been buried to make way for a new entryway, and many of the original frescoes had been covered for years in the underground rubble. We've only recently unearthed the remains of some of the choir benches, originally created by Ranieri."

Engiolo's voice seemed to trail off then, and Angela's gaze focused on a middle-aged Italian woman through the doorway in the inner sanctuary. The woman seemed to be cleaning the pews and was spending a great deal of time washing and polishing the dark wood. Noticing Angela, she smiled and nodded. Angela smiled back, then turned her attention again to Pietro, who was continuing to talk about the discovery of a misericord, a small, ornate bench, rescued from the former excavation site.

According to Pietro, the misericord, and poor Catherine's head, were preserved just up the hill in the Basilica of San Domenico. The rest of her body was for some reason kept in the Santa Maria Sopra Minerva in Rome. Angela thought it was an awkward way to spend eternity. But she just smiled and allowed Pietro to continue. Apparently, they would take a tour of the basilica later that day.

She glanced over at Paul, who seemed to be studying a photograph Engiolo had handed him of the San Domenico misericord. Subtly, she glided over to him to find out what he was looking at so intently.

"Angela." Paul startled briefly, whispering under his breath. "Take a look at this."

Angela took out the round magnifier she carried with her when she examined manuscripts and peered into the photograph. It appeared that carved into the underside of the misericord were the figures of four animals, the same four figures on the outside of the cathedral. Below the carvings seemed to be an inscription. But Angela couldn't make it out on the photograph.

Paul looked at Angela. "We need to get to the basilica."

MOSCOW, RUSSIA

Oksanna sat in the underground room, lit only by the faint cast of oil lamps and candles. Russia's power systems were still down, allowing no access to electrical systems, computerized technology, or even the most rudimentary of customary twenty-first-century comforts.

"What will you do to help the people of Russia and the world?"

One of the members of the Greens stepped forward and took a seat across from Oksanna, challenging her to join them. He continued.

"In the early twentieth century, a man named Alexander Bogdanov discovered that the world could be viewed as a system of relationships—interrelationships—a way of finding the underlying principles that would unify all social, biological, and physical sciences. At the time, it was a form of what some called natural philosophy, a theory of complexity formulated as a social theory fifty years before mathematics would introduce fractals and chaos theory. The premise was that people needed to recognize patterns and think holistically in order to contemplate the complexity of social behavior. Bogdanov called his theory *tectology*. In a sense, it was a call for ethics to outweigh power, to get rid of linear thinking in favor of systems thinking, the knowledge that the complexity of life could be understood only by contemplating the wholeness of its systems, not the forms of its parts. In science, it would mean studying the universe as a whole, getting rid of individual disciplines. In medicine, it would dispose of specialization, return to a way of healing that would see people holistically and interconnectively. As a social movement, it would solve problems based on the good of all people, not the power of a few."

A man from the rear of the room stepped forward now, his hand resting on the chair in front of Oksanna.

"The movement was suppressed under Lenin and Stalin. It was rediscovered only in the 1970s when Gorbachev came to power. What began as a rudimentary tectology developed then into creative forms of advanced systems thinking, what you know now as *synergetics*, cybernetics, the foundations of some of our best creative breakthroughs. But then, what should have resulted in a universal good began to be used, manipulated by big business, government, the scientific elite. The good news is that the twenty-first century took the ideas that fostered huge breakthroughs in communications and technology and used them to create systems like LifeStream that would eliminate controls, allow for a constant flow of intercommunication among people, all with equal access. However, as we also know, that same technology has also been used to manipulate our food supplies, create megacorporations, and foster the new interrelational sciences with the vast array of weaponry, caustic waste, and natural devastation we see today."

The woman began speaking again, more excited now. "Ms. Galina, the Underground Greens are about much more than just replacing our natural food supplies. We want to restore the efficacy, the ethics, if you will, of tectonics, as the theory was meant to be used. We want to use the systems available to communicate to the public what is truly happening now in 2048."

Oksanna smiled. "And what is truly happening now in 2048?"

"Why, the end of the world as we know it, Ms. Galina."

MARSEILLE, PROVENCE-ALPES-CÔTE D'AZUR, FRANCE

St. Seraphim Orthodox Cathedral

Casimir woke to the sounds of the news continuing to blare through the silence of Arnaud's office. He sat up and rubbed his eyes, glancing over at Seraphim. The cockatiel was still sleeping, his yellow plume fluttering softly in the air like the soft spores of a dandelion, his beak nestled securely in his side wing feathers. Exhausted but now hungry, Casimir rose to try to find something to eat from the large kitchen he knew was housed at the rear of the cathedral building. As he headed quietly for the doorway, so as not to disturb the sleeping bird, his attention was captured by a program on the French communications network. "Problems that are created by our current level of thinking cannot be solved by that same level of thinking," he heard a man say.

Albert Einstein, Casimir thought, smiling as the commentator continued talking about the life of the twentieth-century scientist and inventor. Einstein was one of Casimir's favorite scientists. He had learned about him at the institute as one of the forerunners of what was now known in physics to be M-theory, most recently called liminal theory, after the recent discoveries of Horace Milkins. But even in 2048, M-theory was still as much a mystery as its name suggested. The idea of parallel universes, alternative dimensions separated merely by groups of "branes," rippling like waves, creating occasional matrices of matter, was even now hard to get one's head around.

Some thought the entire universe was one great and intelligent thought, an organic infinite, a cosmic musical polyphony. Others, who were more mystical, equated it to a mind of God or a divine potential. Casimir was most interested in Milkins's theory of a universal origin, a causal mystery, a matrix of interwoven relationships with holes and passages intertwining with one another in an evolving complexity. While the eleventh dimension was said to be a unifying dimension for all other strings of reality, Milkins's twelfth extension was the ultimate origin of reality, the liminal zone, the matrix itself. Most fascinating was the matrical idea that shortcuts or tunnels could exist between parallel universes, other systems of time and place coordinates that could even look like our reality and exist beside it but have no one else within it. Or perhaps a past or future version of what we know as the present. There were infinite possibilities in Milkins's theory. And, like Einstein, Milkins also believed that in order to understand that true reality of life, we would need to develop a new mathematical language, a new way of seeing reality that was beyond our current systems thinking.

Casimir smiled again. *Why a mathematical language?*

BEIJING, CHINA
Capitol Building

Matthew Serafino rounded the corner of a back hallway in the central governmental wing of the Capitol Building in Beijing. He needed to find out where Asvaka had hidden the formula for the serum and how much of the stuff they had already made. As he made his way down the central hallway, he could hear voices coming from the president's office. He quietly approached the doorway, leaning in to try to discern if he could find a way to get closer to the inner office. He was getting nowhere this way. Perhaps better to take a look at the National Center for the Study of Genetics lab. He could return to the Capitol Building later during the night and take a look around then.

Just then, Serafino heard footsteps approaching from the main corridor. In an instant, his holotar dissolved into the blackness of the alcove.

Serafino stepped out of the avatar holomorph module back in the Oval Office. He would wait.

23

LIVING WATERS

TUSCANY, ITALY

Village of Siena

After Paul and Angela had left for the Basilica of San Domenico, Arnaud turned to Pietro, who was busying himself about the cathedral, preparing for the morning onslaught of tourists.

"Dr. Engiolo, at what time is the baptism that you asked me here to officiate? Is it today? I hadn't received a time from you."

Engiolo smiled. "Ah, the baptism, yes. When it is time, you will know."

Arnaud looked confused. "Do you want me to stay here, then, at the cathedral? Will the guests be arriving sometime today?"

Engiolo stopped and looked at Arnaud carefully. "Father Chevalier, I ask of you only one thing: awareness. Pay attention to our patron saint. Look deeply inside yourself. The keys to the future are in the kernels of the past. Your faith will guide you. I asked you here to perform a baptism. It may be the most important one you will ever officiate. I cannot tell you the hour or the day. Your faith will reveal that to you. God will lead you. Keep your eyes open, Padre, your ears tuned."

At that, Pietro Engiolo waved and disappeared into the recesses of the sanctuary, leaving Arnaud staring, a restless and odd feeling developing in the pit of his stomach.

Village of Siena, Tuscany, Italy
Basilica of San Domenica

As Angela and Paul climbed the hill leading to the Basilica of San Domenica, Angela looked back toward St. Catherine's Cathedral, its Gothic peaks towering above Siena. It was a feat of architectural beauty, to say the least.

"And a roosting place for pigeons," Paul quipped.

Sometimes Angela could swear he knew what she was thinking.

"Those aren't pigeons, Paul. They're white. They're doves."

"Pigeons are doves."

"Are they?" Angela looked as if she wanted to doubt him but didn't dare.

"Absolutely. Doves are white pigeons."

Angela looked back once more at the cathedral. "Well, whatever they are, the cathedral is home to thousands of them."

In a few minutes, they had reached the entryway to the basilica. Paul immediately pushed open the doors and headed for the place where Engiolo had told him he would find the misericord. It was a beautiful piece of carved wood, adorned with each of the four figures of the Apocalypse: the ox, the eagle, the lion, and the angel. Paul leaned down to read the inscription. It was etched into the wood in an elaborate, thin script, much like the one in the letter Paul had received in Virginia.

The Eagle soars with beauty on the wind
As the Lion roars the truth upon the earth.
The Ox drinks from the goodness of running
waters
And the Angel of fire and love will lead them
through.

The Chosen One will unify them all
And bring them into the land of new beginnings.
Love will prevail.

Underneath the script was a signature and a date.

Leon Battista Alberti, 1452

Paul looked again. "Didn't Engiolo say the misericord was carved for the Cathedral of St. Catherine by Manuello di Ranieri, the architect who built the original cathedral and the original choir benches?"

"I thought so." Angela stooped down to stare at the signature.

"Well, this can't be the misericord from St. Catherine's. It's signed by Alberti."

Paul pulled out his Pearl, touched the screen briefly, and called up information on Leon Battista Alberti.

"According to this," Paul read, "Leon Battista Alberti created a set of twin misericords, one of which had been lost. The other is located in the Santa Maria Novella in Florence."

"Apparently, this is the other one of the two." Angela bit her lip thoughtfully. "I wonder why this one wasn't mentioned. Surely it's common knowledge by now that it's here."

"I don't know." Paul leaned down again and copied the words of the inscription into his notes. He felt around the base and under-side of the bench to see if he had missed any other inscriptions that would give a clue to the bench's history. But he found no other markings.

"So, who is Leon Battista Alberti?" Angela was intrigued.

"Besides a talented sculptor who had a fascination with the four Evangelists and a penchant for creating misericords?" Paul's eyes sparkled playfully. "Well, let's take a look."

Paul accessed the visual device on his Pearl and displayed the text about Leon Battista Alberti on the wall of the basilica.

"According to this, Alberti was a very talented man and a Renaissance thinker."

Paul paused for a moment to read through the text, and then motioned to Angela.

"Look at this. It seems in addition to studying painting and architecture, our man was a Pythagorean, a cryptographer, a musician, a mathematician, an astronomer, and a poet. It says here that Alberti regarded mathematics as the common ground of all the arts and sciences, and he believed that the same numbers that corresponded to the music of the spheres would also correspond to art. For our friend Alberti, beauty was the harmony of all things. And beauty was labyrinthine, same as poetry."

"Well," Angela said with a laugh, "this poem is certainly labyrinthine."

Paul continued. "It says here also that Alberti wrote a manuscript, 'On Painting,' that based all development of art on four main colors: the red of fire, the blue of air, the green of water, and the grey of the earth. The four elements."

Angela was no longer paying attention to the screen but was staring at the poem, written into Paul's notes.

"The elements are all listed here, Paul. But not only that, so are the transcendental attributes that Father Chevalier was telling us about at dinner. Look at this."

Paul leaned down and read the poem again, then leafed through his notes to the chart of the four he had been compiling. The notes he had written matched the words of the poem. The eagle represented air, the ox—water, the lion—earth, and the angel—fire.

"So, in addition to the natural elements, Alberti is adding Arnaud's transcendentals. The four horsemen of the Apocalypse have not only physical traits, but internal characteristics. Could that mean they are more than just symbols? Could they be representative of human traits? Clues to identities of actual personalities or people?"

Paul was barely listening. He was already adding the list of transcendentals into his chart.

Air/Wind	John	Eagle	Sword	Red	War	Beauty
Water	Luke	Ox	Bow & Crown	White	Strife	Goodness
Earth	Mark	Lion	Balances	Black	Famine	Truth
Fire	Matthew	Angel	Scythe	Pale	Disease	Love

"What does it mean to you, Paul?"

Paul was shaking his head slowly. "I have no idea. Maybe nothing. But I know I want to see that second misericord in Florence."

TUSCANY, ITALY

Village of Siena

Paul sat on the villa's balcony, staring out over the hills and fields beyond the vineyard. Angela could see he was troubled. He had been collecting notes and gathering information for some time, both in his Pearl and in his leather binder. But until now, he had tried to gloss over the reality that for some reason, something extraordinary and unusual was happening specifically to him—something that went way beyond explanation and way beyond his ability to pass off the source of the messages as a manipulative scholar. Angela thought he looked defeated. The faculty Paul possessed to make everything easily explainable, rational, factual, or logical had betrayed him this time, and the circumstances of the past few months continued to confound him, provoke him, and now worry him.

As Angela hovered at the entrance to the patio, unsure of whether to disturb him or not, he suddenly turned, as though sensing her presence, and motioned for her to take a seat beside him at the edge of the balcony. Angela sat and waited, knowing Paul would speak when he was ready.

"Something is happening to me—and you with me," he added, "that defies everything I thought I believed in, Angela."

She nodded slowly.

"Do you remember, in Patmos, you asked me if I believed in love?"

Angela smiled. Paul took her hand.

"I do believe in love, Angela. And I suppose that you are right. If, as human beings, we can believe in what we feel inside, without proof, touch, or measurement, then why couldn't we believe that there is more to what exists than what we can see or hear or smell? The question for me is, is that 'something else' just something we experience inside ourselves, or is there something or someone else out there who interacts with our ability to sense, to intuit, or even somehow physically interacts with us and with the world as we know it?"

Paul paused with a silence that betrayed deep thought. "Physics tells us now that our view of reality may be much more limited than we care to think. There's so little we can actually know, be sure of. And what do we do with the rest of it? The parts we have no idea of, can't fathom, that don't make any sense no matter how we look at it? What do we do with all of that?"

Angela ventured a quiet answer. "Perhaps we don't do anything with it. Perhaps it's just there for us to grasp in whatever ways we can. And what we can't grasp, perhaps we just embrace as mystery. Something unexplainable but not necessarily untrue, undefinable but not necessarily unreal. Perhaps we just accept that some things in life may go way beyond what we are able to understand, but despite that, we may play a part in a reality much larger than ourselves. Perhaps our decisions, our lives, our choices are all important, contribute to something we have no idea even exists. We know that everything we do somehow impacts someone else, something else. Even science assures us that nothing exists in a vacuum. Everything is somehow interrelated, interconnected, interdependent. Why would it be so hard, then, to imagine that our circle of influence is much larger than we formerly imagined, or much more complex than we may be able to completely comprehend?"

"So we just accept that we cannot know most everything about everything. Where is the purpose in life to that? Why pursue anything?"

"Because perhaps that's where it only starts getting exciting. Maybe there's a thrill, a purpose"—Angela laughed—"or as our friend

Saint Catherine would say, an ecstasy to life that lies in pursuing what can be known only in part, in holy hypothesis, in what lies beyond the known."

"A part of what we know is our own broadening realization of what lies beyond our knowledge," Paul said.

Angela smiled. "And as Aldous Huxley once said, 'Science has explained nothing; the more we know, the more fantastic the world becomes and the profounder the surrounding darkness.'"

Paul squeezed Angela's hand and sighed. "I've been studying the history of faith all my life, Angela. And yet I've had no idea what it means to have it. Never wanted it. Never believed in it. And now . . ."

Angela looked at Paul. "Do you trust me, Paul?"

Paul looked up, surprised. "Trust you? Of course I trust you. I would trust you with my life."

"Then you do have faith. Perhaps the question is only what you grow to have faith in."

Paul looked up. "Angela, have you ever had the feeling that something you were about to do was really important and vital, even though you didn't know why you felt that way?"

"I think we all have."

Paul hesitated, and Angela could see he was struggling.

"If I accept, despite everything in me that wants to cling to something more rational, that something unusual, something extraordinary is happening to me, that in some way I have been . . . *chosen by God*—the Lamb of God in the prophecy—to do something, find something, discover something that is somehow important, even though I have no idea why or what it means, then my whole worldview, my whole understanding of life and meaning and purpose, will change, Angela."

Angela nodded. "I suppose it would."

"Arnaud's transcendentals: goodness, beauty, ethics, and love. Do you really think they have anything to do with everything else that's been happening? Do they have any connection to the psalms, the elements, the Apocalypse? And if so, is it yet another coincidence that Arnaud is here with us? And what about Engiolo? Who is that guy?"

Paul seemed to become frustrated again, and Angela smiled and reached for his arm.

"All I know is that if people in our world spent more time looking for love, goodness, truth, and beauty, or maybe even God, we probably wouldn't be worried about apocalyptic prophecies."

Angela laughed, trying to lighten the conversation. "And if God is really out there trying to give us a message, I hope those are the attributes that describe God best."

She looked over at Paul and her smile faded. His eyes had glazed over and tears had begun to form.

"Paul," she said quietly, hearing Arnaud enter the patio behind them. Noticing an intent conversation, the priest had moved toward one of the fountains and was sitting on the ledge, waiting for Paul and Angela to notice him. After a while he spoke, his words soft but clear in the evening air.

"For God so loved the world, he sent his only Son, Jesus—the Christ, the Messiah—who dwells with us and lives within us as the Holy Spirit, the Emmanuel, God with us, the Way, the Truth, the Life. And when we are in relationship with him, we are also good, true, loving, and beautiful in God's eyes."

Paul sat up suddenly. "The Lamb."

Arnaud nodded. "Yes, my son, the Lion of the Tribe of Judah is the Lamb of God, who takes away the sins of the world."

Paul turned now, got up, and went over to Arnaud, his face surprised and shining with some kind of revelation.

"Father Chevalier," he said, "It's time. Would you do me the honor of baptizing me?" Arnaud knew immediately that something important had happened, and he didn't want to interrupt the moment with too much conversation.

"Have you never been baptized, my friend?"

"I haven't. And I confess, I'm new to all of this. But I feel . . . I know . . . I have faith"—Paul paused for a moment to look at

Angela—"in God, and . . . the Lamb of God and . . . being baptized is something I need to do, that I must do."

"Then by all means you should," Arnaud replied solemnly. And dipping one hand into the fountain beside them, he turned to Paul and asked him to kneel. He asked Paul if he would allow Christ to live his resurrection life in him, and Paul nodded, his eyes glistening.

Arnaud continued. "Just as the fountain is always moving and still, so also may you find the stillness of Christ in the midst of the flow of life."

Then, pouring the water over Paul's head, Arnaud spoke the ancient Christian words, and a profound sense of release overwhelmed him.

"Paul Binder, I baptize you in the name of the Father, the Son, and the Holy Spirit."

"Amen."

24

THE ROSE AND THE DOVE

TUSCANY, ITALY

Village of Siena

The special news report came onto the large screen as the three guests were having breakfast in the rear sitting room of the villa. Reports of a rapid, flesh-eating streptococcyl bacterial virus in the United States, flooding in the Middle East, a modern version in Russia of the 1859 Carrington Event, and now a massive earthquake and tsunami in India, accompanied the other reports of flooding and storms that followed the political news indicating threats of civil war, genetic warfare, and the recent takeover of China by Afghanistan.

The guests looked exhausted just listening to reports of the onslaught of devastation, and Angela offered to change the station. But Arnaud stood, motioning her aside with a stricken look on his face. "Zero in, please, on India."

Angela motioned to the screen and chose a more detailed news report on the disaster in Chennai.

> Reports are now in that no survivors have been found in the surrounding regions of Chennai, India, and western Bengal, since

the massive tsunami that swept into the Bay of Bengal this week, essentially obliterating parts of India and Bengal, as well as areas of Southeast Asia and the Philippines. Scientists have identified the cause as a violent collision of two tectonic plates, causing an unprecedented amount of pressure from within the Indian Ocean. The resulting underwater quake caused a tsunami so powerful that it literally wiped out the entire region within moments of its impact. The once bustling city of Chennai now lies somewhere in the bottom of the Indian Ocean, and families and friends of those living in the region are gathering in candlelight vigils to commemorate the lost. Scientists confirm that prior to the tectonic shift, a change in marine environment had occurred, causing all known sea life to perish. No cause has yet been identified for the destruction of the ocean's biodiversity.

Arnaud's face had turned pure white. Angela stood up and guided him to a nearby chair. "Did you know someone in Chennai, Arnaud?"
Arnaud sighed. "I did."
The room became quiet, but Arnaud seemed to want to keep his thoughts to himself for the moment, and after a short bout of polite conversation, the others went about their way, leaving him to himself.
"If you need anything, Arnaud . . ."
Arnaud nodded and returned his head to his hands.

The horse races of the night before in the Piazza del Campo had been a relaxing sort of adventure after the long day touring the surrounding cathedrals. The medieval tradition had been part of Siena for as long as anyone could remember. Now, the excitement seemed to fade quickly as reactions to the morning news crept into everyone's demeanor. Especially that of Arnaud. He was still in the sitting room, motionlessly staring out the windows and absentmindedly folding and unfolding his hands, rubbing them on his legs, and then folding them and unfolding them again. His bags had been packed that morning and lay still in the front foyer, waiting for him to embark on his trip back to Marseille.

Paul and Angela had decided to stay in Italy a bit longer, taking a car into Florence to view the second misericord, which was housed at the Dominican basilica of Santa Maria Novella.

As Angela packed their things into the waiting car, she could hear Paul talking with Pietro Engiolo in the main hall. Engiolo had given Paul a gift, a copy of a twentieth-century Bible translation, both the Hebrew and Christian portions. A single bookmark stood out from its thin pages. Paul opened it and read the passage Engiolo had underlined:

> *Shepherd your people with your staff,*
> *the flock of your inheritance, . . .*
> *Let them feed in Bashan and Gilead . . .*
> *Nations . . . deprived of all their power . . .*
> *will lick dust like a snake.* (Micah 7:14–17)

He looked at Paul and nodded respectfully.

Paul hesitated. "May I ask you a question, Dr. Engiolo?"

"Of course, Paul." Engiolo waited.

"Why the messages, the clues, the passages? Why only that? If, as you say, you belong to some kind of Society of Messengers, why don't you all just tell me what's going on, what I need to do? Why all of this?" Paul motioned around him.

Pietro Engiolo reached out his hand and squeezed Paul's arm gently.

"The Society of Messengers is not the kind of society in which all of its members organize together or even subscribe to a certain philosophy or ideology. And yet we have existed since the dawn of time, as carriers, I suppose you could say, passing on information, knowledge, clues, if you will, that would allow you, Paul, at this time and in this place, to do what is necessary to give humanity a chance for survival, an opportunity to find and choose to restore what has been lost. Some of us are aware that we carry these messages. Others of us, brilliant philosophers, artists, sculptors, mathematicians, have no idea we carry the messages vital to your search. Many may never be aware at all that they play a role in the Society or that they belong to a select few who have in some way contributed to the Way of the Seal.

"Paul, God uses people in ways we can only faintly, if at all ever, understand. None of us, not even I, know any more than the few messages we've been chosen to relay. For purposes of safety, protection, preservation of the secrets of time that only upon the birth of the eight had been opened again by Way of the Seal, no one but God knows either the choices or the outcomes of your journey. And only you, the Chosen One, for reasons known only to God, have been designated to fit all the pieces together and to make a way that can offer new hope to our world. Look around you, Paul. The world as you know it is dying. Look for the truth not only in the notes you've been keeping, but look also into your heart, and pay attention to what you find there. Open your mind; follow your intuition. Use your head to construct what you need to know. But use your heart to trust what it tells you."

Engiolo extended his hand then. Paul took it, nodded, and then turned and joined Angela at the car.

"Ready to go?" She smiled at him.

Paul smiled back, and Angela thought he looked surer of himself than she had ever seen him.

"Let's go."

Engiolo went in then to Arnaud. "Father Chevalier."

He handed Arnaud another copy of a similar text in Hebrew and Greek. He, too, had a passage marked. Arnaud read:

There will be signs in the sun, the moon, and the stars. (Luke 21:25)

Arnaud smiled. "Be well, my friend."

Engiolo extended his hand again. Arnaud took it, rose, and he, too, went on his way.

SHORES OF THE WHITE SEA
Near the former Port of Arkhangel'sk, Russia

Oksanna stood at the edge of the inlet along the northern beach of Russia's White Sea. Once one of the most important ports in western Russia, the nearby port town of Arkhangel'sk looked almost like a ghost town now, since the sudden death of marine life from the northern waters. At first Oksanna had thought the change in marine biology was a result of the ice shift that had brought in the floodwaters from the East Siberian Sea to devastate the World Greenhouse Project in Siberia. Or perhaps a result of the strange solar storms that had left odd cosmic lights in the northern skies above Russia. But a similar occurrence had devastated the Indian Ocean, and their discovery had come before, not after, the tsunami that had obliterated half the landmass of the region, sinking it into the ocean's black depths. And more reports were coming in now from the Mediterranean, the Pacific, and the Sea of Japan. It seemed to be only a matter of time before the world's ocean life would be utterly extinct. *How did this happen?* No one had answers. Scientists were baffled and offered up theory after theory, each asserting his or her own as the reason for the sudden reversal of life.

Groups around the world had begun protesting now, certain that the blackening waters were due to some sort of global terrorism. Others presumed some kind of chemical spill or scientific genetics experiment gone awry, the guilty country not willing to admit its deadly and costly error. And now, too, despite years of silence from the vacant and moldering churches in almost every world country, new groups were beginning to form, proclaiming an Apocalypse, their eyes on every prophecy coined since the inception of written text. Oksanna had to laugh. Except for the remnants of the faithful, who had gone underground, meeting in houses and outdoors, the only real operating churches any longer were the huge domes and cathedrals, which mostly survived only as historic sites now. The few who attended actual services or visited the institutions' priests did so only in very small pockets—the superstitious ones, as others called them.

Yet now, so-called believers of every kind seemed to be appearing everywhere to proclaim the end of the world, boasting all kinds of esoteric or prophetic knowledge that had nothing to do with the underground faith of the ancient Christian founders, those claiming to follow Jesus the Nazarene, whom they called a Christ, a Messiah, one sent to save the world from itself. Oksanna shook her head in disgust. Even the Underground Greens had taken to expounding the apocalyptic nonsense. How could they expect her to take them seriously? And yet, the ideas of tectology, complexity theory, holistic emergent phenomenon, systems thinking, seeing the world as an integrated interweaving of events didn't seem wrong either. It was only because of connective systems like the Internet, LifeStream, and holoscience that she could even compare what was happening in Russia to what was happening in India or Egypt or Japan. Perhaps looking at everything happening worldwide would present a better picture of both the problem and the solution, although convincing big businesses, political governments, or the thriving MK BRIC countries to give up their territorialism in favor of holding world hands was not likely anytime soon. In a sense, Oksanna supposed, the world *was* apocalyptic. One big mass of complexity hurtling down in a suicide dive to a lifeless ocean of disconnected solutions.

The Mayans had been systems thinkers, too, hadn't they? Oksanna tried to recall her visit to the National Museum of Anthropology and History in Chapultepec Park in Mexico City. What had they called it? The Divine Plan. Oksanna decided she would look up her notes on the trip when she returned to Moscow. She turned to take one last look at the blackening waters of the White Sea. *Ethics over Power*, she thought. Whose ethics and whose power?

BEIJING, CHINA

The hail began falling at noon in Beijing. Big hail, the size of baseballs and basketballs, crashing hard into roofs, cars, roadways, smashing out streetlamps, blocking intersections. Some pedestrians ran screaming into buildings, others into alleyways and basement enclosures to avoid being hit, injured, or killed by the huge chunks of ice. The roads began to accumulate the scores of hard white balls, now blocking the exits and entryways to the city. Some crashed into shop windows; others piled in heaps on top of patios and fountains. Those with cameras took pictures. Most just watched dumbly in fascination, wondering if the sky was actually falling. Then, as quickly as it had come, the pelting stopped, leaving only a murky, whitish-gray haze that settled over the ravaged city, gradually forming a thick blanket of swirling fog. And through the fog, the sun loomed hot and bright. The bands of light created a luminous glow in the thickening greenhouselike atmosphere.

FLORENCE, ITALY
Basilica di Santa Maria Novella

As they entered the town's historic district, Paul and Angela immediately spotted the Basilica di Santa Maria Novella dominating the town center with its squared structure and domed windows and archways. The basilica was done all in black and white, the colors of the region, and sat in the central square. Angela was pointing to the top of the structure.

"Paul, look at that. It looks like some kind of solar emblem."

"It is. It's the symbol of the Dominicans. You'll find it somewhere in all the Dominican structures, but it's probably most evident here in the Basilica di Santa Maria Novella. It takes up the entire upper level and defines the nature of the basilica."

"And look, Paul, pigeons again. They take up the entire upper level, too." Angela smiled, teasing.

"Those aren't pigeons, Angela; they're doves," Paul replied teasing her back unmercifully.

As they stepped inside, Paul motioned Angela to the right of the sanctuary.

"The Filippo Strozzi Chapel, just right of the main altar, contains vaults covered with paintings of the Evangelists," Paul whispered.

Angela's eyes were still surveying the inside of the sanctuary, which was filled inch for inch with colorful murals and beautiful depictions of saints and other figures. Paul pulled her aside, pointing to the choir stalls.

"There's the misericord."

The bench looked nearly identical to the one at the basilica in Siena, but this one, Paul noticed, had below the carved figures of the four Evangelists in animal form, instead of a poem, the symbols of the four elements. Below the lion was a symbol that looked something like a double leaf, below the eagle was a symbol with flowing strips resembling wind or air, below the ox was a kind of double spiral to resemble water, and below the angel was a kind of triple-tongued fire.

Angela was looking at the figures closely now. "Isn't that interesting?"

"What's interesting?" Paul was perplexed by the way Angela was staring at the symbols.

"Well, look." Angela lifted the cuff of her pants to reveal an odd-shaped birthmark on the inner calf of her leg.

"I've always been annoyed with this ridiculous birthmark. But look at this. Doesn't it look almost like this fire emblem? It has the same kind of strange triple flare. In fact, it's uncanny how similar that looks. What an odd coincidence."

Paul leaned down to examine Angela's leg, then looked back at the symbol on the misericord. "Angela," he said. "That's it."

"What?" She looked, amused, at Paul's serious face.

As Angela was trying to comprehend what Paul was getting at, she glanced to her left, and her eye caught sight of a woman in the sanctuary.

"Paul, shhh. Someone's here."

Suppressing a smile, Angela came out from behind the area of the chapel and back into the main sanctuary. The woman nodded to her. Angela nodded back, and the woman resumed cleaning the pews, wiping them down and then polishing them with some kind of cloth. Angela squinted. *Is that the same woman from the Cathedral of St. Catherine?* But that was ridiculous. It couldn't be the same woman. The woman continued cleaning, looking up now and again and nodding at Angela. Angela looked around. There was no one else, except for her and Paul, in the sanctuary. Curious, she walked toward the woman. Immediately, the woman rose, smiled, leaned over, and kissed Angela on both cheeks. Then she reached down somewhere into one of the pews and brought out a dark yellow rose. She handed it to Angela, nodded again, and smiling, watched as Angela caught up with Paul at the rear of the pews and exited through the sanctuary doors.

"Did you know that woman?" Paul looked astonished.

"No, I've never met her before in my life."

Angela leaned down to breathe in the scent of the rose, which in the noonday sun cast a golden hue onto Angela's face.

As they left the square, one of the white doves rose from the roof, circled the basilica, and landed on the peak of the building, just above the solar emblem.

Part III

XANTHOSIS

We see the brightness of a new page where everything yet can happen.
—RAINER MARIA RILKE

To one who has faith, no explanation is necessary. To one without faith, no explanation is possible.
—THOMAS AQUINAS

The way to see by Faith is to shut the Eye of Reason.
—BENJAMIN FRANKLIN

We are symbols, and inhabit symbols.
—RALPH WALDO EMERSON

We often say how impressive power is. But I do not find it
impressive at all. The guns and the bombs, the rockets and the
warships, are all symbols of human failure. They are necessary
symbols that protect what we cherish.

—LYNDON B. JOHNSON

"Hello darkness, my old friend,
I've come to talk with you again,
Because a vision softly creeping,
Left its seeds while I was sleeping,
And the vision that was planted in my brain
Still remains
Within the sound of silence."

—"THE SOUND OF SILENCE"
PAUL SIMON AND ART GARFUNKEL

25

SOLAR LIGHTS

PORTLAND, OREGON

Jess Farmer stood on his lawn outside Portland and stared up into the sky. He could swear he was seeing aurora borealis. He scratched his head. Only a few isolated reports of seeing the aurora had ever been made as far south as Oregon. *But what else could it be?* The shimmering waves of colored light hovered across the sky like cosmic bands of silk, weaving in and out of the horizon. In the distance, Jess could see the sky light up in flashes, as though a lightning storm were approaching from a distance. He tapped into his Pearl and connected to his sister in South Dakota. She would love this.

She's not going to believe this, Jess thought.

Barely a minute later Jess had disconnected from the call and stood staring, his hand covering his mouth in perplexed amazement. The borealis was not an isolated incident. Janine was seeing it too— over South Dakota. Jess thought for a moment of anyone he knew living in the Northeast. His cousin. He started to communicate again with his Pearl, but this time, the signal was dead. Whatever was over the night skies had just sucked the energy out of the entire atmosphere.

HONOLULU, HAWAII

Waikiki Conservation Center Aquarium

Oksanna had flown to Hawaii as soon as she heard about the Waikiki Center. Apparently they had separated and internalized their aquatic systems the day before the waters of the Pacific had gone putrid, and they now had housed within their tanks the only known living sea life. Oksanna didn't know how long the marine life could live without replenishment from the ocean or whether the center had the resources to filter and duplicate the ecosystem continuously enough to keep the waters vital. And it couldn't be said what would happen if the mammals refused to mate in captivity. But for now, the small remnant swam busily in the huge facility, unaware that their natural habitat had virtually disappeared.

Oksanna had negotiated the job as director of Environmental Restoration, in the hope that she could drive and fund research that would reverse the loss of sea life and in the meantime find new, alternative sources of food for peoples around the globe, particularly in coastal areas. For her, it was a mission that funded life, not death, as the UEM, Underground Environmental Movement, seemed to be focused only on theory and a small kernel of apocalyptic impetus. Without government and private funding, Oksanna knew, they would not and could not do the kind of work that was required to bring change to Russia or anywhere else. All they could do was dream of an ideal systems theory and foster revolutionary anger with their online flyers proclaiming a choice of sustainable ethics or the end of the world. They would not be able to bring those ethics to practical application.

But if Oksanna could somehow be successful here, she would be able to spread those solutions not only to Russia, but to every country. In this mission, she found a new identity and a sense of integrity. Oksanna now knew that it didn't matter what country she worked in; she wanted to work for the citizens of planet Earth. And for the first time in her life, Oksanna had made that choice from her heart and not her head. This time, she was not merely carrying on the traditions of her family, the work that her parents had established, but Oksanna had chosen this mission because it was the right thing to do. The people of the world would need food and water, and Oksanna couldn't turn her back on any of them.

LOS ANGELES, CALIFORNIA

When the rumbling began, Georgiana was sure it was just another of California's usual quakes, a little shake here, a shattering of a glass or two there. Most people who lived here knew how to deal with the everyday "usual." But *that* day, the news report came in too late for anyone to prepare for anything worse. The anchor had just announced that a sudden shift in the Puente Hills thrust fault had seemed to trigger other faults in the area of Los Angeles, and that the city was in immediate danger of succumbing to one of the most destructive earthquakes in its history, when Georgiana's roof suddenly collapsed, and all the houses in the area seemed to dissolve into dust and to fall into a heaping mound of dirt and debris. By eleven that evening, the lower part of California had simply sunk into the sea, as continents across the globe continued to reposition and reshape themselves.

BEIJING, CHINA
National Center for the Study of Genetics
Department of Interrelational Sciences

Matt Serafino had reentered his holomorph module and within minutes found himself in the hallway of the National Center for the Study of Genetics in Beijing. He gained easy access via the holotar and searched every part of the lab's equipment that he could, even the vault. But there was no sign of the formula. None of the digidrives contained it. *Of course.* Matt guessed that at this time, none of the Afghanis would trust the former Chinese scientists with any of the most guarded secrets, even if they originally belonged to them. In order to keep their hold on the country, they needed to tighten their grip, and the ultimate choke hold lay in blackmail. He would need Niú to re-create the formula. He had established Niú in the government's best scientific lab under heavy surveillance. Niú could eat, he could sleep, and he could redevelop that formula. Serafino may not have the formula in hand, but he had something better—its inventor. And after the formula was complete, he would have Niú create something even more powerful than the Angel Cake serum. With this advantage, this new weapon, Matt Serafino would be the one to rule the earth. He would transfer that same power to the new earth the prophecy foretold. Then everyone would bow to him. All he needed to do was find the right gateway. But in order to make it all come to pass, he still needed to find the others, the four.

Matt understood there were others—the four horsemen of the Apocalypse were at this time no doubt spread somewhere across the globe, and he needed to find out how to locate them and bring them to him. Then all he needed was the right coordinates, the right incantations, the right positioning, and he would make it happen. Once his collaborators crossed the gateway, he didn't care anymore what they did or where they went, as long as they didn't impede his carrying out what he needed to do. He needed them. He would use them. And he would discard them at the right moment. But right now, he still had to find them. And Matt Serafino was about as certain of how to do that as he was of how to find the missing serum formula in the haystack of China.

MARSEILLE, PROVENCE-ALPES-CÔTE D'AZUR, FRANCE

St. Seraphim Orthodox Cathedral

Arnaud Chevalier arrived back at the cathedral in Marseille at approximately 5:00 p.m. Exhausted from the drive and his grief, all he wanted was to climb the spiral staircase to his observatory, sit in his large leather chair, and blanket himself in space. The stars were his comforter. The idea that somewhere out there other lands, other people, other worlds might exist had brought Arnaud a sense of companionship, especially after Giselle's death. Now he found himself seeking their solace again.

As he tugged his suitcase from the trunk and dragged it up the back entrance to the cathedral, he suddenly stopped. Seraphim was singing. The bird sang only when Arnaud was present. At times when he would be in the upper levels of the cathedral or in the sanctuary, the bird would stop, preferring instead to nap or wander about his cage, pulling at the wires or chewing on a seedcake. But when Arnaud worked in the office, the cockatiel would sing. Arnaud still couldn't fathom how the bird had learned so many songs or how he remembered all the words. But the bird amused him, and everyone who visited the cathedral seemed to be cheered by its ex cathedra utterances. The feathered genius got so much attention sometimes that Arnaud thought he would begin scheduling performances upon request. But now, from the darkened office, he distinctly heard Seraphim, singing as though from the depths of his small heart.

> *We shall reach the summer land,*
> *Some sweet day, by and by;*
> *We shall press the golden strand,*
> *Some sweet day, by and by;*

Arnaud paused. He hesitated to open the large front doors, wondering if he would disturb the bird. Seraphim was still singing. Arnaud put his ear to the door and listened.

> *At the crystal river's brink,*
> *Some sweet day, by and by;*
> *We shall find each broken link,*
> *Some sweet day, by and by;*
> *Then the star that, fading here,*
> *Left our hearts and homes so drear,*
> *We shall see more bright and clear,*
> *Some sweet day, by and by.*

Arnaud shook his head in amusement. Perhaps the bird had at last gotten lonely in Arnaud's absence and needed to keep himself company. He smiled and prepared to greet his little friend. As he thrust open the large wooden doors, pulling his suitcase in behind him, he looked up to see a short, thin figure standing in the doorway to his study. *Casimir!*

Arnaud dropped his luggage and in an instant had run to the boy, wrapping his arms around him in a giant bear hug. Casimir hugged back, clinging to Arnaud's arm. He tugged his sleeve.

"I hope you're not angry, Père Arnaud. I didn't get on the bus. I wanted to stay here with you, to study some more, to learn."

Arnaud laughed now, his grief tumbling out from the depths of his body so that he could barely breathe. "Casimir! I thought you were lost."

Casimir looked up at Arnaud then, his eyes welling. "But my parents are gone, Père. I didn't know what would happen. And I didn't go home. Chennai . . ."

Tears began to run down Casimir's face. Arnaud hugged the boy close again, then held his face in his hands and looked him in the eyes.

"I know, Casimir. I know what happened in Chennai. It will take some time. Don't be afraid of your tears. They are your heart's way of cleansing itself and making everything fresh again. And don't worry about a thing. My boy, you have a home here with me, as long as ever you want it."

Casimir smiled, and Arnaud thought the young boy breathed a sigh of relief (most of all that he had not gotten into trouble for hiding out in the cathedral). His grief having passed for now, Casimir almost skipped back into Arnaud's office, settling himself once again into Arnaud's large red chair, surrounded by a mountain range of books and papers.

Still laughing, tears running down his face, Arnaud kissed his crossed thumbs and said a prayer. Then he went into the sanctuary and began to play, the notes wafting through the cathedral. It was a song of passion. A song of beauty. A song of hope.

LONDON, ENGLAND

Centre for Manuscript and Print Studies

"The box just reappeared, sir."

The guard looked at the technician with raised eyebrows.

"I swear to you. I was in the lab, and when I came out, the box was back in its case."

The Patmos box, appearing slightly damaged, as its lid seemed unhinged on one end, was indeed back in its original glass case in the Centre for Manuscript and Print Studies, just as though it had never been gone. The guard had seen no one enter or exit the building. He had been in front of the door, his station for the last few weeks, all day long, and he knew no one had come in. Still, the technician looked as though he were telling the truth. And no one had tripped the alarm system that covered the area of the center's main study. The box had somehow simply reappeared. And whoever had returned it was no doubt long gone.

Angela got the call within minutes. Thrilled that the box had been returned, and she would not have to tell Anthony Kontos that it had ever been missing, she prepared to get herself organized after her trip and to come into the center by the afternoon.

She and Paul had arrived back in London late last evening, and she had fallen into an immediate and sound sleep. She thought she had dreamed, but she couldn't remember what about. But Angela had awakened missing home. No matter how long she had lived in England, home was still in Ireland. And, as she unpacked and went about her chores, she found herself thinking now about the fresh air and rolling hills of County Clare. As she dressed, her hand went instinctively to her neck, fingering the golden pendant that her mother had given her. It was a Celtic cross. For those in Ireland, especially Irish Catholics, the Celtic cross was a symbol of eternity, showing the endlessness of God's love and the unending mystery of Christ's resurrection—a symbol of hope. Even though Angela was not a practicing Catholic—even in Ireland, most of the churches had gone by the wayside, unheralded relics in a super New Selfer world—the roots of Angela's heritage still ran deep, and she held deep attachments to Ireland, to the earth, to her family's heritage, and to a kind of mystic view of the world that gave her the ability to see the grit of reality and to find hope in almost any situation. She hadn't been home in a long time. Perhaps it was time.

Angela smiled, locked the apartment door behind her, and walked briskly across the square toward the Centre for Manuscript and Print Studies.

When she arrived, she found Paul waiting in the center's study. After a brief greeting, she went immediately to the glass case and removed the Patmos box, almost hugging it to her body like a lost pet.

She examined the broken hinge, deciding it could be easily repaired. No other damage to the artifact seemed to be obvious, except for a scratch or two along the side of the box. As she moved the lid upward and downward, she noticed the faint scratchings in the wood under the inner hinge. She and Paul hadn't noticed them before, but now she showed them to Paul. They were embedded upward from the side of the box, where they had found the carved 21, 21.

God's Sanctuary
5500

"What do you suppose it means?" Angela stood behind Paul as he examined the box.

"Well, according to what we've learned in Tuscany and from St. Catherine, I'd say God's Sanctuary is somewhere in nature, definitely not where you'd expect."

Angela smiled to herself, thinking about her homeland. "Well, that makes sense to me. What about the numbers—5500?"

"I have no idea." Paul was already scribbling the number into his notes. "But I wonder if someone we know might be able to help us."

Angela looked at Paul curiously. "Who?"

"Our friend Engiolo."

Paul tapped into his Pearl and signaled to connect to Pietro Engiolo. The music on his Pearl played, but wherever Engiolo was, he was not picking up.

"We can try to reach him later." Paul was busy studying the box, looking for any other markings that they may have missed before the box's disappearance.

Angela looked thoughtful. "What about Arnaud?"

"Arnaud?" Paul looked up. "Well, it's worth a try."

MARSEILLE, PROVENCE-ALPES-CÔTE D'AZUR, FRANCE

St. Seraphim Orthodox Cathedral

The observatory was dark except for a faint blue light that escaped from underneath the doorway. Inside, Casimir sat huddled on the floor, the Sefir Yetzirah open in front of him. He appeared to be meditating.

Above in the night sky, ribbons of cosmic light began floating and swirling across the atmosphere, creating membrane-like rainbows that moved like silent sound waves through the darkness. Above Europe, the sky flashed intermittently as a solar storm prepared to unleash itself on the continent.

26

THE APPRENTICE

Goddard Space Flight Center (NASA)

"What is it, sir?"

The sky above Washington, D.C., glowed with an unnatural light, punctured by flashes that lit up the sky.

"It looks like some sort of electrical storm. And it looks like a big one."

"Well, I've never seen a storm like that."

The screen suddenly came to life, and senior scientist Roger Channey's face emerged on the media board.

"Sir, we have new information on the atmospheric disturbances."

"Go ahead, Channey."

"Sir, it appears we are dealing with some sort of solar disturbance, a solar storm."

"Solar storms are regular occurrences, Channey. What's going on with this one?"

"Yes, sir. They are. But normally, they are small eruptions that create the occasional sun spot or cause solar winds to flare through our atmosphere briefly. When they come in contact with our magnetic field, they usually sputter out. Normally, we find the most activity nearest to the north and south poles. It's the same solar winds that cause the aurora borealis over Alaska. But for some reason, which we don't fully understand yet, sir, we're finding this phenomena occurring over most of the northern hemisphere."

"The entire northern hemisphere?"

"Yes, sir; reports are coming in from across the United States and Europe. It's as though the entire north is one large aurora."

"What could cause something like this? Have any of the scientists come up with a hypothesis?"

"Hypotheses, yes, sir. But that's all we have."

"Tell me."

"Well, there are a few. On one hand, it could be just an anomaly. Something similar happened in 1938 in Europe just before World War II, and Greece frequently reports aurora sightings. They had some in 1870, 1938, 1940, 1950 . . . The sightings seem to correspond with some kind of intense solar activity, types of solar storms. The effects can last up to one to two years afterward."

"Would that account for what's happening here?"

"Well, we don't know, sir. It could be that high-velocity solar winds are picking up power or that some intense storm is occurring. The storm could have happened some time ago, and we are only now seeing the effects in the atmosphere. Essentially, the high-velocity gusts, filled with charged electro-particles, are colliding with our atmosphere at an intense rate right now. The movement of the aurora develops as our magnetic fields buckle under the gusts of solar winds. Sometimes you can even hear the crackling as the electricity hits the atmosphere. And it's very powerful. Often, the charge will knock out any electrical or magnetic systems for miles around the phenomenon. In fact, it's so powerful that if we were somehow able to harness that energy, we could power the entire world on one solar storm for years."

"So you're saying it's a temporary anomaly, caused by a time of increased solar activity?"

"Well, that's the one hypothesis, sir."

"What's the other?"

"Well, the other possibility, sir, is that the sun is becoming unstable, that this is a sign of something more about to happen."

"Something more like what, Channey?"

"We really don't know, sir. But . . ." He hesitated.

"Just spit it out, Channey."

"Sir, we could be seeing an explosion that may have already happened years ago. Or a massive change in the sun's energy or gravitational pull. It could be a weakness in our atmosphere, allowing more-powerful winds to connect with our earth's gases, or a sign that the sun is moving closer to the earth, becoming more powerful, more dangerous. Or it could mean we are about to experience increased radiation, holes in our protective atmospheric shield, problems we can only begin to imagine. It could even be a Carrington Event, like we had in 1859."

"Could this threaten any of the earth's life—plant, animal?"

"Sir, in the worst-case scenario, it could be the end of any life on earth."

The room fell silent.

Channey broke in. "But that's just a hypothesis, sir. And a worst-case scenario. We're not there yet."

"I understand, Channey. How soon will you have another update?"

"I'd say in about three hours, sir."

"Thank you, Channey."

"Yes, sir."

The director looked at those gathered in the conferencing room office, hesitated for a moment, and then began shuffling items on his desk. He looked up briefly at those still standing.

"Let's get back to work."

The office cleared.

NEW YORK, NEW YORK

New York University

"It's the Red Dawn."

The professor sat in Washington Square Park with his astronomy students around him, on a small, grassy bit of lawn outside NYU.

"That's what Galileo called it. The Red Dawn, the aurora borealis. There's a twentieth-century story, a myth, a prophecy, call it what you will, about the aurora from a place called Fatima. According to the vision of the time, strange lights would come into the sky before a great disaster. Some say the lights over Europe in the 1930s were a foretelling of World War II. And that the vision in Fatima had predicted it. Whatever it was, the borealis lit up Europe on January 25, 1938. Some say now that the borealis is back to signal a new catastrophe."

Some of the students giggled. Others sat back, amused by the stories. When the laughter abated, one of the girls in the group, a smile still on her face, raised her hand.

"So, what is it really, Professor?"

WICHITA, KANSAS

"What's that?"

Miriam Watson stopped washing dishes and stepped outside.

"I've never seen anything like that in my life." Her husband, Jake, was staring at the sky. "The Indians, the Iroquois, are calling it a sign of the spirits. They're saying it's a sign that something significant is going to happen. That the fire spirits are warning us."

"Oh my! What nonsense." Miriam laughed and stepped back into the house.

Jake pursed his lips together, gave the sky one last look, and began hauling feed into the slop pails for the pens. It was going to be a long morning, and it looked like a storm was brewing.

OUTSIDE CAIRO, EGYPT

Makeshift National Underground Lab

Youhanna Lachier welcomed Hassan Masih and showed him around the new, temporary National Lab. Disfigured from the explosion in the lab, Hassan had lost some of his prior naïveté and seemed now more serious, more mature, perhaps more resigned.

The Moonbeamer Project had taken precedence now. All resources were being diverted to funding the final research that would allow Egypt to build a domelike living structure on the moon's surface. With catastrophic world events compounding daily, Lachier sensed time was of the essence. He would need Hassan. The man may have been injured, but he was a good scientist, smart, able, and loyal to Lachier and the Egyptian government. And now that the floodwaters had ruined Lachier's chances of gaining access to the major power players in the Middle East, he would need his assistant all the more to mind the lab, while Lachier concentrated on other, more personal projects. He was still reeling from the funding and engineering it had taken to drain the marshlands. All that work, and then the results gone in a day. The tsunamis had washed over most of the world's largest oil fields, causing a huge mass of oil and sludge to cover a good portion of the landscape, making it virtually impossible to operate. The cleanup alone would take years. And now, not only had the marsh countries lost their freshwater supply, but even Egypt would have a hard time making enough clean water through the purification plants to provide for their own country, let alone anyone else's. Whatever was in the waters of the tsunamis was not the ocean water he was used to. It had somehow changed in composition and was now as worthless a life source as a drink of metallic mud. But he would let Hassan worry about working on those issues. In the meantime, Lachier needed to find other ways to gain power for Egypt—and prestige for himself as well.

President Mubarak had offered the underground lab as a temporary solution to the destruction of the NRIAA lab in Cairo. The lab had been almost completely demolished, and most of the equipment had been irreparably damaged. The country would need not only manpower but massive funding to rebuild Egypt's most important city. And that put the hold on any other project for the moment. Mubarak was in favor of asking the USA for help. Although USAmerica was in its own turmoil, it had a precedent of handing out funds to nations in catastrophe, and there was no reason to believe that President Serafino wouldn't assist Egypt. The two countries had gotten along for years, and Mubarak had recently attended one of Serafino's White House dinners.

Lachier wasn't so sure. He knew another side to Matthew Serafino, one that would terrorize terrorists. And Serafino had somehow figured out Lachier's role in the destruction of Novitia. Of course, Lachier *did* murder that NASA scientist, but he hadn't done half of what he intended to do, hadn't gotten hold of any of the blueprints he had wanted for the avatar technology he suspected Novitia was harboring. All he had been able to do was stop the United States from building the Nightstreamer. And Lachier thought most of the world would have thanked him for that. He laughed. But not Serafino, of course. Yet he and Serafino were in some ways a lot alike, weren't they?

Both Machiavellians; the end justifies the means.

Perhaps it was time to find a way to work together. Perhaps he and Serafino could join forces. He would ask for the president's assistance for Egypt, and then the president could assist him in getting what he wanted. Seemed fair. But no doubt Serafino would want something in return. Well, perhaps Egypt still had some clout. The way things were going, Serafino may want a guaranteed place in the Moondome. And if that didn't work? If Serafino wasn't interested? Well, then Lachier knew ways to provoke. The United States was already weakening. Most countries expected the start of a US civil war any day. Serafino would have enough on his hands with his country's own internal turmoil. He wouldn't be watching Egypt. If they couldn't tap the power grid in the Middle East, perhaps it was time for a United States of Egypt. Lachier smiled, spreading his arms wide in a satisfied stretch, then leaning back in his chair.

MARSEILLE, PROVENCE-ALPES-CÔTE D'AZUR, FRANCE

St. Seraphim Orthodox Cathedral

As Arnaud's fingers raced across the keyboard of the ebony grand piano, the strains of the *Mazeppa* echoing through the quiet sanctuary, he barely noticed Casimir, who had come in through the side entrance to listen. It wasn't until the boy spoke that Arnaud startled out of his concentration.

"Père Arnaud, what is that song you keep playing?"

Arnaud stopped playing. "It's by Franz Liszt, my boy. One of the Transcendental Études, No. 4, to be exact, the *Mazeppa*, known to be one of the most difficult pieces ever achieved by the composer. For some reason, it's haunted me lately, and I can't seem to get its rhythms out of my head."

"It's so beautiful." Casimir stood awed in the entryway.

"It's unusual, I'll give it that," said Arnaud. "The pounding left hand, the octaves, the rhythms. The difficulty of the piece is astounding. I am amazed myself that I can still play it."

Arnaud laughed, the sound bouncing off the cathedral walls.

"Liszt was a Pythagorean, you know." Arnaud paused to see if Casimir knew what he was talking about. The boy was still listening intently.

"He believed that the polyphony of sounds were transcendental in themselves, were the sounds of the divine. For Liszt, all harmonic relationships could only be expressed in transcendental qualities. Like Gottfried Leibniz more than a century before him, Liszt believed in the unity of one, the transcendental nature of matter, the divine order of all things. I call him a sound theologian."

Arnaud smiled again. Sometimes, he couldn't tell what the boy was thinking. Casimir Marceli seemed to take everything in like a large sponge, processing it quietly and then coming up at times with the most unique thoughts. He wondered what the boy was thinking about now.

The pause was broken by Casimir's unexpected next question. "Can I be your apprentice, Père?"

"My apprentice?"

"Yes," Casimir continued. "I want you to teach me. I have nowhere to go now. Can I really stay here like you said? Assist you? Perhaps learn to be a priest?"

Arnaud laughed heartily now. "There's no need to ask, my boy. Of course you can stay here. As far as I am concerned, this is your home now. Don't think any more about that. I am delighted to have you here. But a priest? I think you have much more to learn and discover before thinking about joining the priesthood, my son. What would make you ask that?"

"I want to learn, Père. About my Jewish heritage. And about Christianity. About truth. And life. About Christ too. The Kabbalah. I've been reading, studying. I've also been reading your notes, the books in your observatory, your scientific journals. I know something big is going to happen, Father Chevalier. And the Kabbalah foretells it, too. I wonder . . . I think . . . perhaps I can help. If I learn, I mean. Be your apprentice. I have no parents now, you know." He lowered his head, his lip quivering.

Chevalier looked thoughtful. "Indeed you could, Casimir. Indeed you could."

Casimir lifted his head, his eyes clearing.

"Can we begin, then?"

Arnaud nodded.

The two were about to leave the sanctuary to climb the rounded stairs to the observatory when the office panel signaled an incoming call. Arnaud had left his Pearl on the table in his study. He hurried in, his red robes flapping about, almost knocking into Seraphim's cage. The bird squawked in protest as Arnaud, with Casimir not far behind him, pulled up the call from the Pearl onto the far wall and greeted Angela Krall from the Centre for Manuscript and Print Studies.

"Miss Angela." Arnaud seemed pleased to hear from one of his new acquaintances so soon after their time together in Tuscany.

"Father Arnaud, pardon my interruption."

"No, not at all," Chevalier burst out loudly. "I'm so glad you've called."

"How are you?" Angela sounded concerned, despite the jovial tone of Arnaud's voice. Or perhaps she was a bit confused by his sudden change of mood. Arnaud realized she hadn't known about

Casimir, his presumed demise, nor his unexpected appearance at the cathedral last night.

"Ah, Ms. Angela, yes. I'm so sorry. I thought I had lost someone very dear to me, but I have since found out my worries were in vain. All is well, and I am delighted to hear your voice. How is Monsieur Paul?"

"He's fine, Father. Listen, we have a question for you. We tried to get hold of Pietro Engiolo, but we've been unable to reach him. I have no idea if you can be of help, but we thought we'd give you a try."

Angela relayed the information they had found on the Patmos box, *God's Sanctuary, 5500*, and asked the padre if he had any idea what the numbers could mean.

"According to Paul, God's Sanctuary seemed to be akin to the poem that Engiolo had given him by Saint Catherine. *God's sanctuary is everywhere.* But we have no idea why the numbers follow."

"What is the date of the box, my dear?"

"Well, it's from Patmos . . . presumably constructed by John of the Apocalypse, as he wrote the book of the Revelation."

Arnaud paused. *God's Sanctuary.*

Casimir, who had been listening quietly, suddenly spoke. "I know what the numbers mean, Père."

Arnaud turned to the boy. "You do?"

"Yes. It's Kabbalah, Father. The numbers correspond to Hebrew letters."

He was paging now through various texts and volumes he had assembled from Arnaud's library and mumbling softly to himself.

"In the gematra, the kabbalistic numerology, the various Hebrew letters correspond to numbers. When you add up the numbers, they indicate something deep and spiritual about the word, something in the divine and mathematical nature of the universe," Casimir explained.

On the other line, Angela had noticed Arnaud's distraction and cleared her throat quietly. Arnaud turned back to the screen.

"Angela, is there any kind of Hebrew word along with the inscription?"

"No, Father. Just the words *God's Sanctuary* and the number."

Angela was interrupted by the sound of talking in the background as Paul spoke.

"Father, as Paul has reminded me, there was a Hebrew word under the title of the sanctuary poem. When we were in Tuscany, we had thought it was the symbol for BSN, Bashan."

"How is it spelled?"

Angela typed out the Hebrew and sent it to Arnaud via her Pearl. Casimir glanced up, continuing to pore through his volumes on Hebrew gematra.

Casimir nodded. "5500—Bashan."

Arnaud turned back to the screen. "Angela, it's Bashan; 5500 is the kabbalistic number for Bashan."

27

THE POTTER'S WHEEL

Centre for Manuscript and Print Studies

Angela returned at noontime with lunch for herself and Paul, who was still in the library, hunched over his notes, sorting through all the documents from the Patmos box, the Diatessaron, and the trip to Siena. He looked up when Angela came in. As she leaned down to set the sandwiches and coffee on the tea table, Paul happened to notice her pendant.

"I don't think I've ever seen you wear that. May I see it?"

Angela removed the pendant and handed it to Paul, who turned it over in his fingers, admiring the artistry.

"It's a Celtic cross, isn't it?"

"Yes." Angela smiled. "A gift from my mother."

"You know, the Irish Catholics believed that the circle enfolding the cross was a symbol of eternity. But the folk will tell you otherwise. In fact, some believe it was taken as a Christian symbol from a solar emblem." Paul stopped short.

"Paul?" Angela could see the surprise in Paul's eyes. Something had caught his attention.

"Of course. The Dominicans. The Basilica di Santa Maria Novella. Saint Catherine, and of course, the diagrams."

He was flipping in his notes now to a portion of one of the psalms. "Listen to this. Remember Psalm 68?"

The hill of God is as the hill of Bashan; an high hill as the hill of Bashan.
Why leap ye, ye high hills? this is the hill which God desireth to dwell in; yea, the Lord will dwell in it for ever.
The chariots of God are twenty thousand, even thousands of angels: the Lord is among them, as in Sinai, in the holy place.

Angela listened. Then, confused, she tried to follow what Paul was telling her.

"Well, we've certainly had enough messages about Bashan to know how important it is. All we need now is to know why."

Paul was excited now. "No. Not Bashan. Look. We've been so engrossed with the other parts of the psalm, the transcendentals, Bashan, that we've ignored the last piece—the chariots."

"The chariots are important?"

"The chariots are all important." Paul continued to rummage through his notes. He brought out the two Dürer drawings.

"See these lines to the top left of the drawing of the four horsemen? It's the sun. Now look at this one." Paul put next to it the second Dürer, *The Adoration of the Lamb*. "Look at the Lamb. It's in the midst of the sun. All the figures are in the midst of celestial fire.

"Now look at this. It's called *Ezekiel's Vision*, by Matthäus Merian. Look at the sun—and the light, the burning, the transporting."

Angela was still not following. Paul pulled out the passages from Ezekiel:

> *And I looked, and, behold, a whirlwind came out of the north, a great cloud, and a fire infolding itself, and a brightness was about it, and out of the midst thereof as the color of amber, out of the midst of the fire.*

"Angela, from within the fire and the whirlwind, Ezekiel sees the four horsemen. They are united together, being transported. Listen."

> *Whithersoever the spirit was to go, they went . . . the fire was bright, and out of the fire went forth lightning . . . and the living creatures ran and returned as the appearance of a flash of lightning . . . Behold one wheel upon the earth . . .*

"It's the sun, Angela. The sun. Something is going to happen with the sun." He pointed again to the four creatures inhabiting the ball of fire in the woodcut. "And somehow, the four horsemen have to unite, so the people can be transported, saved from destruction. Look at what's been happening."

"But Paul, I still don't understand what that has to do with the chariot."

Paul rustled again in his notes and came up with the diagram from the Patmos box.

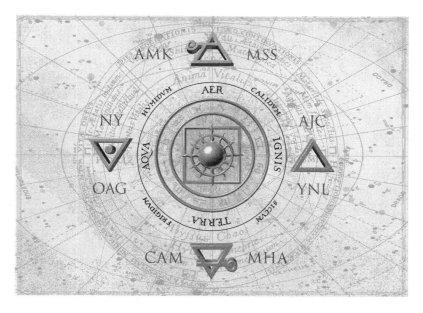

"Look at this diagram. The sun lies also in the center, with the four elements surrounding it. The figures of the four horsemen correspond to the four elements. Now look at the initials inside the inner circle. I couldn't figure out how they correspond. And in the innermost circle are the elements listed again."

Paul pulled out another diagram.

"Look at this one. This one is the same diagram, created by Gottfried Leibniz in the 1600s. What does it look like?"

Angela gasped. "A wheel."

Paul pounded his hand on the table. "Yes! A wheel. Now look at the circles, how everything is interconnected. Leibniz knew. He and Newton disagreed on the theology, but they both knew. And look at the initials by each element."

"They're the same as on the other diagram."

"Yes!" Paul was so excited, Angela thought he would alarm the rest of the technicians, and she cautioned him to be quieter. She had never seen him like this.

"Angela, they're initials."

"Initials," repeated Angela.

"It's the way we will know how to identify the four. They've given us their initials. And—they've told us exactly what will happen. We just need to figure out what it means. But Engiolo was right. Something is going to happen. And that something has to do with the sun. The earth will change. And somehow, the four must unite together in order to somehow save humanity from disaster. Twenty thousand chariots—as many as can be, will be saved. And whatever it is, it's going to happen in Bashan."

Angela tried to follow.

"So, the chariot is the wheel, and the wheel is both the diagram and the sun."

Paul continued. "And our relationships to one another, and to ourselves, and to God. That's why the transcendentals are so important. Leibniz saw that. He saw the interrelationships. He understood, long before the discovery of quantum physics, or chaos theory, or string theory, or M-theory, and now liminal theory—about the interconnectedness of life, the ultimate systems theory. Listen. The chariot in the Jewish faith was called the Merkabah. The fire of the Merkabah wasn't just physical. It was also personal, mystical. The Hebrew and Christian mystics believed that the symbol of fire represented the illumination of the soul that yearns for union with God. Ezekiel's vision was also an ecstatic experience, a revelation, similar to John's. It is an invitation by God or the divine to enter into union. The chariot, the Merkabah, was the vehicle through which to reach a transcendental reality that was beyond what we could know in fact or sensory experience. As you told me, it is intuitive knowledge. The passage can be interpreted both ways. Not only does it depict wind, but also God's Spirit, the vital force of life that Leibniz talked about, the Creator, the sustainer of everything."

Paul paused for a moment. "That's why the Dominicans loved the sun emblem. It represented for them the vital energy and life of God that sustains everything, and it represented the possibility of spiritual unity with God or Christ. For the Jewish and Christian mystics, the seeker was a traveler—therefore the Merkabah. For us, I think it has additional meanings. Something to do with all the solar eruptions we've been experiencing. It's a message about what's going to happen. And whatever it is, it's going to happen soon. And we need to find out when."

Angela waited a few moments to make sure Paul was finished. "So . . . all of that came from my Celtic cross?"

HONOLULU, HAWAII
Waikiki Conservation Center

Oksanna was tired from her first week of work at the Waikiki Conservation Center. It had been going well, and she was busy assembling a team of scientists and funders. But she had been working hard and hadn't had a chance to explore her new home or do anything even vaguely relaxing. As she exited the building, her eyes settled on the Honolulu Academy Museum. Outside the museum was a large placard announcing a special exhibit of Mayan culture and art. *Perfect*. Oksanna had wanted to refresh her memory on what she had seen and learned from her trip to the Mexican museum. Now she would have the ideal opportunity.

Oksanna paid for her ticket to the special exhibit and entered the first room, following and reading each placard, the first of which stated:

THE MAYANS WERE SYSTEMS THINKERS.
ALL OF THEIR SYSTEMS WERE CONCEIVED AS A WHEEL.

28

THE MISSING LINK

National Radio Astronomy Observatory (NRAO)

"Tom, could you take a look at this?"

Arnie King was looking through the space scope. "What's up?"

"Take a look at this. What is that?"

Tom Wade positioned himself in front of the scope's large screen and looked inside. "What the . . . I think that's a solar flare. But no flare like I've ever seen. Something's wrong."

He looked at Arnie. "Better call Majors."

By the time Tim Majors got to the observatory room, the flare had seemed to grow larger and now looked like a huge missile streaking through space toward earth.

"That's the largest solar flare I've ever seen." He continued staring through the scope, now turning it a bit toward the left. "And the sun. It looks three times its usual size. Have you seen this?"

He looked at the others. "Something's going on. Better get NASA on the phone. See if they're seeing what we're seeing."

"Got it." The two accessed the observatory in Greenbelt through their emergency interface panel.

GREENBELT, MARYLAND

Goddard Space Flight Center (NASA)

"Sir, we have another report in from Roger Channey."

"Put him on the screen."

The director stood in the main conferencing room, along with his staff. All eyes seemed transfixed to the screen that showed the huge flare headed for the earth's atmosphere.

"Channey reporting in, sir." Channey's face had appeared on the far wall of the conference room.

"Channey, what is out there? Is that a flare?"

"It is, sir. It appears that we do have some kind of anomaly here, characterized by significantly increased solar activity, which appears to be getting more potent by the day. And we just got word, one of our space satellites is down. The energy's been sucked out of it."

"Where is this going to touch down?"

"According to our current coordinates, it appears that the flare will strike here in the United States, somewhere in or around West Virginia, sir."

"How powerful is this thing? Is the earth's magnetic field going to handle this?"

"Well, that's the problem, sir. The probes have detected that the breach in the earth's magnetic field is getting larger. Back at the turn of the twenty-first century, it was large enough. Now, we can't promise that solar particles won't enter the earth's atmosphere. It all depends on where it comes down. This is a powerful flare. If this one or more of them start pelting us, something's going to get through."

"And the result?"

"Radiation, sir. Big-scale radiation. And it will probably knock out power systems for miles around, maybe more. I . . . advi . . . al . . . should . . . sshhhhhhhhhhhh . . ."

"Channey, you're breaking up. Are you there?"

A loud, low vibrating tone began to echo through the system, sounding like the moan of a theramin. Those in the conferencing room began to hold their ears as the sound increased and then trailed off again.

"What was that?"

The crackling seemed to clear for the moment, and Roger Channey came back on. "Sir?"

"We hear you, Channey. What happened? What was that noise? It sounded like half whale call and half scream."

Channey sounded astonished. "Sir, we believe here in the observatory that we've just heard our first solar vibration."

"Solar vibration?"

"Yes, sir. The sun gives off vibrations all the time, vibrations of the gases—a sort of solar sound waves. Normally, the frequency is so low they could never be heard by the human ear. But whatever is going on, the vibrations have apparently increased enough just now to create a sound audible to the human ear. Our radio waves picked it up. The sun appears to be going through some kind of solar disturbance, and we're just not sure right now what it is."

The sound system cracked again, and once more a low, mournful sound grated through the system, like the turning of a rusty wheel.

One of the scientists in the room spoke up.

"Wow, it is almost like a whale's song."

The system had come back, and Channey replied, "Yes, sir, but I'd say if it is, it's a whale in distress. Oh, and by the way, sir, NRAO just called. They see it coming, sir."

The director looked to one of the men standing near the doorway. "Martins, get the White House on the phone. We've got a national emergency."

HONOLULU, HAWAII
Honolulu Academy Museum

Oksanna moved about the Mayan display. The Mayans had been amazingly astute for the time in which they lived. Oksanna was looking at the Mayan calendar now, which was a round clay tablet with symbols and hieroglyphics that sectioned time into specific elemental cycles. For the Mayans, time was not linear, but cyclical. Each new time period represented a new level of development. She smiled as she noted her birthday, 21 December 2012. The Mayans had thought this date would usher in a new age, in which the world would not end but transform somehow. The process would culminate in 2048, the date on which a total planetary alignment would occur. The Mayans believed in a divine plan, and the final cycle represented spiritual change, a "new heaven and earth," something like the prophecy by John of Patmos, who wrote the Revelation. But for the Mayans, this stage represented a unity of all, an interrelatedness of everything, in which eventually good would win over power.

Oksanna smiled again. Good winning over power. That certainly didn't sound bad.

WASHINGTON, D.C.

National Lab

Matthew Serafino had just entered the National Lab to check on Niú Ye when the call came in from Egypt. President Menes Mubarak was requesting a meeting with the USAmerican president on behalf of his lead astronomer and right-hand adviser, Dr. Youhanna Lachier from the National Research Institute for Astronomy and Astrophysics in Cairo. Egypt was requesting funds to deal with the vast destruction caused by the flooding of its northern banks, and Lachier wanted to update the president on Egypt's vital space-dome project. Lachier would also have information on current solar activity, which the USAmerican president would definitely be interested in hearing. *Why not share information? We are, after all, allied countries,* Matt thought to himself.

Serafino smirked. Youhanna Lachier. *Well, well. At last, my friend, we meet.*

"I'd be glad to meet with him, Mr. President," Matt answered in response to the request.

The Egyptian president nodded and let Matt Serafino know to expect Dr. Lachier later in the day, provided the plane could get through with minimal difficulty. The call then transferred to Mullica to schedule the appointment, and Serafino turned back to Niú Ye.

"How are we coming, Ye?"

"I should have the formula reconstituted within approximately two weeks, Mr. President."

"Aw, Ye, call me Matt. You and I are going to become good allies. Good, strong allies."

"Yes, Mr. President—Matt." Ye bowed his head slightly in feigned respect and went back to his work re-creating the Angel Cake serum.

As Matthew Serafino turned to leave the lab, Niú nervously brushed by one of the lab tables, sending several digidrives to the floor of the lab.

"I'll get that." Niú Ye was already walking briskly toward the edge of the lab table and was bending down to pick up the drives.

Serafino stopped in mid-stride. "What's that? Niú? What's that on your leg?"

Niú, looking surprised, lifted his pant leg slightly to reveal a small birthmark just inside his right calf. The mark looked vaguely like two small swirls, like two half-moons spliced together haphazardly.

"It's nothing. It's just a birthmark. I've had it all my life."

Niú looked wary, unsure of what Serafino was getting at. The man made him extremely nervous, and he wished he would leave the lab.

Serafino stood up and looked Niú Ye square in the face, his dark eyes boring into him.

"We're going to be very good friends indeed."

Serafino thrust out his hand, grabbing Niú Ye's in a tight hand-shake, then turned and exited the lab, leaving a slightly trembling Ye standing in his wake.

As Matt Serafino came around the corner of the hallway, he stopped, lifted his own pant leg, and stared at the birthmark that had defined him since birth. The three small streaks looked almost like tongues of fire, especially whenever the mark became inflamed. *It must be. That has to be the missing piece.* Serafino laughed again. That's how he would identify the others. Of course. They would all bear the mark of their birth: *21 December 2012, at 9:00 p.m.*

Serafino strode back toward the lab, thrust open the door, and poked his head inside. Niú startled and nearly dropped the beaker he was holding.

"When is your birthday, Niú?"

"My birthday?"

"Yes. When is your birthday?"

"Uh, the 21st of December."

"Year?"

"2012." Niú was looking at him oddly.

"Time?"

Niú continued to stare. "Nine p.m., I think."

Serafino smiled, then laughed. "Thank you, Niú. Thank you!"

Serafino returned to the White House then, leaving Niú in a restless relief.

LONDON, ENGLAND

Centre for Manuscript and Print Studies

Paul sat in the center's library, still poring over his notes and materials. The evening news had been disturbing at best. A large solar flare was reportedly headed toward the earth's atmosphere and was set to touch down somewhere near West Virginia, Paul's birthplace and the place he still called home. But more disturbing were the increasing signs of impending disaster he saw as a pattern, leading to what he now knew would be something so significant, it was hard for him to even fathom. Again and again, he had thought of calling someone. But who? Who would believe anything he was talking about? And based on what? He wasn't a physicist, or an astronomer, or even a statistician. He was a historian, an academic. And what he had to say

sounded phenomenal, fantastic. He sounded like one of the dooms-
day prophets lined up along the aerodock hallways.

Finally, he tuned in to his Pearl and made the call. "Congressman
Braddock, please. West Virginia Commonwealth. United States."

Angela's Pearl, meanwhile, was connecting with Arnaud's.

"Father Arnaud, it's Angela again."

Arnaud had answered on the second ring, and even though it was
late in the evening, he sounded jovial as always.

"Do you remember when I asked you about the numbers, the 5500?"

"Yes, of course. God's Sanctuary, 5500, Bashan."

"Well, it just occurred to me, Father—perhaps you could help
with something else."

"Whatever I can do, I will certainly try my best to be of service."
Arnaud was glad for the distraction, as Seraphim had been singing all
evening, and although he loved the bird, his tiny voice was beginning
to get on his nerves.

"Well, Father. We have a box here. The one we told you about. And
the inscription we mentioned was carved into the hinge area of the box.
But also inside were carved two numbers, and we have not been able to
understand what they could mean."

"What are the numbers?"

"21, 21."

Arnaud was silent. His mind was swimming, and he was suddenly feeling an urgency to see Angela and Paul in person.

"Angela, could you and Paul meet me here tomorrow? It's only a
couple of hours by plane, and I really think we ought to talk."

"Of course, Father." She motioned to Paul, who nodded affirma-
tively. "We could be there tomorrow, most likely by dinnertime. And
if the planes are down, we'll take the train."

"Thank you, my dear. And Angela—tell Paul to bring his copies
of all the contents of the box, all of his notes. I have some notes of my
own, and it sounds like it's time we both shared them. I have a feeling
it was no accident that we met. And there's someone else here I think
you should meet as well."

Arnaud looked over at Casimir, curled up asleep on the leather chair in his office, and smiled.

And on and on, Seraphim sang:

> *Awake from your slumber! Arise from your sleep!*
> *A new day is dawning for all those who weep.*
> *The people in darkness have seen a great light.*
> *The Lord of our longing has conquered the night.*
> *Let us build the city of God.*
> *May our tears be turned into dancing!*

29

ROOTS AND SHOOTS

WEST VIRGINIA

The forest had begun burning in the night. Selby had seen the red glow from his window and had alerted his father. He could smell the burning of wood and leaves from his bedroom, even though the edges of the trees were miles and miles away. He climbed up on the edge of his bed and stared out of the window into the night. The sky looked strange. Selby couldn't see the stars. Just a giant mass of waving colored lights rippling through the sky. It looked like the waves that appeared sometimes in the air at high noon when the sun got so hot that it distorted his view of the farmhouse on a summer's day. But this was bigger. The whole sky looked like a giant mass of heat waves.

He climbed down from his bed and flipped the wall switch. They still lived in an old farmhouse with old-fashioned switches. Nothing had been updated in more than a century. But Selby loved the old house. It made him feel the way people who lived long ago must have felt.

No power. He ran into the living room and tried that switch. No light there either. He picked up his father's Pearl from the old television set in the corner of the room. It was dark.

His father was still outside, watching the strange fires, the luminous skies. Selby went out to sit with him on one of the porch chairs in the yard. His father put his arm around him, and together, they stared.

"Do you know what it is, Pop?"

"No, I don't, Selby."

"It looks pretty."

"It does, son. I suppose it does."

GREEN BANK, WEST VIRGINIA

National Radio Astronomy Observatory (NRAO)

"Sir, we have confirmed that solar particles have blown into the earth's atmosphere."

"Do we have any reported effects?"

"Looks like power outages beginning to take effect throughout the western part of the state, and we've had reports of fires spreading throughout the low-lying areas. We don't know yet what kind of radiation we may be talking about. It could be minimal, or it could be frying the area as we speak. Keep the press alert. Better tell people to get to a safe area. If they have a fallout shelter, get in it, and stay there until they hear something different."

"Sir, if power is out, we can't get to the people."

The room was silent as the impact of the situation dawned on the members of the astronomical team.

"Let's go. Everybody out. What's started in the West is going to spread this way. Go home. Get your families. Get out. Get safe. Get underground. Go!"

The NRAO staff left the facility and spread out in different directions, revving their engines to try to beat the oncoming solar fallout.

GREENBELT, MARYLAND

Goddard Space Flight Center (NASA)

"Sir, we've got another flare."

Blake Thompson was on night duty in place of the director and took Channey's incoming message from the central observatory.

"Are you sure?"

"We're sure, sir. And I don't think this is the last one either.

Something big is happening here. And we've got reports now of aurora over the Gulf of Mexico. Pretty soon, it will be everywhere."

"Funny how something so ethereal and beautiful could harness so much power."

"Sir?"

"Nothing, Channey. Good work. Keep us posted."

"Yes, sir."

WASHINGTON, D.C.

The White House

Youhanna Lachier stepped to one side, just barely missing a sideswipe by Matt Serafino as his sword swished through the air, making a slight whistling sound. Lachier put up his hand in a motion to pause, and both men put down their fencing equipment and stood at ease. Lachier lifted his mask and drew in deep breaths.

"Out of shape, I'm afraid," he gasped as he pulled oxygen into his lungs.

Serafino lifted his mask as well and leaned against the side wall while Lachier caught his breath.

"You must practice." Lachier was recovering now, his breath slowing to a moderate pace.

"Occasionally," Serafino replied, amused. "Have you had enough?"

"I think we could go one more round," Lachier said, stretching his wide arms and preparing himself for the next bout.

"All right, then." Matt stepped back into place and began his fencing strategy.

When they had finished and were peeling off clothes and equipment in the White House locker room, Matt glanced at Lachier's leg. Sure enough, the inside of Lachier's calf bore an odd-shaped birthmark—a small group of thin lines, similar to Serafino's, but thinner and facing toward the right.

"So when is your birthday, Monsieur Lachier?"

Lachier looked up, surprised. "My birthday?" Then he laughed. "The 21st of December, 2012. Why?"

"No reason. We just like to keep track of our allies and friends."

Serafino smiled cordially, then motioned to Lachier to join him in the dining room for lunch. The two men left their swords in the locker room, along with their fencing clothes and masks.

SOUTHERN EGYPT

The commander of the Egyptian army looked out at the slaughter taking place outside the treatment facility just inside the border with Sudan. *Border wars*, he thought as he paced up and down. Already, the bodies of hundreds of people seeking water from the plants were being dumped in a makeshift grave site to the west of the region. Soon, it would become a health hazard in itself, having the decomposing flesh so close to the only remaining freshwater in the entire area. The country was having to recycle its water again and again, as no replenishments were available and the plants were running continuously. The surges had picked up. He felt badly for the people. He knew they just wanted to save their families. And Sudan had very few resources for storage or purification of what little water they had. Their primary water source had been the surrounding oceans, with the water brought to Egypt by rivers running through the two countries. But now, those rivers were either dry or poisoned with metallic silt. The only drinkable water was being used by the government, the primary businesses, the wealthy. The others were left to their own devices. And now, many of them were lying dead in Egypt's backyard. He looked out and saw another uprising preparing to be shot down. The commander shook his head and went into his office to continue with his work.

OUTSIDE CAIRO, EGYPT
Underground National Lab

Hassan busied himself in the main lab, working on the blueprints for the space dome. Most of the former lab's equipment was still housed in boxes and crates in the back storage rooms after being rescued from the floods in central Cairo, and he rummaged through them now, looking for a series of digidrives.

Wedged between two boxes was a small metal safe. It was blocking Hassan's way to the back of the storage area, and he gave it a shove to unlodge it from its place. It toppled sideways, and its lid fell open, drives and documents spilling out onto the cement floor in a heap. Hassan climbed over a nearby box to pick up the items and return them to the safe, which for some reason was not locked securely, as it usually was. As he did, he noticed a drive that looked unfamiliar. He placed it into his reader and revealed a document that looked like an accounting sheet. The ones for the lab were kept in a file and drive in the office area. They recorded all the grants and donations for research and the expenses for equipment and usage. But this sheet was filled with personal expenditures—hotels, planes, special equipment, dinners, even the car Lachier had just bought. It didn't take Hassan long to realize that Lachier had been pilfering from the government accounts.

He shook his head, pursing his lips. He was loyal to Lachier. Had been for years. He needed to talk to him first. He would be back in the morning. Hassan would wait.

MARSEILLE, PROVENCE-ALPES-CÔTE D'AZUR, FRANCE

St. Seraphim Orthodox Cathedral

Casimir was staring at the sky from the cathedral observatory. Arnaud stepped inside, careful not to disturb the boy.

Casimir's small voice broke the silence. "A wind is blowing in from the north, clouds with great light are filling the sky, lightning coming out from them. The four must unite. The four with attributes of the divine, with attributes of the earth, water, fire, and air, with attributes of the ox, the eagle, the angel, and the lion. They will be taken up into the wind, and they must be transformed, transported, transcended to another place, the place of the dawn, of the light. They will lead the chariots home."

Arnaud continued to listen, aware now that the boy seemed to be staring, eyes glued to the sky, hands clenched around the Sefir Yetzirah.

"Ezekiel's vision." Arnaud spoke slowly.

Casimir turned.

"Jung called it the rainbow body," Arnaud explained. "The four attributes of God, the four horsemen, four Gospels, four seasons, four elements. Together, they represent total unity, wholeness, the entirety of creation. In the symbolism of the Merkabah, the chariot, the flows of energy join together, just like the earth's magnetic field, transporting the chariot, the All of creation into a new dimension. It's the intersecting center of energy that initiates the transformation. Did you learn this in your books, Casimir?"

"No, Père. I just know. I see it in the sky, from your notes, in what the sun is doing. The Kabbalah is not knowledge itself, Père, but it teaches one to see the inner meanings of things."

"Indeed, my young friend. Casimir, do you know what a *tzadik* is?"

"Yes, Arnaud. It's a seer."

"A seer, yes. But not just any seer. One who has the *ruach hakodesh*, the divine inspiration. The tzadikim can intuit and predict divine events. They may seem to others highly intelligent, but one who knows Kabbalah knows it is much more than intelligence. It is a natural sense of the meaning of things, a natural sense for God."

Casimir looked thoughtful but remained silent.

"Casimir, you are a tzadikim."

Casimir stared at Arnaud with his large, dark eyes. The dark golden curls surrounding his face made him look almost leonine.

"Yes, Père," he said.

LONDON, ENGLAND

Angela was packing so that she and Paul could catch the midmorning plane to Provence. She reached again for the Celtic cross, hanging from her neck, just inside her sweater. She and Paul had been working together for months now, studying the manuscripts, collecting data, investigating the pieces that seemed to be starting to fit together in Paul's mind. But she knew Paul didn't really need her. Her work on the Diatessaron had been finished long ago. And yet, the two of them had continued on together. Angela wasn't really sure what her role was, but she knew she was content to be with Paul. She had grown fond of him, and he of her. And she looked forward to hearing him talk about Patmos, and the transcendentals, and the histories of those who had written age-old prophecies.

She also knew he was onto something, and that somehow he was proving to her—Paul, of all people, Paul, who hadn't initially believed in anything—that something like God really existed, that life wasn't just some random series of events, but that somehow, the world had a fraction of hope. *Doesn't it?* So many catastrophes now. So much disintegration. And it was everywhere now. It wasn't just politics and economics anymore, but something was dreadfully wrong with the earth's balance. *Has humanity helped make it that way?* How would they ever know? But it was clear, something had to change. And it couldn't go back to the way it was. Whatever happened, things could only move forward, onward, or upward, as the prophecy might have it. Angela didn't know what that would ultimately mean.

The only thing she could be sure of was what she knew in her heart. And she knew three things. One: Paul was chosen to do something, fit together the pieces of something important, and to somehow do something that would offer hope to humanity. Two: someone had done the choosing. Whatever happened, they were not alone. And three: whatever happened, she would be at Paul's side. Because when everything else on earth failed, after all, love was the only thing that was still real. Still true. Love and the faith that love existed. And yes, Angela would say it—if love existed, then God existed, too. And Christ? Was the Lamb the center of it all, as the prophecy seemed to indicate? Was the Lamb the center point for all the transcendentals? For all unity? For love? It was the same argument she had used with Paul. Perhaps now she would start trusting it herself.

OUTSIDE CAIRO, EGYPT
Underground National Lab

Hassan was waiting in the lab when Lachier returned. He came into the lab looking pleased with himself, having had, Hassan guessed, a successful meeting with Matthew Serafino, the USAmerican president.

"Did the president accept your offer? Offer his support to us? To Egypt?"

"He did, Hassan." Lachier's smile looked broader than usual.

Hassan looked down at his hands. "Monsieur Lachier, I need to speak with you."

Lachier's smile faded as he realized Hassan was holding the printouts of the altered expenditures for the National Lab.

"What are you doing, Hassan?"

"I want to talk to you, Monsieur Lachier. You know, I've always been loyal to you—"

Lachier interrupted. "Have you shown these to anyone?"

"No, Monsieur Lachier."

"Come here, Hassan. Let's talk." With a flick of his chin, he motioned the assistant to come to the back of the lab.

Hassan reached the end of the hallway and turned to face Lachier. In what seemed less than a fraction of a second, Hassan's eyes had glazed over as Lachier thrust the blade of his dagger through the middle of Hassan's heart. The assistant sighed and fell to the ground in a heap.

Stepping over him, Lachier collected the documents, put them safely back into the locked compartment, and left the lab, locking the door behind him. He had put the dagger neatly and carefully into Hassan's own hand.

It would be hours before the morning security guard called in the emergency.

30

THE RAINBOW

National Center for the Study of Genetics

The storms seemed to come out of nowhere, and Malik Asvaka, now supervising activities in the newly formed Afghani-China's genetics program, ducked into the center's lab, keeping as far away from the windows as he could. In his black garments, his dark gold beard and golden-hazel eyes seemed to gleam in the flashes of light that illuminated the lab, then plunged it again into darkness. Outside, the lightning looked like the thunderbolts he had seen in his childhood picture books of Greek myths, not the usual thin and jagged streaks he had been used to in nature, which now seemed to him mere pencil scratches in comparison. The sky had darkened to an almost pitch blackness, but he could see no clouds. No rain appeared, only the thick, heavy bolts of lightning that seemed to come from everywhere at once, touching down upon streets, buildings, and cars, and leaving them scorched and blackened. *This must be what it would be like to be inside a microwave.* Microwaves were used as the primary cooking ovens up until the mid-twenty-first century, when the nanowave replaced its predecessor. Now, only a few still had the larger dinosaurs, still probably leaking dark energy into the earth's atmosphere.

Malik suddenly brought his hands to his face in pain, shielding his eyes from what appeared to be a bright flash of light that lingered several seconds before leaving the room again in darkness. The lab remained silent. Malik walked cautiously to the window and peered out. The sky had transformed from before the storm and was now filled with a vast series of muted, colored lights rippling about in the atmosphere, like a giant neon fractal or a picture from the Hubble space telescope. *What is it?* Asvaka had heard about it in the news, but he hadn't experienced it firsthand. The scientists and news reports were all calling it aurora borealis. Some reports hinted at something more than that. Asvaka knew what the aurora was. But over China? China had experienced isolated incidents of the borealis in the past, but nothing like this.

Malik tried to get back to work. The lab assistants would be coming in soon for the workday, and he needed to get them on task. But he found himself wishing he were back in Afghanistan.

HOUSTON, TEXAS

Aslow Chemicals Plant

"Many of you know why we've gathered you here today. Our nation is going through a crisis. We have a government that is not listening to our needs, not listening to our voice, ignoring our protests and concerns. And in Texas, we find that unacceptable."

A roar of applause filled the warehouse, in which thousands were gathered for the standing-room-only event.

"In Texas, we know what USAmerica stands for. We know what USAmerica needs, but the United States has been listening to the voices of the wealthy, the greedy, and the tech-hungry, power-hungry voice of Matthew Serafino."

Shrubs yelled out from the crowd. Some threw their fists into the air. Others waved their hats or just nodded in affirmation.

"Today, we ask you to join us in creating a new entity. An entity in which the voice of Texas is the voice of the people, the voice that was always intended to be heard, as the forefathers of the United States believed when they drafted the original Constitution. The United States started off with thirteen British colonies along the Atlantic seaboard. In its early years, based on its founding principles, it grew to encompass fifty states. But the United States of today is a dystopia."

Roars and applause filled the room.

"So today, as we draw up our final document of secession from the United States of America, we ask that you support this contract and its sister document, the Constitution of the New Republic of Texas. And in doing so, offer your loyalty and your voices to a new future for all people within this rich and hopeful land."

The applause continued as citizens lined up in droves to sign the newly constructed documents.

WASHINGTON, D.C.

The White House

Mullica Michaels couldn't keep up with all the calls and e-messages on the president's lines. She finally gave up and slumped back into her chair, her hands over her face. She straightened as the president entered the office and strode past her, as he often did, without even saying good morning. Ted Calahan was on his heels, trying to pin him down on the morning's activities. The president often had his own plans. Unlike former presidents, Serafino liked to do things without consulting anyone, including his own staff, liked to make his own decisions and go his own way, often overriding Ted's meticulous schedule with new appointments and ventures. Sometimes, the president seemed to simply disappear, and Ted would rush around, exasperated, trying to locate him, so as not to appear daft in front of White House guests and dignitaries. But the job paid him well, and right now he suspected Matt Serafino needed him. The country was in a state of civil revolution, and the president didn't seem to notice. Whenever Ted would try to get him to focus on internal affairs, Serafino would laugh and say, "I've got it in hand, Ted." And Ted would not know how to reply. If he tried, Serafino's eyes would darken, and Ted knew he had pushed too far.

When Serafino had become president, the country had hopes of vast change and renewal, had thought Serafino would be the one to bring the United States back to its former glory as a world power. But Serafino no longer seemed interested in that. In fact, Ted couldn't really put his finger on exactly what the president was interested in doing. Another year and he would be voted out of office. Ted was sure of it. In the meantime, he would cover the best he could.

LONDON, ENGLAND
Centre for Manuscript and Print Studies

Before leaving for France, Paul put in another call to the congressman in West Virginia about the solar flares in his home state, but the lines seemed to be down. The call wouldn't go through, and Paul guessed it had something to do with the solar eruption that had radiated throughout most of the western part of the state.

His next call was one well thought out. He disliked Matthew Serafino. But he was, after all, the president. And what Paul knew could save the lives of thousands of people, maybe more. If someone chose to listen. Paul had his Pearl connect to the number for the White House appointment staff.

SAHARA DESERT

The sun beat down on the sands of the Sahara, bringing the temperature that afternoon to 158 degrees Fahrenheit. The highest recorded temperature prior to that had been 136 degrees. The floods and rains that usually would have cooled down the area in the late summer and early fall were nonexistent, due to the absence of water. Without rain, the desert would continue to bake and would soon become uninhabitable even to the few nomadic dwellers and desert animals and plants that normally found a way to survive the intense summer heat. In the skies, bands of cosmic heat waves rippled. And across the dunes, the coarse red sands glittered like tiny metallic chips as the round, red eye of the sun seemed to grow larger and larger in the cloudless atmosphere.

SOUTHWEST SYRIA

The hills outside southern and western Syria rippled with wheat. Now withering from intense heat and lack of water, the grain seemed to make the sound of whispers through the echoing valleys. Over the still-green hills, vast bands of colored light were forming like a giant rainbow in the sky. Those in the surrounding areas thought the rainbow over the hills looked like a domed city. It seemed to center over the tips of the mountains, spewing out colored swirls into the surrounding regions. The place, east of the once-fertile Jordan and near the ghost town of Batanaea, was once called Gilead, the place of soft, fertile land, the place God loved, where thousands once came and were fed on the grassy hillsides—Bashan.

GREENBELT, MARYLAND
Goddard Space Flight Center (NASA)

"The earth's poles reverse every 250,000 years, sir, but we haven't had a reversal in almost 780,000 years now. We're overdue."

Hal Goodman leaned back in his chair. There was only so much they could do. They could observe, but they could essentially do nothing to stop the massive solar eruptions and storms hurling into the earth's atmosphere at a rate of five to eight flares daily. "What can we do to protect the people against the radiation storms? What do we tell them?"

Channey hesitated. "Build shelters, sir. I don't know what else to say."

DES MOINES, IOWA

The solar screams began at noon and continued for almost an hour. Every radio frequency had shut down, emitting only the sound of a rusty chain saw. By that evening, radiation particles had begun to wreak havoc on every electrical and nanowave system in the surrounding areas. As the screams continued from area to area and systems began to shut down, a blanket of stillness filled vast portions of the United States, Europe, Asia, and the Middle East, as twenty-first-century techno-noise ground to a deafeningly silent halt.

MARSEILLE, PROVENCE-ALPES-CÔTE D'AZUR, FRANCE

St. Seraphim Orthodox Cathedral

Casimir was asleep when Paul and Angela arrived, having stayed up most of the night in the observatory, studying and meditating on the wisdom of the Kabbalah. Arnaud invited the two into his study to relax after their trip before having dinner in the cathedral's large dining area. The restaurants in Marseille had all but shut down because of periodic power outages from the solar storms, and the water shortage had prompted a government regulation to cut back on all water usage except for allotted daily amounts. The reservoirs were struggling in every country to conserve drinking water for the citizens. Beyond that, the population was urged to eat fresh, uncooked foods, to reuse bathwater, and to drink water conservatively. Most European countries had made it a crime to engage in any leisure activities using water. And, of course, activities such as washing cars or watering lawns were strictly prohibited.

Angela and Paul set down their bags in the cathedral's narthex area and settled into Arnaud's large leather office chairs as he called up the evening news. The only news available was a readout screen, as most of the news satellites had been rendered inoperable in the last radiation storm. Arnaud knew that soon, even those readouts would be gone, that the most rudimentary electrical systems would eventually shut down.

Angela and Paul had taken one of the last planes of the day. The number of flights had been cut dramatically, due to interference with air-traffic control. Only a few flights were allowed in the air at a time, and only during the daytime hours. The lines at the aerodock had taken hours to maneuver, and Angela and Paul looked tired from the day's flight.

Seraphim was strutting around his cage, stopping now and again to pluck at the seedcake nestled into the side pocket of the metal bars.

"Does he ever come out?" Angela was examining the bird, who looked back at her inquisitively, as though summing her up.

"No," said Arnaud. "I've actually never taken him out. He has seemed perfectly happy to roam about his cage and to sing his heart out whenever he chooses."

"He sings?" Angela was intrigued now.

"He does. But it looks like he's not in the mood today. He often breaks into song as soon as visitors arrive."

Angela peered in at the white-feathered bird. His yellow plume waved about as he nibbled the seedcake, plucking bits off his claw with his beak. His rosy cheeks looked as if someone had smeared him with too much rouge.

"He's a beautiful bird."

"Beautiful," repeated Seraphim.

Angela smiled, found some yogurt drops from the box below his cage, and began offering them to the bird through the bars. Seraphim took each yogurt drop and then seemed to bow his small head, as he stepped back to chew them, neatly breaking them apart with his beak and claws.

After a period of time, Arnaud rose. "Well, let's have a bite to eat ourselves."

The three went into the large cathedral dining area and settled into chairs at the table closest to the kitchen. Arnaud had already prepared the meal and brought it out now on trays that he set in front of them. French cheeses, breads, jams, honey, and sets of homemade crepes with fruit accompanied a bottle of French wine and small glasses of bottled water. There had been a run on bottled water, but the cathedral had been well stocked, due to its oversized pantry and kitchen and its former Easter dinner celebration.

At last, Casimir appeared in the doorway.

"Ah, Casimir, I see you've smelled the food at last!" Arnaud smiled generously. "Please say hello to our guests. This is Dr. Paul Binder from the United States and his lovely partner, Angela Matthews Krall, from the Centre for Manuscript and Print Studies in London, England."

Casimir greeted the guests and then settled in, plucking bits of fruit and cheese from the plates and dipping them into a kind of syrup he made from the honey and jam.

"Casimir is staying here with me—as my apprentice." Arnaud looked at Casimir, nodded, and smiled. "He's quite a brilliant young man and has been a superb assistant to me. I think you will find him eager to engage in our conversation as well."

Paul and Angela nodded in agreement.

"Well, then, shall we begin?"

After Arnaud had cleared the dishes and food from the table, Paul reached into his binder and pulled out the various documents and notes he had been keeping from the time he had received the letter in Virginia until that very day. Most days he kept a makeshift diary and tried to keep track of at least a smattering of current events, in addition to adding thoughts, notes, diagrams, and maps to his collection. At first it felt awkward keeping so many handwritten notes. After all, no one wrote in actual script anymore. Not since the advent of nanocomputers. But now, as most of the systems began to fail, Paul was relieved to have a visible and tangible set of documents to place in front of him. Without them, he would never be able to assemble the various pieces of the message the documents were evidently trying to provide him.

Paul showed Arnaud and Casimir everything he had gathered so far, including the notes he had taken describing the misericords in

Tuscany. In the notes he pointed out his chart, and he explained much of what he himself had realized in his conversations with Angela in the center's library.

"But I haven't been able to figure out what the carved numbers in the Patmos box are for: 21, 21." Paul was looking at the numbers in his notes, trying to connect them.

"I think I can answer that," Arnaud said. He then looked at Casimir, and Casimir nodded.

"21 December 2048, at 9:00 p.m.. The twenty-first of December at the twenty-first hour: 21, 21," Arnaud said.

"How do you know that?" Paul looked surprised.

"Casimir and I have been doing a bit of research ourselves. But I think it's time to compare notes."

31

SILVER AND GOLD

The White House

Matt Serafino sat in the Oval Office, thinking about Paul Binder's call. Thinking hard. Who was Paul Binder? And what made him think he could just walk in and see the president? Was he a nutcase? Was he one of the four? If he was, Matt needed him and needed him soon, especially given all the information Paul seemed to have about upcoming events. Matt supposed the man could have just gathered information and made a hypothesis based on current news reports. It certainly wouldn't take a genius to surmise that the world was headed for some kind of collision, although most people still believed either it was a hoax or the world would somehow just right itself—that everything would go on forever, as it always had, that nothing especially different would ever really happen. Then there were the doomsayers, who always came up with who knows what explanations and speculations on just about anything.

But Paul Binder seemed different. He was intelligent—a history professor from the University of Virginia, and he seemed to have the idea that people would need to evacuate, that they could in some way be saved. *What does he know?* It seemed to Matt there was something

293

Paul Binder wasn't revealing. He had kept to the facts. But Matt could tell by something in his voice that he knew something more. Something he wasn't going to say because it would sound too unusual, too strange, too . . .

Matt paused.

"Mullica."

"Yes, Mr. President."

"Get Dr. Binder back on the line. Ask him to join me for tea at the White House, let's say, in a few days."

"Yes, sir."

Now, let's see. Let's just see who you are.

NEW YORK, NEW YORK

This news report in from the New York Stock Exchange, where the monetary systems of the United States, Europe, and Asia have begun to collapse, a result of the severe and prolonged outages and breaks in the electrical and satellite systems of many of the world's leading economic countries.

"Ted, what can we expect to happen if this doesn't turn around and very soon?"

"Well, Susan, I think we can reasonably expect a collapse of the US dollar, as well as that of the euro, among other currencies. The only commodity going up right now is gold. People aren't spending money. They're stashing gold."

"What about the MK BRIC countries, Ted?"

"The magic bricks aren't so magic anymore, Susan. They're in the same shape as the rest of us, partly because of trouble with the financial systems, but also due to general upheaval right now in the world's natural ecosystems. Gold is the primary solution around the world right now."

"How can we be sure the price of gold will remain stable, Ted?"

"The price of gold will always remain stable, Susan. It's the earth's most prized and valuable mineral. Its uses are only now beginning to be realized. It's still relatively easy to mine, it's available, and it's always going to have some kind of value, no matter what situation the world is in."

"Ted, what happens if the market fails?"

"If the market fails, we all look out for ourselves, Susan."

"Like economic anarchy?"

"Absolutely. It would absolutely be economic anarchy. And I think we're already headed that way, as statistics have shown that people are drawing their money out of banks and investing in gold, Susan."

"Well, it certainly sounds like gold is the way to go, Ted. We'll be back with Ted Holmes in a just a few minutes. Now the weather."

GREENBELT, MARYLAND
Goddard Space Flight Center (NASA)

"How many deflector suits do we have?"

"About fifty thousand I think, sir, but we're making more by the day."

"We need to do better than that. We need to get them on the market and to the population now. Use any facility you need to. Use backup generators. But get those suits built."

"Yes, sir."

"Do we have enough silver and gold resources to pull this off?"

"Right now, I think so, sir. And I think so far, we're the only country making the solar-deflection suits."

"Well, as soon as the rest of the world remembers that gold and silver are the world's best solar deflectors, not to mention electricity conductors, everyone will be rushing to get their hands on one. Get moving."

"Yes, sir."

Director Hal Goodman was tired. He hesitated to call in the report from Roger Channey. It had gotten so that every day, the news just got worse. He almost didn't want to hear it. He sighed and called him up onto the communications screen.

"Channey."

"Yes, sir."

"What have you got for me?"

"Well, sir, we have confirmed that the earth's magnetic poles are in fact in the process of reversal. And the breach in the earth's magnetic field is increasing. We're simply taking too many hits from the solar storms. Fortunately, the radio frequencies have been helping. Whenever the solar screams, as we're calling them now, come onto the frequencies, we know that area has as few as four hours to evacuate before the radiation hits home. It has helped in some areas. In others, where the communications systems are not good or where power has already been compromised, we're losing land and we're losing people, sir."

The director sighed again. "Anything else, Channey?"

"Yes, sir. The astronomers have identified something unusual in the solar system itself. We're not threatened by it, but it's a definite anomaly."

"What's that, Channey?"

"Well, sir, we're trying to narrow down the exact date and time now, but sometime this year, perhaps in just months from now, it seems the planets will fall into a complete and perfect alignment, the first and last time we'll ever see anything like that."

"When is—"

"Sir, I'm sorry to interrupt, but I have to get off the line. We're about to get another 'whale call.'"

"Got it. Thanks for your report, Roger."

"Yes, sir."

MARSEILLE, PROVENCE-ALPES-CÔTE D'AZUR, FRANCE

St. Seraphim Orthodox Cathedral

By the time Arnaud, Casimir, Paul, and Angela shared what they had been experiencing, it was late, and Arnaud invited the group into his office for coffee before retiring to the guest rooms he had prepared for them in the dorm section of the building. Because the cathedral had once housed a monastery, the huge stone building still had accommodations that had been renovated and now could be used for occasional guests. They were small rooms, scant but comfortable, and each of the visitors would have private space in the long corridor connecting the sanctuary to the main tower.

But for now, Arnaud took a moment to relax, stretching his legs in his huge recliner.

Angela, who once again sat beside Seraphim's cage, was looking curiously at Arnaud's leg.

"Father Chevalier, is that a birthmark on your leg? On your inner calf?"

Arnaud looked up, surprised. No one had ever asked him before about his odd-shaped birthmark. Of course, his leg was usually hidden beneath torrents of red robes. But now, he turned his leg slightly to reveal three thin but dark wavelike lines on the inside of his leg.

"I'm sorry for being so personal," Angela apologized. "But it's just that we had an unusual experience in Florence. If you remember, on the misericord there, we found the four figures of the horsemen, but below them were four elemental figures—symbols, it seemed, for fire, earth, water, and air. And I remember, because Paul noticed first that one of them looked strikingly similar to a birthmark that I have on my leg. In fact, it's at the same place approximately as yours."

Angela lifted her right leg to reveal the triple flare that adorned her inner calf.

"I have one, too." Casimir was busy tugging at his pant leg, and he soon extended his calf to show his own birthmark—a symbol resembling a sort of double leaf.

"Wait a minute." Paul was rummaging in his bag and brought out the drawing of the symbols from the misericord.

"All right, all of you. Hold out your legs."

The three dutifully held out their right legs, and Paul took Angela's magnifier and held it over each birthmark. He was shaking his head.

"What do you think they are?" Arnaud looked curious now.

"I think they're part of the answer." Paul was incredulous. "And we've had them all this time. Look at this. Angela, yours looks like the fire symbol. Casimir, yours is exactly like the earth symbol. And Father Chevalier, yours matches the symbol of the air. The only one missing is water."

They all began to stare at Paul's leg.

Paul laughed suddenly. "Oh! Oh, no. I don't have one. I don't have a birthmark."

He lifted his leg to prove his point. The others looked at one another, and then back at Paul.

Angela spoke first. "So, what do you think it means?"

"I think it means," Paul said in amazement, "that you all represent three of the four people I am supposed to bring together. So far, I haven't had to do much of anything. You've all somehow just turned up."

"Then why hasn't the fourth turned up?" Angela looked thoughtful now, as though running everyone they had met through her head as a possible candidate.

"Maybe he or she has. Or maybe not yet," Arnaud offered.

"If he or she hasn't, how do we go about tracking the fourth person down? That's the question." Paul looked worried.

"None of us are from the same country, the same area of work, the same interests."

"But we do all share one thing, I think." Arnaud looked again at his cosmological notes. "The same birthday, 21 December 2012, at 9:00 p.m."

They looked suddenly at Casimir.

"Wait a minute. If Casimir is twelve years old, then he couldn't have been born in 2012. He would have been born in 2036." Angela was shaking her head in confusion.

"But he has the mark."

Arnaud was rising to his feet, a look of incredulity on his face. He walked over to Casimir and cupped his hands around the boy's face. He looked into his eyes and then said slowly, his eyes widening in amazement, "Casimir is not twelve."

BEIJING, CHINA

National Center for the Study of Genetics

Malik Asvaka smiled as he heard the news. Why hadn't he realized before? Of course! The agrofuels industries had failed. The fuel was made from corn, and corn was now a high-priced and rare commodity. Whatever crops were left since the failure of the world's water supplies had to be used for food, which was fast growing to be in huge demand. The agrofuels industry had no more raw material to function. The industries had closed down within weeks of the ocean disasters. Neither was solar nor wind power operable, given the current solar radiation storms. Even electricity had failed sporadically throughout the globe. The nations of the world were fast running out of fuels. And Afghanistan had what they still could use. Oil. Good old oil and gasoline. And Scitheon could capitalize on that! Every country of the world would now be coming to him for help. He needed to get back to Afghanistan. Running the Chinese lab was boring Asvaka. He needed to be where the action was. *And the money.* And if the nations were short on cash, he would take gold. Gold would do just fine. Or silver. But preferably gold.

The day was starting to look up.

WASHINGTON, D.C.

Matt Serafino was trying to think it all through. He knew time was running out. The prophecy had told him he needed to assemble the four. And he had already located two of them. Niú Ye was installed conveniently in his own laboratory, and Lachier could be accessible; he was sure of it. He would need to figure out the formula for the trans-formation, and then take them with him to Jerusalem when the time came. But who was the fourth? Serafino was frustrated. He hadn't a clue how to find one man with a specified birthmark. He, or she— Serafino supposed the fourth horseman could be a woman—could be living in any country of the world. *A woman.* Serafino thought about Doron. He hadn't given much thought to her at all, since the fiasco of a month ago. *What could I have been thinking, trusting her!?* She could have ruined his presidency. Matt was sure she was not the one. But who? Could it be Paul Binder? Matt would be meeting with him the following afternoon. If it was Binder, he would find out. If it wasn't, he would have to figure out a way to find his fourth component. He was running out of time.

He closed the Codex Gigas, still lying on the table, and fingered the golden letters on its cover. If anyone could figure out the spell for transforming the four into one, it was Serafino. And he knew just where to look for it.

32

CONNECTING THE DOTS

St. Seraphim Orthodox Cathedral

"Casimir, do you remember your last birthday?"

Casimir looked thoughtful. "I don't remember, Père," he said slowly.

"And how old are you?"

"I'm twelve."

"Do you remember when you turned twelve, Casimir?"

Casimir appeared to be thinking very hard now. "No."

"How long have you been attending the Institute for the Sciences, Technology, and the Arts, Casimir?"

"I don't know." Casimir was starting to look alarmed now. "What's wrong, Père? Did I do something?"

"No, Casimir. You did nothing."

Arnaud turned to Paul and Angela, who were now looking at each other and trying not to stare at Casimir, who, once Arnaud has reassured him, now seemed mildly curious but otherwise relatively unconcerned with what was going on. He opened one of Arnaud's books and began reading intently.

Paul suddenly seemed to understand and sat up in his seat.

"Astonishing."

"Casimir, would you mind going into the kitchen and bringing back a bottle of water for all of us?"

"Yes, of course, Père."

Casimir jumped down from the chair and left the room. Arnaud turned to the others.

"Technological neoteny."

"Father?" Angela was leaning forward in her seat. Paul was nodding his head, a thin smile coming onto his face.

"At the turn of the twenty-first century, the Human Genetics Project in Poland took a hit for experimenting with human fetuses. Do you remember? Cloning, genetic alterations, the search for youth, cures for diseases—there were all sorts of reasons back then, justifications, if you will, for these experiments. Cyberfetuses. The actual births were few. Most of the experiments went awry, and activist groups knocked down the doorways of the scientific community until the practice was ended around the year 2015. One of the problems was neoteny."

Angela looked perplexed. "But what's neoteny?"

"It was originally a word used for amphibians, but was later applied to the fetuses in the HG Project that wouldn't mature beyond puberty. Juvenilization syndrome. A genetic defect, more or less, that meant once the subject reached adolescence, growth would simply stop. The person would technically age, but his body and mind would stay that of a young prepubescent."

Angela's mouth fell open. "No wonder he appears so intelligent."

Arnaud shook his head. "No, Angela. Casimir *is* intelligent. Beyond intelligent. It's as though his mind has compensated for what has otherwise been done to him. But it's an unusual intelligence. As you see, in many ways, he has the mind of a child. But yet his ability to intuit, to learn, to instinctively understand complex systems, technology, to 'feel' knowledge—that's unique."

Paul was shaking his head now, amazed at what Arnaud was telling them, more amazed to see someone like Casimir in the flesh. Paul had heard about the European genetics projects, but he hadn't known any of the cyberfetuses had survived. But it made sense. All of it made perfect sense.

Arnaud was going on.

"As a neotene, Casimir will also believe he is twelve. His parents probably shielded him as best they could from his condition. I don't think he has a clue. And I'm not going to tell him."

"Frankly, his childlike innocence and naïveté are refreshing." Paul leaned back now, more relaxed.

"So, Casimir is thirty-six years old—like the rest of us." Angela still seemed shocked at the disclosure.

"Indeed." Arnaud shook his head slowly. "And I didn't notice it myself until just now."

"How did you know?" Angela looked curiously at Arnaud, then at Paul.

"The features. The flattened face and nose, the narrow face, broad forehead, almond eyes—all characteristics of neotenes. Otherwise, the rest of their bodies look identical to that of a normally developed child of their age."

Casimir had come back into the room with the bottle of water and handed it to Arnaud.

"Do you know the date of your birthday, Casimir?"

"Yes, of course, Père," Casimir answered pleasantly.

"What is it?"

"21 December 2012."

KABUL, AFGHANISTAN
Scitheon Corporation

As of September 2048, there were 9.1 billion people worldwide. *And they would all need oil.* Malik Asvaka was in an excellent mood. He had talked President Abdul Gulzar into allowing him to come back to Afghanistan to resume the running of the Scitheon Corporation. He had assured the president he could manage the Center for the Study of Genetics' Department of Interrelational Sciences from his home office in

Kabul. Nothing much was happening there anyway. No one seemed to know at the moment what they wanted to do with China, now that they had acquired it. Until they did, the lab would work aimlessly on relatively meaningless projects, waiting for the bureaucratic red tape to clear.

In the meantime, Malik could be capitalizing on the world's fuel crisis. He had, or rather Scitheon had, unlimited access to the nation's oil fields, and with a little finesse, he could team with the other oil-producing countries—his friendly neighbors—and monopolize the world's power sources. He was surprised he hadn't received any requests already, especially from some of the larger countries like India or the United States. Both countries were going through significant unrest, as were most countries now in light of the turbulent economic, political, and natural landscape, but they would soon realize, especially in the United States, that cold-weather months were approaching. And the people of the nation would want heat. Not to mention continued powering of their transportation systems. With a nation as large as the United States, how could they do without oil now? They would need it. They would need Afghanistan.

Malik wondered at the world's slow response to this impending crisis. Was it confusion? Disbelief? Denial? Sooner or later, they'd have to come to the conclusion he knew they would.

Perhaps we could speed up that process, Malik thought as he reached for his interface panel and tested it. For the moment, it was still operational.

"President Matthew Serafino of the United States of America," he said and leaned back in his chair as the computer attempted to connect the call.

GREENBELT, MARYLAND
Goddard Space Flight Center (NASA)

"Can we put the map on the big screen, please?"

The director had called a meeting of NASA staff to update them on the status of the solar interruptions.

"If you look up here on the map, you will see that we have marked with a red dot each place where one of the solar flares has entered the earth's atmosphere. The marks that look like stars indicate the flares that have penetrated the magnetic field and have allowed radiation to enter. The marks surrounded by black indicate the flares that have caused extensive damage. The shaded areas are those locations where power is currently down. The areas in white still have workable systems—for now."

"What about the aurora borealis effect? Is that as widespread as those map points indicate?" Someone from the back was standing now.

"It is. Wider spread, in fact. The aurora is now covering most of the earth's atmosphere. Even where flares have not yet entered the earth's gravitational system, solar particles have become highly prevalent in the gases of the atmosphere as a whole to the extent that our skies essentially now are one large aurora."

Hands were being raised now as questions abounded.

"If the solar onslaught continues, as it looks like it will, how long do we have until the earth itself is significantly compromised?"

The director was silent for a moment. "A few months."

MARSEILLE, PROVENCE-ALPES-CÔTE D'AZUR, FRANCE

St. Seraphim Orthodox Cathedral

Paul was intently studying the notes that he and Arnaud now had spread across the large table in the cathedral dining hall.

"So, there were eight born on 21 December 2012, at 9:00 p.m. That's what the letter said, as well as the Diatessaron prophecy. The birth of the eight. But everything else we've come across seems to correspond with four. And there are four horsemen of the Apocalypse."

Casimir, who seemed to be not listening, suddenly looked up and spoke. "The Kabbalah tells us that everything in the world is one. Of one source. The one divine God. One source, but with what is good, and what is not, all mixed together. For there to be four, there must be eight. The *sitra achra*—negative holiness that comes from God but is not God. It emanates from the divine in creation so as to give humankind free choice. Yet the sitra achra will never win out over God, will not oppose God, but it will reflect the inner ethical and spiritual dilemmas of humankind."

Angela looked up. "What did he just say?"

Paul spoke first. "I believe he means that there may be four horsemen but of two perspectives—two choices. We all have choices in everything we do, between what is good and what is not."

Angela shifted uncomfortably. "But Paul, life is not that simple. How easy would it be if everything were just so easily defined as 'good' and 'bad'?"

"You're right, Angela. I don't think it will be clear. I think that's what makes this all so hard. Good people can sometimes make bad choices, and essentially bad people can occasionally make good choices. And many choices are perhaps what is best out of any number of possibilities that are grey and rainbow-colored in between. But I think in the end, what defines us is what we are inside, and that is what will eventually drive us to make the decisions that will move us in the directions we need to go."

Angela smiled now. "Like love."

Paul smiled back. "Like love. And the rest of Arnaud's transcendentals. Goodness, truth, beauty—but definitely love."

"And what defines us inside, what creates in us those transcendental qualities," Arnaud offered, "is our relationship with the divine, with God, and with Christ."

"So," Paul continued, "eight were born, but only four will need to unite in order to save humankind from destruction."

"Not just any four."

"Four that represent all four horsemen, all four elements . . ."

"And all four must be turned to God. Strive for God's attributes. Must center around the Lamb."

The others were silent.

Angela then spoke quietly. "And the other four?"

"Let's hope we don't encounter them."

Paul broke the mood then, standing and moving around the side of the table to look out of one of the windows in the cathedral dining room. "So, back to practical matters. How do we find our fourth companion?"

Arnaud answered. "I've been thinking about that. Look. We all know we share the same birthday and time of birth. We all share a set of birthmarks. But we're forgetting one more thing."

Paul turned. "What's that?"

Arnaud walked over to Paul's charts spread across the wooden surface. "The elements. They all have initials."

The others got up then and gathered around the chart of elements. "My initials." Angela gasped.

"And mine," said Arnaud.

"And mine," said Casimir.

"There are eight sets. Five more sets."

Paul nodded. "And one of those sets is our fourth companion. OAG."

Angela spoke up again. "But how are we going to locate this someone?"

Paul began to look excited. "Father Arnaud, do we still have power anywhere in Marseille? In France? Anywhere close by?"

Arnaud shrugged. "I don't know. But we could find out. Why?"

"Our Pearls are down here at the cathedral now. But all we need is a working Cloud—even a turn-of-the-century computer will do. If we can access the Cloud, we can find everyone who was born on 21 December 2012, at 9:00 p.m. We can access the census database and find birth records. Then all we need to do is to locate them, meet them, identify the birthmarks."

"Sounds complicated." Angela looked doubtful.

Paul looked around at all three of his companions. "Then we'd better get moving. As for me, I'd better hightail it to the aerodock. Tomorrow afternoon, I meet with President Serafino. Planes are still flying, but they are severely limited and dependent upon the ability of the aviation communications centers to track them. And some pilots are refusing to fly. I may have to wait all night for a private flight in the morning. I'll be back as soon as I can after the meeting."

After Paul left the cathedral, Angela and Casimir piled into Arnaud's car and headed for the Université de Provence Aix-Marseille.

33

THE CHAMELEON

WASHINGTON, D.C.

The White House

Paul arrived at the White House for his afternoon appointment with President Matthew Serafino in a golden-tan suit. The president was waiting for him in one of the lavish conference rooms. A tray with tea service had been left on the center mahogany table, with plates of croissants and biscuits on a highboy to the left of the room.

Matt Serafino greeted Paul with his most charming smile and hand-shake, betraying no sign of whether or not he would be open to hearing what Paul had to say. They settled into elegantly upholstered chairs.

Paul had decided to be cautious. He would let the president know things were going to get much worse, but he would decline to tell him how he knew that or any of the details of the last six months. Paul realized Serafino might not take seriously anything he said without offering proof or reason to back any of it up. But Paul didn't see any way around it. If he told Serafino of the circumstances of his letter, the strange prophecy in the Diatessaron, the documents from the Patmos box, and even more so the events of the past month in particular, he would be thrown out on his ear onto the White House lawn; he was sure of it. He would walk a fine line around what he could say and what was too far-fetched for anyone right now to believe. But yet if people weren't told the truth, how could they be led to Bashan when the time came a few months from now? Would anyone survive? It wouldn't be enough for people to believe that something was going to happen. They needed to trust in a divine power, a God and a Messiah that they hadn't believed in with their minds for years, let alone their hearts. And they would need to follow him, Paul, across the globe to a remote area of the hills, just on that faith. Paul laughed to himself. Even he couldn't see that happening.

Paul looked up to see the president staring at him. He had seen those eyes on the news but never in person. They seemed now to bore right through Paul's mind, as though reading his thoughts. Paul cleared his throat and reached out for a napkin. Serafino watched as Mullica poured the tea and then waved her to leave the room.

The president was a striking figure. He had an air that seemed to put everyone around him in awe. He was tall and lean, and his dark hair and eyes stood out dramatically from his somewhat pale skin. Wearing both his tan suit and confident composure, he looked charismatic, imposing. Paul could see why people were nervous around him.

"Now then, tell me more about why you're here."

Serafino smiled. He looked as if he had no idea why Paul had come. And Paul couldn't read his face. Paul could tell a lot about a person by watching expressions, movements, especially someone's eyes. But not with Serafino. The man threw him off kilter. He didn't seem guarded. He seemed perfectly natural. *Or rather, perfectly unnatural.* Paul drew in his breath.

"I'm sure you've no lack of information about the current state of the solar eruptions," Paul began, "so I won't go into any of that. But I can tell you, they're only the beginning."

Paul watched Serafino, but the president had not moved or even seemed to blink.

"I can't explain how I know this. But I have reason to believe that the earth is entering its last days—at least the earth as we know it—as an inhabitable planet. I believe there's a chance that some of the population can be saved, that they can enter a type of gateway."

Paul paused to think about how to pose his next thoughts. "Are you familiar with M-theory, Mr. President?"

Serafino had crossed his arms and leaned back. He nodded but let Paul continue.

"I have reason to believe that a gateway will become available through, uh, some kind of rare occurrence, and it will happen in just a few months from now at a specific time and place. Those who make it through the gateway can build a new earth in another dimension, another home similar to the one in which we live now. In fact, it may look essentially the same."

Perhaps cleaner would be nice. Paul had to focus to keep his mind from wandering.

"But . . ." Paul hesitated.

The knock at the door startled Paul, and he lost his composure for a moment.

Serafino sat up slightly and called to the doorway to Mullica Michaels. "Yes, Mullica."

Mullica came to the doorway with a short, muscular-looking Asian man next to her. He looked to be about Paul's age, but with a worn, tired-looking countenance. He had beady, dark eyes that shone out from puffy cheeks and a well-defined bone structure. His yellowish-tanned skin accented his dark, black shock of hair. In his hands he held a small digidrive.

"Mr. President, I'm sorry to interrupt. Dr. Niú insisted on seeing you immediately."

Serafino nodded. "Thank you, Mullica."

He turned then to Paul. "Would you excuse me for a moment?"

Paul nodded.

Serafino rose and went to the doorway to speak with Dr. Niú. They spoke for a few moments, and Niú appeared to hand Serafino a small digidrive. Serafino turned toward Paul, smiling.

"Well, not to be rude, Dr. Binder, but I'd like you to meet one of our head scientists, Dr. Niú Ye. Dr. Niú, Dr. Paul Binder. Dr. Binder is a historian and a cultural studies professor from the University of Virginia."

The scientist reached out and grasped Paul's hand briefly, bowing slightly, then backed away toward the door. Serafino beckoned him closer.

"No, please, have a seat for a moment with us, Dr. Niú."

The scientist took a seat across from Paul, looking somewhat uncomfortable. He was not dressed for the occasion, but was wearing a long set of shorts and a kind of knitted polo shirt.

Serafino continued. "Dr. Binder was just telling me that he believes the earth is not going to be able to handle a continuation of the intense solar activity we are experiencing, especially in addition to the other natural phenomena that have been occurring recently."

He looked to Paul for affirmation.

"What do you think about that, Niú?"

Niú Ye seemed to squirm in his seat, and Paul thought he sensed the smell of sweat from the short, stocky man.

"I'd have to agree, we are certainly experiencing something we've never encountered before." Niú seemed to be trying to tactfully say something useful, or perhaps skillfully to say nothing at all.

Paul felt sorry for the Asian man, and he was beginning to feel uncomfortable himself, not certain of where Serafino was planning to go with the conversation, when he glanced down toward the tea table and his eye caught sight of the side of Niú Ye's leg. Paul wanted to look more closely, but he couldn't risk the oddity of overtly staring. He was sure he was seeing one of the marks. One of the birthmarks. This one appeared to be a type of nonenclosed circle, or perhaps two semicircles, enmeshed in a type of whirlpool design. *Water.* Paul nervously sat back so as not to call attention to his gaze. But he could not help but study the man's face, trying to discern whether or not he was the one they were looking for. How would he know?

Matthew Serafino was talking again now, and Paul turned his attention back to the president.

"So, what is it you suggest I do, Dr. Binder?"

"Honestly, I'm not sure, Mr. President. It's just that . . . I wasn't sure you were aware . . . I just thought you should know . . . what, uh, could happen."

"Well, let's keep in touch." Serafino rose, ending the conversation and ushering Paul out the door toward the corridor, where Mullica met him to escort him to the outer entrance. Paul turned back for a moment, but Matthew Serafino had already gone back inside and was shutting the conference room door. He had seen no birthmark on Paul Binder. He was not the one.

MARSEILLE, PROVENCE-ALPES-CÔTE D'AZUR, FRANCE

Université de Provence Aix-Marseille

Arnaud thanked the dean for allowing them to use the university office computer. Most of the systems in the area were down, but the university was running temporarily on a backup generator and could manage to access the Cloud at select times of day, depending upon the solar activity. Angela, Arnaud, and Casimir gathered around the office desk to try to collect the information on births from 21 December 2012, at 2100. Since they needed worldwide statistics, Angela tried several sites, including LifeStream, to try to assemble the information. Despite nearing the midpoint of the century, searching the virtual network was still partly a hit-and-miss experience, or perhaps a game of skill to find the right combination of keywords that would place one into the right virtuality at the right time.

At first, Angela could find only general and broad statistics. After about an hour, she finally came upon statistics that conformed more closely to what they needed, but she would need to search each country separately for the information. She looked around at Arnaud and Casimir. There was a lunchroom and snack station down the hall. She motioned and pointed, smiling.

"This may take a while."

CHARLOTTESVILLE, VIRGINIA

University of Virginia

Dandelions. The hills were covered in yellow and gold. Paul had forgotten how beautiful these simple weeds could look decorating the landscape. And they seemed to need very little care. Even despite the shortage of rain and fresh water, the hardy plants seemed to thrive throughout the state of Virginia. Most of them would be fading now, as the weather was turning fast toward fall. Paul wondered if he would ever see a dandelion again. If the prophecy turned out to be true, then who knew what kind of world would lie beyond December? Would it have dandelions? Plants at all? Or would it look just like this, with rolling hills and golden fields? For a moment, Paul felt the enormity of what might occur in the next few months, and a feeling of profound sadness swept over him, a blanket of sorrow, not just for the earth but for everyone in it. It was a feeling of great loss, of grief, as though the world had already died and had left Paul alone in a barren wilderness. He tried to shake it off. He couldn't afford to embrace this feeling right now. He had too much to think about. And if he could save a portion of humanity, even a few thousand people, it would be worth every ounce of energy he had. The weight of this responsibility seemed to wake him from his sadness and restore his balance, at least for the moment. Although, he thought, it was appropriate to allow for sadness. The earth may not be dead, but if not dead, then certainly in its death throes.

Paul had not been back at the university in the prior semester, and now, as he went in to see the dean of faculty, he knew he needed to request a leave of absence for the fall. He hoped they would understand and grant the leave. Then again, would anyone be here after the fall semester to care?

MARSEILLE, PROVENCE-ALPES-CÔTE D'AZUR, FRANCE

Université de Provence Aix-Marseille

"Got it!"

Angela printed out the list of names. Arnaud and Casimir hurried to look.

"In that particular year, on that particular date, and at that very time, down to the minute, only eight people were born. Our horsemen."

Arnaud read the list of names aloud:

"Angela Matthews Krall, born 21.12.12 at 2100 hours, Galway Bay, Ireland.

"Malik Haider Asvaka, born 21.12.12 at 2100 hours, Kabul, Afghanistan.

"Casimir Ariel Marcelli, born 21.12.12 at 2100 hours, Gdańsk, Poland.

"Youhanna Nasim Lachier, born 21.12.12 at 2100 hours, Lyon, France.

"Arnaud Jerome Chevalier, born 21.12.12 at 2100 hours, Paris, France.

"Niú Ye, born 21.12.12 at 2100 hours, Hangzhou, China.

"Oksanna Anya Galina, born 21.12.12 at 2100 hours, Siberia, Russia.

"Matthew Samael Serafino, born 21.12.12 at 2100 hours, Trona, California."

The three were quiet for several minutes as they stared at the printout. Angela broke the silence. "So this is real."

Arnaud answered softly. "So it seems."

Angela's eyes filled with tears as she turned and looked at Arnaud. "Father Arnaud, Paul is not listed. I know his birthday is also 21.12.12. I know it is. But he's not listed with the rest of us."

"I know, my dear. I don't believe Paul is one of the eight. He's not one of the horsemen. He doesn't have the birthmark. But the prophecy called him the Chosen One. Don't worry, Angela. Don't worry about Paul. He's the one. The one who is going to lead us all to Bashan. I don't know why everything is happening the way it is. But Paul has a special role. Not the same one as the rest of us. But a very important role that will, I'm sure, become clear. You said yourself, sometimes when you can't know something, you just have to trust what you feel, what you intuit with your faith. We all have to walk on, Angela. And Paul will be the one to walk with us. Trust."

After several tries, Angela was able to access her Pearl through the university's communications system.

"I'd better send this information to Paul."

CHARLOTTESVILLE, VIRGINIA
University of Virginia

Paul took out the elemental charts from his leather binder and stared at the initials surrounding the spheres. All of them matched the list Angela had just given him.

AMK and MSS were both fire elements. MHA and CAM were earth elements. YNL and AJC were air elements. NY and OAG were water elements. Paul wrote the initials and the names next to the rest of his chart.

Three of them corresponded: Angela, Arnaud, and Casimir. The fourth missing element was water. Paul examined the list. The missing horseman had to be Niú Ye or Oksanna Anya Galina. He would need to be very careful. One of them would unite them. And one of them could divide them.

He knew where to find Niú Ye. Now he would need contact information for Ms. Galina.

The university systems were still up and operating, although with occasional interruptions, and he was fortunate to get through to Angela again on the first ring.

"Angela, I need an address and contact information for Oksanna Anya Galina. And I'm going to need you to do some research. I'm going to need to know everything possible about the life, the history, the education, the jobs—everything—of Dr. Niú Ye and Ms. Galina. Let me know when you've got it. Oh, and Angela, I think we'd better plan on staying at the cathedral from now on. I have a feeling we need to stay together."

34

TWISTS AND TURNS

University of Virginia

Paul was still staring at the names Angela had given him. *Matthew Samael Serafino, born 21.12.12 at 2100, in Trona, California. Matt Serafino.* Paul shivered. What had he been thinking?! He could have told Serafino something that would allow the man to infiltrate everything they were discovering. Paul didn't know what exactly that might mean, but he knew it wouldn't be good. Serafino was interested only in power. It made perfect sense. Paul looked again at the symbols. Fire. Serafino was fire, the angel horseman, the agent of death, the one who tramples everyone under his feet. Who was his counterpart? Paul stared at the sheet. Angela.

Angela was the key figure for all of them. Angela. Paul guessed she had no idea how important she would be.

He would need to find a way to get to the people, to try to find those who might have enough trust inside them to listen to him. But he couldn't do it through public channels. Certainly not through Serafino. *The remnant of those still with faith. Of course. The sanctuaries.* He would contact the priests, who would know how to get in touch with the underground faithful. Lead the people to the sanctuaries.

Serafino wouldn't follow anyone there, would think they were just engaging in rituals, praying, gathering. He might even think they chose to go on their own. Paul needed to make sure Serafino wouldn't find out that Paul had called them there. And then when they were gathered, at the right time, he could somehow get them to Bashan. The priests could get word to the people. And they might listen. Trust what Paul was telling them. He had to try.

NEW HAVEN, CONNECTICUT

The city of New Haven lay deserted, bits of red tape blowing into the gutters and flapping from the still-present wooden posts surrounding the city. The staph virus had taken its toll and had transformed the once-vibrant city into a ghost town. Above the empty streets, the sky shimmered with swirls and bands of rainbow colors.

If the virus hadn't eradicated the population, the sun would have, as solar particles immersed the area for miles around in a radiation bath, moving out northward toward Hartford and southwest toward New York.

MARSEILLE, PROVENCE-ALPES-CÔTE D'AZUR, FRANCE

St. Seraphim Orthodox Cathedral

Angela, Arnaud, and Casimir arrived back at the cathedral in Marseille that evening and found Paul sitting in Arnaud's office, surveying maps of the Middle East and Syria. He stood up as they arrived, greeting them and motioning for them all to have a seat in the crowded office. Seraphim squawked and moved back and forth in his cage excitedly at the arrival of his master and the rest of his audience. Casimir went over to the cockatiel's cage and held up a seedcake. Seraphim reached out and plucked some seeds from the cake in Casimir's fingers, settling onto his perch.

Angela brought out the research she had done at the university in Marseille. Paul nodded for her to begin.

"Niú Ye was born in Hangzhou, a small village outside Beijing in China. From what I could find out, he was given to an orphanage as a young child and raised working in the rice fields. No money to speak of. Seems to have spent a lifetime trying to locate his family, but has never found them. He made friends with the Christian missionaries there near Hangzhou, and they apparently recognized him as a bright and reputable young man. They sent him to the university in Beijing, where he studied biogenetics. He was apparently an outstanding student. Straight honors. And he was recruited by the government after receiving his doctoral degree to work as head scientist for the new emerging interrelational sciences research team at the National Center for the Study of Genetics in Beijing. There was some talk then that he had engaged in some kind of illegal or underhanded activity while at the center in China, and that he recently had been experimenting with some very potent and dangerous genetic-altering technologies. But other than that, he seems to have led a pretty quiet life. He normally attends most of the world's bioethics and interrelational sciences conferences, and he apparently made China the leading biogenetics center in the world, until recently."

"What happened recently?" Paul looked up.

"He disappeared. The news reports in China indicate he simply vanished from the country without a word. That was right before the Afghani takeover. No one has been able to locate him since."

Paul smiled. "Well, someone has. What about Galina?"

Angela looked perplexed by Paul's comment but went on.

"Oksanna Anya Galina was born in Siberia, Russia, to very famous parents—I know you've heard of this in the news—they revolutionized the return to biofarming by building a giant agridome called the World Greenhouse in Siberian Russia near the turn of the century. They were essentially the reason Russia became the humanitarian country it did—and the only country capable of feeding its inhabitants with its own food supply. When they died, their only daughter, Oksanna, took over the enterprise, called the IEO, a nonprofit funded by the government and private investors. The IEO had plans for a humanitarian project on behalf of Russia to build a sister greenhouse in a host country, when Galina was shot at a fund-raising event in Moscow. From what I can find out, there's been no arrest and no leads on who attempted the assassination. But soon after her recovery, the World Greenhouse in Siberia was completely obliterated by the iceberg devastation and flooding in the northern seas. I'm sure you remember that from the news. Galina chose not to rebuild, and the IEO seems to have simply dissolved. Russia has been looking at other ways of supplementing their food supplies, and Galina left the country about a month ago to take a new position"—Angela paused—"at the Conservation Center in Waikiki. Oksanna Anya Galina is in Hawaii. I have an address."

"Excellent work, Angela." Paul was impressed.

"Now." He looked around at the group. "Which of these two do you think is our final horseman?"

WASHINGTON, D.C.

The White House

Matt Serafino followed the narrow underground tunnel to the small room where he still kept the Codex Gigas, the Devil's Bible, which lay on the single wooden table in the center of the space. He didn't think anyone knew about these underground passages anymore. They had no doubt served a purpose when the White House was built, perhaps for safety, perhaps for some kind of other, more-clandestine reasons. But Matt had come across the labyrinthine cloister of passageways almost immediately, sensing them out like a bloodhound.

Here, he laid out his collection of books, treatises on alchemy by authors from Paracelsus to Newton. Serafino needed to figure out how to unify the four horsemen of the Apocalypse and transport them into the new age, where he, Serafino, would lead a new world, a world of wealth, prosperity, and unity; a world where everyone would come under one rule, his rule—that of the New Unified States of the World. His vision. He had known he was destined for this almost from birth, could sense it, feel it. He always knew that someday he would lead all people into a new kind of age. And it was coming now.

Binder was right about that. Something was going to happen, and it would happen soon. He needed to find the last missing piece, the last player in this game of roulette. And then he needed to get his three compatriots to the temple in Jerusalem, to the Court of the Priests, the center square of the golden dome.

In Jerusalem, the Dome of the Rock is located in the very place where the temple had been, over the cave of souls. Serafino would need all of them to assemble there, inside the octagon-shaped structure. They would need to stand each on one end of the octagon, east, west, north, and south, representing the four elements, earth, wind, fire, and water. And they would need to say the alchemical incantations at precisely 9:00 p.m., the twenty-first hour. And then they would be transported into the new age. Matt wasn't sure if the entire temple would go along with them, or whether they would simply disappear and reappear in the new reality, the new dimension. But he needed to put all his energy now into finding the last horseman—and into finding the incantation. For years, the alchemists knew. They knew this day would come, as did the Aztecs and the Mayans, and so many others throughout history. The prophecy would soon come to pass. All the prophecies were one. They were all from different cultures, different times, different perspectives. But they all essentially came to the same conclusions if one knew how to read the signs. In December 2012, the seals were broken. It was now the Time of Becoming, the Age of the Seraph, and soon, it would be the Age of All Beginnings. And he, Matthew Serafino, was destined to be at the center of it all.

MARSEILLE, PROVENCE-ALPES-CÔTE D'AZUR, FRANCE
St. Seraphim Orthodox Cathedral
Seraphim had been singing all evening. The group had moved into the sanctuary and was sitting in the foremost wooden chairs, relaxing and sipping glasses of French wine.

"What is that strange tune?" The bird had caught Angela's attention, and she had been listening to him sing for the last hour.

Arnaud laughed. "It's the *Mazeppa*. Liszt's Transcendental Étude No. 4. I've been playing it far too often lately, and Seraphim must have heard it and memorized the tune."

"It's haunting."

"Indeed. But I'm afraid small Seraphim doesn't do the entire piece justice. Allow me."

Arnaud relocated himself to the bench at the large ebony piano, placed his hands carefully and contemplatively at the keyboard, and then burst into the rich and astounding complexity that is the *Mazeppa*.

Angela and Paul were flabbergasted.

"I had no idea Arnaud could play like that," Angela whispered, her voice echoing in the almost empty sanctuary.

The tones resounded within the cathedral walls, building to a climax. Angela felt the sound surround them. If she closed her eyes, she could almost imagine the music enclosing them all inside a cacophony of horses, chariots, and the rush of the winds and storms. In her mind, they were all together, unified, being lifted, transported upon the waves of the wind, the waves of sound, the beautiful music of the universe. The music was the music of love, the music of everything, the music of God.

As the piece ended, Angela sat up, a smile still on her face. She blinked her eyes, needing to clear her head. The music had been an almost mystical experience. She had never heard anything like it. She looked over at Paul. He had the same look of disorientation, as though returning from someplace far away.

They both glanced to the far wall, where Casimir had been sitting, playing with a large nautilus shell from Arnaud's study. He, too, looked contemplative, dazed, mesmerized by the music, which he had no doubt heard many times before.

Paul suddenly sat up. He was staring at Casimir's shell.

"Fibonacci's golden ratio, the golden squares. The basis for all beauty, all complexity in nature. Truth, beauty, goodness, love all lead to the unity of all things, a transcendental of reality. Leibniz's labyrinth. The labyrinth of the continuum."

Angela glanced over at Arnaud, who was leaning around the piano, listening intently to Paul. Casimir looked up as well, his alert, inquisitive eyes staring calm and unconcerned from his broad face.

Arnaud spoke up. "The labyrinth. Of course. It's the connection we've been looking for. In the cathedrals, the labyrinth symbolizes the path to the Holy Land, to spiritual awareness and unity. It's both an individual and a communal process. It is the act of trusting the path of faith that brings the follower home. *Le chemin de Jerusalem.* The Platonists built them first. But our historic cathedrals have them. It's the perfect meeting place."

Casimir spoke up now. "In the Kabbalah, the labyrinth is the journey of the heart. The labyrinth of the Kabbalah was similar to the Indian medicine wheels—it offered a way to wholeness."

"The Mayan prophecy." Angela joined in. "The wheel."

"Yes," said Paul. "And just like the Mayan wheel, the labyrinths have eleven circuits, four quadrants all arranged around the cross, with the rose in the center."

"The rose. I had forgotten about that." Angela sat up now, listening, before saying, "The wheel you've been talking about, Paul. The chariots of the four horsemen. They are all symbols also of the labyrinth. The path to the infinite. The path to God and Christ and the Holy Spirit, the unity of all creation—all people, all that is."

Arnaud joined in. "Excellent thought, Ms. Angela." He continued, "You know, I am a member of the Labyrinth Society."

They all turned and looked at Arnaud. Angela's eyes got wide. "You are?"

Paul was smiling, then laughing. "That's it! That's it."

He got up and strode over to Father Chevalier, throwing his arms around the large priest and hugging him. A surprised Arnaud stepped back, blinking. He looked confused.

"Father Arnaud, can you contact all of your priests, the ones in the Labyrinth Society, those with labyrinths inside their cathedrals and sanctuaries?"

"Well, yes, of course."

"It's the gathering places. We'll have all those who want to make the pilgrimage of faith to Bashan come to the labyrinths. No one else will know. The New Selfers won't pay any attention to those gathering around the labyrinths.

"Father, we need to get to work. We need a list of all the cathedrals with labyrinths. Then we need to find a way to transport those who gather at these various locations to Bashan." Paul hesitated only a moment. "Planes. We need planes."

The three were distracted then by a knock on the cathedral door. It was late.

"Who could be here at this hour, I wonder?" Father Arnaud rose from the bench and walked slowly and quietly to the narthex door. He opened the large wooden doors to find a woman with dark hair and dark eyes, in a heavy fur coat, standing in the doorway.

"I'm sorry to bother you so late, Father. But I received a letter."

35

SIGNS

MARSEILLE, PROVENCE-ALPES-CÔTE D'AZUR,
FRANCE

St. Seraphim Orthodox Cathedral

Angela was busy helping Father Arnaud gather the lists of priests from the Labyrinth Societies.

"I didn't know there was a labyrinth in Washington, D.C., Father."

"Yes. The Washington National Cathedral. There are many more of them than I'm sure you realize, my dear. In France alone, there are several. The most famous are those at Chartres, Reims, and Sens. But even in England you have Alkborough Church in North Lincolnshire, the Ely Cathedral in Cambridgeshire, St. Mary Redcliffe in Bristol, Ichenstoke in Hampshire."

"And St. Paul's in London, of course."

"Of course. The labyrinths are a symbol for us that, although the world has changed, the light of hope for humanity will never die. The labyrinth will always lead the trusting to God. And the cathedrals, the sanctuaries—they've always been a place where those of faith come to follow the path of God. You must find as many as you can, Angela. Russia, Syria, San Francisco, throughout Europe, Asia, the Middle East, Africa, the Americas . . . all across the world, you must find them. We will need at least one gathering place per country. At least. Wherever there are faithful, those still with their hearts rooted in the Lamb, they must be brought to Bashan."

Paul came in the door then with their newest guest.

"Ah, Ms. Galina. Have you slept well?"

"Yes, thank you, Father."

Paul interrupted. His attention was drawn to a symbol and a sheet of music that Father Chevalier was preparing on his Pearl.

"Father Arnaud, what is that?"

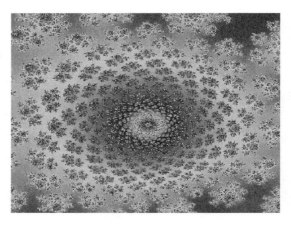

"This," Arnaud explained, "is our message."

"It looks like some kind of fractal." Angela was looking too now. "It's beautiful."

"Yes." Arnaud laughed. "Almost everything in creation is in some way beautiful—and created from the same types of sequences used here."

"Sequences?"

"Yes. You see, the message is encoded. The letters have been assigned numbers and developed into an algorithm, a labyrinth of language, if you will. The fractal that is generated can also be expressed in sound—in music, as you see here."

Arnaud touched the side of his Pearl, and the encoded numbers burst into an odd melody.

"Music. The universal language." Arnaud smiled.

Paul laughed. "Leibniz would have loved this."

"He may have, yes. Leibniz wanted to discover a *characteristica universalis*, a symbolic universal language to express reality. In a sense, we have that now in our combined knowledge of physics and mathematics."

"Well, I still think the universal language is love." Angela smiled.

"So it is, Ms. Krall. So it is."

Paul looked puzzled. "But Father Arnaud, how is anyone going to know what the message says?"

Arnaud smiled. "All the members of the Labyrinth Society will know how to decode this message, Paul. And so will all the priests. Remember, the church went underground years ago. The cathedrals have been nothing much more than historic sites to just about everyone except the select few. And those are the few from everywhere whom we will gather together. The priests know them. In order for the church to function, for the faithful to follow their pilgrimages, the priests needed a way to communicate. The Labyrinth Society has provided that. They are the 'keepers of the faith.' They will understand your message. And they will communicate the word to others."

Paul looked at the seemingly random numbers on the page Arnaud had prepared:

3, 1, 12, 12, 9, 14, 7, 1, 12, 12, 6, 1, 9, 20, 8, 6, 21, 12, 20, 15, 7, 15, 4
21, 12, 48, 2100
13, 5, 5, 20, 1, 20, 12, 1, 2, 25, 18, 9, 14, 20, 8
1, 12, 12, 23, 8, 15, 3, 15, 13, 5, 23, 9, 12, 12, 2, 5, 19, 1, 22, 5, 4

"What does the message say, Father?"

"It's very simple," said Arnaud before translating the numbered code for Paul:

Calling all faithful to God
21 December 2048, at 2100
Meet at Labyrinth.
All who come will be saved.

"And you believe the network of the Labyrinth Society will understand that, be able to pass it on?" Paul looked hesitant.

"I know they will. We must do the difficult thing and give control to God, trusting that the message will make it through the communications system, and trusting that it will reach those who need to hear it."

HAWAIIAN ISLANDS

The explosion came unexpectedly in the early hours of the morning. Blinding flashes of light crackled through the still-darkened sky over the metallic soup that was the Pacific. The red ball of the sun appeared to expand to three times its size as it hovered over the Hawaiian Islands. The blast of solar radiation seemed to stir something inside the earth and its subterranean waters, like fire under a closed pot, and the Mauna Kea erupted, sending molten rock into the air for miles.

Te Tama, kahuna for the remaining Kanaka Maoli on the island, dropped to his knees along the beaches of Oahu.

"It's a sign."

WASHINGTON, D.C.

The White House

"Oil?" Serafino laughed.

Malik Asvaka had joined Matthew Serafino in the Oval Office and was taken aback by the president's reaction to his offer.

"Why would you think the United States would want to buy oil at a time like this?"

Malik hadn't expected this reaction, and he was temporarily at a loss for words.

"Mr. President, with the state of the world, the earth at the moment, I would think—"

Serafino interrupted Asvaka. "Could you excuse me for a moment, sir?"

"Yes, of course." Malik looked confused. He *was* confused. He had known to expect the unexpected from someone like Matthew Serafino. Their prior encounter upon the president's visit to Scitheon had proved that. However, he couldn't imagine the USAmerican president turning down an offer to buy the only workable fuel now available. What was Malik missing? Did Serafino know something he didn't? Nevertheless, the president's behavior was odd, to say the least. And it was about to get stranger still.

Matthew Serafino seemed to have lost all sense of the need for presidential decorum. He strode back into the office, stood directly in front of Asvaka, and folded his arms.

"May I ask, when is your birthday, Mr. Asvaka?"

"My birthday?"

TEHRAN, IRAN

"Where did you get that suit?" Ali was staring at Sarv's protective covering.

"My uncle has connections in the government. The prime minister bought five thousand of them from the United States last week."

"Hard on the eye!"

"Yes, well, it's solar-deflective. You're not meant to stare at the suit."

Ali continued digging.

"So, when the radiation shelters are completed, how many of us do you think are going to get to use them?"

Sarv looked at his companion and smirked. "None of *us*."

MARSEILLE, PROVENCE-ALPES-CÔTE D'AZUR, FRANCE

St. Seraphim Orthodox Cathedral

Oksanna had joined the others in the dining room that evening. It was getting colder as the fall progressed, and they all sat in the drafty hall, huddled in sweaters and blankets. Heat would be a rare commodity in the coming months. As the electrical systems continued to fluctuate, sometimes working, sometimes not, depending upon solar activity, the price to attempt to heat something like a cathedral was out of the question. Arnaud suspected they might have to go back to using the huge fireplaces that stood in most of the older rooms, and eventually they would most likely have to dispense with their single rooms and huddle together in Arnaud's office for heat. But for now, blankets would suffice.

"So, I'm still not clear on how you found us." Paul had taken a slice of cheese from the table and was nibbling on the end of it.

"Sometimes I'm not sure either." Oksanna smiled wanly. "I'm not exactly one to do anything spontaneous. I'm more of a practical person, I would say."

"A practical person with a 'save the world' mentality and an optimism that would fool any realist," Angela said and smiled.

Oksanna laughed. "Touché, Ms. Krall. But I'm afraid I am a realist in one sense. No matter how much kindness and concern I may have for the world, nothing can be done without money. At least not on a large scale. It is the generosity of many that has always funded my humanitarian efforts. It is the community and not the individual who ultimately creates change."

"Well said, Ms. Galina." Paul nodded respectfully.

"But," she continued, "despite my realist attitude, I have been lately fascinated with something I came across in my studies of the Mayan culture—about the sun. And then I got this letter."

Oksanna pulled out a letter that she had kept in the pocket of her large coat. She unfolded it and laid it on the table, where the others could see it. The script looked similar to that in the letter Paul had received.

"The Society of Messengers." Angela smiled.

"Perhaps," said Arnaud.

The letter was brief and simple, but Paul could see why Oksanna would respond.

Dear Ms. Oksanna Anya Galina,
You have been chosen to help guide others to safety.
A new world is waiting and you will become part of

*it. There are others like you. All born on the 21st day
of December 20-12, at 21-00. All with the characteristic
birthmark on the right calf. You are not alone.
At this time tomorrow, Hawaii will be gone. It
will sink into the sea at dawn. Go to the Syrian
Orthodox cathedral in Marseille tonight. The others
are awaiting your arrival. Trust not what you know or
even what I tell you. Trust your heart. Read the signs.*

Paul was nodding.

Oksanna continued. "I had just come from the Mayan exhibit in Waikiki. The signs. Well, the prophecy, and the sun, what's been happening . . . I have no real explanation for why I left and came here. At this point, I suppose, I have no reason to believe that knowledge is only what we learn in books, or from scientific experiments, or from what we can physically touch. I trusted my intuition."

Angela reached over and put her hand over Oksanna's long fingers.

Arnaud looked around the table. "And Hawaii?"

Oksanna looked up. "It's gone."

OUTSIDE CAIRO, EGYPT

Underground National Lab

Youhanna Lachier received the message from Matthew Serafino that evening via messenger.

"The president of the United States is inviting me to dinner."

Youhanna's voice echoed in the empty lab. He was used to having Hassan there to speak to. Now he had gotten into the habit of talking to himself.

What could Serafino want now?

Youhanna thought they had come to an agreement. The United States would offer Egypt financial support in return for the president's place in the Moondome. Yet Serafino turned down the offer.

He said he wasn't interested in the dome. But he would assist Egypt no matter what. Now Youhanna wasn't sure what Serafino really wanted. But he knew the president wouldn't make a deal that was one-sided. Perhaps, it was now time for Serafino to tell him what he really wanted. Youhanna frowned. Serafino made him nervous.

THE GATHERING

MARSEILLE, PROVENCE-ALPES-CÔTE D'AZUR, FRANCE

St. Seraphim Orthodox Cathedral

The five sat around the table in the cathedral kitchen, the dining area having become too drafty for comfort. The kitchen had a warm glow to it, and the fire in the old stone hearth kept the entire room heated and comfortable. Arnaud had toasted the French bread over the wood in the hearth, and he brought it out now, warm and steaming, to the table in a blue cloth. Fresh butter in a crock, along with jams and honey, adorned the side table. Paul began the meal by passing the warm bread, as Arnaud poured the dark, red wine into small, rounded wine glasses. The mood was jovial but solemn, as they all joined hands around the small but welcome meal.

Outside the cathedral, the windows showed flickering firelight and cast a deep, red glow onto the newly falling snow.

Oksanna was the first to notice the white flakes falling outside the cathedral windows.

"It's snowing!" Her eyes lit up as she gazed toward the window.

"How can that be?" Arnaud seemed confused. "There's no water to evaporate. What kind of snow is that?"

They all rose from the table and gathered around the window. The white substance was beginning to form a thin layer across the dry grass of the cathedral's lawn.

"I don't think that's snow." Angela looked doubtful. Pressing her face against the window, she strained to examine the flakes.

"What do you mean?" Oksanna appeared disappointed and worried at the same time.

"Look how it's falling. Snow doesn't fall like that," said Angela.

Paul watched the small, odd-shaped flakes gently fall to the ground, blowing slightly in the evening breeze.

"Angela's right. Snow is heavier than that. It falls directly downward. This looks lighter. What is that?" Paul turned to the others. "Should I go outside and—"

"No!" They all jumped slightly as Arnaud's voice demanded attention.

"Something's wrong. That's not snow. That's ash."

"And where there's ash . . ." Paul began.

"There's fire," said Angela.

WASHINGTON, D.C.

The White House

Matt looked at his watch. Another twenty minutes, and he would have all of them at one table. He had asked Mullica to create a special menu with the White House chefs. He wanted this meal to be perfect. He needed the cooperation of all three of his new colleagues, and he couldn't have anything go wrong.

The table was decked in gold and red with shell black plates and gold-plated dinnerware. Before the meal was to begin, Serafino would plan to meet the group for a small pre-dinner drink in the adjoining sitting room. After dessert, they would retire to the smoking room for cordials and cigars. And then Serafino would pitch his proposal.

The chefs had done well. Serafino nodded in approval as the kitchen staff prepared the presentation of the evening meal.

Roast lamb with mint and parsley potatoes adorned a large tray in the center of the long table. Bottles of sparkling water stood on the side table nearby, and the waiter had carefully filled each guest's glass, allowing the small bubbles to erupt into tiny fountains at each place setting. For dessert, a large chocolate lava cake waited on the sideboard.

Serafino had gone to great difficulty to make sure the chefs could acquire all the ingredients needed to create the meal. He still had his connections, which was good, because food was short, especially fresh vegetables and herbs. And meat was fast becoming a rare commodity as animals perished from lack of food and water. Farms were virtually nonexistent now, and the only foodstuffs available were packaged and canned items or stored grains and fruits. Soon those would diminish. *But by that time, I won't have to worry about it,* Serafino thought as he curled his lip. *As long as everything goes all right tonight.*

Niú Ye was the first to arrive, having come from the lab. He was followed closely by Malik Asvaka. After his meeting two days before with the president, Serafino had insisted that the Afghan man stay as his guest in the White House East Wing. So Asvaka had donned his best suit and strode through the long hallways to the president's quarters at the appropriate time. Youhanna Lachier had been scheduled to arrive by plane earlier that afternoon and was staying in a nearby hotel. Serafino asked Mullica to find out if the French-Egyptian would be delayed, and Mullica quickly hurried from the room to make the call.

"Well, my friends, while we are waiting for our colleague Dr. Lachier, let us have a drink together. A toast, to our allied nations. *Euan, euoi!*" Serafino raised his glass.

Niú gave the president an odd glance but raised his glass appropriately. Malik Asvaka couldn't be sure what Serafino was up to. And it bothered him. It confused him. Why were they all here? A Chinese biogeneticist, an Egyptian astronomer, and himself—an Afghani technoscientist. What did the president want?

They had just gathered in the small dining room when Youhanna Lachier arrived. The president welcomed him and led him to a seat at the table with the others. Matt Serafino lifted yet another toast to the future of the coming new age, met by another set of strange and confused looks from all around the table, and the meal was thereby commenced.

While feasting on the lamb, the four eventually grew somewhat comfortable with one another, although each distrusted Serafino in his own way and for his own reasons. At the end of the meal, the president invited the group into the adjoining chamber, an octagon-shaped area with leather furniture and dark wood lining the walls that Matt Serafino used as his smoking room.

Serafino handed a gold humidor with its heavy scent of tobacco to Niú and asked him to pass the box around, so that each could choose a cigar of his liking. Matt had reserved his own cigar of the evening in a special box that he kept in his private rooms. It was a Padron Anniversario 1964, a rare brand, almost a century old, with a woody and nutty flavor like chocolate and coffee rolled up into a sheath of smoked spices. He sat back now, enjoying his treat and watching his companions begin to relax. And like a panther observing his prey, Serafino waited.

BOULDER, COLORADO

"I don't think anyone is going to suspect anything with us meeting here."

"I think you're right, but let's check the room for bugs just in case."

The gathering of the western states in Boulder that morning was not one anyone took lightly. One by one, Oklahoma, Kansas, Nebraska, South Dakota, North Dakota, Montana, Wyoming, Colorado, New Mexico, and Arizona had taken the initiative. What was left of California mercenaries soon joined forces, as did Nevada, followed closely by Oregon and Washington. Idaho and Utah were the last to sign on, knowing it was useless at that point to remain neutral in the midst of the others gathering in the West. Although Texas had already seceded from the States, New Texas had offered their assistance if and when fighting broke out. They had at the very least promised to serve as a solid boundary, preventing the east from crossing Texan country in order to reach the western south.

The speaker, Governor Jerry Campbell from Oklahoma, had organized the group and served as temporary leader of the movement to launch what was only the second civil war the United States had ever seen, this time between the West and the East—two areas that had always been as different as night and day and that had grown even more so during the last century. Now they were like two completely different countries, despising each other for what the other was not.

But this time there were also bigger fish to fry. The agricultural West was dying, and most blamed big industry in the Northeast, believing it must have been the fault of pollution, toxic waste, or inattention to global warming that had destroyed the earth's waters, threatened the nation's food supply, and cast the less wealthy into ground-creeping poverty. Radiation from solar rays was destroying the nation's forests, killing whole areas at a time with radiation baths, and drenching the states in a panic they had never before imagined. Most lived almost totally in the radiation fallout shelters they had either just built or had adapted from a century before for protection against twisters and other natural phenomena. The natural resources they had come to depend upon were depleting fast, and already an entire portion of California had fallen into a murky sea. The people may not have thought the government in the East had caused each disaster, but they did think nothing was being done about any of it. The current president seemed unaware, unconcerned, and distracted from the concerns of the people, as though he had bigger and better things to think about than his nation. For most states, it had long become unacceptable. For the West, it was cause for civil war. They might not have all the solutions, but they felt they would and could do better themselves, and they took it upon themselves to form mercenary groups and to spend the last several years training from young to old in renegade-style forms of combat. That was their thought the day the petition was signed and the West officially declared war on the Eastern states.

MOBILE, ALABAMA

Windows were smashed and the alarms went off for the eleventh time that night. Ethan Shaw motioned for his family to be quiet. His wife and their daughter were huddled at the far side of the room, trying to sleep. No one felt safe anymore. Even if there was nothing to be had, the looters would break in anyway, damaging property, taking whatever could be eaten or drunk and wreaking havoc, sometimes even committing murder in their wake. It was not a good time to be in USAmerica. It was not a good time to be anywhere in the world, for that matter. And people were scared. For the first time since the Great Depression in the United States more than a century before, there was simply no food to be had. And now it was so much worse. The water supplies were next to depleted, and the replenishing and purifying plants couldn't keep up with the demand. In place of what used to be heavy fall and winter rains was now only a gray sort of ash that came down from the sky in the aftermath of a radiation bath. And people were getting sick. Radiation diseases were becoming prevalent, some showing up long after the assumed exposure. The government had mass-produced radiation-deflecting suits and masks, but only the wealthy and connected had access to those. The rest of the people—most of the people—suffered silently in the dry and cracking landscape that they had called home.

Ethan had heard that the West was gathering for civil war. And he wondered what that would mean for him in the nation's South. Would he have to go to war? What would happen to his family, left alone in a city now full of crime and looting, as if that were the daily norm? He looked over at his wife and daughter, now sleeping fitfully, arm over arm on the makeshift bed. And Ethan Shaw cried.

MARSEILLE, PROVENCE-ALPES-CÔTE D'AZUR, FRANCE

St. Seraphim Orthodox Cathedral

The red dawn had moved in thicker over Europe, and the skies shone golden, orange, and red, casting a strange glow over the landscape.

To Paul, it was like looking through red plastic foil. And out of the red came the ash. White falling flakes that seemed to gather like snow in heaps everywhere. Paul guessed the ash was filled with radiation particles. Arnaud was right; they needed to stay inside for now. Needed to gather their resources, and within the week they would need to be on their way to Bashan. It would be safer there.

Paul still hadn't figured out where to get the planes they would need to transport the people from the labyrinths—from the cathedrals and sanctuaries—to the hillsides of Bashan. They would need whatever they could get their hands on. Planes. Helicopters. And they would need to be ones that used oil and gasoline and required pilots, some that could be retrofitted, not the new high-tech solar, sonic, and nano planes that needed energy that was no longer reliable for power. The solar flares would also knock out communication. They would need to be very careful.

Arnaud had said the priests were organizing the people. More people than Paul had estimated were already making the pilgrimages to the sanctuaries. For some, they felt safer in the sanctuaries than at home, and people were beginning to camp out not only inside the cathedrals, but in their large courtyards and even on their former lawns. Paul was astounded. Could that many people have that kind of trust? He had thought the world had completely dispensed with faith—with any thought of God. Perhaps they had only dispensed with the churches, had been disappointed by them, let down. But now the sanctuaries again offered a hope, and for most people, it was the only hope available. And they continued to gather.

GREENBELT, MARYLAND
Goddard Space Flight Center (NASA)

The team of astronomers, scientists, and astronauts watched helplessly as the screen showed the footage of the last satellite to record data before the solar explosion that knocked out the satellite's power and fried the power grids of most of the northern hemisphere. They were running now on archaic, century-old generators, and even that power threatened to fizzle out at any time. With the explosion of the satellite, a bright flash of light had lit up the northern skies, as though the very atmosphere of the earth itself had opened up and allowed the eye of God to peek through. Everyone who had looked directly at the flash had gone blind immediately. The force of the light had been so powerful it had exceeded the amount of light the eye could absorb by millions of times. People were becoming fearful to be outside, instead opting to hide away in underground rooms, caves, passages, wherever they could find places away from the bizarre effects of the sun. Solar winds were kicking up again, creating anomalies in every weather system. News reports had long given up trying to predict the weather, which was now as random as the core of black energy that exuded from it. Fierce tornadoes had been making their way across the western United States and throughout Asia, Africa, and the Middle East. The now dry landscapes were ripe for major dust storms, hauling huge mounds of putrid earth into the air and slamming it down upon buildings, cars, and industries. The deserts were baking at temperatures never before heard of, and the magnetic shift had caused major upheavals on the poles, which were fast growing thick, dark, and cold. Geomagnetic storms were raging across the entire globe, sending tsunamis of metallic sea into the land. Volcanoes erupted daily. Ash fell from the sky. And the borealis was turning ever redder as the sun approached the earth. And still more storm clouds were gathering. The time had come, and everyone knew it. The earth was dying.

Part IV

IOSIS

My task, as a sincere Christian and musician, is to seek and to cultivate the True, the Good, and the Beautiful.

—Franz Liszt

Love is the only gold.

—Alfred Lord Tennyson

There are things so deep and complex that only intuition can reach it in our stage of development as human beings.

—John Astin

We must become the change we want to see.

—Mahatma Gandhi

On tops of mountains, as everywhere to hopeful souls,
it is always morning.

—Henry David Thoreau

37

TURNING ON THE HEAT

St. Seraphim Orthodox Cathedral

Angela found Paul in Arnaud's office, looking at old maps. He was busy drawing red circles where each of them had been born, and tracing lines from their places of birth to their present meeting place at the cathedral in Marseille.

"Good morning, Paul."

Paul looked up and smiled. "Morning, Angela."

"That looks like a giant triangle with a thousand interlocking strands."

Paul laughed. "I suppose it does. Look at this." He held out one of the maps for Angela. "Hibernia. That was the name for Ireland when Ptolemy drew up his map of the world in the second century. That's what Tatian, maybe even John of Patmos, would have thought of that place that they envisioned, where you were to be born in 2012."

Angela was impressed. "What's this one?"

"Sarmatia—later known as Polonia in Bulane. Casimir's birthplace. You would like this, Angela. In the second century, what is now Poland was the land of the early Celts. They lived there first, long before the Germanic migrations took them west and north, where they settled into your homeland—Ireland."

"That's amazing, Paul. What else? Where was Oksanna's birth-place? What was Russia?"

"Over here. Probably Sarmatia, too. The area was so widespread, it's hard to say where borders may have started and ended. Germania could have stretched over that way, or Hyperborei a bit farther north."

"And Father Arnaud?"

"Here, where we are now. Gallia."

Angela smiled, shaking her head. So many years ago, and yet the earth was in many ways more familiar in Tatian's time than it was becoming now.

They suddenly felt a rumbling in the floor, followed by a violent shaking that lasted between five and six minutes. They fell to the ground and sought shelter under the table, while Seraphim squawked and flew about his cage in alarm. After it was over, Angela went over to the bird, petting him and soothing him, while Paul picked up the pieces of bro-ken pottery and books that had fallen from Father Arnaud's shelves.

The others rushed in.

"Is everyone all right?" Father Arnaud looked around, making sure everyone was accounted for.

"Fine," said Paul. "The quake was a small one. But I have a feeling it's only the beginning of a lot worse to come. We need to be ready."

"Speaking of ready, I think I have an answer for you about the planes, Paul."

Oksanna had run into the office, wearing her large musk-ox fur coat and in bare feet. Her thick, dark hair hung around her face and shoulders.

"The Underground Greens in Russia have some connections—I think with Aeroflot. I might be able to get you the planes you need for 21 December."

"How many? There are thousands gathering."

"I'm not sure. But I'll get hold of them right now."

"Excellent."

Angela looked at Paul. "That's it, then, isn't it? The last piece. We're ready."

"Not quite." Paul motioned to the windows. The skies were a deep red, and heaps of ash covered the ground throughout the area of the cathedral and no doubt through Marseille and beyond.

"We don't know how much radiation is out there and in that ash. We don't even know how safe we've been in here, although I suspect the gold on the cathedral's facade has served as a deflector and has shielded us for the most part. But until we figure out a way to deal with the radiation and get to Bashan safely, we can't go out there."

Angela looked alarmed. "I hadn't thought of that."

"Neither had I," echoed Oksanna, turning from her Pearl, where she was still trying to make a connection.

Just then, Arnaud's office panel rang. Paul jumped slightly, not expecting a call.

Arnaud answered and then looked at Paul. "It's for you."

"Me? Who knows I'm here?"

Arnaud was shaking his head. Paul took the call.

"Paul Binder."

"Dr. Binder, this is Niú Ye. We met briefly when you came to the White House last week."

Paul looked worried. He motioned for the others to leave the room, and they all quietly exited the office, shutting the door behind them.

"Yes, I remember." Paul was listening intently through the somewhat bad connection, hoping the crackling didn't worsen and cause him to miss what the Chinese scientist had to say.

"Look, Mr. Binder. I don't have a lot of time right now. But I think I know who you are, what you are going to try to do. And I need to warn you that Matthew Serafino . . ."

"Wait a minute. Dr. Niú, with all due respect, sir, before we have this conversation, don't you work for President Serafino?"

"Look, Mr. Binder. There's someone I've been in touch with here who has given me some very valuable information about Matthew Serafino. And what I haven't learned from my source, I've now confirmed after a dinner several of us had with the president last evening. What I'm trying to say is, I know where your meeting place is."

Paul looked alarmed now. "My meeting place?"

"Please, I'm not threatening you. Serafino doesn't know. No one will know. I promise you. I think I can help you."

"Help me how?"

"Let me think about that. I have some calls to make. I just want you to know I'm on your side."

"On *my* side? Dr. Niú, there are no sides in this. Only destruction for everyone, unless . . ."

"Yes, you are quite right. But Serafino will lead the four of us his way."

"Then you *are* part of Serafino's entourage."

"I just want you to know, when the time comes, I'll do what I can. I was once helped. Long ago. It . . . changed the course of my life. I'll get back to you."

The line went dead, and Paul found himself more confused than ever. He was still staring straight ahead, thinking over his conversation with Niú Ye, when Oksanna knocked at the door and Paul motioned for them all to come back in.

"What was that about?" Arnaud took a seat at the far side of the office.

"I'm not sure. I'm just not sure."

Oksanna looked up suddenly, excitedly waving her Pearl. "I've got them."

BEIJING, CHINA

Capitol Building

"Niú, my God, where have you been?"

Murong Gui took the call to his private number in the middle of the night. "I have to be careful, Niú. I'm being watched."

"I know, Mr. President. So am I. And I only have a moment. The lines are unstable. Can you get to the lab?"

"I don't know. Why?"

"I have a formula. I need you to get it to Jian Chen in the lab. Is he still there? They haven't gotten rid of him, have they?"

"I don't think so. Most of the scientists have been feigning loyalty, to stay in their positions—or stay alive."

"Listen. I'm going to send it through my Pearl, if I can, to the lab's mainframe. Jian Chen knows how to get to it when they're not looking. The formula is different from Angel Cake. This one is more lethal, much stronger. It mimics a virus. I got the idea from a flesh-eating staph that has been wiping out the Northeast here in the United States."

"You're in the United States?"

"Mr. President, please, sir. I only have a moment. I need you to have Jian Chen make the serum in two vials and then get one of them sent to Ri Long in Islamabad in Pakistan. Put it to her attention, at H-2 Markaz in Islamabad. Label it private and confidential. She'll know what to do. It's our only hope."

"What about the second vial?"

"That one is for you, sir. Use it wisely. Take back our country, Mr. President."

Murong Gui smiled for the first time in months. "Are you safe, Niú?"

"For now. But I don't know for how long. And one more thing, sir. I need a favor. And it's big."

"Yes, Niú, whatever you need."

WASHINGTON, D.C.

The White House

"If you want, I'll buy your oil, Mr. Asvaka. In exchange for your loyalty. A short trip to Jerusalem on 21 December. How's that?"

Asvaka was certain that the president had lost whatever marbles he had left in his head. What he had told them last night was ridiculous, far-fetched, delusional at best. But Malik also saw a way to make a lot of money based on this delusion. And if Serafino needed him to make a trip to Jerusalem on the twenty-first of December in order to recite some cultic mumbo jumbo in exchange for buying the huge quantities of oil Asvaka was offering, then he would do it. He smiled his large, toothy smile and held out his hand.

Youhanna Lachier was not convinced. He was familiar with M-theory and certainly saw the current situation in the world as dangerous, urgent. But an end to the world now? And exactly on 21 December? He wouldn't have expected someone like Serafino to fall for petty prophecies. And yet it seemed the only thing Serafino wanted from him, in exchange for the cash Egypt needed, was for him to remain this last month in Washington, D.C., and to fly with Serafino and the others to Jerusalem to the Temple of the Dome on 21 December. Serafino said the trip would only take a day, and then Lachier would be free to do as he wished. Although Lachier didn't trust the USAmerican president one iota, the offer sounded easy. Maybe too easy. But for now, he would go along with his host. He had dealt with more eccentric leaders than Serafino to get what he wanted. In the meantime, he would get word to the Egyptian president that funds were on the way. He had accomplished his goal.

RICHMOND, VIRGINIA

The gunfire broke out first in Virginia, as armed troops in trucks, tanks, and army and marine gear rolled past Richmond toward Washington, D.C. Serafino had alerted his military, and they had been waiting for the Westerners with troops from the East. With no time or resources to make new uniforms or equipment, both sides appeared in the same colors and in the same styles of equipment, so that it became difficult at times to detect which side one was fighting for—or against. But fight they did. USAmerica's civil war had begun, and it had begun on southeastern soil.

NUREMBERG, GERMANY

The earthquake that began at noon lasted longer this time, devastating most of the factories and transportation systems in the city. Although the air felt cool now in December, intense pockets of heat would travel through the atmosphere in waves, creating what people were calling radiation baths. The hospitals were filled with burn victims, some who had only briefly gone out of their homes and encountered the intense radiation. Most had taken to wearing as much protective clothing as they could. It was rare to find a pedestrian, and when one did, the unfortunate traveler was usually covered head to toe with clothes, hats, scarves, and ski masks lined with solar-deflective material. At times it was just too dangerous to be outside. Medical staff were in demand, and what had been factories, especially those that had processed food items, now became makeshift hospitals, treating rare forms of cancers, deformities, burns, and other radiation-related illnesses. But without power most of the time, and without adequate water, fuel, and supplies, the doctors, nurses, and volunteers were at the minimum burned out, stressed, and depressed. They could do little to help.

In Germany, people were flocking to St. Lamberticus in Mingolsheim, presumably to take sanctuary from the oppressive damage of the sun, which was continuing to puncture through the earth's magnetic layers. With the reversal of the poles, what had been a beautiful aurora had turned into a thick, red layer that permeated the earth's atmosphere like blood, casting a strange glow across the cities and the landscape.

The people wondered why the government was doing nothing. Why would no one do anything?

BEIJING, CHINA
Center for the Study of Genetics

Jian Chen accessed Niú's private files using his password and hacked into the encoded file Niú had sent through President Murong Gui.

He had known how to do it, because Niú himself had once shown him how to get around the algorithm. He thought Niú must be very glad at this point to have taught his assistant scientist this otherwise perhaps questionable skill.

As soon as he found the encrypted formula, he went to work. He would have the serum ready by the following day. Then he just needed to get one of the vials to Murong Gui. The package going to Pakistan could pose a problem. There was still rudimentary parcel service in their part of the world. As long as Jian Chen stayed relatively out of sight and didn't call any attention to himself, he should be able to mail it with no problem from the Beijing central postal center. He hoped the mail was still being delivered in Pakistan. The radiation was increasing, and deliveries were decreasing, as well as any kind of public transportation. But so far, the mail was still moving. It might be slower than usual, but Jian Chen prayed for speed. Once he put the second vial into Murong Gui's hands, things would move quickly, and their operative in Afghanistan would need to act quickly. He suspected she would.

He had always admired Niú Ye but thought the older scientist was somewhat of a nervous sort, not the type to rebel. He liked this side of his mentor. If this worked, China would be back in the hands of Murong Gui, and Afghanistan would be at the mercy of China.

38

IN THE RED

The White House

"We don't have the resources, Mr. President."

Ted Calahan was following Matthew Serafino down the hallway of the White House, trying desperately to get the president's attention and keep it for more than five minutes.

"Don't worry so much, Ted."

"Don't worry? Sir? We're in the midst of a civil war, sir."

Matt Serafino stopped and turned to Ted Calahan.

"Mr. Calahan. I need you to go back to your office to alert the press that everything is being taken care of, and then I need you to schedule a plane to take me to Jerusalem on 21 December."

"A plane? To Jerusalem?"

"Is that going to be a problem, Mr. Calahan?"

"No, Mr. President. I'm sure the presidential hybrid-aerocraft, Osprey I, will be in order and available."

"Thank you, Ted."

Matt Serafino strode down the hallway, leaving his chief of staff exasperated and confused in the middle of the White House corridor.

WASHINGTON, D.C.
Washington National Cathedral

A dark figure was slowly walking the path of the labyrinth among the many others in the center sanctuary of the Washington National Cathedral. From under her hooded coat, her long, dark hair hung loosely to her shoulders. Her left arm seemed to droop a bit, but she held her hands together in front of her, clasped in a prayerlike posture, keeping her head lowered as she followed the turning pathway. And as she walked, she thought about what she knew. More than he had thought she did. And she had kept track of *him*, watched his every move. She had even followed him several times, attended his public events. He never noticed her. At first, she didn't know what he was doing. Didn't know what the pictures meant. Until she came to the cathedral. Now it was clear to her who he was. What he was. And she regretted her time with him. Understood so much more now than she had. The priest at the cathedral had helped her. Father Millard had made her understand so many things. Most of all to trust her intuition.

She would take the trip with the others. No one would say where they were going. For security, she guessed. They had to go on trust. She had looked up the man who was leading the people to safety. Paul Binder. A historian from Virginia. He was staying at the cathedral in Marseille with Arnaud Chevalier. She knew Arnaud. Everyone in the astronomy and cosmology field knew him. Perhaps he would talk to her. Perhaps in some way, she could help. She thought perhaps she knew a way it could be a kind of penance, or at the very least, one small token of defiance.

GREENBELT, MARYLAND
Goddard Space Flight Center (NASA)

"What are we seeing, Channey?"

"Meteorites, sir."

The director had been in a bad mood that morning and was grumbling to himself. He hated having no control. What next? How could this be happening? He was tired. The sky was falling in, and they were essentially helpless to do anything about it. He could feel his staff looking to him for guidance, answers, and he had none. He was just as confounded, confused, and frightened as the rest of them. He swore under his breath.

"Sir?"

"Never mind, Channey." He regained his composure. "So what can we expect to happen?"

"Well, best-case scenario, sir, a couple of meteorites fall to the ground and we get a couple of big rocks in our backyard."

"And the worst?"

"Worst-case scenario, we're pelted with massive fireballs. I don't think I have to tell you the result of that, sir."

"No, Channey." The director paused. "Thank you."

"Yes, sir."

He looked out at his staff, turned silently, and left the room, leaving them to look at one another in stillness.

CHARTRES, FRANCE

Chartres Cathedral

Father Gautier could see the line of people coming from far down the road in both directions. They seemed to be coming from everywhere. The cathedrals had been virtually empty for years, but now people swarmed for miles around to reach the labyrinths. The Chartres cathedral was large, would accommodate thousands if it had to. *And*, Father Gautier thought to himself, *it might have to.*

He stood for a moment looking up at the sculptured carving of Christ, surrounded by the four horsemen of the Apocalypse. For many, this would be their last journey of hope.

He bowed to the statue, crossing himself as he turned to go out to meet the oncoming pilgrimage.

MARSEILLE, PROVENCE-ALPES-CÔTE D'AZUR, FRANCE

St. Seraphim Orthodox Cathedral

"Backed out?" Angela, usually composed, looked like she would burst into tears. "What do you mean, they backed out?"

"They're afraid of the Russian government." Oksanna looked distressed.

"But Aeroflot is private, isn't it?"

"I'm not sure what's happening in Russia now. Things have changed since the World Greenhouse collapsed. And I haven't been back . . . I'm sorry, Angela." Oksanna looked as though she would burst into tears at any moment.

"Oh, Oksanna, it's not your fault." Angela hurried to Oksanna's side and put her arm around her shoulder. "I didn't mean to imply . . ."

"It's fine, Angela. I'm disappointed, too."

The two women stood together for a moment, comforting each other, as Paul came into the office.

"What's wrong?"

"The Underground backed out. We have no planes."

Paul was silent. He was exhausted. The preparations and the stress of the last six months were taking a toll on him, and he suddenly looked tired and haggard. He looked up at the two women, their eyes stricken. "We'll find a way."

"But how? *How* are we going to find a way?" Oksanna was frustrated. She had depended on her contacts in Russia, and they had let her down. She supposed she couldn't expect much else. She had not signed on to their project, and they had no great loyalty to her.

Paul looked calm again, a strange quiet coming over his face.

"You know, we've come all this way, and mostly not on our own." He looked at Angela. "You know that, Angela."

She smiled and nodded, remembering the events of the last months with Paul.

"We're asking all those people out there to trust in a God they haven't been in touch with for years, to trust us, too, that we're going to lead them to a place where all this destruction will end. Ask Father Arnaud how many are gathering. Thousands. Thousands upon thousands. All coming to the sanctuaries, ready to give up everything they've believed in as real and to follow a new truth, one that will require them to trust their hearts, their intuition, to imagine that love and truth and goodness and beauty still exist somewhere in a world they can access with the help of this God. Many of them wouldn't even know who the Lamb in the center is, who the Christ is, who has been the saving mediary of all humankind for centuries. Many of them have never heard of him. They're coming, most of them, because they have nothing else to believe in. But, they're coming. And that is the beginning step of faith. We have to trust, too. I can't believe that we would have been brought here all this way just to fail now. I know, I'm as new at this faith thing as anyone. But I can't imagine that God, as the source of love and resurrection life, would not give us every opportunity. We just have to find it. And sometimes"—Paul looked at Angela again and nodded—"many times, the opportunities find us."

Arnaud had walked into the office and was listening to Paul. Now he spoke as well.

"Paul Binder, you have done more for my own faith, in this moment, than I experienced in many years of being a priest. And I agree with you. If God didn't want to give humanity yet another chance, all of this wouldn't be happening."

Oksanna agreed. "You're right. You're all right. We need to trust not in what we thought was real, but in what is more than real in ways we can't possibly fathom right now. And whatever is happening, we're all part of it. And we need to stick together. We need one another."

Arnaud nodded. "Indeed."

The three joined hands, pulling in Casimir, who had just come in from the sanctuary.

"Together no matter what," said Paul.

"No matter what," the others echoed.

GREENBELT, MARYLAND

Goddard Space Flight Center (NASA)

"Someone's been in the storage room, sir. I know I locked it earlier."

"Has anything been taken?"

"I really can't tell, sir. I'd have to do an inventory."

"Well, we have a lot more important things on our plates right now than worrying about supplies. Let it go, Johnson. If a problem comes up, we'll deal with it then."

"Yes, sir."

MARSEILLE, PROVENCE-ALPES-CÔTE D'AZUR, FRANCE

St. Seraphim Orthodox Cathedral

As Angela came through the cathedral's narthex, she saw Casimir slowly coming through the large wooden front doors. His left arm and neck were bright red.

"Casimir! Were you outside?"

"I just wanted to take a peek. It hurts."

"Oh, no. Paul! Arnaud! Oksanna! Come quickly!"

Oksanna ran in from the sanctuary. The others followed soon afterward from the kitchen, where they had been preparing the evening meal.

She stooped to examine the boy's skin. "We need to get some wrappings, some gauze. Paul, there's a first-aid kit in the kitchen. Father Arnaud, please, would you get some cool water. Not too cold. Angela, I have salve in the bathroom."

She guided Casimir to the leather chair, just as Arnaud was returning with the water. Arnaud sat at the boy's side and held his hand while Oksanna cleaned his burns.

"Casimir, why did you go out?"

"I'm sorry, Father Arnaud. I just was curious. It just looked so pretty out there, with all the red, and the white snow."

"Oh, my boy. How long were you out?"

"Just for a few minutes. It wasn't long. It hurts."

"Yes, it will hurt for a while. I'm glad you were only out for a few minutes. But please, don't go out again, yes?"

"I won't, Father."

The four worked together to finish bathing and dressing Casimir's arm and neck. They checked the rest of him, but it looked as though only a small portion of his body had been exposed to the sun's rays. They hoped the damage wasn't too deep.

"You rest here now, Casimir. We need to start packing for our trip. But one of us will come in to check on you. All right?"

"All right, Père. I'll be fine."

"I know you will, my boy." Arnaud smiled.

Paul was the first to speak. "We need to think about what protection we are going to use to get to Bashan. Apparently, some areas are worse than others, and we're surrounded by one of the worst of them."

"So it seems." Arnaud glanced out the window at the thick, reddening sky.

"And we need supplies. Our resources are nearly depleted. We're going to be out of water and food very soon," Oksanna added.

Paul looked around at them. "Well, I don't think we can wait any longer. In fact, we still need to find the right location, so that we can tell the planes where to go."

"You're right, Paul. We can't afford to stay here any longer." Arnaud was nodding. "We need to go."

"Do we have an aerojet? And can you fly it?"

"We do, praise God!" Arnaud spoke up. "Compliments of my friend, the president of the Université de Provence. It's his private jet. All we need to do is get to the private airfield on the other side of Marseille. And yes"—he smiled—"I can."

Arnaud was busy reminiscing about his days in the French aero troops, when Casimir stumbled through the doorway.

"But look at what just happened to Casimir!" Oksanna looked frightened.

The four were interrupted by the ringing of the cathedral door chimes.

Arnaud excused himself and walked to the entryway. Outside in the enclosed area was a large box. Arnaud looked toward the gate. He could see a small mail truck backing out of the cathedral's main drive. The driver could barely be seen, due to the heavy deflective covering he wore in order to do his job. Arnaud hauled the heavy box inside, and Paul helped him get it into the office area.

"What is it?" Casimir sat up, curious.

"Well, let's see," said Paul.

Arnaud slit open the box. Inside were five golden suits.

"What is it, Father Arnaud?" Casimir was trying to poke his head around to see what was in the box.

Arnaud held up one of the suits. "They're radiation-deflector suits. Government standard." He again looked inside the box. "Five of them. With headpieces."

"They're gold?" Angela was amazed, touching the material, its golden flecks sparkling in the dim light of the office.

"They're gold. The best radiation deflector in the world. But these are expensive—and rare." Paul wasn't sure whether to laugh or cry.

Arnaud was smiling. He picked up the card lying at the bottom of the box.

On it was scrawled in simple printed script:

I'll see you in Bashan.
Doron Anderson

39

THE GOLDEN GRIFFIN

SÃO PAULO, BRAZIL

The balls of fire came down like fiery hail. Martin Ruiz saw them coming and ran inside before the first rock landed three feet from his front doorway.

"Mariana, look!"

Mariana came to the doorway, saw the smoldering rock, and backed away, crossing herself and clutching the pink rosary beads around her neck. Paulo and Jorge were playing in the other room, and she went to them and put her arms around them protectively.

"What is it, Martin?"

"I don't know. I don't know."

SALT LAKE CITY, UTAH

"What is it, Jared? Is it the Easterners?"

"I don't know, Martha. But it doesn't look like anything I've ever seen."

Martha Turner went to the window and peered out. One of the meterorites had fallen to the ground nearby, and the red-hot rock was smoldering, letting off black smoke into the red hazy atmosphere.

Martha whispered, "I think it's a bomb." She turned to her husband. "What'll we do?"

Jared Turner joined his wife at the window, keeping back so as not to encounter any of the sun's rays.

"I don't think that's a bomb, Martha. Look at it. It looks like a rock."

"Well, maybe they make them that way now."

Her husband was shaking his head.

"What if it goes off?"

"Well, what are our options? We can't go out there." He gestured to the outdoors. "We'll have to stay in here and see what happens."

They sat together on the couch in the small living room and waited.

"Jared."

"Yes, Martha."

"Do you believe in God?"

MARSEILLE, PROVENCE-ALPES-CÔTE D'AZUR, FRANCE

St. Seraphim Orthodox Cathedral

"Who's Doron Anderson?" Angela looked up at Father Arnaud.

"An old friend and fellow astronomer. She's head of an astronomy lab in Washington, too." Arnaud smiled. "She called me the other day, because of you, Paul."

"Me?"

"Let's just say, she wanted to help."

Paul nodded. Whatever Father Chevalier and Doron Anderson had talked about, it must have been confidential, and Paul didn't want to ask him to breach his confidence.

"Well, I'm so glad she did."

"Are we ready to go, then?" Arnaud had brought the small collection of supplies they would take with them. They couldn't take much, only a simple sack for each of them, with water, a change of clothes, and some food. They would need to go on from there, trusting that whatever lay on the other side of Bashan had food and water.

"Where's Casimir?" Angela looked around but didn't see the boy.

"I think I know." Arnaud climbed the spiral staircase to the observatory. Casimir was inside, sitting on the wooden floor, hunched over something he seemed to be building.

"What are you making, Casimir?"

"It's a cover, Père Arnaud."

"A cover?"

"Yes. For Seraphim. I figured out how to make a deflector suit for him, too. I'm afraid I may have melted down one of your chalices. But I learned how to do it in here." He motioned to one of the books lying nearby on the floor. "I inserted the gold like threads into this small tablecloth, lined with foil. See, Père? I can put it over Seraphim's cage and take him with us."

Arnaud nodded, laying his hand gently on the boy's head. "Thank you, Casimir."

The boy smiled.

"Come now; it's time to go."

Kabul, Afghanistan

Scitheon Corporation

When the guard came into the lobby, the receptionist was lying face-down on the front desk. Her face had turned an ugly sort of black, and her tongue protruded from her mouth. Her eyes were still open and bugged out, as though trying to grasp a last breath of oxygen. Her hands had gripped the side of the desk and frozen there, stiff and still.

Fahran backed away, alarmed. The building seemed quiet. Going back down the long hallway where the labs and offices were located, he could hear nothing. He peered into one of the offices. Jeb, one of the scientists, was sprawled across his desk as well, his face and neck swollen and blackening. His left hand had crumpled a paper towel, and in his right, his coffee cup still sat balanced on the desktop. The guard went on. Every office looked essentially the same, each with a dead office staffer or scientist laid out within it, still in the midst of morning coffee.

"The coffee."

Fahran looked down at the cup he had poured for himself and set it down on one of the desks. He had poured it when he entered the building but hadn't had a chance to drink it since discovering the mass of bodies in the building. Now he looked at it suspiciously.

He heard the front doors open as someone entered the lobby. He grabbed the cup and ran back down the hallway toward the front entryway.

Masoud had just come in to work in the lab. Fahran waved him down. Masoud stopped short, almost falling over a nearby chair after spying the receptionist at the front desk.

"Masoud."

The scientist looked relieved to see Fahran. "What's going on?"

Fahran was out of breath and stopped for a moment to regain his composure. "Can you test this coffee?"

The scientist held it to his nose to sniff it. And Fahran put up his hand.

"No!"

Masoud lowered the cup and stepped back.

Fahran was shaking his head. "The coffee. I think the coffee is poisoned. Can you test it? In the lab?" Fahran continued, "Everyone's dead. The scientists, lab assistants, office staff. It's not a pretty sight. I think they drank the coffee."

Masoud nodded, speechless with shock, and walked quickly down the hallway, taking the coffee cup with him. Fahren remained at the front lobby, hoping to prevent any further casualties.

In the city of Kabul, already two-thirds of the city's population lay dead and blackening at their breakfast tables and office desks.

BEIJING, CHINA

Capitol Building

"Will you join me for tea, gentlemen?"

Murong Gui had gathered his Afghani colleagues in the presidential dining room and was serving each a cup of the steaming tea. He nodded to Abdul Gulzar as the Afghan president took his first sip of the morning brew. The others followed, nodding politely. No one noticed that Murong Gui did not partake in the morning ritual.

In less than three minutes, all of his colleagues were dead. Murong rose calmly, gathered his things, and went into the presidential office to officially reinstate himself as the official president of the People's Republic of China.

MARSEILLE, PROVENCE-ALPES-CÔTE D'AZUR, FRANCE

St. Seraphim Orthodox Cathedral

The five all looked like glittering golden statues after they donned the heavy deflector suits. They looked at one another, then held up their hands and legs, each amazed at the strange material. They would need to travel together in Arnaud's car across town and into the outskirts of Marseille to the airfield, where the private jet waited to take them to the Syrian airport. From there, they would need to find their way to the area called the Golan Heights, formerly known as Bashan. All they knew was that it was somewhere northeast of the Sea of Galilee and south of Mount Hermon. The Yarmuk River lay to the south. The area was currently divided into four territories: Batanea, Gaulanitis, Geshur, and Karnaim. But Paul was particularly interested in a landmark called the Rogem Hiri. Located in the center of the Golan Heights area, in the grassy hills still strewn with large oaks, was a group of stones that had been built into walls. They now lay in four concentric circles that led to a central core. Believed to be an early astronomical observation center, the site was located about ten miles east of the Sea of Galilee. *Could that be the wheel? Could that be the location where they would need to gather?* Paul hoped that when the time came, they would know what to do, where to go. He knew now to get them to Bashan, but beyond that, he hadn't a clue. But then again, even Jesus hadn't known the time or place of his own coming either, had he?

KABUL, AFGHANISTAN

DON'T DRINK THE WATER.

The signs were everywhere as the city officials attempted to let people know the city's water supply had been compromised.

Because communications were down due to the solar storms, it was hard to tell how widespread the infiltration had been. Was it all of Afghanistan? Only Kabul? Those who could get through on make-shift communications devices tried to warn whomever they could reach. Those who couldn't resorted to primitive methods, like large signs, paper flyers, messengers. Most were stymied by the fact that they no longer had any idea how to communicate without technology.

The serum, when mixed with water, was immediately lethal and virtually undetectable. And compared to the speed of the symptoms, without technology there was no way to compete. The devastation was unstoppable. It was only a matter of time until much of Afghanistan had been eliminated, the corpses of its people blackening and rotting in the solar heat.

MARSEILLE, FRANCE

Avignon Private Airfield

When the five arrived at the airfield, Arnaud led them to the num-bered areas where the private planes were parked. They walked along, looking at each plane and jet, wondering which one would carry them to southern Syria. At last, they reached space number 137.

"That's not a plane." Paul laughed.

Arnaud looked at the paper again. "It says 137."

"Do you have the code?" Paul was walking toward the huge golden craft, wondering at its unusual construction.

"I don't," said Arnaud, fumbling in his pocket. "I have a key." Arnaud smiled. "I guess our benefactor thought the jet, which runs on electrical waves, wouldn't operate in the solar disturbances. He sent us to his helicopter instead."

"I've never seen anything like this." Angela was running her suited hand over the copter's main golden-colored body. "It's beautiful."

Angela looked up then and quoted from the passage in the Ezekiel prophecy: "The wheels sparkled as if made of beryl . . . a wheel intersecting another wheel."

Arnaud chimed in. "Yes, golden beryl or perhaps topaz, the golden stone, chrysolite, the Tarshish stone—all words the prophecy uses to describe the chariot's wheels. The golden beryl, heliodor . . . gift from the sun. And don't forget the word *helicopter*."

"Helicopter?" Angela looked at Arnaud.

"Yes, from the French *hélicoptère*. The ancient Greek words are ἕλιξ—*helix* or 'spiral'—plus πτερόν—*pteron*, or 'wing.' The prophecy from Ezekiel!"

"I think we've got the right aircraft." Paul nodded.

"Indeed, I believe we do." Arnaud motioned for the four to get into the craft, and the five golden figures prepared to board their golden chariot.

Casimir handed Seraphim's cage in the shining coverlet to Angela and climbed aboard. The rest followed. Arnaud climbed into the cockpit of the helicopter and inserted the key into the ignition. It roared to life. He laughed.

"These haven't been around for fifty years."

Within minutes, the helicopter had risen into the red sky and was headed southward toward Bashan.

From the back of the copter, Casimir could hear Seraphim singing:

Yes, we'll gather at the river
the beautiful, the beautiful river,
gather with the saints at the river
that flows by the throne of God.

40

THE INHERITANCE

EN ROUTE TO SOUTHERN SYRIA

"Père, where do you suppose we're really going?"

Casimir had moved toward the front of the helicopter and was sitting next to Arnaud, petting and soothing Seraphim. He looked deep in thought. Arnaud paused, trying to think of the right words to explain to the boy what even he didn't understand.

"I think . . ." Arnaud paused again. "I think we are going to do exactly what you thought we would when you told me about the M-theory you were studying, Casimir. I think we are going to enter a new dimension somehow, another place. I don't know if it will look like this one, or different. But I think it will be a place where we will have food, water, and can build a new life. All of us. Together."

"Why are we going, Père? Why do you suppose this is happening? To all of us? Do you know?"

"What I know, Casimir, is that the sun is dying. And we have the opportunity to start again. In another place. Why some of us and not others? I don't know."

"Yes," said Casimir. He continued to stroke Seraphim's small head through the bars of the cage.

Arnaud looked at the boy, thought for a moment, and then said slowly, "What is your intuition telling you, Casimir? What does your heart know?"

Casimir looked up, his eyes wise for his small frame. "I think . . . it's a gift. I think God is giving us another chance. And some of us were chosen to let people know about it."

Arnaud's eyes began to fill, and he hastily brushed the tears away with the back of his hand. "I think you're right, Casimir. I trust . . . you're absolutely right."

Arnaud waited a moment before continuing, "Casimir, do you know what a covenant is?"

"Like a pact?"

Arnaud smiled. "Like a pact, yes. And a pact is always between two or more people. From the very beginning of time, God made a pact, a covenant with all of us, all of humanity."

"But we didn't do so well." Casimir had obviously been studying the Torah, along with his books on the Kabbalah.

"No, we didn't. We didn't do so well. In fact, we seem to have a knack for not keeping our end of the pact almost every time."

"But God keeps on trying."

"So it seems, Casimir. God keeps on trying. Even when it looks like we've managed to destroy everything possible, to lose all our faith, to not even remember how to recognize God anymore, God remembers us. And finds ways to give us new chances."

"And the way to keep the pact, Père—it's love, isn't it?"

"Yes, I think so," said Arnaud. "I think love is what binds everything in the universe together, binds us to one another, and binds us to God. And the one who symbolizes love is Jesus. The Christ. The Messiah."

"It seems so simple, Père."

Arnaud's eyes grew sad. He looked up at Casimir, nodding. "It does, doesn't it?"

WASHINGTON, D.C.
National Lab

In his dream, Niú Ye is walking through the fields of rice. He can hear the voices calling to him from over the hill. He tries to find his way through the rows of rice, but the grain is so high, it's hard to see. He cups his hands over his eyes and stares at the hill in front of him. But the glare of the sun is too strong. He can't see. He can still hear them calling him. He grabs his pails of rice and starts up the hill, struggling. Then he sees the woman. She's standing at the top of the hill, waving. Ye drops the buckets and starts running to her. Tries to get up the hill. He can see her better now. Smiling and waving with both hands. Calling his name. *Niú Ye, come!* He is almost at the top of the hill. She reaches out to him, and he tries to grasp her hand. But then he loses his footing and slides. Slides down the hill. She is calling after him, calling his name. But he can't see her any longer. By the time he looks up, she's gone. He calls to her. *"Yu ma ma!"* But he is alone in the field.

WASHINGTON, D.C.
The White House

Matthew Serafino wrote down the incantations in the small note-book he would take with him on the trip. He was ready. Now all he needed was to get them all to Jerusalem. He had gathered supplies and had already packed them aboard the presidential aerocraft. Thanks to his Afghani comrade, he would have oil and gasoline for the convertible Osprey I. Serafino was glad he had gotten these first deliveries of oil from the Middle Eastern country, because now the Afghan government had more pertinent matters to attend to in Afghanistan, as their water supply had been compromised, presumably by China. Serafino was perplexed how China was so industrious and creative as to come up with such a brilliant bio-genetic serum and to apply it with such finesse, especially when he, Serafino, had possession of their lead scientist and clearly the one who had brought them into the forefront in the manipulation technologies to begin with. But nevertheless, they had, and the Chinese president, Murong Gui, had reclaimed his country for China. It would remain to be seen whether Afghanistan would now be subject to China's beck and call. At the moment, they had no president, and a strong portion of their population, especially their working population, was dead. Not a promising situation right now. Serafino was relieved that Malik Asvaka had been here with him during the whole fiasco. What if he had succumbed to the poison? Serafino needed all of them in order to make the alchemical process work.

All of them had agreed to make the trip to Jerusalem with little coercion on Serafino's part. He had something they wanted, and except for Niú, he knew they would see the trip as a small price to pay for Serafino's generosity. Matt smiled to himself. Once they had entered the gateway into the new city, he would see just how loyal they would be. Matt had assumed that the city of Jerusalem would be transported along with him. After all, whom would he rule? He wasn't exactly sure how it worked, but he was confident that as long as he did everything right, the power of the earth would be his. It was, after all, his birthright.

The rest would take care of itself. The country, now enmeshed in civil war, would keep on fighting until the sun swallowed up the earth. He was sure of it. Serafino wasn't interested. He had sent enough Eastern troops to hold the Westerners back until he could be safely out of Washington, D.C. After that, it wasn't his concern.

Serafino looked around at the cases of water and food, bags of supplies, and his maps. He had brought along the large Codex Gigas, just in case, wrapping it in red cloth and stuffing it under the front area of the plane. He was ready. He motioned to Ted Calahan to call the others.

DAMASCUS, SYRIA

The golden helicopter touched down at the private airfield outside Damascus. They would leave it there for now, going out by SUV and then on foot to investigate the area, known as Rogem Hiri, or in Hebrew, *Gilgal Refaim*, meaning "the wheel of spirit." Then, they would return for the copter the morning of 21 December and lead the others into the hills of Bashan. Paul had shown the map of the ancient site to the others, and they had gasped at the wheel-like circle made of basalt in the midst of the hills of Bashan. The site comprised four stone concentric circles with a rounded center. Dated from approximately 3000 BCE, it had been a worship center, an ancient calendar, and an astronomical and religious guide to the early Hebrew people in Bashan. The area was surrounded by beautiful hills and volcanoes. At the winter solstice, 21 December, the sun would shine through the stones, illuminating the ancient structure. Paul wasn't sure how he knew, but he was certain it was here that the gateway would occur.

The Sea of Galilee, located ten miles to the west of the wheel of Gilgal Refaim, was a freshwater lake and had not suffered the devastation of the oceans and seas. The land appeared surprisingly fertile, and they would have access to water and food for the next few days as they explored the area. Although the weather should have been fairly mild in December, it was warmer than usual, due to the solar heat. Yet the sky over the Bashan hills, now called Golan Heights, shimmered in rainbow colors, as the aurora borealis had not yet descended into the deep, thick red of solar radiation, as it had over Europe. But Paul knew it was just a matter of time until it did. And most likely, according to schedule, a matter of hours.

The five grabbed their backpacks from the helicopter, adjusted their suits, and headed into Damascus for a last meal before their excursion. They would spend the night in Damascus and then rent a vehicle in the morning for their excursion into the hills of the southern Golan Heights. The trip was about forty miles, only thirty to sixty minutes south of Damascus, depending upon the terrain.

As they shared a meal of falafel, hummus, tabouleh, and meat with egg, the five also shared stories of the circumstances that had led them together. Soon, everything would change.

"As long as we have each other, I know everything will be all right." Angela squeezed Paul's hand.

Paul took her hand in his, and they all sat in silence for a moment, contemplating the beauty of the landscape and enjoying what would probably be their last formal meal together on the earth as they knew it now.

Oksanna pointed to the north. The sky was already changing from its rainbow hue to a deepening golden orange. Soon the red would descend like a blanket as the sun reached toward the equator. The Golan Heights area where the Rogem Hiri was located in Syria was only 32 degrees north of the equator. When the sun reached Bashan at the winter solstice, when all the planets would be aligned, the time and space of the earth would change.

Oksanna looked at Paul and spoke almost in a whisper. "Do we have planes yet? For the people meeting at the labyrinths, the sanctuaries?"

Paul shook his head. "I'm going on faith," he said. He didn't elaborate, and no one said a word. But Oksanna could tell it was on everyone's mind. How would the people come? Had they done all this just for themselves? It couldn't be.

Paul said finally, "I would give all the gold in the world to be sure we had those planes right now. I just need to trust that perhaps the Russians will reconsider and come through."

Oksanna looked doubtful but remained silent.

Angela looked at Paul. "Something will come through. I know it will. And we don't need gold or any other kind of money. At this point, gold doesn't even matter anymore. Nothing that we thought was most important matters anymore. When it comes down to it, love is the only gold."

"Thank you, Angela." Oksanna smiled at her new friend.

Arnaud raised his cup and toasted their last meal together. "To love."

"To love."

WASHINGTON, D.C.

National Lab

While the USAmerican president was readying for their journey, Niú Ye had managed to slip away and make a last static-filled call to the reinstated president of China, Murong Gui. Murong was in good spirits and thanked his lead scientist.

"You are loyal, Niú Ye. I will never forget this."

"Thank you, Mr. President, sir. I wish I could have done something sooner."

"What you did was brilliant, Niú, brilliant. Now, when will you be returning to China?"

"I'm not sure, Mr. President. I have promised to accompany the USAmerican president on a trip to Jerusalem. In fact, I leave in a few moments."

"Jerusalem? Why?"

"Mr. President, it's a long story to explain. And I'm not certain I understand all of it, although I think I understand more than my traveling companions."

"But you will return after your trip? Reassume your position as head of the National Center for Genetic Studies here in Beijing?"

Niú's eyes grew sad. "I hope so, sir. Sir, I'm so glad everything worked out for you, and for China."

"It wouldn't have if not for you, Niú Ye."

"It is the least I could do for my beloved country, Mr. President."

Although Murong Gui couldn't see him through his portal, Niú bowed his head in a gesture of respect.

"Sir, I must go. I can hear them looking for me. There's one last thing. The favor that I told you I would need to ask from you."

Niú didn't mention the call he had received from an anonymous woman, a lead astronomer at the Goddard Space Center, a few days before, giving him details of what was needed. He didn't have time to explain any of that to the Chinese president. As long as he kept his word, that was all Niú needed to know.

"Niú Ye, whatever you ask, you will have it."

"Then, sir, here is what I need. And I will need them within twenty-four hours."

SOUTHERN SYRIA

Golan Heights

The sun sparkled off the five travelers as they donned their golden solar-deflection suits and masks and set off in their rented SUV toward the Golan Heights. The suits felt somewhat hot and uncomfortable, but Paul didn't want to take any chances, not knowing how much radiation could be in the atmosphere and when the sun would begin to descend on Bashan.

As they approached the area of the Golan Heights, they could see the rolling hills and the majestic peaks of Mount Hermon in the distance.

"It's beautiful," Angela gasped.

Paul stopped the SUV, and they got out onto the grassy turf.

"The hills that God loved."

41

THE FINAL JOURNEY

Youhanna Lachier, Niú Ye, and Malik Asvaka boarded the Osprey I along with Matthew Serafino and headed for Jerusalem. The flight would take approximately seventeen hours under normal conditions, but Serafino expected, given the atmospheric difficulties, they might need to use alternate routes. They had prepared for a twenty-four-hour trip. The Osprey would arrive in Jerusalem the twentieth of December. They would gather at the Dome of the Rock, the site of the Jerusalem temple, the morning of the twenty-first. And Serafino was sure everything would fall into place from there.

The others looked either annoyed or bored, or perhaps both— Serafino wasn't sure which. Except for Niú Ye. Niú was chewing the top of his fingernail, and staring out of the plane window at the smoldering atmosphere. Serafino wondered what he was thinking. But Niú Ye seemed always to be nervous. Serafino smiled to himself. The little man had the guts of a feather pillow. He couldn't imagine how Niú had managed to accomplish what he did at the Center for Genetics. It seemed to Serafino the man didn't have the stature to compete with anyone. *Less to worry about*, he thought. Serafino had enough to worry about, making sure the others would comply with his plans.

Lachier and Asvaka were much more predatory, much more ruthless, and definitely much more decisive than Niú. He guessed either one of them would gladly stab him in the back, given the opportunity. He would need to keep his eye on them at all times.

But gold talks. And he had essentially bought both of them. Both of them had needed him. And that was exactly how he liked it.

SOUTHERN SYRIA

Golan Heights

Paul took the call on his Pearl, which was miraculously still functioning in Syria, although crackling with static most of the time. His face broke out into a smile that could have rivaled the sun.

Angela noticed and walked over to him as he put the device back into his pocket, where he had been keeping it safe. He looked up at everyone gathered. "We've got planes."

Oksanna clapped with glee. Casimir, usually off to the side of the group, guarding Seraphim in his cloth-covered cage, looked up and smiled broadly. Arnaud was nodding. His long nose looked especially prominent when he smiled. Angela hugged Paul, a look of relief spreading across her face.

Oksanna spoke first. "Has the Underground reconsidered?"

"I'm not sure. Father Gautier didn't say where they were coming from, and the connection was difficult. But he clearly said they had planes and were organizing the people now, and they have the coordinates to get here."

Arnaud looked around. "Well, that's good enough."

"Yes, it is." Paul sat down for a moment on one of the rocks. As he did, a small brown snake slithered out from underneath it and moved quickly across the ground cover. Angela screamed softly, cupping her hands over her mouth.

"You'd think I would be used to anything by now," she apologized.

Paul laughed. "Just a brown whip snake. They're not poisonous. Probably a lot of them out here."

At that, Angela looked around her nervously.

"I wouldn't worry about it." Paul motioned to the west. "It's a good sign."

"A good sign?" Angela was always amazed at Paul's knowledge base.

"Of course. Where there are snakes, there is bound to be water. Good water."

He motioned again to the west. "The Sea of Galilee is a freshwater lake. No doubt it hasn't been compromised in the same way the seas have been. You can see it from here. Look!"

The others turned and looked out at the horizon. They could see what they thought to be the large lake in the distance, sparkling in the rays of light that emanated from the aurora-filled skies.

"That's why this area looks better than anywhere else. It's still being nourished by the water."

Paul paused and seemed to look around him at the surrounding landscape. "And I'll bet there are freshwater springs somewhere under here."

"Speaking of water, could we pause for some lunch?" Oksanna was leaning against the SUV, looking slightly peaked from the morning's excursions.

"Good idea." Paul unpacked the food, along with the remaining water bottles they had brought from the cathedral in Marseille. They had bought additional supplies in Damascus, trading the gold from their watches and jewelry for the more valuable commodity, bottled water. They had enough now to last them well into the following day.

As the five sat sharing their meal under the shade of the Golan oaks, Paul pulled out a sheath of diagrams from his leather binder. He still carried the leather satchel with him wherever he went. Angela guessed it was like a personal, almost spiritual, diary for Paul, not just a log of the events of the past months and the information that had led him here with them to Bashan, but a kind of personal witness of his own journey. He never left it out of his sight.

He was consulting the maps now that would take them to the Rogem Hiri—the Gilgal Refaim. As he stared at the wheel-like formation, one of the diagrams slipped from his hands and fell to the ground.

Angela picked it up. "Paul, what's this one?"

Paul looked up. "Ah, that's the Ptolemaic Universe, his version of the solar system."

Angela stared at the diagram. "So many people seemed to know, Paul. In every age, there seemed to be those who knew something of what is happening now. But no one seemed to be able to put all the pieces together."

"Perhaps because this kind of knowledge has always been meant to be known together, in unity. Perhaps it takes putting together what many have learned in order to really see."

Arnaud looked thoughtful. "I've always thought that we as humans have such a narrow picture of the world because that's the way we choose to see it. But yet each of us sees something the other doesn't. When we think together, feel together"—he looked at Casimir and smiled—"our world opens up to a whole different picture. A different reality."

"Love," said Angela, pointing to the center of the diagram. "All unity is bound by the force of love. Look at the diagram. Even Ptolemy knew that. He knew already in the second century that the entire motion of the universe was driven by divine love."

"The harmonious macrocosm." Arnaud smiled.

Paul looked around at all of them gathered, still finishing the last of their lunch together. "Well, it's no mistake that the only hope for humanity lies in the unity of the four horsemen of the Apocalypse, is it? It's the unity of everything, all creation, all elements of the earth, an entire universe of divine creativity that brings everything that exists into some kind of unified relationship. We're in a way perhaps a symbol of that unity, a living semiotic. We know that everything that exists does so in waves of movement. Perhaps our being here in Bashan is the start of another wave. One that our unity will initiate. A response of humankind to the divine song of the universe. To God."

Arnaud blinked. "That's incredible, Paul."

"I think so, too." Angela was shaking her head in amazement.

Casimir sat smiling, clutching the Sephir Yetzirah close to his heart. He looked over at Oksanna, reached out, and took her hand. She smiled and sat down beside him.

From inside the heavily covered cage, she could hear Seraphim singing a muffled song.

GREENBELT, MARYLAND
Goddard Space Flight Center (NASA)

"We need to evacuate, sir. We can't wait any longer."

The director sat with his face in his hands. Everyone was gathered for what would be their last meeting at the center.

The final report from the observation crew had been clear and concise. The sun was going to be destroyed, and the earth along with it. In less than two days, the planetary alignment would fall into place at the same time that the sun would become unstable, imploding from the inside out and sending everything around it into a cosmic cacophony.

The director guessed the kindest thing to do would be to allow everyone to leave, go home, find those they most wanted to be with, and to wait.

He wouldn't make the announcement to the press. It would only cause widespread panic, alarm. He thought to himself, *Let the people live until the last second, as they always have. Let them die in the midst of living.*

He stood slowly, turning to face the staff he had worked with for almost thirty years at NASA. "All right everyone, let's go home."

EN ROUTE TO THE GOLAN HEIGHTS

"It's time, everyone."

The planes had arrived at each location as requested. Around the world, those who gathered in the sanctuaries and cathedrals, where the labyrinths served as a final symbol of their pilgrimage, prepared to board their golden chariots to the Holy Land.

The sun was wide in the sky, casting a luminous glow on the metallic paint of the waiting planes as, one by one, the multitudes gathered and approached the areas for takeoff.

In some areas, people were transported in buses and vans to local private airfields. In others, they drove out to nearby fields, plateaus, anywhere strategically viable for the planes to take off. The mass exodus was not one of panic, but the people moved in an almost prayerlike fashion, as though assured that their journey would end in the hope they imagined when they gathered in the great sanctuaries.

Although the priests who guided each group had prepared them, letting them know what would be happening, no one could have guessed that so many would travel the road to Bashan in blind faith. And yet they did. By the thousands, they boarded the planes. And as the rumbling began, the air filled with thousands of planes, all heading to the hills of the Golan Heights.

Paul had told them where to go, had given them the coordinates. Had told them to circle the Gilgal Refaim. To keep circling until the twenty-first hour.

It was almost time.

SOUTHERN SYRIA
Golan Heights

As they were arriving that afternoon at the site of the Gilgal Refaim, the rumbling began. Paul could feel it vibrating under his feet, as though the very earth wanted to speak. He looked over at the others. They felt it too. They walked onto the edge of the circular formation, silently moving along through the rings toward the center of the wheel. The center was a large flat area that looked out over the rounded exterior of the wheel-like formation.

Paul looked over at the others again. "This is it," he said.

From the place they were standing, they could see out across the still-green of the land and the surrounding hills. An air of quiet seemed to pervade the space, as though separate from the rest of the world.

"This is the place," he repeated. "We're here."

42

QUAKING FIELDS

Outside Baltimore, in the fields that used to wave golden with wheat and corn, the Western and Eastern forces were raging a final battle.

Gunfire and explosions cast black smoke into the bloodred atmosphere. Detonating land mines shook the earth, and flashes of light punctuated the skies as far as Richmond, Virginia, to the south and Washington, D.C., to the southwest.

The West had fashioned a new flag, converting the red, white, and blue into a set of sixteen broad red and blue stripes with a white round center to represent the sixteen Western states. The East had maintained the traditional flag, and both were determined to win the battle that they thought would set the course for the nation's future.

Several of the central Midwestern states had not known which way they wanted to go and preferred to do nothing, relegating themselves to the Eastern side.

The military in the West was strong. The United States had traditionally recruited heavily from the Western states for army and other military units, and they appeared now well trained and significantly more motivated than the Eastern troops, who seemed to be taking a stance of defense without having worked through a solid set of reasons for supporting the current government. Most of the soldiers were young boys, confused not only by the current state of US affairs, but also afraid for their lives as they fought in heavy uniforms and gear in the heat of the reddening sky.

Radiation sickness was commonplace now, and the troops continually complained of symptoms that sounded at first like sunstroke, then developed quickly into pervading bouts of radiation illness. But they did as they were told, and the battle raged onward.

They thought the battle would continue until the moment of decision. Most had no idea that the moment of decision would come long before they would imagine.

NIGERIA, AFRICA

The ground shook violently. Those in the city ran for cover but found nowhere safe to go. Within minutes the city's buildings were falling and dissolving into rubble. Huge ruptures heaved the ground upward in jagged protrusions, as though the earth's plates wanted to reorganize themselves beneath their feet. A low, grating sound could be heard as the earth seemed to groan in labor. In the center of towns, huge crevices separated people from their homes and families. Roads became impassable. The quake went on for almost an hour, slicing the center core of Africa straight down the middle. And then the storms came.

The lightning destroyed what the earthquake hadn't, hurling bolts that burst into flames and spread like wildfire across the landscape. What hadn't already been singed by the solar and radiation storms was now fast blackening, then cooling into a gray ash that blew furiously in the solar wind.

NORTHERN HEMISPHERE

Throughout the northern part of the hemisphere, the blanket of red thickened even more and spread like fog until the cloudless skies showed no signs of the aurora, only the blood crimson of solar radiation. It seemed to be moving downward across the globe, as though a large shadow were descending upon the earth, covering it in darkness.

EN ROUTE TO JERUSALEM

Through the darkening red skies, the presidential plane approached the continent of Africa. It would still be hours before they landed outside Jerusalem. The plane jolted, and even Serafino looked pale as the plane struggled to hold its own in the strange and unfamiliar atmosphere.

Suddenly, a group of planes whizzed by them on their western side, causing the pilot to fear for their safety. He swerved to the right to allow space.

Air traffic communications were nonexistent, and visibility in the thickening atmosphere was difficult at best.

Matthew Serafino leaned forward to see more of the yellow-gold planes roaring past them. He knew something had to be happening. Were people gathering? Were they going to Jerusalem? How could they know?

He looked over at the others. Lachier was paying no attention to the planes. Asvaka looked curious but unconcerned. Serafino watched Niú Ye. He thought the man had a thin smile on his face. Just for a moment, until he saw Serafino looking at him. But Serafino was sure he had seen it. Perhaps he didn't know the Chinese scientist as well as he thought he did.

"What do you think of the planes, Niú?"

Serafino's voice broke the silence, and Niú Ye seemed to jump, startled. But he looked over at Serafino, calmer than he usually was.

"Quite a lot of them, aren't there?"

"I'd say so," said Niú. He looked back nonchalantly to the plane's window on his right.

"Strange for a group of planes to be out here in this, isn't it? Most have been grounded I thought." Serafino continued to stare at Niú, hoping to get a glimpse of something that would tell him if the scientist knew something.

But Niú kept his face toward the window, answering simply and quite calmly, "Strange, yes."

Serafino was feeling agitated. But he wasn't sure how to probe further at the moment. He still needed Niú Ye in Jerusalem, and he couldn't risk alienating him now. Serafino looked back at the others. They were still looking bored. Lachier had stretched out his legs and was leaning back in his seat, his arms spread across the adjoining rows. Asvaka looked tired but alert, his dark eyes scanning the plane for something to distract him from the long journey.

The plane jolted again and dipped suddenly in the air. Lachier sat up and checked his seat belt to make sure it was secure. Niú appeared to be gripping the sides of his seat, his knuckles turning white.

"Only a few more hours." Serafino motioned to the plane's assistant, then looked back at the other three. "Let's have a drink, shall we?"

GOLAN HEIGHTS, SYRIA

Gilgal Refaim

The ground was rumbling harder now, and Paul thought he could see the volcanic mountains smoking yellow in the distance.

"We'd better get back to Damascus. We need the helicopter to lead the others in."

The five climbed back into the SUV and headed toward the main road that would lead north to the city. The quakes were getting harder now, and Paul imagined the surrounding areas were suffering damage already from the earth moving beneath them.

Overhead, the aurora had deepened into hues of gold, orange, and red.

43

THE QUINTESSENCE

DAMASCUS, SYRIA

Back in Damascus, Paul made arrangements for them all to spend the night. As the solar storms began rolling in, the city became quiet. Those who had access retreated to their lower levels, basements, and underground shelters. Shops and restaurants had closed down, windows and doors were tightly shut, and no one dared go outside. As most had no protective covering, the streets became as vacant as a ghost town.

When the five were safely indoors, they removed their protective suits and lounged together in the upstairs bedroom they had been able to rent from one of the small, private hotels that was still taking guests. The room was small and windowless, but it offered safety and privacy.

Outside, they could hear the rumbling of the earth and the crackling of the skies as solar lightning began to descend upon Syria and the Middle East.

"I hope the planes will be all right." Angela looked worried, glancing toward the outer walls. "They'll still be en route now."

Paul nodded. The others looked at one another in silence.

"We still don't know where the planes are coming from, whose they are. Do you really think the environmentalists came through?" Oksanna was sitting hunched on one of the cots with her head against the back wall, her long dark hair almost covering her body.

Paul answered, "There's no way to know. Perhaps. Or perhaps groups of private owners. The connection was too bad to clearly hear all the details, but it sounded like our contacts in Chartres felt everything was in hand, that they had enough planes for everyone in all the locations, and that Chartres had been able to complete the organization of the flights."

The others nodded.

"What time do we leave tomorrow, Paul?" Father Arnaud was sitting against the far wall with Casimir. The boy had removed the covering from Seraphim's cage, and the cockatiel was hungrily nibbling on a seedcake and sipping water from one of Casimir's bottle caps.

"I think we should leave in the afternoon. I don't want anything to go wrong. We can land the helicopter near Gilgal Refaim and wait. When the time gets close, I'll get into the craft and take it up so the planes can see us. They'll be circling the wheel of Rogem Hiri."

"And then?" Oksanna looked up.

"And then, we'll see." Paul looked around at them all. "I think we'd all better try to get some rest. It's going to be a long day tomorrow, and we have no idea what to expect."

OUTSIDE JERUSALEM

Tel Aviv Airport

Matt Serafino's plane landed on the airfield in the midst of one of the solar storms. The four exited the plane quickly, running for cover through the ramp and into the aerodock waiting area. They would be staying at a local hotel adjacent to the airfield, and Serafino led the group down one of the long hallways to the exit that would transport them to their quarters for the night. As they headed for their rooms, Serafino handed each of them a solar radiation-deflector suit.

"You're going to need these."

"What is this for?" Malik Asvaka was eyeing the suit suspiciously, turning it over in his hands.

"You see what's already happening out there." Serafino motioned to the outside. "By tomorrow, it will be worse. If you don't want to be instantly incinerated by the radiation, you will need to keep this on, at least until we get into the temple."

Malik and Youhanna Lachier took the suits and headgear and headed into their rooms for the night. They didn't bother to complain. They would do what Serafino wanted, and the next day, after he had had his fun, they would return to their countries and resume business as usual. At least they hoped so. They'd had enough of Serafino to last them for a long time.

Niú Ye reached for his suit. But Serafino paused. "I can trust you, can't I, Niú?"

The scientist bowed his head slightly and reached for the suit.

Serafino continued, "Because if I find out I can't trust you, Niú, there will be consequences. Even in the next age—especially in the next age, when the power of the world is in my hands, those whom I can trust will have positions with me. Those whom I can't—well, let's just say I will have no use for those people. Do you understand me, Niú?"

Niú nodded again, sensing it was best to say nothing if possible.

Serafino handed him the suit, and the man scurried off down the hallway, closing his door behind him. Serafino scowled. Something was up. He could sense it. Smell it, as a predator smells prey. He would find out what Niú was up to soon enough. But as long as he showed up at the Jerusalem temple tomorrow, Matt was going to let it ride. He could be patient. For now. He went into his room, shutting the door tightly and locking it. Then he fell into a restless sleep.

DAMASCUS, SYRIA

It was late. The others had fallen asleep. Casimir lay next to Seraphim's cage. The bird was also still, his beak buried into his side feathers. Oksanna lay sprawled on the far cot under her large fur coat. Angela had fallen asleep sitting up, her head leaning over on Paul's shoulder. Only Paul and Father Arnaud were still awake. Paul was propped on some pillows against the back wall, and Arnaud lay sideways, his arm under his head. He looked over at Paul.

"Are you ready for this, Paul?"

Paul smiled. "Do I have a choice?"

Arnaud nodded. "We always have choices."

Paul nodded back. He waited awhile and then spoke again. "It seems so far-fetched sometimes. So hard to believe that all of this is happening this way."

Arnaud sat up a bit, leaning onto his pillow.

"I wonder what it will be like—in the new world," Paul said.

"I think our scientists have been wondering that for centuries. But no one much likes or even believes the answers. When Horace Milkins, the twenty-first-century physicist, started talking about the twelfth dimension, the liminal zone, parallel universes with short-cuts and paths between them, even most of the scientific community didn't want to listen."

"What is the twelfth dimension, do you think, Arnaud?" Paul looked curious but wary.

"I really don't know. Some call it the mind of God, the absolute. The M-theory scientists who subscribe to Milkins's theory call it the quintessence."

"The quintessence?"

"Yes. Dark energy. The energy that has been the cause of the accelerating universe. The mystery force. In fact, those who subscribe to M-theory have many names for it: the matrix, mystery, membrane, master, the universal mind. But whatever you want to call it, the quintessence represents the origin, the spark, the source of everything and all other energy. Some say it's the music of the universe."

"Like the music of the spheres that Pythagoras subscribed to? Or Kepler?" Paul looked interested now.

"Not exactly." Arnaud explained further. "Their concept of the music of the universe was much more rudimentary. And remember, at that time, they still thought the planets revolved around the earth. But they did see the unity of things. They knew that somehow everything was related."

"Although related in a mathematical system." Paul was more alert now.

"Exactly, yes. Kepler believed that sacred geometry, cosmology, astrology, and the harmonies of music all worked together in a similar kind of system, but one that could be deciphered by humankind. M-theory knows its limits, is aware of what it does not know. In a way, humankind has come a bit further. We've perhaps realized how much we really do not know, cannot know. We've in a sense come to a place where we may be ready to embrace the mystery of life, rather than trying to insist on defining it."

Paul looked skeptical. "And yet, we still spend most of our time trying to define it—or to control it."

"Ah, control it, yes." Arnaud nodded. "And yet it is when we let go of our control that we find we are aware of so much more."

"Faith."

"Faith, yes."

"Then, really knowing something, being aware of something, means simply to be open to God's possibilities." Paul's eyes looked heavier now, and his eyelids struggled to stay open.

"Exactly," said Arnaud. "Or it may mean knowing we are part of something much larger than ourselves, and allowing ourselves to be content in that awareness."

Arnaud looked over at Paul. His eyes were closed. Arnaud turned onto his back, his hands lifted above his head, and tried to go to sleep.

44

SONG OF THE SERAPH

Angela woke, her head still on Paul's shoulder. She could hear a low groaning coming from somewhere outside that sounded like a huge, rusty wheel. It seemed to come in long, agonizing waves, like the sound of a distant foghorn, as if the earth were sighing. She leaned over, gently shaking Paul awake.

"Paul. Listen."

Paul sat up. The sound was like nothing he had ever heard before. It was accompanied by the somewhat distant rumblings of the quakes, but the frequency grew and diminished like something vibrating deep within the earth's core.

Arnaud had sat up and was listening as well. "It's the earth's voice," he said.

Angela looked over. Father Arnaud continued. "Scientists know now that the universe and everything in it is made up of movement, of vibrating waves."

"Like sound waves?" Angela looked interested.

"Exactly like sound waves. But most all of the waves, especially those of the solar system, move so very slowly that they could never be discerned by the human ear. If we were to actually hear every sound,

393

we wouldn't be able to function. The world would be a cacophony, or a polyphony—depending on how you look at it—of sound." Arnaud had stopped to smile.

The others heard them talking and were waking up as well now, stirring from their cots and rubbing their eyes. Arnaud went on.

"Even the membranes, what M-theory calls the branes of the universe that flow and sometimes meld together, creating mass, they also move, ripple like waves."

Paul was paying attention now as well. "The *musica universalis*, as Kepler would have called it."

Arnaud nodded. "In a way, yes. More like the music of the universe, cosmic music, the song of life."

Angela spoke up again. "So, what we're hearing, perhaps it is the earth's song."

"Perhaps. Or perhaps the sun's song. Astronomers call it the cosmic scream, the sound the solar particles make as they penetrate the earth's magnetic field."

"That sounds frightening." Oksanna had sat up and was rummaging in her knapsack for a block of cheese she had brought with her from the cathedral in Marseille.

Angela looked thoughtful. "I suppose we're part of the song too, now."

"Indeed." Arnaud smiled. "We all participate in the energy of life, in the mystery of everything that breathes and moves."

Paul had pulled himself up now and was becoming alert. "So, in a way, as we attune ourselves to God's song, we also attune ourselves to the song of life."

"And carry the resurrection of Christ within ourselves," Arnaud added. "In a sense, all life is a continual resurrection. By subscribing to life, one subscribes to the sense of new beginnings."

"New beginnings. I like that." Oksanna smiled, biting into her cheese.

The low groaning began again, and the four looked around at one another in silence. Paul stood then, stretching his hands behind his back.

"We'd better wake Casimir."

He looked over. The boy was still sleeping, his arm around Seraphim's cage. Arnaud smiled. Casimir was less fearful than any of them. He had an innocence about him Arnaud had often admired over the past months as he had gotten to know the young man. He watched him sleeping. Seraphim had practically become his bird. Casimir had grown attached to the little cockatiel, and Seraphim in return seemed to remain calm and content at the boy's side.

"I'll wake him in a moment," Arnaud replied.

"What time is it?" Oksanna looked around. "Does anyone have a watch?"

"It's 10:00 a.m.," said Angela.

Oksanna began to rustle through her knapsack again, extracting a small bottle of water.

"I believe we may be able to find some breakfast downstairs." Arnaud had risen and was heading for the door.

"Good idea." Before Paul followed, he turned to the others. "Let's all meet downstairs by eleven. We'll make sure to eat something, gather our things, and meet outside by 1:00 p.m. Oh—and don't forget to put on your suits."

The others nodded.

TEL AVIV, ISRAEL

Matthew Serafino had risen early and knocked on the doors of the others, rousing them awake and alerting them to meet him downstairs. He had arranged for a car to take them to Jerusalem, but during the night the air had become condensed, its red glow settling on the area like a thick blanket, so pervasive that no driver would agree to take them. So Serafino consented to driving himself, pulling the large black limousine to the edge of the entryway and waiting for the others to come out. He had donned his suit and reminded the others to do the same. He was sure the radiation had risen to a dangerous level. He had no way to measure it, but he wasn't taking any chances.

The three came out within fifteen minutes. The car lurched forward as Serafino drove toward Jerusalem, which he expected would take less than an hour. They would reach the dome in plenty of time to look around inside and make sure of their positions for that evening.

The drive was silent. No cars were on the roads, and no sounds of the city could be heard. It was as though the people had vanished. Serafino knew they were hiding inside, afraid of the sun. He wondered what they thought would happen now, if they thought the problems would just disappear. End in a few days. That everything would just somehow return to normal. Or if, somewhere inside themselves, they knew they would die a few hours from now.

The earth began to rumble loudly. Matt Serafino, jolting from his thoughts, suddenly steered the car to the left as a section of the roadway seemed to vanish from underneath the car. His passengers started and clung to their seats, their eyes wide and staring. The earth was cracking open, as though some internal fissure had suddenly snapped, as if the entire core was ready to split in two. A low groaning sound filled the air. Lachier covered his ears. They would need to hurry.

DAMASCUS, SYRIA

By the time the five piled into their SUV, left the town, and headed for the airfield, the rumbling had increased. A loud crackling filled the skies, as though the entire atmosphere were charged with ions. The roads were beginning to shift. Hairline fissures crept across the ground in jagged paths, as though some invisible hand were cracking the earth like an egg. Paul had to shout to be heard above the din. "We can't take the car. We can't risk it. We're going to have to get to the copter on foot."

The four adults took the lead. Casimir followed behind, shielding Seraphim's cage against his chest. He had replaced the cage's heavy solar cover, and now Seraphim squawked in protest as the sounds of thunderous cracking preceded bolts of lightning so large, they looked like enormous white claws reaching down from the sky. Above them, the red had descended.

They ran for the fields, staying away from the cracking macadam of the roadways.

"Over here," Paul shouted and motioned for the others to follow. "We can get to the airfield this way."

The five golden-clad figures ran through the trenches of dried wheat, the solar storm descending around them. At last they reached the airfield.

"We just need to climb up over this hill," Paul was saying. He lowered and shielded his head with his hands.

The meteorites had begun to fall.

45

THE HILLS OF BASHAN

OUTSIDE DAMASCUS

The meteorites fell like hail, raining balls of fire on the surrounding terrain. Angela screamed and huddled over, holding her hands over her head. She yelled for Paul, but none of them could be heard through the sounds of the pounding quakes and crackling atmosphere. Paul motioned for them to follow. He led them to a small overhang where they would be safe for the moment.

Casimir was clutching Seraphim's cage protectively, shielding the bird from the falling debris. Arnaud could hear him comforting the bird, singing softly into the cage the melody of the *Mazeppa*.

Angela pointed to the eastern horizon. "Paul, look!"

The sun had risen for the last time on the earth's horizon. It appeared to be at least seven times its usual size and looked like a giant spreading red stain in the rusty-red of the gaseous atmosphere. Clouds had been nonexistent for months, as the aurora had displaced the blue of the sky and no rain could accumulate. The thickness was something stranger, a mixture of solar particles and the earth's gases, blended in now with a kind of heated solar waves. *Radiation*, Paul thought.

At last there was a reprieve, and Paul motioned for the four of them to climb the hill to the airfield. The sun's waves were shining off the golden helicopter, making it look like a brilliant ball of fire. They ran for the copter, dodging the last falling bits of cosmic debris, and climbed inside. They needed to get to Gilgal Refaim. They could find shelter there until the time came.

Arnaud locked the key into the ignition, and the copter started up with a roar. In moments, the golden vehicle had risen into the red sky and was heading away from Damascus toward the hills of Bashan.

JERUSALEM

Matt Serafino abandoned the limousine a few blocks away and motioned for the others to follow him up to the entrance of the Dome of the Rock, the site of the Jerusalem temple. The octagonal structure was huge and towered above the city, its golden dome shining brilliantly in the heat of the sun's rays. The solar storm was descending upon the area, and bolts of lightning charged around the dome as though it were emitting them itself. The sun was growing larger and now filled the eastern sky.

Inside the deserted dome, Matt Serafino instructed his cohorts to sit down in the entryway as he scouted out the building and deciphered which direction was north, which was south, east, and west. They would need to be in the right positions for the transformation to take place. No one was inside the structure. No one dared go outside. The earth's atmosphere looked like something out of a science-fiction movie and, Serafino presumed, probably felt like it, too. Their suits protected them from the sun's radiation. Without them, Serafino guessed, they would be fried.

Niú Ye stood at the entryway looking out at the solar storm. He took off his glove and was biting the tip of his fingernail, occasionally looking back at Matthew Serafino as he strode about the inner sanctum of the dome. He hadn't seen or heard the planes since they had passed them in the air, and he wondered if they had gotten to the area safely. Perhaps they had been forced to land and wait out the meteorite storm. Niú had never prayed in his life. He had watched the missionaries praying hundreds of times growing up and had even pretended to pray along with them. But at the time, he had thought it a silly and meaningless gesture, and he had done what he needed to in order to please his benefactors. Now he tried. Tried hard. He squeezed his eyes shut and with everything he had, he put his mind—and his heart—to task.

HILLS OF BASHAN

"There they are." Paul pointed to the east of the helicopter as they approached. "The hills God loved. The hills of Bashan."

The golden helicopter whizzed through the red sky over the rolling hills and valleys of the Golan Heights. As they approached Gilgal Refaim (the Rogem Hiri), Angela motioned to the others. "Look at that!"

From the air, the circular landmark was clearly visible. It looked like a giant wheel, or a stone version of a crop circle. Its four circular dark rings were joined together by thin inner spokes, and it stood out boldly against the still-verdant pasture.

The center of the wheel was slightly raised. In the reddish-orange atmosphere, with the risen sun shining hotly on the landscape, the basalt stones seemed almost crystallized and glowed a deep golden tone.

"The 'wheel of spirits,'" said Arnaud. He steered toward the formation and set the copter down in the field adjacent to the stones. He turned to the others.

"We'll wait here," Paul said. "We'll have a few hours until it's time."

"Paul, I don't see any planes." Angela was holding her hands over her eye-shield to minimize the intense glare, trying to discern any movement in the thickening skies.

Oksanna looked worried. "What if they really did back out?"

Paul looked over briefly and nodded to the Russian woman. "They'll be here."

Oksanna sat back quietly, biting her lower lip.

Arnaud leaned over to Paul. "What do we do now?"

He looked around at everyone, his eyes reassuring. "We wait."

46

FORMATIONS

Dome of the Rock

Serafino had called each of them to the center of the dome and was pointing to each quarter of the sanctuary, which formed a circle around the center rock.

Earth, wind, fire, water. North, east, south, west. Eagle, lion, ox, angel.

Youhanna Lachier looked over at Malik Asvaka and rolled his eyes. He was worried about what was going on outside. All communications were down now, and he couldn't get hold of anyone in Egypt. He had no idea how they were weathering the radiation or if anyone had figured out what to do about it. Surely one of the world's astronomy labs would have come up with something by now. He was fast beginning to regret having promised to make this trip with the USAmerican president. Whatever mumbo jumbo he was into, Lachier belonged back in his lab, where he could be doing something to help. He thought of leaving. But at this point, he couldn't imagine how to get anywhere. He had no plane. For the moment, he was completely dependent on Serafino. He sighed and leaned against one of the pillars.

Malik Asvaka thought the president had gone off the deep end, but he continued to humor him. The money was worth it, he thought. When the storms had cleared, he would be the one returning home with the largest oil sale of the century. And he could easily convince the Afghan government to give him a fair cut; he was sure of it. *Whatever government that will be*, he thought sardonically. Malik had no idea what he was returning home to. China had somehow double-crossed Gulzar, and now his own country was almost completely obliterated by genetic terrorism. And what hadn't killed them through the water system would soon take its toll in famine. Oil was essentially the only thing they did have left. Asvaka jolted back to the present as he heard Serafino talking to him, telling him where to stand. The man was clearly a nutcase. But for now, Asvaka would play along. When the storm ended, Serafino had better keep his end of the bargain.

Niú Ye had been standing slightly to the side of the others and now perked up as he heard the sound of jets roaring through the atmosphere. They had to be jets. *What else could it be?* A slight smile came onto Niú's broad face, and his eyes lit up for a moment in relief. Serafino looked over, catching the man's expression, and he walked over to him now.

"What was that, Niú?"

Niú Ye shook his head. It was almost 7:00 p.m. now. Almost time. And it would all be done.

As though reading his mind, Matt Serafino suddenly shoved the scientist into the nearest pillar. His hands were tight around his neck. Asvaka and Lachier backed away, not knowing what to do.

"You know something, and you're going to tell me now."

HILLS OF BASHAN

"Paul, we need to know what to do."

Angela was shouting to Paul above the din of the raging storm. The solar storm felt strange. No winds were blowing the trees, no rain falling from the skies, and yet lightning and thunder crashed around them. Bits of falling fire dotted the landscape, and everywhere the earth cracked open, rumbling from beneath as though about to implode.

"The planes are late. What do we do?"

Paul shook his head. They sat huddled together in the center of the Gilgal Refaim, frightened but determined. Paul stood to the side, staring up into the sky.

Just then, the sound of roaring seemed to cut through even the crackling of the skies. They all cocked their heads and listened.

Angela pointed. "Look! There! Paul, look! It's the planes!"

They all stood, waving with both arms, laughing and shouting as hundreds of golden planes roared by. They came in droves and began circling the Rogem Hiri in a wide arc.

Oksanna was peering up at them. "Those are not Russian planes."

Paul was shaking his head in astonishment. "They're Chinese." He looked again and gasped. "It's the Chinese air force."

Paul began to laugh uncontrollably, tears running down his face. "What? How?" He looked over at the others in unbelief. "Niú Ye! They sent the entire Chinese air force!"

Paul snapped out of his shock and, running to the copter, got in and raised it into the air above the Rogem Hiri as the planes came, more and more of them, circling and circling.

JERUSALEM

Serafino was furious. "No!" he shouted. "NO! What have you done?" He threw the Chinese man to the floor and strode to the doorway of the temple. *"No!"* Then, turning, he shouted angrily, "Come on; let's go. We're going now."

"Going where?" Lachier had even begun to look frightened of Serafino, who resembled a wild panther deprived of his meat.

"Let's get to the limousine. We need to get back to Tel Aviv. We've got very little time."

"Little time for what? What about this ritual is so vital?" Malik had to run to keep up with Serafino as he darted through the disintegrating streets where they had left the limousine.

"We need to get to the Osprey I and fast. We're going to the Golan Heights. We're supposed to be there, not here!"

Malik and Youhanna Lachier exchanged glances but didn't say another word. Both wondered, at the same time, if they could somehow break free from Serafino, perhaps when they arrived back in Tel Aviv, and wait until the aerodock could transport them out.

"Come!" Serafino motioned for them all to get into the back of the limo, and then he jumped in and floored the engine, speeding past debris and trenches back in the direction of Tel Aviv.

Serafino began mumbling under his breath. To Malik, it sounded like some kind of strange incantations. He glanced over at Youhanna Lachier. Youhanna gave him a knowing look, raised his eyebrows, and shrugged slightly. Neither of them was certain what to do, but they knew they didn't want to remain with the USAmerican president at this point, no matter how much money he represented. Niú Ye was riding in the front of the car next to Serafino. He was flattened so tightly against the passenger-side car door that if it were to open, he would fall out immediately onto the sidewalk. The car sped along, bumping wildly over ridges and gaps in the roadway. As the car approached a major fissure in the highway, Serafino suddenly veered left and began driving across the field, the limousine bouncing up and down over the terrain.

At last they reached the airfield. But Serafino didn't stop at the aerodock entrance. Instead, he drove right up to the Osprey I. The president leaped out of the car and ran around to the other side, pulling Niú roughly out of the passenger side. He angrily motioned for the others to get into the Osprey.

Youhanna Lachier turned briefly, glancing back toward the aerodock. He looked at Malik. He shook his head slightly, his eyes narrowing. Just as Lachier considered making a run for it, Serafino turned, grabbed the Egyptian's arm and shoved him forward toward the plane's steps. He motioned for Malik to follow. Locking the doors, he jumped into the cockpit and prepared the plane for takeoff.

Malik looked at Lachier. "Can he fly this?"

Lachier shrugged, his eyes widening. As the plane rose in the thickening air, they glanced over at Niú Ye. The man sat rigidly on the opposite side of the plane, looking terrified. But he appeared to be thinking. His hands were folding over each other again and again, and his eyes began darting back and forth, as though he were considering some desperate act.

Lachier began to look alarmed.

Niú Ye was reaching for the emergency door.

Malik got up. "Niú?"

In what seemed like less than a second, Niú thrust open the emergency door of the plane, stepped forward, and threw himself out of the soaring plane.

Malik gasped, his breath being sucked away by the vacuum that suddenly overtook the interior of the plane.

Lachier clutched at a seat for support and began to shout, as he and Malik slammed the emergency door shut.

Matt Serafino looked around, hearing the noise. But he couldn't leave the cockpit. They were soaring over the Jordan River now and would soon arrive at Rogem Hiri. Matt could see the mass of planes already circling the area.

Youhanna went to the cockpit door. Serafino unlocked it. He was shaking his head violently.

"Niú's gone."

47

ENDINGS AND BEGINNINGS

GOLAN HEIGHTS (BASHAN)

Gilgal Refaim (Rogem Hiri)

Paul saw the Osprey first from the helicopter. It was the only one not of a golden color, and as it flew closer, Paul could see the red, white, and blue emblem on the side. He pulled out binoculars. *Serafino.* He couldn't let Serafino near Gilgal Refaim. He pulled the helicopter upward and headed toward the Sea of Galilee.

"What's he doing?" Angela watched Paul soar the helicopter away from the center of Gilgal Refaim. She looked at the others. It was almost 9:00 p.m. The huge rays of the sun were beginning to pour through the stone walls of Gilgal Refaim, as the twenty-first hour of the winter solstice approached and the planets aligned for the first time in millions of years.

Oksanna gasped. "Angela, it's beautiful."

The light was brightening, and the entire rock formation now glowed a brilliant gold, shining as though made of some kind of reflective metal. The four held hands in the center of the wheel and looked toward the sky.

Casimir kept Seraphim's cage in the center of all of them, occasionally peeking under the thick blanket to check on the bird, who seemed restless in the din of the surrounding solar storm.

Paul flew the helicopter toward Serafino's Osprey, hovering directly in his path. Serafino dodged the copter, swerving over the Sea of Galilee and then circling back around. Paul tried to head him off again. Again, Serafino dodged the copter and circled back. Paul lifted his binoculars again and could see the anger and determination on Serafino's face.

It was five minutes until 2100 hours. The sun had completely filled the Rogem Hiri, lighting it a brilliant gold that shone upward underneath the bloodred sky. The Chinese planes continued to circle above in formation and looked almost like a large golden wheel themselves. Lightning streaked in and out among the crafts but didn't strike them. The thunder roared loudly now, and Paul heard the earth begin to crack beneath them. The bright round ball of the sun seemed suddenly to be lowering and growing larger, a ring of white light forming around the edges of it.

On the ground, Angela was becoming frantic. "Why isn't Paul coming?"

She stood and began waving her arms.

Oksanna stood beside her, cupping her hands over her brows.

Arnaud stood then as well, looking toward the Sea of Galilee to the west. "It's got to be Matthew Serafino," he said, looking at Angela. "Paul's keeping him away. He's doing what he needs to do."

Angela was sobbing now. "But it's two minutes of nine, Arnaud!"

She grasped hold of his arm, watching as the copter swerved and swooped in front of the oncoming plane.

Behind them, Casimir was lifting the cover off Seraphim's cage. He looked at the bird tenderly, and then quickly unlatched the cage and raised it high over his head. The cockatiel stepped to the edge of the cage, seemed to look around, and then suddenly flew from the cage up into the air above them, landing on a small twiglike oak tree that had grown up between the rocks in one of the circles, and began to sing.

At one minute before nine, Arnaud turned to the others, and they joined hands. Angela was still staring at the golden helicopter.

"He's not going to make it back, is he?"

Arnaud looked as if his eyes would fill, but instead he hugged Angela, pulling her into the center with the others.

*
* *

Matthew Serafino was angry now, angrier than he had ever been. If the copter wouldn't move, then he wouldn't swerve away this time. There was no more time to fool around. He circled for the last time and drove the Osprey forward.

The helicopter sat in position, waiting.

The sun seemed to grow larger and larger, expanding by the minute. Then there was a blinding flash of light, followed by a deafening crack.

The last thing Angela saw was the speeding plane and the helicopter as they came together, and fell.

The light consumed them, and suddenly all sound seemed to vanish, swallowed up as though in a vacuum. And the world went black.

48

THE NEW DAWN

Angela woke as if from a long sleep to the sound of singing. She sat up. She seemed to be sitting under a large oak tree on the greenest, softest grass she had ever seen. She looked up. The sky was a brilliant color of blue. Nimbus clouds glowed sapphire with swelling rain. The meadows were filled with wildflowers, and the trees swayed gently in a warm breeze. Nearby, she could hear the sound of water. Angela stood up and walked to the edge of the clearing. The waterfall was stunning. Blue water fell into a white froth that bubbled over the stones of the brook. She could see fish swimming beneath the surface, and water lilies grew within the clear water. She looked up. The sun was small in the sky, as though it had always been that way. Barely a cloud could be seen. In the background, Angela could see the tips of white on the mountains. She turned around again.

Oksanna and Arnaud were coming toward her. Oksanna began running when she saw Angela, laughing. "We made it, Angela. We're here. And it's beautiful."

Arnaud was carrying what appeared to be apples in one arm. "Fruit trees," he said, motioning to the opposite field.

"Where are the others?" Angela looked around.

"They're over there, over the next hills," replied Oksanna. "There are many of us, Angela. But we'll figure it all out." She laughed.

"And Paul?" Angela looked at the two of them. Their eyes lowered. "He didn't make it."

The tears began running down Angela's face before she could stop them. Arnaud put his arms around her, comforting her. Oksanna stroked her hair.

"These are new beginnings here, Angela. A new age."

Arnaud lifted her chin and looked into her eyes. "He saved your life. All of our lives. He's the reason we're here."

Angela nodded, blinking.

The three turned and walked through the flowered fields toward the others. As they passed the oak tree, Casimir ran toward them, smiling. He looked happier than Angela had ever seen him.

He grabbed Oksanna's hand and began pulling her forward through the grassy meadow. Then, at last, he let go and began to run, faster and faster, until he was just a small figure ahead of them in the fields. They could see his golden hair reflecting in the sun as he ran, laughing.

And as they walked, Angela could still hear Seraphim. He was sitting in the giant oak by the base of the clearing. And he was still singing.

> *My life flows on in endless song*
> *Above earth's lamentations,*
> *I hear the sweet, though far-off hymn*
> *That hails a new creation.*
>
> *Through all the tumult and the strife*
> *I hear its music ringing,*
> *It sounds an echo in my soul,*
> *How can I keep from singing?*
>
> *What though the tempest round me roars,*
> *I know the truth, it liveth,*
> *What though the darkness round me close,*
> *Songs in the night it giveth.*

No storm can shake my inmost calm
While to that rock I'm clinging
Since love is Lord of heaven and earth
How can I keep from singing?

I lift my eyes, the cloud grows thin
I see the blue above it;
And day by day this pathway smoothes
Since first I learned to love it.

The peace of Christ makes fresh my heart,
A fountain ever springing.
All things are mine since I am his—
How can I keep from singing?

EPILOGUE

The Fossor's Find

4 JANUARY 2011

CHARLESTON, WEST VIRGINIA

Ethan Burroughs finished with the burial and sat down to examine the contents of the large cardboard box. He had been digging graves now for almost forty years. It wasn't as if he couldn't have done almost anything else. He had been well educated—gifted, even, one could say, in literature, art, and music. But there was something about honoring the dead that Ethan found fulfilling. The work was hard, and he was getting older now. But he loved being outdoors under the firs and willows in the quiet of God's sanctuary. And for him, it was a way to serve the church and the people who had gathered within it for centuries before and would continue gathering for centuries more. Ethan had been a member of the church since he was born, and his family had attended before him for generations.

Ethan had dug and attended many a burial in his time, but this was the first time anyone had left him someone's personal effects. The funeral director had said the woman had no family. If Ethan wasn't interested in what was inside, he could discard it if he wished.

Gingerly, he lifted the lid of the cardboard box, its edges

weathered from years of storage. The woman had been 108 years old. Angela Binder. Born in 1903. Inside was an old silver watch, tarnished a bit on the edges, some papers and documents, and a large brown leather binder cracked with age. He blew the dust from the cover. The documents in the box seemed to be family records. There was a birth certificate for Angela Binder from the hospital in Charleston, and the death records of her parents. Her mother, Maria, died, it seemed, when Angela was still young. Her father had been eighty-four. Ethan strained to see the writing, which was partially smudged.

Paul Binder
Born 1861
Died 1945
Charleston, West Virginia

Ethan located the birth certificate for Maria as well. But he could find none for Paul. *Perhaps it was lost.* The final document was an ordination certificate, issued by the Methodist Church of the Conference of West Virginia. It was dated 1898 to Paul Binder, pastor.

Ethan put the papers aside, lifting out the large brown leather binder. It was thick with papers. He opened it carefully, so as not to damage whatever was inside. The sheets looked old and yellowed. The first page was a kind of title page.

The Journals and Notes of Paul Binder
March 2048

Ethan stared at the page: March 2048. He looked around, sure he must have read it wrong. The leaves were blowing through the willows, and the sun shone through the clouds, making rainbow colors on the grassy lawn of the cemetery. He looked back down. It *was* March 2048.

He ran inside to the church office and pulled up a chair at the computer. Putting in the name Paul Binder, he waited.

Paul Binder
Born 1861
Died at the age of 84 in 1945
Pastor of the Methodist Church of West Virginia
Ordained 1898 by the West Virginia Conference
Founded the Church of the Lamb of Bashan in 1900
Wife, Maria
Born 1865, died 1913
Daughter, Angela
Born 1903, died _____

Since Angela had just died, her death information was not yet available on the Web. He scrolled down to another article. This one was dated from 1945 and appeared to be some kind of memorial statement for Paul Binder.

PAUL BINDER, 1861–1945

Today, we honor the passing of Rev. Paul Binder. Reverend Binder founded the Methodist Church of the Lamb of Bashan in the hills surrounding Charleston, West Virginia, in the year 1900. A well-remembered and well-respected figure in Charleston and in the entire South, Reverend Binder was only thirty-nine years old when he founded the small church on the grassy knoll of what he later named Bashan Hill. The congregation grew from fifteen to fifteen hundred people at the time of Reverend Binder's death. In his lifetime, he traveled the countryside, preaching in every area he could where people would listen to the word of Christ. He was one of the most sincere and powerful preachers the South has ever known. As a result of his dedication and commitment to the Word of God, Reverend Binder led a religious revival that changed the course of the history of the church. He is survived by his daughter, Angela Binder, 42, of Charleston, West Virginia.

Ethan sat back with his hand covering his mouth and chin. He looked down again at the leather binder. Slowly, he opened it once again and paged through the thick sheath of notes and papers inside. There were news clippings from the year 2048, manuscript documents, copies of letters and diagrams, and a journal, dated from 3 March 2048. Ethan paged to the end. The last entry was made on 21 December 2048.

Sticking out of the back of the journal, the corner of a small piece of folded paper caught Ethan's attention. The entirety was wedged into the binding, and he had to gently tug at it to unloose it from the notebook. It appeared to be an additional journal entry, but this one was dated 22 December 1897.

Yesterday, on 21 December 2048, I witnessed the destruction of the planet and the fulfillment of the Seraph Seal. Yet today, I find myself in the year 1897 in an earth still lush and green with life. I can only assume that Horace Milkin's theory was right and that there are multiple dimensions and realities to God's universe—the Lord's way of always providing new chances to begin again, perhaps. None of the others are with me, and I can only hope they were successfully transported into the new dawn. I have faith that they were. Somehow, I have entered a different gateway, but it is not one I disdain. I see an opportunity, and perhaps it is God's continued plan for me, to help build a different outcome for humanity this time—one that finds a new beginning in Christ, not in the face of destruction but in the here and the now. The beauty of Bashan and the promise of Christ are eternal. And the key to it all is love. Angela will always reside in my heart.

—Paul Binder, 1897

Ethan Burroughs paused for a moment, his fingers still splayed across his face, as he contemplated the words in front of him. Then he pulled his chair closer to the computer, placed the leather binder in front of him, and he began to read—and to write.

Part V

THE QUINTA ESSENTIA

Is the world already headed to a path of destruction?
—TITUS LIVIUS, AD 26

I believe first-century insights and people can solve twenty-first-century problems.
—LEONARD SWEET

A world ends when its metaphor has died.
—ARCHIBALD MACLEISH

In the time of universal deceit, speaking the truth is a revolutionary act.
—GEORGE ORWELL

The Journals and Notes of Paul Binder

March 2048

Notes, Charts, and Symbols
Elements

Air   Earth   Fire   Water

Found in the Patmos box, this chart contains the initials of the eight.

The birthmarks of the four horsemen.

The unity of the elements.

The Mayan wheel or almanac, containing the prophecy of 2012.

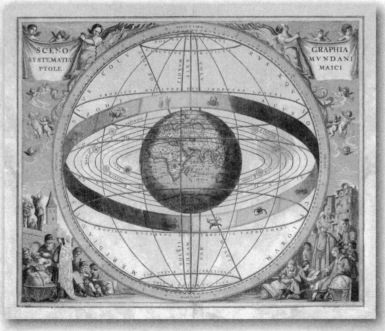

Ptolomeic spacial system. The outermost sphere was known as _Primum Mobile_, the "first moved," because, driven by divine love, it caused the motion of all other spheres.

PICTURES, DRAWINGS, AND DIAGRAMS

Four Horsemen of the Apocalypse
Facade of St. Catherine's Cathedral in Sienna

Dürer woodcut, The Four Horsemen of the Apocalypse

Dürer woodcut, The Adoration of the Lamb

Ezekiel's Vision, by Matthäus Merian

Clues

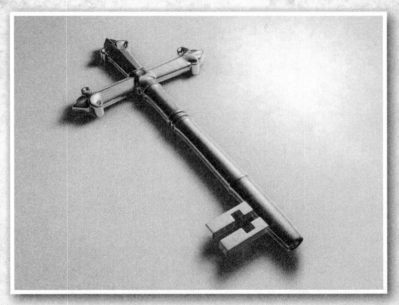

The Cross Key

The Solar Symbol of the Dominicans

Maps

Patmos, where the Cave of St. Anne is located and where John wrote the Revelation prophecy. The Patmos box was found here by Casimir Marceli.

This is an ancient map showing Patmos and the names of the original areas during Tatian's time.

Map showing the location of Damascus and the area of the Golan Heights to the right of the Sea of Galilee.

Rogem Hiri
Gilgal Refaim

SCRAPS, THOUGHTS, NOTES, ARTICLES, NEWS CLIPS, AND OTHER MISCELLANY

CERASTES – Horned viper native to the Sahara desert. Can be lethal.

BANANA SPIDER – Native to Brazil, the spider is extremely deadly and aggressive.

TRANSCENDENTALS – truth, goodness, beauty, bound in unity by love

CODEX GIGAS – The Devil's Bible. Contains a type of almanac and spells.

2, 1, 19, 8, 1, 14 – Bashan

MAZEPPA – Liszt's Transcendental Etude No. 4

RHYTON – A drinking cup in the shape of an animal.

MOONBEAMER PROJECT – Egyptian space jet; space vacuum and interspace domestication.

ATBA – Anti-Technology Biological Alliance (underground Old World doctors)

INSTITUTE FOR TECHNOLOGY, THE SCIENCES, AND THE ARTS – Chennai, India 48758 – where Cassimir is educated

PYTHAGORAS'S TETRACTYS – 4:3, the perfect fourth.

NOTES

STREPTOCOCCUS PYOGENES: This is the strain of virus that broke out on campus of Yale University, New Haven, Connecticut, in the New United States. The virus is a rare and new strain of flesh-eating strep. The symptoms are severe, and death follows usually within hours. The virus is extremely contagious, and it wiped out most of the area surrounding New Haven before being contained.

SOLAR FLARES: Solar flares or solar wind are charged particles that emit from the sun and can enter the earth's atmosphere. Normally, the earth's magnetic field blocks radiation from these flares. However, scientists have discovered a breach in the earth's magnetic shield, allowing for radiation to enter. Effects from flares can wipe out electrical systems and networks for miles around. If harnessed, they would contain enough energy to power the entire United States.

KABBALAH: The Kabbalah is a form of mystical Judaism and is studied in conjunction with the Torah in order to gain insight and wisdom. Sefir Yetzirah is one of the major documents. The Hebrews believed that the Kabbalah revealed a secret knowledge of God, that the Kabbalah was imparted to Moses by God. The Kabbalah emphasizes universal salvation.

MUSIC OF THE SPHERES: Pythagoras believed that the universe was a harmony based on mathematics and music.

TETRASOMIA: The doctrine of the four elements. Coined by Empedocles in the fifth century.

CHARIOT/WHEEL (MERKABAH): The chariot (symbolized by the wheel) is a common symbol in most of the apocalyptic prophecies.

ALBRECHT DÜRER: The artist created woodcuts of <u>The Four Horsemen of the Apocalypse</u> and <u>The Adoration of the Lamb</u>. Both give clues as to the horsemen's identities.

ISAAC NEWTON: Newton wrote a book on the prophecy of Daniel in which he describes the seals and four horsemen. Newton regarded the universe as a cryptogram set by God that could be discerned through introspective imagination. According to turn-of-the century historian and semiotician Leonard Sweet, Newton spent more time ruminating on biblical prophecies than on scientific experiments. ("The Revelation of Saint John and History," in <u>Christianity Today</u> 11 [1973]: 9–10)

GOTTFRIED LEIBNIZ: Leibniz's Monadologie was written at a time when he was influenced by neoplatonic mysticism, alchemy, and Kabbalah. He developed an alchemical view of resurrection (the quintessence). Leibniz's mysticism, however, was combined with a rational form of inquiry. Love and unity with the Divine were important themes for Leibniz. Imitating Christ's love for all humanity is the foundation of Leibniz's theology and ethics. The progress of humanity through the advancement of the arts and sciences. Not a mystic himself, Leibniz associated with the mystics and favored a mystical practice that would promote unity with God.

TATIAN: Resided for a while in Greece. Established school in Mesopotamia. Influence in Syria. Took clandestine trip to Patmos just before his death.

WORLD LEADERS

President Abdul Gulzar, Afghanistan
President Aishwarya Kapoor, India
President Matthew Serafino, USAmerica
President Kim Sun Lee, South Korea
President Igor Petrov, Russia
President Ernesto Alvarez, Brazil
President Murong Gui, People's Republic of China
President Bernino Bruno, Mexico
President Menes Mubarak, Egypt

NEWS CLIPPINGS

STATE OF TEXAS SECEDES FROM THE UNITED STATES

WORLD NEWS

October 2048

The state of Texas has voted today to secede from the New United States of America and has formed the Republic of New Texas, an independent country. The decision came after several meetings of top officials who are unhappy with President Matthew Serafino's leadership of USAmerica. Rumblings of further secessions are prevalent, and it may be only a matter of time before other states choose to secede, or the nation is plunged into its second civil war.

BREACH IN EARTH'S MAGNETIC FIELD YIELDS RADIATION BATHS

US NEWS REPORT

June 2048

NASA has reported a significant breach in the earth's magnetic field just at a time when an increase of solar flares is beginning to pummel the planet's atmosphere. Citizens are advised to build or use available fallout shelters to avoid possible radiation exposure. NASA correspondent Mitch Mayer assures that the government will make every effort to inform people of upcoming radiation baths caused by the solar storms. An increase in the manufacture of gold-plated solar suits is in production, and the suits will be available to the public within the next few weeks.

UNITED STATES PREPARES FOR CIVIL WAR

NETWORK NEWS, NEW YORK

November 2048

Led by Colorado, the Western states of USAmerica have declared war on the Eastern states. Sources reveal a first battle is brewing in the area of Richmond, Virginia. President Matthew Serafino seems to have no comment on the war, and he has not made any address to the public about the pending war.

NEW BREAKTHROUGHS IN BIOINFORMATICS IN AFGHANISTAN

WORLD NEWS ABROAD

April 2048

The Scitheon Corporation, the largest manufacturer of weapons in Afghanistan, is making unheard-of strides in new weapons manufacturing, combining genetics with information technology. Although Scitheon has not revealed the nature of these new weapons, sources believe they may be a future threat to the welfare of the other world nations, should they be tested or released to the public.

MASSIVE EXPLOSION IN BRAZILIAN AGROFUELS COMPANY

LONDON GAZETTE

April 2048

An explosion in Brazil's Agrimar Bioenergia filled the skies over Brasilia as a leak of evaporated ethanol collided within the enclosed boiler room of the company. Sulfuric acid vapors additionally leaked into the plant's warehouses and offices, causing immediate deaths. The cause seems to be linked to pipes that had been intentionally sawed off, allowing the fumes into the plant. Agrimar Bioenergia was the largest agrofuels industry in Brazil.

WORLD GREENHOUSE OBLITERATED BY ICEBERG TSUNAMI

RUSSIAN POST

April 2048

On Tuesday evening, massive icebergs from the East Siberian Sea caused a huge tsunami to crash into the shores of Siberia with a force that has caused the ocean to flood the entire region, wiping out Russia's environmental project, the World Greenhouse. The Greenhouse had been the only naturally and nationally grown food source in the world, and its director, Oksanna Anya Galina, had been committed to Russia's humanitarian efforts to assist neighboring nations in increasing their food supplies and growing independently viable food sources for their citizens.

BAY OF BENGAL SUCCUMBS TO EARTHQUAKE

NEW DELHI NEWS

June 2048

Yesterday a massive tsunami crashed over the area sur-rounding the Bay of Bengal, wiping out entire regions, including Chennai, India, western Bengal, Southeast Asia, and the Philippines. Scientists are attributing the tsunami to the violent collision of two tectonic plates lying beneath the Indian Ocean. The tectonic shift caused an earthquake, in turn provoking a powerful tusanmi. Just before the shift occurred, scientists in the Bay of Bengal region had reported a change in marine environment, similar to the elimination of ocean life found also in the Mediterranean, Pacific, and the North Seas. Marine biologists are still searching for answers as to the causes of these increasing natural phenomena.

TERRORIST ATTACK ON US WEAPONS MANUFACTURER

US NEWS

April 2048

Novitia, the US's prime weapons manufacturer, with its production center in Texas, was the target of a terrorist attack last night. The fires lit up the skies as the company burned to the ground. No report as of yet has been offered concerning who was responsible for the attack or why.

NASA SCIENTIST FOUND IN SAHARA

NEW YORK TIMES

March 2048

The body of NASA scientist Jonathan Maslow was found today in a remote part of the Sahara Desert. An autopsy revealed that the cause of death was multiple bites of a rare desert horned viper. The death is being investigated as a homicide. NASA has declined comment. Maslow is survived by his wife, Ann, and a daughter, Rachel.

WATER WARS CONTINUE IN SOUTHERN EGYPT

CAIRO NEWS

September 2048

The deaths increase in southern Egypt today as the Sudanese continue their run on the Egyptian water-treatment facility just inside the border. The Egyptian army has been ordered to shoot and kill all raiders. Bodies are being stacked in a nearby ravine. The shortage of water, due to the oceans' demise, has been causing extreme conflicts throughout the world as people fight for access to clean drinking water.

Letters, Clues, Poems, and Other Items of Interest
(scraps and documents)

2-1 March 2048

Dear Mr. Binder,

If you are receiving this letter, the year will be 2048, thirty-six years after your birth and the birth of the eight. The Seal that was associated with the Time of Becoming has now come to fruition. Locate the manuscript of the Diatessaron. You have been chosen to unlock the future of your world. The Cross key will guide you. Use it wisely.

Matthew Serafino's inaugural Scripture

For the Lord will come in fire,
　　and his chariots like the whirlwind,
to pay back his anger in fury,
　　and his rebuke in flames of fire.
For by fire will the Lord execute judgment,
　　and by his sword, on all flesh;
　　and those slain by the Lord shall be many.

For as the new heavens and the new earth,
　　which I will make,
shall remain before me, says the Lord,
　　so shall your descendants and your name remain.
From new moon to new moon.

The additional portion of the Palimpsest prophecy:

To the One chosen by the Seraph's Seal: At the appointed time, you will find this prophecy. When you do, you must find the others. You will know them by their attributes. Use the key. Find the box of John of Patmos. From there, you will know what to do. The Society of Messengers will help you and guide you on your way. They are entrusted to carry the Way of the Seal into the Time of Becoming. You are not alone. Start now. Choose well, Paul.

—Patmos, 723

PSALM 151:

Praise to God on high who
Sends the Holy Seal upon us.
All of the people shall praise him.
Let the hills rejoice and
May the chosen see the dawn of the new day.
Find the
Hidden hills.

PSALM NOTES FROM THE PSALM BOOK IN THE PATMOS MATERIALS:

Lord, who May dwell in your sanctuary? Who may live on your holy hill? He whose walk is blameless, and who does what is righteous, who speaks the truth from his heart. (Psalm 15:1–2)

Who may ascend the hill of the Lord? Who may stand in his holy place? (Psalm 24:3)

How good and pleasant it is when brothers live together in unity! (Psalm 133:1)

The hill of God is as the hill of Bashan; an high hill as the hill of Bashan. The chariots of God are twenty thousand, even thousands of angels: the Lord is among them, as in Sinai, in the holy place.

Poems by Saint Catherine of Siena:

The Sanctuary

וְשֵׁב

It could be said that God's foot is so vast
That this entire earth is but a field on His
Toe,
And all the forests in this world
Came from the same root of just
A single hair
Of His.
What then is not a sanctuary?
Where can I not kneel
And pray at a shrine
Made holy by His
Presence?

"Everything comes from love,
All is ordained for the salvation of man,
God does nothing without this goal in mind."
2, 1, 19, 8, 1, 14

POEM FROM THE MISERICORD AT THE BASILICA IN SIENA:

The Eagle soars with beauty on the wind
As the Lion roars the truth upon the earth.
The Ox drinks from the goodness of running waters
And the Angel of fire and love will lead them through.
The Chosen One will unify them All
And bring them into the land of new beginnings.
Love will prevail.

(Leon Battista Alberti, 1452)

EZEKIEL'S PROPHECY:

And I looked, and, behold, a whirlwind came out of the
   north,
A great cloud, and a fire infolding itself, and a brightness
   was about it, and out of the midst thereof as the color
   of amber,
Out of the midst of the fire.
Whither the spirit was to go, they went . . . the fire was
   bright,
And out of the fire went forth lightning . . . and the
   living creatures ran and returned as the appearance
   of a flash of lightning . . .
Behold one wheel upon the earth . . .

Oksanna's Letter, October 2048:

Dear Ms. Oksanna Anya Galina,

    You have been chosen to help guide others to safety. A new world is waiting and you will become part of it. There are others like you. All born on the 21st day of December 2012, at 2100 hours. All with the characteristic birthmark on the right calf. You are not alone.

    At this time tomorrow, Hawaii will be gone. It will sink into the sea at dawn. Go to the Syrian Orthodox Cathedral in Marseille tonight. The others are awaiting your arrival. Trust not what you know or even what I tell you. Trust your heart. Read the signs.

ALPHABET OF THE APOCALYPSE: READING THE SIGNS OF THE TIMES

This is a "Culture Sign Watch," tracking the shadows cast ahead. Certain events cast shadows ahead, not just behind, and they can be seen if you have the eyes to see them.

*
* *

Knowledge will increase.

—DANIEL 12:4

Abaddon [Social]

Abaddon (in Hebrew; Apollyon in Greek) means "Angel of the Bottomless Pit," or Prince of Destruction, one of the biblical names for the devil. John Bunyan used the Greek form, Apollyon, for Satan in *Pilgrim's Progress.*

Other names for the devil include:

Aliboron—popular in the Middle Ages

Azazel—in Leviticus, this is the devil to whom you sacrifice the scapegoat; also used in Muslim demonology

Beelzebub—Prince of the Devils, Lord of the Flies

Mephistopheles—tempter who wants you to sell your soul

Seirizzim—rabbinical writers called the devil this; the word means "goat" or unclean animal

ABC (Anything but Christianity) [Social]

The editor in chief of the *Encyclopedia of Christian Civilization* is filing a class-action lawsuit against the publisher Wiley-Blackwell because the publisher demanded changes that make its tone less Christian. Editor in chief George Kurian is suing on behalf of the four hundred contributors to the encyclopedia: the complaint of the publisher is that the "encyclopedia of Christian civilization" came out "too Christian." In particular, the publisher doesn't want negative historical references to the persecution and massacres of Christians by Muslims.[2]

The ABC syndrome is a reflection of the collapse of Christian culture and the rise of a post-Christian culture and increasingly anti-Christian culture where the ruins of a great religion are in evidence everywhere from assaults on church property (loot the looters) to extended families and self-patrolled homeless communities now living in what used to be church buildings to mocking movies like Bill Maher's *Religulous* (2009), now a cult film in which two-thirds of the film attacks Christianity, and only gingerly approaches Judaism or Islam. Writer P. J. Kavanagh admits that he is a head-down Christian—"those of us who think we believe, or try to believe, or at special memorable moments *believe* we believe, but for the most part keep our heads down."[3]

In Iraq, the glorious historic Christian presence is a whimper. Ten of Baghdad's eighty Christian churches have closed since 2003. Almost half of those Iraqis who flee the country each month are Christian, while Christians make up only 5 percent of the population. Attacks on Christians by radical Islamic groups are of epidemic proportions. In the words of the Chaldean archbishop Louis Sako of Kirkuk, "Christians are suffering from forced evacuation, rape, kidnap, blackmail, scarring, and killing."[4]

The Russian poet Yevgeny Yevtushenko once asked the English novelist Kingsley Amis: "You atheist?" "Well yes," he replied, "but it's more that I hate him."[5]

In Western cultures, the norm is either ABC or atheism. Yet signs of spiritual revival are everywhere. This is not a Christian great awakening but a Global Generic Spirituality (GGS) great awakening. Check out Oneness University in India or Naropa Institute in Boulder, Colorado.

Addictions [Social]

In this highly addictive culture, trying to get people free of their addictions is like trying to cut the green bits of mold out of blue cheese. At any given time, 0.7 percent of the world's population is drunk. Culture is such a toxic pool that as soon as a child enters it, he or she gets poisoned. Ten percent of fourth graders in the USA—that's 1 in 10 of our ten-year-olds, are already drinking. It's 3 in 10 by sixth grade.[6] We face the classic junkie dilemma: our problems are so intertwined with our existence, our everyday lives, that we don't try to solve them but escape them, and we become masters of denial and deception.

AIDS [Environmental]

The HIV/AIDS pandemic continues on an upward trajectory, with fifty million and counting currently living with HIV in the world. The disease is now largely treatable with the proper (and expensive) medicine. According to Professor Richard Feachem, director of the Global Fund to Fight AIDS, TB, and malaria, "HIV/AIDS globally is already the worst disaster in recorded human history. It is already worse than the Black Death in Europe in the fourteenth century."[7]

Alchemy [Social]

Alchemy was an early protoscientific practice combining elements of chemistry, physics, cosmology, art, semiotics, metallurgy, medicine, mysticism, and religion. God's alchemy is the creation of eternal life by the transformation of earth and humanity, and the redemption of creation in "the wound is the gift" process of transmuting hardships and handicaps by the grace of God into precious gold. The four stages of alchemy are blackening, or Melanosis; whitening, or Leukosis; yellowing, or Xanthosis; and reddening, or Iosis.

Apocalypse [Social]

Literally means an unveiling of that which is hidden; or a connecting of disparate dots and a reading of theological signs that lifts the veil to reveal concealed scenarios.

Artilects [Technological]

Artificial intellects, including those found in robots like the tens of thousands of those currently deployed in the Middle East, Pakistan, and Afghanistan, are devices such as bomb-sniffing robots, high-flying drones, and so on. FedEx and UPS are becoming the world's biggest users of artilects.

When artilects mate, they sire SAMs: Self-Aware Machines.

God is of no importance unless God is of supreme importance.
—ABRAHAM HESCHEL

Atheism [Social]

There is only one thing worse than the cant of piety. That's the recant of piety.

All "isms" are "wasms," as Dwight Eisenhower used to say, with the exception of atheism. Increasing numbers dismiss religious faith as a brain dysfunction or a viral infection. In best-selling books Richard Dawkins, Christopher Hitchens, Sam Harris, Daniel Dennett, Frederick Crews, and others say religion is a corrupting delusion and call people of faith "malevolent, barking mad, mendacious, deluded."[8]

Not all the new atheists are as angry as Dawkins, from whom this howl of rage is taken. Dawkins not only calls people of faith "goons" and "fools," but he equates religious education of the young with child abuse. Of course, there have always been atheists. But the new atheism has more of an edge to it, more willing to ridicule and scorn people of faith and to treat other faiths in a more aggressive, hostile, and mocking way. Of course, all the new atheists crack a common whip against Christianity, their number one enemy. All contend in some form that all religion corrupts, and absolute religion corrupts absolutely. Beware the "isms," atheists counsel. They turn to "schisms." Of course, they exempt atheism from their caveat emptor.

Seven percent of the world's 6.8 billion people live in countries with high restrictions on religion,[9] many of which are supporting the passage by the UN General Assembly of the defamation of religion resolution, which says that liberty of expression can be curbed by law when it comes to religion.[10]

Scientists are proving to be surprising hold-outs to the new atheist orthodoxy. Scientists are increasingly finding that the universe is spiritual in character.[11] Although some like Marvin Minsky argue that because religion has retarded the progress of science, "religions have deprived you of the option of having an afterlife!" Minsky believes that science is moving toward a form of immortality when mind meets machine.[12]

Three of the greatest evil-doers of the twentieth century, between them responsible for the loss of tens of millions of lives, were atheists: Hitler, Stalin, and Mao.

Three of the greatest do-gooders of the twentieth century were religious: Mahatma Gandhi, Mother Teresa, and Martin Luther King Jr.

The new atheism has created . . . a perfect sport. NO one can win in the game called "God": everyone can land blows.
—MARK VERNON[13]

Autogeddon [Environmental]

Such is the impact of the auto-cratic (car is king) suburbia on the environment. Suburban developments were named after the flora and fauna, the animal and plants that they killed to make room for the McMansions with their six-car garages: Turtle Creek, Fox Run, Oak Forest, and so on. Suburbia is a succubus that takes its toll of truth and daily drains beauty out of being.

Lewis Mumford's prophecy that the flight to the suburbs "carries no hope or promise of life at a higher level"[14] now rings true. Only those suburbs that grow into cozy, dozy small towns and vibrant cities with arts and pedestrian-friendly businesses will enjoy a future. Density, diversity, and mixed use are no longer swearwords in urban planning.

Bailout Bubble [Economic; political]

All bubbles burst. Dot-coms, real estate, bailout—they all pop and wreak havoc. But there is nothing left to inflate any more bubbles that will postpone the inevitable chaos. If some scapegoat cannot be found, the only diversion left to politicians is war. War is the $14 trillion question. That's the amount earmarked for the various bailouts for the bad bets made by the "too bigs to fail."

*I accept this award today, with an abiding faith in America
and an audacious faith in the future of mankind. I
refuse to accept the idea that the "isness" of man's present
nature makes him morally incapable of reaching up for
the eternal "oughtness" that forever confronts him.*
—MARTIN LUTHER KING JR.
(ACCEPTING NOBEL PEACE PRIZE, DECEMBER 1964)[15]

Beta [Social]

Everything now is conditional, transient, fleeting. Life is lived in beta.
Marshall McLuhan said, "If it works, it's obsolete."[16] When you start
hearing from the media about some topic or some social phenomenon, it's a clear sign that the phenomenon has fallen into irreversible
decline. In a beta world, there is *no* Next Big Thing. There are only
one hundred thousand Next Little Things, some of which will become
the one thousand Next Big Things.

Bicameral Mind [Social]

Also known as split-brain theory, this burgeoning literature on how our
two brains function is as significant as Freudianism in earlier generations.
    We dream with the right side of our brains. We read with our left
hemisphere. Therefore, we never read in our dreams. (If the church
has only half a brain, it's the wrong half.)

Bioinformatics [Technological]

This scientific field is a fusion of biology and information technology;
it is a digitization of information, including chemical information.

Biomimetics [Technological]

Manufacturing modeled on nature. It observes how nature works and
attempts to replicate it with organic components that self-assemble

in order to grow complex, self-adapting, self-replicating systems; the downside danger is that biological systems are notoriously hard to control (e.g., "gray goo": biosphere-eating toxic sludge), and our risk-taking is far beyond what any safety standards can address, as we learned with BP in the Gulf of Mexico.

Examples of safe biology-based systems: Second Life is a biological model for human interaction; Wikipedia; user-generated games; "evolutionary design" approaches like Microsoft, which put imperfect products on the market and rely on feedback to improve them.

Bioregionalism [Political]

Local is the new global; people are staying home. Shipping costs are exorbitant; airline travel harrying; terrorism and kidnapping ever-present dangers. Besides, you can go anywhere in the world virtually. So when you do travel, it's seldom and a big deal.

This circle-the-wagons phenomenon also goes by the name of locavore, re-incarnation, or more academically, "reinhabitation," the process of learning about one's home area and then resolving to help improve local and regional conditions as a prime priority. The nationalistic "Buy Local/Country First" has devolved into the locavore slogan of "Buy Local/County First" or "Build it, grow it, live it, and buy it local." This process of residents of a bioregion becoming "rein-habitants" or partners in the life-sustaining functions of the region and its natural assets and ecosystems has led to locavores' implementing on a neighborhood scale what we once wished our government would do on a national and international scale. The upper classes are now almost all locavores. They buy "clean."

In 1900, 40 percent of the US population lived on farms and were self-sufficient on their land. In 2005, only 2 percent of the US population lived on Old-MacDonald-Had-A-Farm farms. That 2 percent is climbing back upward, with the prolifeation of both homesteads and "doomsteads," although the difference between home farms and factory farms is significant.

In 2006, only 40 US cities or regions hosted buy-local groups. In

2010, that figure has jumped to 130 cities, representing 30,000 businesses.[17] "For every $100 spent at a locally owned store, $45 remains in the local economy, compared with about $13 per $100 spent at a big-box store.[18] "Every dollar spent at a locally owned business generates two to four times more economic benefit, measured in income, wealth, jobs, and tax revenue—than a dollar spent at a globally owned business does."[19]

Of course, sometimes the wagons are circled more to control the battle within than to repel attacks from without.

Bitprints [Technological]

Every digital transaction leaves a print. Every supermarket checkout, every postal delivery, every movie you've rented at home and at hotels, all these are digitally accessible and can create a digital imprint, or a bitprint. Bitprints are becoming the new app for dating, but it's so much more than putting in a name, a phone number, or an e-mail. Bitprints provide immediate knowledge about everybody, including what they're worth, what they're known for, and what they're bad at.

Bonsai [Social]

Bonsai is the new buzz. Everything is bonsai: bonsai business, bonsai church, bonsai art. (A throwback to the past? The Harley Psalter, one of the great masterpieces of the medieval world, has colored line drawings that took eight craftsmen over a period of one hundred years to draw.)[20]

In a bonsai world, spare and bare are beautiful again.

Book of Revelation [Social]

Also known as the Apocalypse of John, this is the only book of the Bible that John Calvin didn't write a commentary on. Martin Luther initially dismissed it as "neither apostolic nor prophetic," though later in life, he came to appreciate this testimony to the future written by John on the prison-camp island called Patmos.

In Eastern Orthodox churches, while they recognize the book of Revelation as part of the canon, they refuse to read from it in their services.

Bottom Billion [Economic]

A phrase coined by Paul Collier[21] to describe the fifty-eight countries, mostly in sub-Saharan Africa, that comprise the bottom billion, namely, those people who live on less than $1 a day. The three richest people in the world possess a combined fortune greater than the combined total GDP of the forty-eight poorest countries.

It is not that these fifty-eight countries have not mastered modernity or received aid. Since 1960 the world has dumped $450 billion in aid on the forty-eight countries of sub-Saharan Africa. Between 1975 and 2000, aid to Africa averaged $24 per capita, while aid to South Asia was $5. During those twenty-five years, the per capita GDP in Africa sank, while South Asia's per capita GDP more than doubled.

Mallam Nuhu Ribadu, chairman of Nigeria's Economic and Financial Crimes Commission, reported that nearly $400 billion in African aid had been squandered through bribes, money laundering, and thefts between 1960 and 2000.[22]

Brain-Controlled Remotes [Technological]

First available to disabled people, these headsets using near-infrared rays and optical fibers are becoming widespread. A revolution is turning the human body into the ultimate identification card (e.g., biometric payment systems where your fingertip is linked directly to your checking account). Marshall McLuhan's view of the telephone as an extension of the ear has become literally true with earrings and earplugs now doing what cell phones used to do.

Bureaucracy [Political]

In the Enlightenment pursuit of perfection and efficiency, bureaucracy became valued more than goals of best and resilience. The government bureaucracy running Medicare eats up approximately 30–40 cents of every Medicare dollar.

Bureaucracies are also known as "cretins," and the philosophy behind the formation of bureau drawers for every aspect of life "cretinism." The transition from command-and-control hierarchies to connect-and-collaborate networks is going full steam in almost every sector of society with the notable exception of the church. The motto of the National Association for Professional Bureaucrats: "When in charge, ponder; when in trouble, delegate; when in doubt, mumble." USAmerica (see "USAmerica") is now paying a quarter of a million of its citizens to devise new but implement old federal rules.[23]

In public choice theory, the government is no better or worse than a business. Forget virtuous government and bad businesspeople. The government is a competitor to business.

The government is like a lobster. It will eat anything. It wants to survive, it will compete with anything, and it can be a cannibal.
—AMITY SHLAES[24]

Candlemaker Fallacy [Social]

A preservation of the old that leads to an opposition to the new (e.g., electric lighting, because it will put candlemakers out of business).

Carrington Event [Environmental]

See Magnetic Reversals.

Casino Culture [Social]

One that entertains oneself to death. If "idle hands are the devil's workshop," then US homes are the holiest places on the planet.

Michael Bywater calls entertainment "the fourth horsemen of the apocalypse": "We don't live; we watch living being done. We don't play; we see others playing; even our minds are filled, not with our own inner narrative, but with other people's voices."[25]

Our ancestors were too busy living to have a lifestyle.

Chimera [Social]

Any organism that carries more than one set of genes. The word came into use after the 2004 "Stuart Little Experiment" of Irving Weissman, in which he placed some human cells in a mouse brain.[26] Named after the composite creature of Greek mythology that was part-lion, part-goat, part-serpent. Michael Crichton's 2006 thriller *Next* was built on the premise of what happens when you mix human and chimpanzee DNA.

Chinafication [Economics]

There is an old saying that needs updating: "As American as apple pie." The new saying? "As American as Chinese food." Nobody eats or makes apple pie anymore. But many do eat Chinese food. Lots. There are nearly forty-one thousand Chinese restaurants in the United States—more than McDonald's, KFC, and Burger King combined.[27]

China is taking over the world, not one country at a time, but one company at a time. China has gone from wanting the things of the West, to making the things for the West, to owning the companies that make the things for the West—including the IBM computer on which I am typing. China is the most global country in the world today.

In the "Chinafication" of the world's economy, China now consumes 40 percent of the world's cement, a third of its coal, and a quarter of its steel. China accounts for half of all the construction activity on the planet today. Intermittently, China may be the most innovative country in the world. Once its restrictions on free speech were brought down by the Internet, the flood of previously dammed-up creativity and entrepreneurial activity burst forth. For example, the International Institute of Semiotic Studies was established in China at Nanjing Normal University in 2007. What slowed the flood of innovation was the absence of any legal structure or history respecting contracts and patents.

China's economy is growing at 10 percent a year, while the United States has 10 percent unemployment. With rising job losses in the

United States, hostility toward China increases. Hence the presence of NOT MADE IN CHINA labels.

There are those in China who are praying for China to become a Christian nation. One hundred thousand people a week are becoming Christians in China, although figures out of China are notoriously unreliable. There is the aboveground "patriotic church," and there is the underground church. Officially, there are twelve to fifteen million Chinese Catholics and one hundred million Protestants. These official figures are all-encompassing of the state-controlled Chinese Patriotic Catholic Association, the Protestant Three-Self Patriotic Movement, and the underground Catholic and Protestant churches.

Why has China emerged so quickly to become such a global powerhouse? John and Doris Naisbitt give their explanation by a retelling of a third-century Chinese legend. General Zhuge Liang sat on the banks of the Yangtze River facing the enemy army of Cao Cao on the other side. Rather than attack directly, Zhuge sent over various boats packed with straw. Cao Cao's archers, perceiving an attack, sent a hail of some one hundred thousand arrows down onto the boats, whereupon Zhuge retrieved the vessels and stole his enemy's ammunition,

The late premier Deng Xiaoping in the 1980s employed the same "borrowing arrows" strategy when he invited foreign capital and industry into the country, starting with Volkswagen in 1978. Other large Western firms followed, including Boeing and IBM. The arrangement provided abundant cheap labor for US companies. China secured capital and, more important, technological expertise—arrows that the West valued cheaply, it turns out. In 2005, Lenovo, which had done subcontracting work for IBM under a different name, became the world's third-largest computer manufacturer when it acquired IBM's PC division. The Naisbitts forecast that China "plans to turn itself into one of the leading producers of hybrid and all-electric vehicles within three years, with the goal of being the world leader in electric cars and buses," thanks in part to lessons learned building automobile parts for foreign companies.[28]

Chindia [Political]

China and India contain two-fifths or 40 percent of the world's population.

China dominates global manufacturing.

India dominates information technology.

Put differently: China is #1 in hardware; India is #1 in software.

Choosing Times [Social]

Puritans called times spent in the valley of decision "choosing times." We are living in one of the most important choosing times in all of history. "Multitudes, multitudes in the valley of decision" (Joel 3:14). Rather than "I think, therefore I am," it is now "I choose, therefore I am."

We make the future day by day. Responsibility and choice make the future. What's coming down the pipes? We choose. If we choose wrong? Then what is the worst that you can imagine? It's going to be much worse than that.

Cloning [Technological]

Cloning is becoming widespread globally. It is one of science's best-kept secrets. In the not-too-distant future, almost every human born to a rich family will have a spare human being, a clone of themselves, kept in a cryogenic container to be harvested when body parts of the host give out. There is a vast and growing worldwide market for extra organs, with kidneys already exported from Africa and Southeast Asia to rich Westerners.

The Cloud [Technological]

The word *Cloud* will soon replace the word *Internet*. Whatever you do online, whether update on Facebook (in our book, called "Life Stream") or upload to YouTube, you are in the Cloud. There is a public Cloud (Finland was the first to make broadband a legal right), which means that every human being now has the Library of Congress at their beck and call. There are private Clouds, customized data Clouds for each person with a closed internal network and protected fire-wall. And there are hybrid Clouds. Some people have very powerful Clouds, which you can tap into if you follow or fan them.

The best way to think of the Cloud is as a living entity. It grows and gets stronger, gathering more personality as it collects more infor-mation. What we are calling "FirePillar Protection" is our name for the new combined antivirus, 911, security system, protecting both your body and your Cloud, which follows you wherever you go.

The Cloud is entered through the "Pearl." (See "Pearl" entry)

Complex Emergency [Social]

"Complex Emergency" is the UN/NGO euphemism for war, now fought as much on the mediated fields of image as the muddy fields of battle.

Of non-Jewish German males born in 1920, more than 40 per-cent died in the Second World War. In some places, the Second World War is still going on: Russians are still fighting the Chechens; Eastern Ukraine is still fighting Western Ukraine; Serbs are still fighting everyone.

Ten nations from 1914 to 1945 managed to kill 100 million people. That is twice the entire population of the Roman Empire.[29]

If North Korea can build a bomb, then anyone can, and anyone can bomb anyone else. The nuclear bomb promises the destruction of the planet as we know it; but a world without the bomb isn't neces-sarily a safer world.

Based on accounts of refugees fleeing into China, at least three million North Koreans perished in the famines of the mid-1990s. Kim Jong Il has created a generation of chronically malnourished and stunted children, smaller than their predecessors in the Japanese colonial era eighty years ago. At present, a seven-year-old South Korean boy would weigh roughly two-thirds more than a North Korean boy of the same age, and would be some twelve inches (thirty centimeters) taller.

The greatest "complex emergency" in the world today is not the war of armaments but the war of minds and the war of spirits, a warfare the terrorists are waging better than anyone.

War is the means by which Americans learn geography.
—ATTRIBUTED TO AMBROSE BIERCE

Consumerism [Economics]

We're all consumers now.

Go to a hospital, and you're not a patient; you're a customer.

Get on a plane, and you're not a passenger; you're a customer.

Go to a restaurant, and you're not a patron; you're a customer.

Go to college, and you're not a student; you're a customer.

We shop for a wife or a husband like we shop for cookies or handbags.

For the past fifty years in contemporary Western societies, being a consumer has trumped being a citizen. Our social duty is to do as we are told and go shopping. Look around you. We did. We went shopping for everything and anything, and we are suffering the consequences. We're shopped out. We shopped till we dropped. Now we're picking up the droppings.

The shopping life, the bling-bling life, is doomed to binges and splurges, like a middle-aged man who tries periodically to hold his tummy in. The brown paper bag is trendy again, replacing those loud shopping bags with brand names emblazoned on them. *Cosmopolitan* magazine, once the epitome of hedonism, has just hired a spirituality editor, its first, for the British edition of the magazine. The editor is named Hannah Borno, and she writes, "I've come to the painful realization that men and shoes are not enough to make me happy."[30]

Wall Street led the nation off the wall because of too much credit and too much easy money. So what is the government's solution to the problem? More easy money and more credit. Federal obligations have USAmericans in debt to the tune of $546,000 per household.[31]

The United States is less prepared than Greece for radical lifestyle changes.

Hedonistic consumerism seems built into the system as a vested interest, since both large corporations and the federal government promote greed and more goods, so that the economy does not collapse.

Cooper's Law [Technological]

Spectral efficiency (the amount of information that can be crammed into a given slice of radio spectrum) has doubled every thirty months since Marconi patented the wireless telegraph in 1897. The law continues to hold. Devices in 2048 will have a spectral efficiency more than one trillion times greater than Marconi's successor devices did in 2009.

The law was named after Martin Cooper, once called "the most influential person no one has ever heard of," who almost single-handedly invented the wireless industry. Planet Earth now has a central nervous system because of Marty Cooper, whose name today is as magic as that of Alexander Graham Bell once was. The son of Ukranian immigrants, he invented the cell phone in 1973 and the commercial use of that phone in 1983 (list price $4,000). 3 April 1973, the day Cooper took the phone into the streets and made the first call, is now on everyone's calendar.

Co-ops [Economics]

When I was born, there were almost five hundred food co-ops (most organic, but not all). Between 1969 and 1979, it is estimated that between five thousand and ten thousand food co-ops were established in the United States, but by the middle of the first decade of the twenty-first century, such things as poor business management had reduced that number to about three hundred.[32]

Corporations [Economics]

Don't think companies; think nonrecognized states. Economic entities have much more power than political entities.

CPC (Center Point of Christianity) [Social]

The Center Point of Christianity—the center of gravity for the gospel, the spot on the planet where there are an equal number of Christians north, south, east, west—changed from northern Italy in 1800 to Timbuktu in 2010. It will continue to move eastward—to Nigeria in 2020, to Addis Abbaba in Ethiopia in 2048.

Crisis Management [Social]

An oxymoron if ever there was one. In 2000, only four US universities offered courses devoted to disaster management; it is now an academic growth industry, with 115 degree programs available and hundreds more under consideration.

The futuristic sublime has a disconcerting habit of turning into the antiquarian ridiculous.
—MAX SAUNDERS[33]

Cybernetic Genies [Technological]

Invention is increasingly automated, with inventors spending now as much time deciding what to "wish" for as in actual product design. "Be careful what you wish for; you might get it."

Invention Automation Technology (or IAT) is in the midst of many court battles. Can IAT be patented? What about the artificial wishes that human inventors give to computer-generated inventions and artificial-invention technology? Are they patentable?

Cyborg [Technological]

The marriage of the born and the made. Computers are becoming more human, and humans are becoming more cyborgian. The world of matter is becoming animated, and the world of animation is materializing. We're all cyborgs now. Or to implement a more user-friendly word, we're all transhuman now.

It's harder to see the latter than the former. Epileptics now have cyberonic devices implanted in their necks and chests. Vocal implants go into a hole in the thyroid cartilage to repair damaged voices. Quadriplegics get NeuroControl's Freehand System. Hip replacement, anyone? Pacemakers? Prozac? Eyeglasses? We live in a hybrid world, a world that straddles the boundaries between nature and culture, the born and the made. Very few of us any longer are not borgs in some way. The line between physical and virtual reality is getting thinner every day.

Decentralization [Social]

A mediatized world and decarbonized economy are forcing decentralization on everyone and everything. All top-down authorities are being replaced by bottom-ups. The triumph of the nano is reflected in every aspect of life, including the bull market in personal coaches, personal trainers, self-improvement books, image consultants, and so on.

If the last three decades of the twentieth century were characterized by the rise of "mega-churches," the first two decades of the twenty-first century will be characterized by the rise of "satellite churches" and "house churches."

If the story of the twentieth century was the struggle to get homes "on the system," the story of the twenty-first century will be the struggle to get homes "off the grid." Homes will aim at zero or low carbon and will generate their own energy.

The dismal failure of all centralized statist and collectivist approaches is birthing new decentralized models; Chinese communists abandoned socialist economics in favor of an indigenous form of capitalism, very different from that of the United States, with no inclusion of "democracy" but an authoritarian political order with a redistributive ethic.

Even terrorist groups are not liberation armies but open-source, decentralized conglomerates of small, quasi-independent units.

Denominations [Social]

Church assemblies too often conducting dramas of insignificance and denial.

Devil's Dung [Environmental]

The number one spice in the world is now asafoetida, making the seven Stans where it is now grown (Azerbaijan, Turkmenistan, Uzbekistan, Kazakhstan, Kyrgyzstan, Pakistan, Afghanistan) economic power-houses. It's also famous as the world's smelliest spice, which is why for many years Westerners knew nothing of it, not even that it was in Worcestershire sauce. Strong underground markets even traffic in what some profess to be the long-thought predecessor spice but then extinct silphium-seeds. I have seen one, and indeed it is a heart-shaped seed, just like the ancient Libyan silphium. Sold commercially as *bandhani hing*, this spice has been found to be a natural contraceptive and to bring fountain of youth properties when taken in pill form. It exerts special healing power on the lungs, which have replaced the heart in illnesses causing death. The only resin that costs more is maple syrup.[34]

Devolution Revolution [Political]

In an asymmetric world, what used to be reserved for nations is now available to individuals. Nation-states are collapsing everywhere. Secessionist movements can be found in every country. Transnational financial interests now not only rival but trump the power of nations.

There are now NGOs for everything—26,000 international NGOs, 90 percent of them created between 2000 and 2010. NGOs are now a superpower with almost the same clout and stature as multinational companies and nation-states.

Domotics [Technological]

Home automation systems that feature voice-activated and emotion-sensitive technologies are in various states of implementation. Prototypes already exist of domotic homes where your playlist can read your mood and put on the right music; your kitchen can read your hunger level and suggest menus; your clothes and jewelry can read your stress level and change their character. Domotic homes are already built where lights switch on or off and curtains can open or close, all on commands given in your own voice. By connecting to your home by cell phone, you can change the temperature, switch off the coffee maker, and turn on the TV. The options are limitless.

Dunbar's Formula [Social]

Dunbar's formula: 150 (147.8) is the maximum number of individuals with whom we can have a real relationship, in which they know us and we know them.

A cultural mosh pit is not a community, at least not a harmonious one that generates creative energy.

No country has ever been greater or purer than ours or richer in good citizens and noble deeds; none have been free for so long many generations from the vices of avarice and luxury; nowhere have thrift and plain living been for so long held in such esteem. Indeed poverty with us went hand in hand with contentment. Of late years wealth has made us greedy, and self-indulgence has brought us, through every form of sensual excess, to be, if I may say so, in love with death both individual and collective.

—Titus Livius (26 CE), on the Roman Empire[38]

Ecopolis [Social]

Towns and toxins went together in history. Now cities are becoming the most ecofriendly and healthy places to live, with some green urban environments called ecopolis vying for the lowest carbon footprint. The US, mired in industrial era technologies of wires and poles, is far behind burgeoning cities in the East that are being built green from the ground up.

Residents of the ecopolis hate all packaging with a passion. The only acceptable packaging contains reusable and recyclable components that can be reclaimed; in the ecopolis, conspicuous consumerism is being seen as not only bad manners but as a sin, as a spiritual defect.

Two saints of the ecopolis are architect William McDonough and chemist Michael Braungart, authors of the landmark book *Cradle to Cradle* (2002). They contend that "every material used in the manufacturing process should ultimately either biodegrade harmlessly or be reusable with no loss of quality (unlike today's recycling, which is actually downcycling)."[35]

Ecotiques [Environmental]

Fancy name for Dumpster-diving, which itself is a pejorative way of putting waste collection or the crusade by "waste collectors" not to let waste go to waste and to convert garbage into energy . . . When a culture throws away a third of all the food it buys, collecting garbage starts to make sense.

Mining waste is big business. Japan recycles cell phones. They can get a one kilogram gold bar worth about $10,000 out of 120,000 recycled cell phones. The United States could generate about 2.4 percent of its electricity from the trash it produces.

Two other facts are fueling this new form of mining: (1) there is no "away" in which to "throw away" (Great Britain has only seven years' worth of landfill space left); (2) airless black bags housing rotting food create methane, a greenhouse gas twenty-three times more powerful than carbon dioxide.

---

*We live in a world where half of us are killing ourselves
with excess calories while the other half starve.*
—KATE COLQUHOUN[36]

Electronic Monitoring [Technological]

Ninety percent of all probationers are now on electronic monitoring surveillance, with many others hooked up to it as well. Who would ever have thought that a New Mexico district court judge reading a *Superman* comic strip, when a character was tracked by a transmitter affixed to his wrist, would prompt the judge to request an engineer to design an electronic bracelet to emit a signal picked up by a receiver placed in a home telephone, and with any movement of 150 feet from the telephone, the signal would be broken and the authorities notified.[37] We predict even Martha Stewart will get on board, with a trademarked line of ankle bracelets.

Empire USAmerica Dissolving and Devolving [Government]

Adam Smith declared that the discovery of America ranked as one of the two "greatest and most important events recorded in the history of mankind."[39] In the United States, *dream* and *nation* are interchangeable words. When the dream dies, so does the nation.

Empire America is now on the downhill. The United States is not in charge anymore. Arab money and Asian money rule the world. They are also what is building this new world. In virtually every quantifiable comparison to other developed nations, the USAmerican standard doesn't win, place, or show. Once the gold standard, the United States is now the plastic standard, living off credit and cards.

The parallels between USAmerica and Rome are being pointed out by everyone: Borders and immigration (Romans faced the invasions of barbarians), a bloated state bureaucracy (the highly centralized Roman Empire), privatization and outsourcing (the economic exchange of influence), the emergence of a gap between civilian and military leadership (increased use of mercenaries and emperors ceasing to lead troops), and the ultimate failure of a reliance on "shock and awe" (the fall of the Roman Empire).

The United States is not in the top ten of any good "Top Ten" (from economics to quality of life) list, and it is plummeting in the ranks of countries in terms of per capita GDP.

The United States now is a fantasizing project, a twilight zone of denial and delusion.

Those over age thirty-five can't shake the idea of the United States as the singular dominant power.

Those under age thirty-five have only known a world where China is the dominant economic superpower, and India the second.

Those under age thirty-five are angry at their elders for failing to face the demise of the supremacy of the United States and to prepare for a new kind of national and international order.

What is certain is that, for some years, you have strangely abused the advantages given to you by God.
—ALEXIS DE TOCQUEVILLE (1805–1859)[40]

Encyclopedias [Social]

Surprisingly, this is an age of encyclopedias, with more than fifteen thousand new editions in the first decade of the twenty-first century, a reflection of the fact that people need help in navigating new waters and their retching human and technological initiatives.

Evil [Social]

The more violence, injustice, and discord that run rampant in the world, the more the church seems unprepared to address the reality of evil, having long abandoned a language to talk and address the enormity of wickedness (Satan, sin, devil, demons, etc.). Indeed, the evil viewpoint has all too often become the "good" viewpoint: "There is no good and evil, there is only power, and those too weak to seek it" is how Professor Quirrell sums up the evil viewpoint for Harry Potter.[41]

For those Pollyannas who think humans are all good and "all's well with the world," Welsh priest/poet R. S. Thomas asks, "And where do the viruses come from?"[42] Ninety percent of the 140 billion e-mails sent daily are spam or spear-phishing scams.[43] Or try surfing the Web without a firewall or antivirus software. Soon someone will write the sequel to *Moral Man, Immoral Society*, adding a third category: "More Immoral Robots." Even in robotics, the talk of "original sin" underestimates the scope of the problem, if recent research on the emergence of evil in evolutionary robots is to be taken seriously.[44]

The doctrine of "original sin" is secondary to a doctrine of original innocence, an Edenic primordial paradise of peace and harmony where the genie of "good and evil" had not been released.[45] Even so, evil and suffering cannot be explained. They can only be circled around, and sometimes these circles can get closer and closer to the original Tree of Life.

If you are a good economist, a virtuous economist . . .
you are reborn as a physicist. But if you are an evil,
wicked economist, you are reborn as a sociologist.
—ANONYMOUS INDIAN-BORN HINDU ECONOMIST[46]

Enhanced Singular Individuals (ESIs) [Technological]

In a sense, almost every Westerner alive today is an ESI, since our very life depends on chemical (antibiotics, etc.) and technological (glasses, anyone) enhancements. But in the future there will be pioneers of the "Human Singularity" who will take the merger of the "born and made" to its greatest degree, people with advanced capabilities of mental acuity and physical ability. Perhaps known as Goliaths, those who refuse to become ESIs may be known as Norms.

What terrifies us is not the explosive force of the atomic
bomb, but the power of the wickedness of the human heart.
—ATTRIBUTED TO ALBERT EINSTEIN

Environmental Refugees [Environmental]

By the mid 1990s, there were 25 million environmental refugees. In 2010, there are 50 million environmental refugees. In 2040 there will likely be 200 million or more. Most are displaced due to climate change, as the world is being choked to death on carbon dioxide and methane. Refugees of unprotected populations are rife with rape, human trafficking, theft, and murder.

Everyone now is an environmentalist. But environmentalism is in the midst of a civil war, with two competing saints: John Muir and Theodore Roosevelt. John Muir is the saint of the Yosemite movement (female/lover). Theodore Roosevelt is the saint of the Yellowstone movement (male/hunter). Very few bridges are being built between Yosemite and Yellowstone, although a few are starting to realize that maybe the movement needs both.

When you check out at the supermarket, you have two choices: Do you want to destroy the oceans and kill fish with the plastic bag, or do you want to destroy the land and kill trees with the paper sack?

Felo de Se = *"Felon of Oneself" [Social]*

An archaic legal term for suicide, *felo de se* is becoming such a problem it is birthing a new discipline, the science of suicidology. Twice as many people in the United States die from *felo de se* than AIDS. Suicide is the eleventh-leading cause of death, the third-leading cause of death in people ten to twenty-four years of age. In the past three decades, the number of suicides committed by people ages fifteen to twenty-four has tripled. And the number of suicide bombers in every religious tradition is skyrocketing. It is estimated that 90 percent of all known suicide bombings have occurred in the last ten years. "We love death the way you love life," said twenty-year-old Shezhad Tanweer, one of the seven July 2005 London suicide bombers in a video released posthumously.[47]

Six people took their own lives in the Bible:

1. Samson (Judges 16:23–31)
2. Saul (1 Sam. 31:3–4)
3. Saul's armor-bearer (1 Sam. 31:5)
4. Ahithophel, who sided with Absalom in his rebellion against David (2 Sam. 17:23)

5. Israelite king Zimri (1 Kings 16:18–19)
6. Judas Iscariot (Matt. 27:3–5)

As a reward for suicide, the Koran promises martyrs a paradise of orgiastic sex with both women and boys.[48]

The suicide rate among Vietnam vets from the war's conclusion to 1983 was only slightly less than the number of those killed in the war: 58,000.

In 2005 alone, 6,256 veterans who served in Iraq and Afghanistan committed suicide. The U.S. Army confirmed this in their Suicide Event Report. It was the highest rate in twenty-six years. Those soldiers who served in multiple deployments had the highest rates of suicide.

Among elderly women, which ethnicity is most likely to commit suicide, at least in New York? Asians! The reason, according to the Samaritans Suicide-Prevention League, is that these ladies hail from a part of the world that respects the elderly. Then they end up here, where being old is almost criminal.[49]

German-Jewish cultural thinker Walter Benjamin argued for apocalyptic violence in order to bring about the messianic age. He believed a fallen world needed some cathartic violence to initiate a paradise. But Benjamin himself committed suicide in 1940 in order to escape the Nazis. He opted out rather than fighting.

Fibonacci Numbers [Economics]

These are sequences of numbers that appear throughout nature almost as a rhythmic pattern, and that also help to explain and predict the financial markets. The Fibonacci sequence ultimately forms a golden spiral, one of the most beautiful images mathematics can produce.[50]

Florida [Social]

The US state with the prettiest name is now either the world's number one "sunny place for shady people,"[51] or "The Last Resort," the place where people go to die. Florida is "the state that floats in brackish water/held together by mangrove roots."[52]

Four Horsemen of the Apocalpyse [Social]

The four horsemen of the Apocalypse are griffinlike creatures in human form, as expressed in the visions of Ezekiel in the Hebrew Bible and the Apocalypse of John (Revelation) in the Christian Bible. In both Ezekiel and Revelation, the four resemble an ox (or bull), an eagle, a lion, and a human (sometimes represented as the angel of death). These animals have been typically and historically associated with the four elements: fire, water, air, and earth. In both the Hebrew and Christian texts, they ride colored horses and carry specific tools or weapons that define them. They are also depicted with the symbol of the chariot or Hebrew Merkabah (the wheel). German artist Albrecht Dürer created two woodcuts depicting the four horsemen. One is called *The Four Horsemen of the Apocalypse* and shows the four figures on their horses, carrying their weapons. The second, *The Adoration of the Lamb*, has the Lamb of God as the center, surrounded by the four horsemen figures. Matthäeus Merian the Elder's *The Four Horsemen of the Apocalypse* creates the vision of the Merkabah, the fire surrounding the chariots, and the horsemen as they are transported to heaven. Merian also created a piece called *The Seals*, in which the horsemen and the sun also stand prominent.

The first horseman was on a white horse carrying a bow and a crown, with which to conquer; the second horseman was on a red horse and was given a sword to take peace from the earth; the third horseman rode a black horse and carried a pair of scales. He represented famine. The fourth horseman rode a pale (sometimes depicted as a yellow, sallow, or greenish) horse and represented Death. This rider was of human form and could kill by famine, sword, plague, and wild beasts. The ox was represented by the color white or water, the eagle was represented by the color red and air. The lion was represented by the color black and earth, and the human/angel was represented by the color of pale or sallow and represented fire.

In the end all corruption will come
from the natural sciences.
—SØREN KIERKEGAARD[53]

Frankenfood [Technological]

Genetically modified foods.

Freeconomics [Economics]

A culture of free gives away the basic version, but charges for upgrades. It is also known as the gratis economy where the people who pay for premium services and apps underwrite the rest.

Gendercide [Social]

One hundred million women are missing from the world's population.

China is facing some really hard times based on its one-child policy. There are hundreds of millions of aging parents with no children to take care of them. There is a shrinking workforce. There are millions of males with no mates. China will soon have as many unmarried young men ("bare branches") as the entire population of the young men in the USA.[54] You want to talk about an aggressive culture? You want to talk about a culture where testosterone reigns and has no release?

Genetically Modified Organisms (GMOs) [Technological]

Genetically modified crops (e.g., "golden rice") could feed the poor and prevent disease at the same time (prevent blindness). But swelling fears of "Frankenfoods" releasing mutant crops with unpredictable consequences and poison food products are creating wave after wave of food scares, alienating people from agribusiness and attracting many toward bioregionalism.

An organism is only DNA's way of making more DNA.
—E. O. Wilson

Genetic Enhancements [Technological]

The encoding of what scientists call the "God gene" into human embryos with vitamin supplements that stimulate the "God zone" of the brain, while adamantly opposed by atheists, is supported by many secularists, because religious people live healthier, happier, longer lives than anyone else. They also make better parents.

Instead of "The Devil made me do it," it's now "My DNA made me do it."

As beautiful as that word brainbow (your brain on God) is, faith is more than a quirk of neurochemistry produced by the stochastic interplay of genes, epigenetics, and developmental environment.

Geoethics [Government]

A companion to geopolitics: What ethical guidelines will shape future decisions relating to global governance or government? Some want world government. Others want world governance, like Strobe Talbott, who argues, "Individual states will increasingly see it in their interest to form an international system."[55]

Gertrudes [Social]

People named after Gertrude Stein, who, when asked how she liked Oakland, California, responded, "There is no there there."[56] For a lot of Gertrudes, who are all descendants of Louis XVI, there is no one at home. "Is anyone in there? Is anyone awake to your world?" (*See* "Louis XVI.") More and more people are walking zombies, drugged into compliance and franchised into conformity by medicine and media.

In a world of Gertrudes, the highest compliment may well be: "There's a there there."

Globalization [Social]

Some things are a choice; some things are a condition. Globalization is a condition. Once the globalization genie was let out of the bottle, there was no return. We sink or swim together.

For some globalization is another word for interdependence and interconnectedness. For others, globalization is a roiling, boiling source of tension because of its association with free trade and free-flowing capital. For conspiracy theorists, globalization is a euphemism for Jewish world government. For the Taliban, as well as for many academics, globalization is another name for injustice, exploitation, international capitalism, and Westernization.[57]

Marc Leland, a former US Treasury official, put it best when he said, "Globalization is like the two institutions we know as democracy and marriage. Both institutions at times can be problematic, but the alternatives are highly unattractive."[58]

What can bring about the demise of globalization? The constriction of free-flowing capital, protectionism, isolationism, and distrust of "foreigners."

God [Social]

Except for the atheists, people now recycle rather than reject God. God is in nature, in the market, in products, in people. Indeed, virtually everything in life now is goddified.

Greying of the Globe [Social]

The globe is greying. We are fast approaching the time when, for the first time in human history, people ages sixty-five and older will outnumber children under age five (by 2030).

Tax battles are starting between those without children (the aging) and those with children in the public schools. People increasingly resist paying to educate other people's children, leading to school tax rebellions.

A greying globe requires greening.

Greener Than Thou [Environmental]

"Live green or die." Green is now the new way of life. Green is the new black. Eco-mania is everywhere.

"Climageddon" books abound. Is humanity now taking its final exam? Extreme weather patterns are a cause for worry: severe flooding in some areas, brutal droughts in others, increasing percentages of the planet's surface will no longer support agriculture.

For James Lovelock, now age eighty-six, in his book *The Revenge of Gaia*, it's already too late. "We're doomed," he states. "Only a handful of the teeming billions now alive will survive. It is much too late for sustainable development; what we need is a sustainable retreat."[59]

The old environmental movement focused on things like pollution, for example, GHGs (Green House Gases), rather than issues of sustainability, green technology, and so on. Well into the digital age, we still lived in the industrial age, as the world's industrial blast furnaces continued roaring full tilt to power the planet.

Ecuador passed the world's first constitution in September 2008 to extend inalienable rights to nature.[60]

All non-hybrid cars will be heavily taxed. Fossil fuels will still be needed, but the oil supply will peak in 2040, making gas prices their highest in history at $20 a gallon. The chickens will come home to roost after decades of burning six gallons of gas for every gallon found.

Gas-sippers are the new glass slippers for a green economy.

Griffin [Social]

A composite being comprised of at least two of the four animals highlighted in Genesis 2 and Ezekiel 10. The king of the land is the lion. The king of the air is the eagle. The king of the fields is the bull or the ox. The king of the planet is the human. Each one of these four animal "kings" became associated with one of the four Gospels:

Matthew = human
Mark = lion
Luke = bull
John = eagle

Often in Hebrew and Christian art, the cherubim and seraphim are portrayed as griffins in various combinations of animals. These hybrid creatures, or "bi-formed animals" (as Dante called them), also were used to symbolize the beauty, goodness, and truth of Christ. Medieval Christians brought the eagle and the lion together as a reminder of the dual natures of Jesus—its aquiline-leonine body the symbol also of two of the four elements, earth and air, and hence of the two kingdoms of Christ, heaven and earth.

From the twelfth to the sixteenth centuries, the possession of griffins' eggs, ornamented and carved, was highly prized and associated with magical powers. In estate inventories of nobility these cups were called "grypeseye." Griffins were also guardians of hidden treasures, especially emeralds, which were associated with the Last Supper, because by some accounts the Holy Grail was an enormous carved emerald.

To make things even more interesting, depending on how certain features of the griffin were pictured, the griffin could also be a symbol of Satan.

GRIN [Technological]

An acronym that stands for *genetics, robotics, information technology, and nanotechnology,* GRIN is a reflection of the dramatic shift from a mechanical to a biological paradigm. A few frown at every GRIN. Most people, however, fall into two camps. There are some who want some moral drag on a runaway train. There are others who want to speed that train on (nanotechnology leadership is now full-speed-ahead in places like Japan, Hong Kong, Singapore, China, Taiwan, and Israel).

Erwin Chargaff, DNA researcher, warned colleagues before his death at age ninety-two (2002) that they should stop "sticking their clumsy fingers into the incredibly fine web of human fate." He added: "Scientific curiosity is not an unbounded good. Restraint in asking necessary questions is one of the sacrifices that even the scientist ought to be willing to make to human dignity."[61]

The more science and technology move us forward, they also move us backward in their potential for evil. A move forward in GRIN is amoral. It may or may not be a moral advance for the human species, as any look at the history of twentieth-century genocide and environmental degradation makes clear.[62]

Scientists want to own the rights to the successes of what happens with all their playing and GRINning around, but they don't want to own the problems that might be tossed forth by their experimentation.

Some humans seem less bent on worshipping our Creator than on remaking gods of our own creation.

---

11 September was essentially a collision of early 20th century technology: the aeroplane and the skyscraper. We don't want to see a collision of 21st century technology.
—BILL JOY, SUN SYSTEMS COFOUNDER

Gulf Stream [Environmental]

"There is a river in the ocean," said nineteenth-century oceanographer Matthew Maury,[63] and that river is now being cited as the Achilles' heel of the global climate system. The Gulf Stream and associated thermohaline circulation in the North Atlantic, which flows from North America to northern Europe, is decreasing in density and reducing or potentially even shutting off this thermohaline circulation. Paradoxically, the result of this could plunge northern Europe into a mini ice age.[64]

The oil-sodden waters of the Gulf Coast and the troubled Gulf Stream turbulence make their impact on the future no less important than it has been in the past.

Here Comes Everybody [Social]

James Joyce's prophecy "Here Comes Everybody"[65] is now being lived out in spades. Back in the twentieth century, filmmaker Francis Ford Coppola predicted a day when anyone could make films because technology would lower the barrier of entry to practically nothing. That day is here, not just in film but in music, art, everything. No clean line between the "pro" and the person in the street. Both making and enjoying music have now returned to every Tom, Denice, and Harriet. Ditto authors and artists and architects (and that's only the start of the a's).

You need a lot of spades to bury truth.
—SERBIAN POET VASKO POPA[66]

Herschelites [Social]

Followers of William Herschel, the musician who doubled the size of the solar system with a single discovery in 1781,[67] these are scientists who see themselves first as artists: as poets, musicians, painters, and sculptors, and for whom formulas are more like musical notes and palettes than anything else.

High Finance [Economics]

Shorthand now for financial fraud. Corporate capitalism is routinely lambasted for its focus on short-term profits, unfettered faith in free markets, and compensation packages that ignore cross-the-lines ethics, for example, the line workers and the bottom lines of business.

House of Cards Effect [Political]

Civilizations often fall quite suddenly. It's called the House of Cards effect. When things go, they go quickly. For example, after three days and three nights in August 1991, there was no Communist Party anymore, no Soviet Union, no Warsaw Pact, only a bloodless revolution against one of the bloodiest political systems in history.

Overnight, the financial industry fell back to zero.

Overnight, the independent investment banking business model on Wall Street ended.

Overnight, the largest thrifts and mortgage lenders of the country collapsed.

Overnight the securitization industry disappeared.

What emerges from overnight? Two extremes: a few large, diversified, global firms; thousands of small, local community banks.

Overnight, the world is different. Here are some examples of overnights:

- 16 June: South African uprising began in Soweto on that day in 1976, making the black township south of Johannesburg famous throughout the world for popular resistance to apartheid.
- 9 November (Germany) 1989: fall of Berlin Wall.
- 9/11, 3/11, 7/7: terrorist attacks in New York, Madrid, London.

The overnight implications of the House of Cards effect are still to come on many more personal levels. Medical experts worry that nature may swat us overnight with disease. Billions of "overcrowded primates," many sick, malnourished, with weak immunity systems and connected by air travel, are a free lunch waiting for an enterprising microbe. "Mother nature always comes to the rescue of a society stricken with overpopulation," Alfred Crosby sardonically observed, "and her ministrations are never gentle."[68]

Hyderabad [Political]

The city with the largest concentration of scientific talent in the world reflects the transition from West to East in terms of eds and meds. Hyderabad is in India, the new global center of medical tourism.

Hydroponics [Environmental]

Hydroponic growing is becoming the norm, as the future of food as we know it is in jeopardy from water shortages, diseases in the animals we eat, crop failure, climate change, commodity price increase, food contamination, soaring energy costs, armed conflict, disrupted delivery systems, and the disruption of our food supply.

In the twentieth century, rather than becoming widely distributed, the food supply became increasingly centralized among a few corporations, making it weak and vulnerable and creating a backlash to bolster local food sources.

Food is now a security issue, and food security is no longer left to the markets. Food ethics has become a burgeoning academic discipline, as a three-pillar system of food production based on cheap oil, abundant water, and chemical fertilizer is crumbling.

We depend just as much on our gas-guzzling, chilled, plug-in, "just-in-time" food deliveries, as ancient Romans did on foreign conquests, shipping and slaves—and our food system is no more secure, ethical or sustainable than Rome's was.
— CAROLYN STREET[69]

Hyper [Social]

Everything is hyper—hypercentralization, hypercompetition, hyperconnectivity, hypersensitivity, hyperactivity, hyperliteracy— with microbursts of activity in every arena of existence generating its own whiplash and giving birth to the name Age of Turbulence.

Three of the most significant "hypers":

1. Hyperinflation: The only buyer left for US debt is the Federal Reserve. Every Ponzi scheme must come to an end. The Greece Ponzi scheme ended in 2010. The rest of the Ponzi PIGS (Portugal, Ireland, Greece, Spain) ended in 2010. The US Ponzi scheme ended not long after.

2. Hyperthymia: More and more people are always "up," as if they were on uppers, but the joy is natural due to an abundance of serontonin and dopamine available as food supplements.

3. Hyperconnectivity: As you read this, three-quarters of the earth's population is connected through cells and the Cloud, and soon a digital skin will cover the entire globe.

*Hyperconnectivity begets hypermimesis begets
hyperempowerment. After the arms race comes the war.*
—AUSTRALIAN FUTURIST MARK PESCE[70]

iMuslim [Social]

A phrase invented by Gary R. Bunt, who argues that the Web, now known as The Cloud, is the natural home for Muslims because they have no central authority.[71] Fatwa portals and Web site portals have become the new mosques, with the entire corpus of Islamic knowledge now online. In fact, it is now possible to convert to Islam online, so long as one keeps to the rules of the electronic form of the shahada, or prayer of conversion. Ironically, al Qaeda and other jihadists evangelize using technology that was pioneered by the US military.

Muslims account for 23 percent of the world's population of 6.8 billion people, but 60 percent of that number live not in the Islamic heartlands of the Middle East and North Africa, but in Asia. Sixty-two percent of the world's Muslims live in the Asia-Pacific region. Israel's one million Muslims make up 17 percent of the country's people: 4 million Muslims, in Palestinian territories.

Indabas [Social]

Zulu-style "indabas," or listening groups of forty or less people, seem to be the proposed solutions to everything, often replacing voting. For example, in Rwanda they are called *"Inkiko Gacaca"* (gacaca [pronounced ga-chacah] courts), or public truth-telling, where every week, in villages all over the country, Rwandans have gathered to heal from the genocide that began on 8 April 1994, when almost a million Tutsis were slaughtered by Hutus. All over Rwanda there are billboards that read INKIKO GACACA: ukuri kurakiza (gacaca courts; truth heals).

Intersexuals [Social]

Intersexual is the more recent description of those who used to be called androgynes, hemaphrodites, or in the Bible, eunuchs (Matt. 19:12). This not insignificant percentage of the human population (from 350 to 700 million people in a population of 7 billion) is increasingly claiming legal rights to be known as a "third gender" and suing physicians who perform gratuitous surgery on them as infants to force a male or female gender choice on them.

Invisibility [Social]

The art of "invisibility" is the new pursuit . . . and not just invisible to negative criticism but to positive celebration as well. In a world where everyone is famous for fifteen minutes, and where everyone visible is naked to the world, and where people are fighting Facebook fatigue, the most prized possession is the scarcest: invisibility or anonymity. Even the *Oxford Dictionary of National Biography* (*DNB*), in its newest incarnation, includes the delicious new category of "wealth at death," whenever possible letting you know the amounts left behind in the estates of the deceased.

Light refracts off objects and illuminates them (because the object is denser than the light), so if light doesn't bounce but instead goes through, objects, things, and people become invisible. It's the principle behind a window. The glass is not what is seen, but what is beyond the glass. It's also the cloaking theories being explored in quantum physics. The key is to bend the light or absorb it, not to refract or reflect it.

If you're confused by this, don't worry; so is everyone else, and so am I.

Irony [Social]

As soon as you can say something has "gone the way of the hula hoop," there is the hula hoop, making a comeback.

In the midst of chaos and psychosis, the gaps in reality—between what you expect and what actually happens—start making themselves seen and heard. For example, the great irony of Iraq was this: a war against Islamic terrorism took on the one Arab country that was the most secular and the greatest barrier to the spread of Islamism. Unfortunately, as the Polish poet Adam Zagejewski points out, irony as a strategy for survival is seeing without penetrating, without struggling with the gaps in reality.

Irony can turn into tragedy, and Reinhold Niebuhr addressed that possibility in the last sentence of his classic 1952 book:

> If we should perish, the ruthlessness of the foe would be only the secondary cause of the disaster. The primary cause would be that the strength of a giant nation was directed by eyes too blind to see all the hazards of the struggle; and the blindness would be induced not by some accident of nature or history but by hatred and vainglory.[72]

Jugaad [Economics]

No longer a management fad from India (Hindi slang word pronounced joo-gaardh), this improvisational style of innovation reigns supreme everywhere you look—business, church, even academe. Jugaad presupposes scarce resources and existential needs, not lifestyle wants. Where people used to say KISS (Keep it simple, stupid), they now say JUGAAD. Seventy-five percent solutions trump 99 percent exquisite systems. Inexpensive invention on the fly is now the norm, though there is a downside that is delicate to discuss: Jugaad can be an excuse for shoddy construction and cutting corners.

Kaitag [Economics]

These embroideries on Soumakh carpets are now big business. There are three ritual uses for the Kaitag embroideries: protect a newborn child from the evil eye; wrap up the dowry of a bride on her way to the new marital home; and cover the faces of the dead before burial.

In a time of universal deceit,
telling the truth is a revolutionary act.
—George Orwell

Karaoke Culture [Social]

You go to a show, not so much to watch the show as to be the show. Everything now is interactive—user-generated, copyleft, free content, open source, and wiki.

A backlash of elitism despises the mediocrity, unreliability, and erosion of authority that are endemic to a karaoke culture, which makes everyone an expert, every amateur a professional. A karaoke culture is a world without gatekeepers—for example, how do you assess the worthiness of the 175,000 new blogs that appear every day?

Kidnappings (bosnappings) [Economics]

In Latin American countries, enterprising professionals have created a niche business: delivering ransom to kidnappers in exchange for hostages. There are so many kidnappings in Mexico, Brazil, Colombia, Haiti, the Philippines, India, Russia, Nigeria, and South Africa, that these small-business ransom couriers are thriving alongside homegrown terrorism, which is now a big business.

Hatred is a very light sleeper.

Large Hadron Collidor (LHC) [Technological]

The LHC went online 10 September 2008. Protons took their first lap around its 27 kilometers crisscrossing the French-Swiss border more than ten thousand times. Fifteen years earlier, the United States abandoned the larger SSC (Superconducting SuperCollider) outside Dallas in Waxahachie for financial and political reasons.

Libertarianism [Political]

Town officials across the United States are refusing to spend money on doughnuts and pastries for senior citizens' morning coffee clubs because it's a health issue. "Let them eat carrot sticks and grapes."

Seniors respond with pickets: "We want doughnuts."

Libertarians differ from liberals and conservatives in the following ways:

- Liberals want moral freedom, but market regulations.
- Conservatives want market freedom, but moral regulations.
- Libertarians don't like any form of regulation except for external benefits (e.g., protection from mad cow disease, environmental protection, police and fire protection, etc.).
- Libertarians are anti-NWO (New World Order). They don't believe in world government, saying, "We have enough trouble with government already." They are committed to the spread of open societies and free markets.

Reagan has become not only a Republican hero but a Libertarian saint. He is famous for saying, "Government's view of the economy could be summed up in a few short phrases: If it moves, tax it; if it keeps moving, regulate it; and if it stops moving, subsidize it."[73]

Liszt [Social]

Hungarian composer Franz Liszt was the most accomplished pianist of the nineteenth century, and a composer who equated harmony with spirituality, culminating in his taking minor orders in the Roman Catholic Church. "The mind's tides are not like those of the sea; they have not been ordered: 'Thus far shalt thou go, and no further'; on the contrary, 'the spirit bloweth where it listeth,' and this century's art has its word to contribute, just as much as had that of earlier centuries—and it will do it inevitably."[74]

Louis XVI Prize [Social]

The Louis XVI Prize is given out to the person most out of touch, most unable to connect the dots, most *not* paying attention. This is in ironic honor to French king Louis XVI's diary entry on 14 July 1789, the day the Bastille was stormed: *"Rien,"* or in English, "Nothing." He was clueless as to what was going on around him.

This book is dedicated to Louis XVI and his hoards of descendants.

As a child, an astrologer warned him to be on guard, especially on the twenty-first day of each month. Usually the twenty-first so struck terror in him that he refused to do any business that day, and he took it as a Sabbath. But, once again, in keeping with his cluelessness, on 21 June 1791, he and the queen were arrested in Varennes while trying to escape France. On 21 September 1791, France abolished the institution of royalty and proclaimed itself a republic. Then on 21 January 1793, he was beheaded by guillotine.

Machiavelli [Social]

The "end-justifies-means" Machiavelli actually put the phrase a little differently than what we're used to: "When the act accuses, the result excuses."[75] Political theorist Niccolo Machiavelli is supposed to have dreamed that he had to choose between going to paradise with holy people, like monks, hermits, and the ragged poor, or going to hell with people like popes, kings, princes, and philosophers. He chose hell.

Magnetic Reversals [Environmental]

Also called *geomagnetic reversals,* for reasons no one knows, planet Earth's magnetic field irregularly flips its polarity every ten thousand years or so. The magnetic history of earth reveals in fossil form, and rock records the story of the South and North poles swapping places. A reduced magnetic field on earth exposes the planet to increased and disruptive solar cosmic radiation (solar wind).

But geomagnetic storms, which are tied to peaks in the sun spot cycle, could produce a global catastrophe like the solar superstorm of 1859, also known as the Carrington Event. The National Academy of Sciences says that the recovery time from another such Carrington Event would be four to ten years because of its effect on power grids, along with a domino effect on everything that draws energy from the grids.[76]

Mahatma [Social]

Mahatmas are everywhere. The word is borrowed from the Hindus, who called someone who became "large-souled" Mahatma, as in Mahatma Gandhi. The highest level of sainthood reached in this new global generic spirituality is "Mahatma." Spirituality is now mostly divorced from any specific religious context and has become a smorgasbord of spiritual traditions that you dip into according to your tastes, preferences, and lifestyle.

Marketolatry [Social]

In a theomarket religion, the market is god. We refer to the market as though it were a living being. The market is nervous or happy or skeptical. In Old Testament times, the Israelites feared Yahweh's reaction to their actions. Today, it is the market's reaction that is feared and is the ultimate arbiter of whether something is good or bad. Like all deities, the market is all-powerful and deserving of worship.[77]

A few "heretics" remain who refuse to worship the market and decry the market as a false god, making the distinction between the market god's "Good Life" vs. the Maker God's "Abundant Life." But even many churches have come around to marketolatry.

Marquez, Gabriel Garcia [Social]

Gabriel Garcia Marquez, or "Gabo" as he is affectionately called, is celebrated as the new Cervantes by virtually everyone. He is Latin America's first truly global writer, with many now following in his wake. Like Fidel Castro, his close personal friend, and like Hugo Chavez, who calls Jesus "the greatest socialist," Gabo symbolizes the new leftward drift and resurgence of socialism in Venezuela, Bolivia, Ecuador, and Paraguay (its president a former bishop and key supporter of liberation theology). The rise of socialism is running in parallel with the growth of evangelical churches in Latin America. The symbol of this is the $20 million temple built in Guatemala by the Protestant Church Fraternidad Cristiana. It is the largest building in Central America, with a Burger King drive-in and parking for more than thirty-five hundred cars. There are a million Bible study groups in Brazil alone.

Masters of Business Apocalypse (MBA) [Economics]

MBA now stands for Masters of Business Apocalpyse, with attacks from all sides for teaching methods and models that are causing apocalypytic scenarios of all sizes and sides. One business periodical asked this question at the one-hundredth anniversary of Harvard Business School: "Business schools are largely responsible for the US financial crisis. Pro or con?"[78]

McMansions [Social]

Also known as Hummer Houses, these houses-on-steroids are emptying and becoming a new form of the Victorian boardinghouse as part of the migration from suburban to urban living. Car ownership is expensive. People are hungering for more of the pedestrian life, found in urban and small-town living.

If our houses are the mirrors of our soul, then a lot of souls are big, sterile, marbleized, gold-plated, treeless, artless boxes.

Medical Tourism [Social]

Medical tourism has snuck up on everyone without being noticed.[79] Popular medical destinations include India, Thailand, Malaysia, Brazil, Costa Rica, Argentina, and South Africa. Johns Hopkins University's affiliation with a major Singapore hospital was the first wave of outsourced medical treatments.

The Mayo Clinic of the future is in Shanghai today. In Shanghai, you can get a physical in one hour, which includes full blood work, EKG, chest X-ray, eye and hearing tests, blood pressure reading, ultrasound, and an interview with a physician, followed three days later by a computerized report in Chinese and English. Escorts Heart Institute and Research Center in India reports a death rate of patients during surgery that is less than half that of most major hospitals in the United States.

A bone marrow transplant that would cost $200,000 in the United States costs only $30,000 in India. Increased medical tourism is proving to be a boon for third-world medicine, not to mention third-world economies, which are now pouring money into funding upgrades to hospital facilities and medical research. It is not forcing lower costs in the home countries, as some predicted.

Megacity [Social]

A city of more than ten million people. New York City was the first to reach this figure in 1940. By 2010, there were twenty megacities—including three in India, and two in China. By 2025, China will have 235 cities with more than one million people.

Mein Kampf [Political]

Mein Kampf, a perennial best seller in Arab lands since it was translated into Arabic in the 1990s, now ranks number one or number two on many best-seller lists among Palestinian Arabs and Iranians. The Arabic kiss-both-cheeks greeting is increasingly followed by the Nazi salute.

Merian, Matthäus [Social]

Seventeenth-century engraver whose picture of *Ezekiel's Vision,* with the shimmering Four Evangelists and the Mystic Wheel, is an apocalyptic masterpiece.[80]

Methane Hydrates [Environmental]

Vast deposits of volatile blends of natural gas and water lie trapped on continental shelves. As the globe warms, the potential release of these deposits, now stabilized by low temperatures and high pressure, could result in a catastrophic toxic belch. Some scientists argue that this is what happened eons ago to destroy most of the life on planet Earth. This scenario is at the heart of Liz Jensen's novel *The Rapture* (2009).[81]

Microbivore [Technological]

Medical nanorobots the size of a bacterium are now replacing drugs as the preferred therapy. They have no side effects, work with digital precision, and send warning flares from constant medical monitoring.[82] Nanomedicine, or the application of nanotechnology to medicine and the creation of healing molecular machines, is becoming a cottage industry.

Micro-Farming [Environmental]

The "do-little-large" phenomenon is taking hold and leading to all sorts of new hungers for long-term loving connections with the local and the creation of sustainable communities. From-the-source, clean foods and artisan food movements are generating farms dedicated to serving a one-hundred-mile radius.[83]

Rooftop farming, green roofs, and sky gardens are turning up in surprising places. According to the Census of Agriculture, the most productive farmland in the United States is in the borough of the Bronx! The second most productive farmland is in the city of San Francisco! You can earn up to eight times the average personal income on as little as one acre of land.[84]

Micronation [Political]

Self-proclaimed independent states that renounce citizenship in the country where they find themselves in favor of self-government, self-determination, and self-protection. The ultimate in the devolution revolution and tribalism, these micronations, which once existed only on the Internet or in the imagination, are now actual legal entities in so many places that Wikipedia is listing them. Nowhere do micronations yet have official recognition by international bodies. But families, clans, and eco-villages are popping up all over the globe, claiming sovereignty over some physical territory and declaring themselves a micronation (often named after the founding family or founding figurehead).

Middle-Class Millionaires [Economic]

Lewis Schiff defines this group (which on a bell-curve would fit into the "middle" but in a well-curve would become part of one end), as people who have earned (i.e., didn't inherit) a net worth of $1–10 million.[85]

MK BRIC [Political]

The MK BRIC countries include Mexico, Korea (South), Brazil, Russia, India, and China (also known as "magic bricks"). As the West heads toward stagflation, terrorism, and civil conflict, these nations are moving into positions of power and influence. Could one key to the current MK BRIC's boom and bloom be the doom and gloom that pervade elsewhere? These countries boast impressive strides in mathematics, engineering, and science education in their school systems. The West's persistence in deploying an industrial, factory-model of learning helps to explain the growing poverty, increased illegal drug use, rising unemployment, and mushrooming gang crime. Magic brick-building relationships are essential to the economic welfare of Western nations.

Moore's Law [Technological]

In April 1965, Gordon Moore, cofounder of a company called Intel, was asked to write about the future. So he threw together some prophecies, in which he predicted home computers, electronic watches, and a doubling of microprocessing power every eighteen months (this was added later, as was the codicil that microprocessors would halve in price). In other words, Moore's Law posits an exponential curve of improvement, which has proved true, not just for computer-processing power, but in some ways even more so for bandwidth and storage (as streaming video on cell phones reveals).

Nanowire transistors will replace silicon-based semiconductors, extending Moore's Law well into the future. There is an end point to Moore's Law, however, because no transistor, not even a nanowire one, can be smaller than an atom.

M-Theory [Technological]

Often called the *membrane theory*. The omnipresent attribute of God is mathematically demonstrated in M-theory by physicists. Omnipresence is now a quantifiable scientific fact, although not necessarily attributed to God by the scientists. M-theory (so named by Edward Whitten) is the successor to string theory and heavy gravity theory.[86] One of the things M-theory states is that there is a group of thin membranes that connect all matter in the universe. They exist in the eleventh dimension, the unifying dimension of the first ten dimensions. Thus some of the more mysterious attributes of theology are becoming measurable and quantifiable.

The eleventh dimension is jammed with membranes (branes) of varying dimensions (P branes). Each renders a possible other universe. Parallel universes may be different or close to ours. Some could look just like ours. The M-theory offers the prospect of an infinite number of universes. By an exchange of gravity waves, scientists believe we could communicate between worlds. Physicists also believe that these branes may yield holes or passages between them, which could allow for entry into other dimensions. We live in a membrane in this current dimension, and if we were to find the right passage, another dimension or brane may exist in which we could find ourselves alone in a similar but new environment.

Murphy's Law [Social]

The more Moore's Law applies, the more Murphy's Law kicks in. In Moore's Law, it keeps getting better and better. In Murphy's Law, anything bad that can happen will happen.

Behind Murphy's Law lies the Law of Unintended Consequences.

For example, LEDs or compact fluorescent lights last ten times longer and use 75 percent less energy than regular bulbs. But these intestine lights contain small amounts of mercury, so should not simply be thrown out with the garbage, but treated as radioactive waste. In fact, in some states it is illegal to throw them away.

Here's another example: Professional social workers want to help those who need it the most. Who's that? Single mothers raising children by themselves. How to help? Arrange for single mothers to jump to the front of the line for neighborhood housing, which in turn gives an incentive for single mothers to stay single and to become mothers, privileging one-parent families.

Here's progress for you:

- In 1907, horse-drawn vehicles in NYC moved at an average of 11.5 miles an hour.
- In 2007, automobiles in NYC crawled along at the average daytime speed of 10 miles an hour.

When you take into account the time required for check-in and security clearance, an airline flight from Philadelphia to Los Angeles now takes nearly an hour longer than it did forty years ago.

Myanmar (formerly Burma) [Political]

Myanmar is a devoutly Buddhist country. That doesn't stop it from enslaving more than eight hundred thousand or so of its people, or of being the biggest producer of opium after Afghanistan. For the Buddha, the first truth was this: all life is suffering.

Mycoplasma mycoides [Technological]

A modified version of this bacterial genome became the world's first synthetic cell, created by the Minimal Genome Project at the J. Craig Venter Institute in Maryland in 2010.[87] As significant to ethics as splitting the atom or cloning Dolly the sheep, this creation of a self-replicating bacteria opens the door to genetically manufactured diseases.

Natural Capitalism [Economic]

After 9/11, some attempt was made to shift from consumer capitalism to natural capitalism, in which the environment is recognized as a valuable asset that produces $33 trillion in economic benefits annually.[88] Pope Benedict XVI likes to take a different tack and distinguish between a market economy and a capitalist economy.[89] The latter is one form of the former, but there are other models of market economies, including the civil market economy.

Neuromarketing [Economic]

The use of brain science and tools that monitor the brain (electroencephalography, biometrics, magnetic resonance imaging) to test-market products has replaced focus groups. Everything is brain-tested, which has birthed a backlash of regulations called *neuropolicy* to oversee costs, privacy, and interpretation.

New Selfers [Social]

The New Selfer creed, in which the sacred becomes an appendate of the individual and where everybody is out for what is best for oneself, comes with a shiny veneer of care and concern. Sometimes that shine is expressed in terms of the global environment and global government. Other times the care and concern are expressed in terms of a new nationalism.

The global New Selfers come spiritually well-endowed. All clamor for One World government and One World ecology. But that clamor takes many forms. Old *Star Wars* films became the sacred texts for some New Selfers, who, like Van Gogh, when they had a need for religion, went outside to paint the stars. The same with Harry Potter films and *Avatar*, which inspired a whole new style of religiosity in home architecture and accents. Reality entertainment has become more than a social phenomenon, as have sports teams, with arenas the new cathedrals and cities the new denominations. For many New Selfers, food is a religion; chefs, high priests; kitchens, temples; and the quality of life measured out in what's worn and eaten, when and where.

Norms [Social]

Norms is our name for people who shun unnecessary technological or chemical enhancements, as compared to ESIs—enhanced singular individuals—people who have fused carbon and silicon, flesh-and-blood with technology.

Noughties [Social]

Also known as the naughty noughties, the decade from 2001 to 2009, in which economic meltdown, subprime debacle, terrorism (9/11), climate change, wars, the collapse of Wall Street, and the collapse of the US auto industry prevailed. Some call it the "wasted decade" of the twenty-first century. Some call it the "good ole days," when only 155,000 people died on the planet every day (from hunger, disease, war, accidents, old age, etc.). Others call it the "Decade Debacle." Who would ever think that the notion of history as "progress" would suddenly seem old-fashioned?

Non-Malicious Criminals (NMC) [Political]

A new category deems people to be non-malicious criminals if they have committed crimes against humanity, but the crimes they've committed were not considered crimes in their own ethically inferior cultures.

Obesity [Social]

USAmerica is home to 23 percent of the planet's excessively overweight individuals. According to WHO figures and definitions, obesity is now the condition of more than 60 percent of Americans. Over the course of their lifetimes, 9 out of 10 men will become overweight, along with 7 out of 10 women.[90]

OncoMouse® [Technological]

The OncoMouse® is a Harvard-engineered animal with a human gene inserted and a registered trademark for a name.[91]

Pandemics [Environmental]

Along with bioterrorism, global connectivity, and climate change, pandemics are currently a global concern. Today's pandemics are not the first planet Earth has faced. In the years 1348 and 1349, the Black

Death killed more than 50 percent of the inhabitants of Europe.[92] Influenza pandemics occur regularly, every ten to fifty years. If a virus similar to the 1918–20 influenza pandemic appeared, there would be 60 million deaths worldwide. The avian H5N1 influenza has a high fatality rate (around 60 percent) and is spreading globally into areas where dangerous genetic recombinations are likely.

The only predictable thing about pandemics is their unpredictability. In the words of the *Economist*, "The generals of global health assumed that the enemy would be avian flu, probably passed from hens to humans, and that it would strike first in southern China or Southeast Asia. In fact, the flu started in an unknown pig, and the attack came in Mexico, not Asia."[93]

Parkour (PK) [Social]

Parkour, or "the art of movement," is becoming the number one individual sport, with a new book out on Sebastien Foucan, one of the inventors of free running,[94] almost every month. Parkour is also a survival mechanism in many places around the world.

The Pearl [Technological]

The Pearl is our name for the biometric portal into the Cloud. It is activated by your voice, chemical changes in your body, or in the future, BMI (Body-Mind-Interfaces). We are close to The Pearl in the Ford SYNC system, a revolutionary new technology for 2010 cars developed in partnership with Microsoft. The Pearl (or something similar) will soon replace PCs, PDAs, smart phones, and navigation systems, all of which are engulfed in the Cloud. The Pearl will be worn as a piece of jewelry. Some prefer earrings; others prefer bracelets around the wrist or ankle. A few have Pearl bio-chip implants, but Christians in particular refuse any human chipping for fear of bearing the Mark of the Beast.

Pedestrian [Social]

Pedestrian is the new buzzword. Pedestrian churches are replacing parking lot churches, bringing back pastors and priests in contrast with leaders and CEOs that dominated parking lot churches—those being roundly criticized for their reflection of the soul-numbing blandness of suburbanized America with its generic franchises and placeless malls.

A reflection of the quest for pedestrian living is the fact that the number of housing permits being issued in major US cities is growing by leaps and bounds. The urban core share of all housing permits in Chicago rose from 23 percent in 2002 to 46 percent in 2005. New York, Philadelphia, Los Angeles, and Washington, D.C., report similar trends.[95]

The better your city's public transportation system, the brighter its future.

Polarization Entrepreneurs (PoENTS) [Political]

Terrorism is so common that there is now a politically correct phrase for a terrorist: polarization entrepreneurs. First suggested by Cass R. Sunstein, it is they rather than mainstream politicians who have had the vision to exploit the spaces left by continually subdividing digital populations.[96] Debates remain over how many polarization entrepreneurs are also Samsonites. Every major cosmopolitan city now has its cadre of PoENTS. The proximity of sublimity and terror continues.

The death camp Buchenwald was designed to be near Weimar, the city romanticized as the pinnacle of German culture. Goethe, Schiller, Wagner, Liszt, and Bach all lived there.

Pole Dancing [Social]

On college campuses in Europe, pole dancing is replacing yoga, with courses on the art of stripping becoming as popular as yoga used to be (e.g., Swindon University in England has partnered with strip nightclubs). Who would ever have imagined that strippers could be on our next faculty?

Yoga is now little more than an exercise choice for anyone who would rather not break a sweat.

Prepone [Social]

Preponing is a new survival skill: arranging for an event to take place earlier than planned. The opposite of postpone, the term is often used with *prepotent*, the opposite of *impotent*.

Prison [Political]

The United States has more people incarcerated than any nation on earth (2.1 million), a figure that has quadrupled since 1980. In the words of Judge Richard Posner, the US "criminalizes more conduct than most, maybe than any, non-Islamic nation."[97] More than 50 percent of those in prison are African Americans. One out of three African American males are in prison. Prisons can no longer be called correctional institutions. Since 95 percent of all inmates return to society without learning any new skills while in prison, and continue to be angry and bitter once out of prison, the rest of society pays the price.

Project 365 [Technological]

Project 365, which started out as an attempt to document life by taking a picture per day and posting it online, has now become a 24/7/365 vlog or what we are calling "life logging" that is posted on Facebook, so that your entire life, or as much of it as you want documented, is now available online for public or private screening. The automatic indexing and editing of life experiences is primitive but is producing immense wealth for those pioneering this technology. There is no unedited story.

Quantum Entanglement [Technological]

The linking together of two quantum properties, such as electrons, so that if you observe the properties of one, the other simultaneously syncs into the same quantum state regardless of distance or time.[98] Einstein called this "spooky action at a distance,"[99] making possible instantaneous travel similar to the *Star Trek* transporter.

Rationality [Social]

Throwing away old copies of *Economist* magazine, of which I'm a back-door reader, I opened one to find the obituary of Robert

McNamara, who is quoted as reflecting on his role in the Cuban missile crisis of 1962. Present on a cabinet level and having seen it all, here are McNamara's reflections: "Kennedy was rational. Kruschev was rational. Castro was rational." Yet their rationality pushed the world to the brink of Armageddon. "Rationality," he concluded, "will not save us."[100] The lethal folly of our rational ways is well documented in the twentieth century's monstrous rational conurbations.

Reality Mining [Technological]

This is a new term for data mining, reflecting new holographic technologies, in which the boundaries of what is "real" are severely blurred.

Renaissance America Aborning [Political]

Some say Empire America is dying. What if Renaissance America is being born? Renaissance means rebirth, revival, or what one might call future-fitting the old into the new.

So what's being reborn? What's being future-fitted? "America the Beautiful," the old model "when the US led the world in quality of life, education, health, income, upward mobility . . . and was the most egalitarian and most envied nation in the world."

That number-one USAmerica was a time when the following rang true:

1. Main Street, not Wall Street, was the role model.
2. Blue-collar workers wore blue collars and worked in jobs that gave them middle-class incomes.
3. Moms and pops worked at their own shops, not as minimum-wage chain-store clerks.
4. Family farms, not factory farms, fed USAmerica.
5. Americans ate real food, not Frankenfood. (See "Frankenfood.")
6. Quality counted, not just the bottom line.
7. A tightly knit community/neighborhood spirit prevailed, not vanilla suburban anonymity.[101]

Retro [Social]

Retro is more than cool: it's a convention. Old school is back with a vengeance. People are dressing up: formal is now "in." All that boomer talk about the formaldehyde of formal has been silenced. When tank tops and flip-flops started showing up at work, the corporate climate boomeranged back to formal and against sloppy and floppy.

The retro trend is partly fueled by technology. Camera phones are making us dress up more, be more "presentable," since we never know when our picture will be snapped and plastered all over YouTube. French cuffs and cuff links (the New York City store named Tender Buttons is becoming a pilgrimage site) will in the future appear on nanotechnology never-iron shirts.

A majority of people see the 1950s, 1960s, and 1970s as "happy days" and "better times" than they're living in.[102] People now want the "tried-and-true," leading to a huge nostalgia boom. But twenty-first-century retro is more than "romancing the past"; it's a celebration of the halcyon days when the "American dream" was magic and magnetic, not sick and sagging. Hence the desire to bring back the old-world elegance and fine design (in food, fashion, art, construction, entertainment). "Make it better" rather than Walmart's "make it cheaper."

People are also tired of screaming voices on TV that spew venom and vituperation wedded to political correctness and talking points. Among some there is a return to graces and maturity, away from rancor and toward respect and listening to one another.

Reverts [Social]

Reverts are what Islam calls *converts*. Islam professes to be the religion of nature (*din al-fitr*). The Qur'an argues that Adam and Eve were Muslim. That's why there are no "conversions" in Islam, only reversions to the original condition. New Muslims are called *reverts*.

Islam argues that every human being is born Muslim; we just don't know it yet.

Rogem Hiri (Gilgal Refaim) [Social]

Located ten miles east of the Sea of Galilee in the Golan Heights (formerly Bashan), Rogem Hiri is known as *Gilgal Refaim* in Hebrew and means "the wheel of spirit." The ancient formation was used as a worship center, ancient calendar, and an astronomical and religious guide for the early Hebrew people. The site dates from approximately 3000 BC. The basalt rocks form a wheel-like structure with four concentric circles and a rounded raised center.

Rumi [Social]

This thirteenth-century Sufi mystic—perhaps most known for his lines "out beyond ideas of wrong doing and/right doing/There's a field, I'll meet you there"[103]—continues his fifty-year trend as the best-selling poet in translation in the United States, in spite of a spate of powerful English-speaking poets, including Wendell Berry, Derek Walcott, W. S. Merwin, Lucy Shaw, Bob Dylan, and Nathalie Handal.

Samsonites [Social]

Suicide bombers are increasingly known as Samsonites, named after the first suicide, that of Samson (Judges 16:23–31), who killed himself and three thousand others by destroying a building. A Samsonite begins each day with a greeting: "This is a good day to die."

Scarcity [Environmental]

Scarcity abounds. In a world of nine billion people (1948 data), everywhere you look there is scarcity: scarcity of water, credit, energy, minerals, and food, leading some already to call the decades from 2008 to 2048 the Age of Scarcity, just as 1975–2008 was known as the Age of Abundance.

It appears for Western nations that the price of a tank of gas and a tanking economy go together.

Secularization Theory [Social]

The biggest academic hoax perpetrated in the twentieth century? The notion that what distinguishes today from yesterday is that modern became "a secular age" is not true. Religion didn't decline, but it is now diffused and suffused throughout culture, attached to anything and everything.

People like David Lynch (filmmaker) and Carter Phipps (executive director of WIE) call themselves "spiritual practitioners" even though they aren't religious.

Peter Berger, the preeminent US sociologist and proponent of secularization theory, now has repented with a big *oops!* "We don't live in an age of secularity," he admits. "We live in an age of explosive, pervasive religiosity."[104]

One of the biggest questions of the future is whether by 2050 there will be billions or millions of Christians in the world. In 1900, Africa had 10 million Christians representing 10 percent of the population; by 2000, that was up 360 million, or 46 percent of the population. "That is the largest quantitative change that has ever occurred in the history of religion."[105] In 1950, only 2.4 percent of South Koreans were Christians; now the figure is 30 percent.

If there will be billions of Christians in the future, they won't be in Europe. Why is Europe the exception? The European Enlightenment was all about freedom *from* belief. The USAmerican Enlightenment was all about the freedom *to* believe.

Throw religion out of the door; / It flies back by the window
—JONATHAN BENTHALL[106]

Seals [Social]

The seal has both literal and metaphorical meanings in *The Seraph Seal*. In the book of Daniel, the scroll containing the end-time prophecies is sealed with seven seals until the time when the Lamb of God will open them and the apocalyptic time period will commence. In the Apocalypse of John, otherwise known as the book of Revelation, the last book in the Bible canon, the seals on the scroll are opened by the Lamb, first releasing the four horsemen of the Apocalypse, who are given a third of the earth to influence in various ways according to their natures. The next seals opened contain prophecies of earthquakes and a blackening sun. After that, more disasters follow with the opening of the final group of seals. In addition to the literal seal on the scroll, the word *seal* also means "decision." Symbolically, in *The Seraph Seal* the sealing and unsealing of the scrolls represent God's decision to both create and follow through with the prophecy of the Apocalypse. However, as the seals are opened, humankind is still given opportunities to participate in the course of events leading to the final decision or outcome. In this way, God is neither fatalistic and deterministic nor is humankind completely free from God's influence in the world and beyond.

In ancient Hebrew times, seals were also physical objects and symbols of identity. Seals were typically signets cut into stones. In alchemy, the seal of Solomon was a six-pointed star (a combination of the fire and water symbols, also symbolic of the air and earth) and was said to invoke the magic of the Kabbalah. The seal of Solomon represented a symbolic transmutation or the perfect balance of unity, the spirit wheel. Likewise, the Aries seal was an alchemical symbol related to early Christianity that was typically worn as an amulet or used as a seal. The sacred symbol was said to bring safety to the one possessing it. The seal typically bore the Greek letters *alpha* and the *omega*, the symbol of the ram, and the words, "The Word was made flesh, and dwelt among us" (John 1:14 KJV).

Secessionist Movements [Political]

Part of the decentralization stampede, secessionist movements are growing. November 2006 witnessed the First North American Secessionist Convention in Burlington, Vermont, hosted by Middlebury Institute. From Hawaii to Maine, from North to South, eighteen states sent delegates. The "Second Vermont Republic" is not alone—the Alaskans, Hawaiians, and Texans want their countries back, not to mention Arizona, Idaho, and others.

Selective Reduction [Social]

One of the best–kept secrets of the assisted-reproductive industry is selective reduction, as highly skilled sonographers "delete" from the screen selected fetuses in the womb when too many appear or when abnormalities surface. Genetic engineering is now designing children for success before they exist. In a designer world that won't pick up anything that isn't designed, including toilet bowl brushes, designer children are babies-as-products that we strategically purchase and plan. In a world where *90 percent* of unborn babies that test positive for Down syndrome are aborted, some people still have distant, dim memories of when children were created according to God's images and dreams, not according to the parents' images and dreams.[107]

Seraph [Social]

The seraphim (plural of seraph) occupy the highest rank of angels in Christian theology. Where the cherubim protect the mercy seat of the ark of the covenant, the seraphim are the direct caretakers of God's throne. Circling the heavenly seat, they are locked in an eternal song referred to as the *Trisagion* (Thrice Holy) song, based on Isaiah 6:1–3, where the Seraphim sing in unending praise, "Holy, holy, holy, is the Lord of hosts: the whole earth is full of his glory" (KJV). In the Christian liturgy there are only a few occasions that warrant triple hallelujahs.

The first mention of the seraphim within the New Testament is in the book of Revelation, chapter 4, verses 6 through 8.

Slavery [Political]

The extent of slavery in the twenty-first century is mind-boggling. There are an estimated twenty-seven million slaves in the world today,[108] which means that there are more slaves at work around the globe, and in more countries, than ever before in history.

On top of this horror, the price of a slave is at an all-time low: $100 on average, but in some places as low as $10.

Soft Power [Social]

Power and influence based on culture and ideas is called *soft power.*
Cultural flows are now primarily from East to West. Trends such as
feng shui, ethnic cuisine, chai tea, alternative medicine, *American Idol,*
Antiques Road Show, Ugly Betty (an ABC hit stolen from a Colombian
telenovela, a melodramatic soap opera) come from Eastern cultural
influences. In the words of designer Tom Ford about the fashion
industry: "We are finished here in the West."[109]

Solar Thermal Power Stations [Technological]

A major target for terrorists in the future will be the solar thermal
industry, which will replace nuclear power in the 2030s. Solar thermal manufacturers have some of the most sophisticated security
systems in the world, and every heliostat has a hidden alarm. Seville,
Spain, opened its first power tower in 2007. Power towers are now
art structures, and just as almost every architect in the twentieth
century wanted to do a cathedral, almost every artist now wants to
be commissioned to do a power tower. Cities will compete for the
most beautiful power towers in the same way they compete for best-
designed museums today.

Spaghettification [Environmental]

This term in physics has nothing to do with pasta or with highway
intersections. It refers to the process by which an object is gravitation-
ally torn apart upon falling into a black hole.

STEM (Science, Technology, Engineering, Mathematics) [Technological]

These are the major contributors to the knowledge economy and the
major foci of universities around the world. The humanities are lan-
guishing, and many universities offer no courses in pre-1900 European
history.

USAmerica is falling behind in the training of people in STEM.
From 1980 to 2000:

- Chinese engineering graduates increased 161 percent to 207,500.
- Japanese engineering graduates increased 42 percent to 103,000.
- South Korean engineering graduates increased 140 percent to 56,500.
- India produces more than 100,000 engineers a year.
- US engineering graduates declined 20 percent to 59,500.[110]

By the first decade of the twenty-first century, China was graduating three times as many engineers as the United States.[111]

Surveillance [Technological]

Fly-on-the-wall, eye-in-the-sky surveillance is omnipresent and omniscient. The average Londoner is caught on government surveillance cameras about three hundred times a day.[112] "Big Brother" is already watching.

But Little Brother is watching, too, through citizen monitoring, where cell phones capture events as they happen and where nothing is off the record or out of sight.

But will this make us act better? Stick a camera in someone's face, and what do you get? *Girls Gone Wild, Cops,* and *Survivor.* Cameras don't seem to bring out the best in us.

Survivalism [Social]

Survivalism has now gone mainstream and become a "don't trust the system" religion with an ethical framework based on withdrawal as the best moral strategy in the face of evil. Maybe the worst thing we can do is to participate, to engage, to involve ourselves in processes that are destructive either way. The writings of Alasdair McIntyre are the lodestars of this movement.[113]

For this reason, more and more people are committing Facebook suicide, ducking under the radar, and forming secure communities in head-for-the-hills hideaways and remote island locations.

Switch of Life [Environmental]

The "Switch of Life" is turning off, and in the future new meters will be everywhere that look like lungs, one side measuring carbon dioxide in the ocean, the other measuring carbon dioxide in the air. Our two-part lungs: trees and plankton. One-third of carbon dioxide emissions goes into the oceans and increases PH levels of the water. The more the oceans become acidic, the more plankton is killed off in a cascade effect. Plankton life is in danger of collapsing. Anything that needs to use calcium to build a shell is in danger of collapsing, and if plankton can't make its shells . . . Not good!

Tenth Angel [Social]

According to the eleventh-century Persian physician and philosopher Ibn Sina (known to the West as Avicenna), the prime mover of the universe is energy, or desire, and the Tenth Angel is the one who communicates human desires between our world and the nine heavenly spheres. Music is what the Tenth Angel uses to materialize energy into matter, and vice versa.

Tetramorph [Social]

When all four animal "kings" unite to form a unique being of incredible powers and majesty, it is called the Tetramorph ("the Four Forms"). See Ezekiel 1:1, 4–14; and Revelation 4:2, 6–8.

TGIF Syndrome [Social]

A new condition of shell shock, partly created by a 24/7 news/info cycle where information is spreading faster in TGIF (Twitter/Google/Internet/Facebook) than people can digest.

Three-Block Wars [Political]

Three-block wars are "smile-shoot-smile" conflicts in which the soldier is one moment fighting for his life and the next administering goodies to civilians. Has any three-block war ever been won?

Too Big (TB) [Social]

In this "big is bad" backlash, everything is TB—cars, homes, waistlines, deficits, theater popcorn, military, businesses, and so on. Gigantism is now anathema. Every Goliath has Davids circling, wanting to be the first to bring down the too-big-to-fail mammoths. Big trees fall over in the storm, not the little ones.

The "too big to fail" or "anything you can do I can do mega" days of the early twenty-first century are still vivid in some people's minds. The resolve is that no institution should be allowed to become so mega that it can blackmail the world (read: taxpayers) into bailing it out. There is one strange exception: banking. In 2007, the world's ten biggest banks accounted for 59 percent of global banking assets. By 2010 that figure had climbed to 70 percent and is still rising quickly.

The old economy of scale doctrine based on "bigger is better" or "get big or get out" no longer holds. In the new economy of human scale, there is a right size for everything—that's the true economy of scale, whether you're a mouse or an elephant. The mantra of the future is "Do little large," or as some are shorthanding it, "Shape UP."

The *New York Times* dubs this the "app store effect" because Apple encourages programmers writing iPhone applications to set a very low price for apps, no more than one dollar, because nobody blinks at a buck. In the first eighteen months after the first app was available, more than three billion apps were downloaded just from Apple's App Store. Want to become a millionaire in a month? Write an iPhone app. Little adds up to big in this new economy of scale.

Tribal [Political]

Globalization is producing an equal and opposite reaction: tribalization. The more global we become, the more local we need to live. And the local church is not nearly local enough.

Marshall McLuhan was right: Planet Earth is now a global small town. The Cloud has connected even the most remote places of the global village, giving us all common experiences in real time for the first time in history. This global small town has many neighborhoods, or what could be better called tribes. The largest and most powerful neighborhoods are in the East.

Forget Rudyard Kipling's "Oh, East is East, and West is West, and never the twain shall meet."[114] It's now the Wild, Wild East, and the most powerful tribe in this hood is China, with India a close second (*see* "Chindia").

The greater the integration of the world community, the greater the hunger to hold on to identity markers: languages, cultures, traditions, and histories. For example, Japanese Americans don't want to blend into whiteness, hence the birth of young people participating in tea ceremonies, learning kimono etiquette and the art of taiko drumming, not to mention pilgrimages back to Japan. Countries that encourage (and sometimes subsidize) hegiras back to homelands and mother countries include Mexico, Israel, Taiwan, and South Korea.

There are many tribulations of tribalizations, but there are many benefits as well. These include: (1) the rebirth of local food tastes and the rise of ethnic foods; (2) the rebirth of the homemade and homespun, as reflected in the sewing resurgence,[115] which is less about saving money (you don't) and more about personal customization in a mallified, massified world hungry for empowerment and creative expression and the celebration of diversity and plurality over homogeneity and uniformity, as any stop at a Traveler's Aid desk at almost any international airport will reveal. You can request help in Spanish, French, German, Italian, and eleven languages from India. But you can also get help in Khamu, Mien, Tigrinya, Tajiki, Pashto, Dari, Pangasinan, Pampangan, Waray-Waray, Bambara, Twi, and Bicolano.

The success of New York City, arguably the most cosmopolitan city in the world, is that it is also one of the most insular and tribal cities in the world.

USAmerica [Political]

This is one part of the Americas, which include all the peoples of North and South America, a region of the globe that covers 8.3 percent of the earth's total surface area (28.4 percent of its land area) and contains about 13.5 percent of the human population (about 900 million people).

The United States is only one of thirty-five nations that make up the Americas, which include the people of North America, South America, Latin America, and Central America. These thirty-four other American nations often resent the United States of America's arrogating to itself the name for the entire continent. Hence the need for the term *USAmerica.*

Video Games [Technological; Social]

Two thousand eight was the year when the sales of video games surpassed the sales of music and video combined in the United Kingdom, and the year it surpassed total UK book turnovers singly. Some hospitals have started making headsets available to kids before surgery so they can play video games or listen to music while awaiting anesthesia. They found that it calms kids down. The University Hospital in Newark, New Jersey, is already doing this.

Shigeru Miyamoto is a genius no one has heard of. He invented Mario, Donkey Kong, Zelda, and Nintendogs. You might call him the "Walt Disney" of the video-game world. "Miyamoto has dedicated his career to the Japanese console-maker Nintendo, for whom all of his games have been designed. Nintendo began life in the late nineteenth century as a maker of card games. The emphasis on gaming, and their transition to newer technologies, has ensured their survival."[116]

Virtual Water [Environmental]

All goods and services have an aquatic rucksack.[117] For example, the production of a thirty-two-megabyte computer chip weighing two grams requires the consumption of thirty-two liters of water. The manufacture of a motor car soaks up as much as 400,000 liters. The heaviest user of all is agriculture, which accounts for 65 to 70 percent of the global consumption of fresh water. Depending on the region of origin, one kilo of grain conceals 1,000 to 2,000 liters of virtual water, depending on the local climate; 5,000 to 55,000 liters go into the production of one kilo of cheese, and as much as 16,000 liters go into a kilo of beef. Water consumption figures for various nations must therefore include virtual water in the reckoning; they cannot limit themselves to the direct consumption of water for drinking, bathing, or car washing. An average citizen of the United States, for example, uses about 20,000 liters of water a day just for his or her consumption of beef.

A study in 2000 put the price of cleaning up the UK water supply after one year of farm pollution at 200 million pounds. Such are the hidden costs of every nation that get shrugged off or passed on to the future or the world's poor. Markets treasure what they measure, so the movement to track human wastestreams is gaining strength for those who believe we must be accountable for our waste. Or in Lester Brown's elegant phrase: "Get the market to 'tell the ecological truth.'"[118]

VUCA [Social]

This is US Army war college jargon for the world we live in: a VUCA world is characterized by volatility, uncertainty, complexity, and ambiguity.

"Water, water everywhere, nor any drop to drink."
—SAMUEL TAYLOR COLERIDGE[119]

Water [Environmental]

Three billion people now are without access to fresh water, and half the world's population is living in areas of acute water shortage.

Millions die annually from bad water and water-related diseases.

Water problems have led to a boon in tourism to the Arctic. Because of iceless Arctic summers and melting sea-ice, there is until September a sea-ice-free Arctic. The ice extent in the oceans has shrunk to 1 million square kilometers (620,000 square miles), down from 4.6 million square kilometers in 2012.

Wiihabilitation [Technological]

Virtually every hospital now boasts game therapy for its rehabilitation patients. From stroke to mental illness to orthopedic injuries to Alzheimer's, Wiihabilitation takes therapy from something you have to work at into something you enjoy playing at.

Wikipedia Principle [Social]

You can fix your mistakes, but you can't hide your making of them.

This is the key to Wikipedia's success. Personal responsibility for particular mistakes can't be erased, but the mistakes themselves can be. Thus the incentive to introduce errors or to play mischief with the facts is muted.

The English-language version of Wikipedia currently has more than 2,870,000 entries, a number that increases by 500,000 over a twelve-month period. The English-language version is only one of more than 250 different versions in other languages. The German, French, Italian, Polish, Dutch, and Japanese Wikipedia sites all have more than half a million entries each. The Xhosa Wikipedia currently has 110.

Wild Cards [Social]

These are the unintended, unanticipated consequences of our choices that force change overnight, because they are destabilizing, life-altering, paradigm-busting and system-disrupting. Whatever keeps you awake at night, knowing that when the consequences hit, we are in for the fight of our lives, that's a wild card. Or some would call them "black swans."[120]

It would be hard to overestimate the wildness in wild cards. Humans delude themselves by belittling the role that hazard and happenstance play in life. Orson Welles defined a film director as someone whose job it is "to preside over accidents."[121] Example: Deep Horizon in the Gulf of Mexico (2010).

Wild cards appear sometimes at a dizzying clip. Many times they seem like Jokers (Y2K). Their scenarios can be good or bad—bonanzas or disasters, asteroids or ahhhs (pleasant surprises)! The challenge is to recognize these wild cards as soon as they are dealt, then deal with them as quickly as they appear.[122]

When you watch for wild cards, you prepare for the worst-case scenarios, but plan for the best. Some major wild cards include political upheaval in China, pandemics, disruptions to food supplies, artificial intelligence, implosion of market economies, and the very exponential nature of the rate of change itself. From 2012 to 2048, there will be more growth in scientific knowledge than in the years from 1812 to 2012. Ray Kurzweil and John Smart predict that by 2048 $1,000 will buy you computing power comparable to the processing power of all the human brains on earth.[123]

Change is happening so fast that our outmoded social systems can't handle it. We need a social revolution to go along with our technological revolutions.

Nothing dates like the future.

WITWIGO [Social]

Short for "What in the world is going on?" which has become the new "'Go figure'figure" phrase. With so many ill winds blowing from every direction, and with Chicken Little wearing a hard hat, so many things falling from the sky—such as resource depletion, climate craziness, disease pandemics, technological anarchy, geopolitical tensions, economic instability, social upheaval, increasing world population— this phrase is becoming more and more commonplace.

Yottabytes [Technological]

A yottabyte is one septillion bytes of data. Yottabytes will be common by 2050, making it possible that no digital information need ever be thrown away. You can store your whole life on a computer or post it on Facebook.

These technologies bring us long-distance killing as well as long-distance kisses . . .

Zero [Social]

When paradigms shift, they go back to zero.

One of the most important people out there: the zero-to-one person. It is harder to get from 0 to 1 than from 1 to any other number. At 1 there is movement and momentum and a model to start with. But at 0 there is nothing, only nil and inertia.

ZPE Revolution [Technological]

Zero-Point Energy is the energy that remains when all other energy is removed from a system. Zero-Point Energy will be as significant as the discovery of fire, and patents have already been issued (e.g. U.S. Patent 7,379,286) and experiments underway (e.g. University of Colorado) that are exploring how to use the energy of a system at temperature T=0. ZPE will change everything. It's the ultimate Wild Card!

This is not the end, not even the beginning of the end, but perhaps it is the end of the beginning.
—WINSTON CHURCHILL[124]

NOTES

Engaging the Apocalypse: A Nonfiction Essay on Scenarios and Semiotics for the 21st Century

1. Mark Vickers, "TrendWatcher: The Fiction Effect: Plausible Scenarios That Shock," HR World, 17 July 2009, http://www.hrworld.com/features/trendwatcher-scenario-planning-072009.
2. Matthew Hertenstein, et al, "Smile intensity in photographs predicts divorce later in life," *Motivation & Emotion*, 2009, 99–105.
3. Josh Levin, "How Is America Going To End?: The world's leading futurologists have four theories," *Slate*, 3 August 2009, http://www.slate.com/id/2223962, p. 4.
4. Ibid.

Alphabet of the Apocalypse: Reading the Signs of the Times

1. Heinrich Heine, Paris, 12 July 1842, in his *Lutetia*, vol. 2 of *French Affairs: Letters from Paris, The Works of Heinrich Heine* 8, trans. Charles Godfrey Leland (London: William Heinemann, 1893), 305.
2. See, for example, Edward Feser, "'Too Christian' for Academia?" National Review Online, 11 February 2009. http:/article.nationalreview.com/385529/too-christian-for-academia/edward-feser.
3. P. J. Kavanagh, "Bywords," *TLS: Times Literary Supplement*, 20 July 2001, 16.
4. Michael Hirst, "Iraq: Christians Flee Worst Sectarian Violence Since War," *Tablet*, 28 April 2007, 38.
5. As referenced in Martin Amis, *Experience: A Memoir* (New York: Talk Miramax: Hyperion, 2000), 189.
6. Edward Hill, Past President of AMA, "The Coming Revolution in Healthcare," *Vital Speeches of the Day*, December 2006, 776.
7. Richard Feachem, speaking to the All-party Parliamentary Group on Africa, as quoted in Alex De Waal, "Sex in Summertown," *Times Literary Supplement*, 6 August 2004, 5.

8. John Polkinghorne, "One of the Hosts," *TLS: Times Literary Supplement*, 2 November 2007, 27.

9. So says Pew Forum on Religion and Public Life, "Global Restrictions on Religion" (2009), http://pewforum.org/Government/Global-Restrictions-on-Religion.aspx.

10. This resolution has been promoted by the fifty-seven-nation Organization of the Islamic Conference.

11. Philosopher Robert Nozick discusses this phenomenon among physicists in *The Nature of Rationality* (Princeton UP, 1993). Also see Edward J. Larson and Larry Withan, "Scientists are Still Keeping the Faith," *Nature* 386 (3 April 1997), 435ff.

12. Marvin Minsky, "New Prospects of Immortality," in *What Are You Optimistic About?* ed. John Brockman (New York: Pocket Books, 2008), 195.

13. Mark Vernon, "Incredible Views," *Times Literary Supplement*, April 2, 2010, 8.

14. Louis Mumford, *The City in History: Its Origins, Its Transformations, and Its Prospects* (San Diego: Harcourt, 1961), 503.

15. Martin Luther King Jr., "Nobel Prize Acceptance Speech," in *A Testament of Hope: The Essential Writings and Speeches of Martin Luther King*, ed. James M. Washington (San Francisco: HarperSanFrancisco, 1986), 225.

16. Quoted in a letter dated 20 February 1970, in *Letters of Marshall McLuhan*, ed., Matie Molinaro, Corinne McLuhan, William Toye (New York: Oxford University Press, 1987), 398.

17. According to the Institute for Local Self-Reliance (ILSR). For more see Kimberly Weisul, "Consumers Buy Into 'Buy Local,'" *Bloomsberg Businessweek*, 18 February 2010, http://www.businessweek.com/magazine/content/10_09/b4168057813351.htm.

18. *Trend Letter* 29 (July 2010): 1. For more see Weisul, "Consumers Buy Into 'Buy Local.'"

19. So says Business Alliance for Local Living Economies (BALLE) research and public policy director Michael Shuman. See Barbara Bedway, "Slow Money: A New Community Movement is Picking Up Steam," *Fiscal Times*, http://www.thefiscaltimes.com/Issues/Life-and-Money/2010/06/11/Slow-Money-How-a-New-Community-Movement-is-Picking-Up-Steam.aspx.

20. For a sampling of the manuscripts, see "Facimilies of Manuscripts in the British Isles: The Harley Psalter," http://libraries.slu.edu/archives/digcoll/mssexhibit07/manuscripts/harley.html.

21. Paul Collier, *The Bottom Billion* (New York: Oxford University Press, 2007).

22. Ronand Bailey, "Data: Aiding and Indebting," *Reason*, October 2005, 16, http://www.reason.com/0510/data.shtml.

23. *The Economist*, January 23, 2010, 11.

24. Nick Gillespie, "Remembering 'The Forgotten Man': Amity Shlaes, Author of a New History of the Great Depression, Talks About Franklin D. Roosevelt's Baleful Economic Legacy, the Growth of Government, and the Death of Classical Liberalism," *Reason*, January 2008, 34–42, http://reason.com/archives/2007/12/18/remembering-the-forgotten-man.

25. Michael Bywater, *Big Babies, Or: Why Can't We Just Grow Up* (London: Granta, 2007), 114.

26. John Rennie, "Human-Animal Chimeras," *Scientific American*, 27 (June 2005): A8. http://www.scientificamerican.com/article.cfm?id=human-animal-chimeras.

27. "Chinese Cuisine, American Eats," in *Life in the USA: The Complete Guide for Immigrants and Americans*, http://www.lifeintheusa.com/food/chinese.htm.

28. See John and Doris Naisbitt, *China's Megatrends: The 8 Pillars of a New Society* (Harper Business, 2010), 74–75, 97, quote on 211.

29. Ronald Wright, *A Short History of Progress* (New York: Carroll & Graf, 2005), 121.

30. Cullen Murphy, "Fatwa City," *Atlantic Monthly*, November 2005, 169.

31. The U.S. National Debt Clock estimate as of 6 July 2010 is that each citizen's share of just the national debt is $42,733.71. See http://www.brillig.com/debt_clock/.

32. See Elyse Friedman, "Food Cooperatives in the United States," in *Oxford Companion to American Food and Drink*, ed. Andrew F Smith (New York: Oxford University Press, 2007), 166.

33. Max Saunders, "Future Sublime," *TLS: Times Literary Supplement*, 26 June 2009, 14.

34. The timing of cold nights and warm days needed for a successful sap run is shifting due to global warming in such a way that it can't support the making of maple syrup. And that doesn't even address the way the shifting temperatures affect the health of the trees themselves. See the work of the Proctor Maple Research Center at the University of Vermont: www.uvm.edu/~pmrc.

35. Chip Giller and David Roberts, "Resources: The Revolution Begins," *Fast Company* (March 2006), 77, http://www.fastcompany.com/magazine/103/essay-resources.html. See also William McDonough and Michael Braungart, *Cradle to Cradle: Remaking the Way We Make Things* (New York: Macmillan, 2002), 56, 105.

36. As quoted in Jenny Turner, "Stick in a Pie for Tomorrow," *London Review of Books*, 14 May 2009, 23–24. The quote is found in the introductory pages of Kate Colquhoun, *The Thrifty Cookbook* (London: Bloomsbury, 2009).

37. The judge was Jack Love. See George Mair and Claire Lee, *Electronic Monitoring: The Trials and Their Results* (London: H. M. S. O., 1990), 4.

38. Titus Livius, *The Early History of Rome* (New York: Penguin, 2002), 30.

39. Adam Smith, *An Inquiry into the Nature and Causes of the Wealth of Nations* (Dublin: William Porter, 1801), 2: 134.

40. Alexis de Tocqueville, "Tocqueville to Theodore Sedgwick, 29 August 1856," in *Tocqueville on America After 1840: Letters and Other Writings*, eds. and trans. Aurelian Craiutu and Jeremy Jennings (New York: Cambridge University Press, 2009), 183.

41. J. K. Rowling, *Harry Potter and the Sorcerer's Stone* (New York: Scholastic, 1997), 291.

42. R. S. Thomas, "This Page Should Be Left Blank" in his *Counterpoint* (Newcastle upon Tyne: Bloodaxe Books, 1990), 8.

43. "War in the Fifth Domain," *Economist*, 3 July 2010, 26.

44. See Steven Johnson's book *Emergence: The Connected Lives of Ants, Brains, Cities, and Software* (New York: Scribner, 2002) and "Robots Forming Human-like Societies," *Electronic Evolution*, 28 May 2009, http://current.com/items/90119924_robots-forming-human-like-societies-electronic-evolution.htm; or the same title from the *Daily Galaxy*, 19 May 2009, http://www.dailygalaxy.com/my_weblog/2009/05/a-robot-hitler.html.

45. For more on this, see John Milbank, *The Future of Love: Essays in Political Theology* (Eugene, OR: Cascade Bookes, 2009), 185–86.

46. Quoted in Paul Krugman, *Peddling Prosperity: Economic Sense and Nonsense in the Age of Diministed Expectations* (New York: W. W. Norton, 1994), xi.

47. Quoted by Peter Harriot, *Religious Fundamentalism: Global, Local and Personal* (New York: Rougledge, 2009), 158.

48. Here is what is in store for dead jihadists:
   - Koran 51–55: "We shall wed them to dark-eyed houris."
   - Koran 55:56–57: "Bashful virgins neither man nor Jinn will have touched before. Then which of the favors of your Lord will you deny?"
   - Koran 55:57–58: "Virgins as fair as corals and rubies."
   - Koran 55:70–77: "Dark eyed virgins sheltered in their tents."
   - Koran 78:31: "Gardens and vineyards, and high-bosomed virgins for companions."
   - Koran 52:24: "Round about them will serve . . . boys handsome as pearls well-guarded."
   - Koran 76:19: "Boys of perpetual freshness; if thou seest them, thou wouldst think them scattered pearls."

49. www.samaritansofboston.org.

50. See "Fibonacci Numbers and Nature," http://www.maths.surrey.ac.uk/hosted-sites/R.Knott/Fibonacci/fibnat.html.

51. First attributed to the Riviera by W. Sumerset Maugham in E. S. Turner, "Travel," *Times Literary Supplement*, April 2, 2004, 32. But also attributed to Monaco.

52. The first line of Elizabeth Butler's, "Florida," in her *Complete Poems 1927–1979* (New York: Farrar Straus, Giroux, 1983), 32.

53. Søren Kierkegaard's prophetic remark in *The Journals of Søren Kierkegaard*, ed. Alexander Dru (New York: Oxford University Press, 1938), 181, sec. 617. As opposed to social sciences, the natural sciences are those that use the scientific method—biology, chemistry, physics, the "hard sciences" are the driving forces, driving us to our destruction.

54. *TLS*, 6 March 2010, 13.

55. Strobe Talbott, *The Great Experiment: The Story of Ancient Empires, Modern States, and the Quest for a Global Nation* (New York: Simon & Schuster, 2009), 126.

56. Gertrude Stein, *Everybody's Autobiography* (New York: Cooper Square, 1971), 289.

57. See for example Naomi Klein, *The Shock Doctrine: The Rise of Disaster Capitalism* (Toronto: Vintage Canada, 2008).
58. Quoted in David M. Smick, *The World is Curved: Hidden Dangers to the Global Economy* (New York: Portfolio, 2008), 273.
59. James Lovelock, *The Revenge of Gaia: Earth's Comate Crisis and the Fate of Humanity* (New York: Basic Books, 2006), quotes are on 109, 147, 7 respectively.
60. Ecuador used as a consultant a US-based nonprofit, CELDF or Community Environment Legal Defense Fund. Jennifer Koons, "Ecuador's New Constitution Gives Inalienable Rights to Nature," http://www.greenchange. org/article.php?id=3389.
61. Quoted in Chet Raymo, *When God Is Gone Everything Is Holy: The Making of a Religious Naturalist* (Notre Dame, IN; Sorin Books, 2008), 40–41.
62. John Gray, *Black Mass: Apocalypic Religion and the Death of Utopia* (New York: Farrar, Straus and Giroux, 2007).
63. Matthew Fontaine Maury, *The Physical Geography of the Sea, and Its Meteorogy* (London: Sampson Low, 1891), 22.
64. For more see "Shutdown of Circulation Pattern Could Be Disastrous, Researchers Say," Science Daily, 20 December 2004, http://www.science-daily.com/releases/2004/12/041219153611.htm; and Ian Sample, "Alarm over Dramatic Weakening of Gult Stream," *The Guardian*, 1 December 2005, http://www.guardian.co.uk/environment/2005/dec/01/science.climatechange.
65. James Joyce, *Finnegan's Wake* (New York: Penguin books, 1999), 32.
66. Quoted in J. C., "Bash Street Kid," *TLS: Times Literary Supplement*, 19 March 2010, 32.
67. Richard Holmes, *The Age of Wonder: How the Romantic Generation Discovered the Beauty and Terror of Science* (New York: Vintage Books, 2010), 63–64.
68. Ronald Wright, *A Short History of Progress* (New York: Carroll & Graf, 2005), 130.
69. Carolyn Steel, *Hungry City: How Food Shapes Our Lives* (London: Chatto & Windus, 2008), 102.
70. Mark Pesce, "Hyperpolitics (American Style)," address presented at the Personal Democracy Forum on 24 June 2008, available at http://blog.futurestreetconsulting.com/?p=61.
71. See the Introduction to Gary R. Bunt, *iMuslims: Rewiring the House of Islam* (Chapel Hill: University of North Carolina Press, 2009), 1–6.
72. Reinhold Niebuhr, *The Irony of American History* (New York: Charles Scribner's Sons, 1952, repr. Chicago: University of Chicago Press, 2008), 174.
73. Ronald Reagan, *Ronald Reagan: The Great Communicator*, ed. Frederick J. Ryan Jr. (New York: HarperPerennial, 2001), 62.
74. Liszt to Agnes, 16 November 1860, in *Franz Liszt and Agnes Street-Klindworth: A Correspondence 1854–1886*, ed. and trans. Pauline Pocknell (Hillsdale, NY: Pendragon Press, 2000), 187. Here is that idea put into musical form: http://www.youtube.com/watch?v=ozLu94tW_bk.

75. Niccolò Machiavelli, *The Prince and The Discourses* (New York: Modern Library, 1950), 139: "when the act accuses him, the result should excuse him."
76. See, for example, http://en.wikipedia.org/wiki/Geomagnetic_storm (accessed 17 July 2010).
77. "Even the Communists couldn't beat it. It outlasted them and now flourishes in the ruins of their regimes. And the Market as God is omnipresent, it is everywhere, turning the whole of creation into a commodity. It dominates every area of life. For instance, traditional religions have regarded human beings as sacred, but long ago the Market reduced them to an inventory of spare parts to be sold a piece at a time—blood, sperm, fertilizable eggs, and no doubt human genes will soon be added. And if in spite of having bought a spanking new body you are still unhappy, the Market can sell you peace of mind and personal fulfilment offered by some psychological guru or life-style consultant. Just like the Christian God, the Market loves sinners . . . . Celebrity itself has been turned into a form of currency . . . 'the Market God is insatiable': its motto is 'there is never enough.'" Colin Morris, *Things Shaken—Things Unshaken: Reflections on Faith and Terror* (Epworth, 2006), 126–27.
78. "The Debate Room: Financial Crisis: Blame B-Schools," Pro, by Jay Lorsch and Rakesh Khurana; Con, by Andrew W. Lo, *Bloomberg BusinessWeek*, http://www.businessweek.com/debateroom/archives/2008/11/us_financial_cr.html.
79. For a Medical Tourism travel agency see http://www.medretreat.com/.
80. "Ezekiel Sees the Glory of God," http://home.halden.net/rolf/merian/m125.jpg.
81. Liz Jensen, *The Rapture* (New York: Doubleday, 2009).
82. For more see Robert A. Freitas Jr., *Nanomedicine: Volume IIA Biocompatibility* (Austin, TX: Landes Bioscience, 2003).
83. Barbara Kingsolver tells of her locavore project to "feed ourselves [only] vegetables and animals whose provenance we really knew" and to eat only what was produced within striking distance of where they lived. See Barbara Kingsolver, with Steven L. Hopp and Camille Kingsolver, *Animal, Vegetable, Miracle: A Year of Seasonal Eating* (New York: HarperCollins, 2007), 10.
84. See Michael Olson, *MetroFarm: The Guide to Growing for Profit in or Near the City* (Santa Cruz, CA: TS Books, 1994). See also MetroFarm: *The Online Magazine of Metropolitan Agriculture*, 10 September 2009, http://www.metrofarm.com/index.php.
85. Russ Alan Prince and Lewis Schiff, *The Middle-Class Millionaire: The Rise of the New Rich and How They Are Changing America* (New York: Random House, 2008).
86. Katrin Becker, Melanie Becker, and John H. Schwarz, *String Theory and M-Theory: A Modern Introduction* (Cambridge University Press, 2007), 329–30.
87. J. Craig Venter Institute, "First Self-Replicating Synthetic Bacterial Cell," http://www.jcvi.org/cms/research/projects/first-self-replicating-synthetic-bacterial-cell.
88. Paul Hawken, Amory Lovins, and L. Hunter Lovins call it this; see their *Natural Capitalism: Creating the Next Industrial Revolution* (Boston: Little, Brown and Co.), 1999.

89. "Encyclical Letter *Caritas in Veritate* of the Supreme Pontiff Benedict XVI to the Bishops, Priests, and Deacons, Men and Women Religious, the Lay Faithful, and All People of Good Will on Integral Human Development in Charity and Truth," 29 June 2009, http://www.vatican.va/holy_father/benedict_xvi/encyclicals/documents/hf_ben-xvi_enc_20090629_caritas-in-veritate_en.html.

90. Amy D. Bernstein and Peter W. Bernstein, eds., *The New York Times Practical Guide to Practically Everything: The Essential Companion for Everyday Life* (New York: St. Martin's Press, 2006), 3.

91. See, for example, "Bioethics and Patent Law: The Case of the Oncomouse," *WIPO Magazine* 3 (June 2006), http://www.wipo.int/wipo_magazine/en/2006/03/article_0006.html.

92. For an account focusing on the experiences of just one small village in England, see John Hatcher, *The Black Death: A Personal History* (Cambridge, MA: Da Capo Press, 2008).

93. "The Pandemic Threat," *The Economist*, 2 May 2009, 11.

94. Sébastian Foucan, *Freerunning: The Urban Landscape is Your Playground* (Berkeley, CA: Ulysses Press, 2008).

95. David Pearce Snyder, "Big Changes for Living and Work Spaces," *Trend Letter*, March 2010, 3.

96. Cass R. Sunstein, *Republic.com 2.0* (Princeton, NJ: Princeton University Press, 2007).

97. Richard A. Posner, "The Most Punitive Nation," *Times Literary Supplement*, 1 September 1995, 3–4.

98. For the implications of QE on travel, see Marvin J. Cetron, "Vision: Teleportation," *Futurist*, September-October 2008, 34–36.

99. Walter Isaacson, *Einstein: His Life and Universe* (New York: Simon & Schuster, 2007), 458.

100. Quoted in "Robert McNamara" (Obituary), *Economist*, 11 July 2009, 80.

101. Gerald Celente, "Renaissance 2012," *Trends Journal*, Autumn 2009, 9, http://issuu.com/publishgold/docs/tj-autumn-09.

102. The June 2006 Roper Poll came up with the 66 percent figure. Also see the Pew Research Center poll, which reveals that half of the adults believe that their children's future will be worse than theirs. *Parade Magazine* polled its audience and found that half said they were worse off than their parents. For more see Tom Von Riper, "The Average American: 1967 and Today," 10 October 2006, http://www.forbes.com/2006/10/16/demographics-income-population-biz_cx_tvr_1017median.html.

103. *Rumi: The Book of Love: Poems of Ecstasy and Longing* (San Francisco: HarperSanFrancisco, 2003), 123.

104. Quoted in *Blindspot: When Journalists Don't Get Religion*, ed, Paul Marshall, Lela Gibert, and Roberta Green Ahmanson (New York: Oxford University Press, 2009), 163.

105. Francis Campbell, "No Future in the Ghetto," *The Tablet*, 2 February 2008, 12, http://www.thetablet.co.uk/article/10955.

106. The title of chapter 7 of Jonathan Benthall, *Returning to Religion: Why a Secular Age Is Haunted by Faith* (New York: I. B. Tauris, 2008), 169.

107. "Science moves faster than moral understanding" (9) writes Michael J. Sandel in *The Case Against Perfection: Ethics in the Age of Genetic Engineering* (Cambridge, MA: Belknap Press of Harvard University Press, 2007), 9, 46. In this thin volume, Sandel eloquently contends that "children ought to be valued in their unbidden givenness rather than designed" (Michele Pridmore-Brown, "Ironing Out the Glitches," *Times Literary Supplement*, April 18, 2008, 28–29). His argument is that to design children is to "disfigure" the parent-child relationship and deprive the parent of the "enlarged human sympathies" that "openness to the unbidden" cultivates (Sandel, 46).

108. According to Kevin Bales, *Understanding Global Slavery: A Reader* (Berkeley: Univeristy of California Press, 2005), 4.

109. Quoted in Dana Thomas, *Deluxe: How Luxury Lost Its Luster* (New York: Penguin Press, 2007), 300.

110. www.samaritansofboston.org.

111. As referenced by Carl Camden, "Workplace and Workforce Trends: The Future is Now," *Vital Speeches of the Day* 71 (15 August 2005): 650.

112. Michael Bywater, *Big Babies: Or, Why Can't We Just Grow Up* (London: Granta, 2007), 191–92.

113. Alisdair McIntyre supports this somewhere . . . He argued that US citizens should consider sitting out the last US election because "when offered a choice between two politically intolerable alternatives, it is important to choose neither. And when that choice is presented to rival arguments and debates that exclude from public consideration any other set of possibilities, it becomes a duty to withdraw from those arguments and debates, so as to resist the imposition of this false choice by those who have arrogated to themselves the power of framing the alternatives." (As quoted in Constantine Sandis, "Torn Away from Sureness," *Times Literary Supplement*, 15 August 2008, 23.)

114. Rudyard Kipling, "The Ballad of East and West."

115. Sales of Singer machines doubled from 1999 to 2006.

116. John Lanchester, "Is It Art?" *London Review of Books*, 01 January 2009, 18.

117. I first encountered this in Wolfgang Sachs's *Fair Future: Resource Conflicts, Security, and Global Justice* (New York: Zed Books, 2007), 103.

118. Lester R. Brown, *Eco-Economy: Buiding an Economy for the Earth* (New York: W. W. Norton, 2001), 7.

119. Samuel Taylor Coleridge, "The Rime of the Ancient Mariner," in *The Complete Works of Samuel Taylor Coleridge*, ed. W. T. T. Shedd (New York: Harper Brothers, 1994), 7:233.

120. Nassim Nicholas Talab, *The Black Swan: The Impact of the Highly Improbable* (New York: Random House, 2007), xvii–xviii.

121. As quoted in Frank Brady, *Citizen Welles: A Biography of Orson Welles* (New York: Anchor Books, 1990), 593.

122. See John L. Petersen, "How 'Wild Cards' May Reshape Our Future," *The Futurist* 43 (May–June 2009): 19–20.

123. Ronald Bailey, "Creative Accounting Taking Stock of Big Ideas," *Reason*, October 16, 2005, http://www.reason.com/0510/ci.rb.creative.shtml.

124. Winston Churchill, "The End of the Beginning, A Speech at the Lord Mayor's Day Luncheon at the Mansion House, London, 10 November 1942," in his *The End of the Beginning: War Speeches*, ed. Charles Eade (Boston: Little Brown, 1943), 266.

Read this book and see Jesus
like you've never seen Him before.

RESTORING THE SUPREMACY AND SOVEREIGNTY OF JESUS CHRIST

JESUS MANIFESTO

LEONARD SWEET
FRANK VIOLA

Visit www.thejesusmanifesto.com to learn more.
Available wherever books and e-books are sold.